CONCEPTS AND CHALLENGES

EARTH AND SPACE

Leonard Bernstein ◆ Martin Schachter ◆ Alan Winkler ◆ Stanley Wolfe

Stanley Wolfe
Project Coordinator

GLOBE FEARON
Pearson Learning Group

The following people have contributed to the development of this product:

Art and Design: Evelyn Bauer, Susan Brorein, Tracey Gerber, Bernadette Hruby, Carol Marie Kiernan, Mindy Klarman, Judy Mahoney, Karen Mancinelli, Elbaliz Mendez, April Okano, Dan Thomas, Jennifer Visco

Editorial: Stephanie P. Cahill, Gina Dalessio, Nija Dixon, Martha Feehan, Theresa McCarthy, Maurice Sabean, Marilyn Sarch, Maury Solomon, Jeffrey Wickersty, Shirley C. White, S. Adrienn Vegh-Soti

Manufacturing: Mark Cirillo, Tom Dunne

Marketing: Douglas Falk, Maureen Christensen

Production: Irene Belinsky, Linda Bierniak, Carlos Blas, Karen Edmonds, Cheryl Golding, Leslie Greenberg, Roxanne Knoll, Susan Levine, Cynthia Lynch, Jennifer Murphy, Lisa Svoronos, Susan Tamm

Publishing Operations: Carolyn Coyle, Thomas Daning, Richetta Lobban

Technology: Jessie Lin, Ellen Strain, Joanne Saito

About the Cover: Our Sun is one of about 100 billion stars in the Milky Way Galaxy, part of which is shown in the larger photograph. Orbiting the Sun are nine planets, including Earth. The smaller photograph shows Earth as seen from space, where it appears to be rising above its only natural satellite, the Moon.

ISBN: 0-13-024202-0

Printed in the United States of America

1 2 3 4 5 6 7 8 9 10 06 05 04 03

1-800-321-3106
www.pearsonlearning.com

Acknowledgments

Science Consultants

Gregory L. Vogt, Ed.D.
Associate Professor
Colorado State University
Fort Collins, CO

Stephen T. Lofthouse
Pace University
New York, NY

Laboratory Consultants

Sean M. Devine
Science Teacher
Ridge High School
Basking Ridge, NJ

Vincent R. Dionisio
Science Teacher
Clifton High School
Clifton, NJ

Reading Consultant

Sharon Cook
Consultant
Leadership in Literacy

Internet Consultant

Janet M. Gaudino
Science Teacher
Montgomery Middle School
Skillman, NJ

ESL/ELL Consultant

Elizabeth Jimenez
Consultant
Pomona, CA

Content Reviewers

Sharon Danielsen (pp. 24–25)
Site Manager
Darrin Fresh Water Institute
Rensselaer Polytechnic Institute
Troy, NY

Dr. Charles Liu (Chs. 2, 3, 4)
Astrophysicist
Department of Astrophysics and Hayden Planetarium
American Museum of Natural History
New York, NY

Hugh P. Taylor, Jr. (Ch. 1)
Robert P. Sharp Professor of Geology
Division of Geological and Planetary Sciences
MS 100-23, California Institute of Technology
Pasadena, CA

Dr. Raymond C. Turner (Ch. 1)
Alumni Distinguished Professor Emeritus of Physics
Department of Physics and Astronomy
Clemson University
Clemson, SC

Todd Woerner (pp. 72–73)
Department of Chemistry
Duke University
Durham, NC

Teacher Reviewers

Peggy L. Cook
Lakeworth Middle School
Lakeworth, FL

Claudia Toback
Consultant/Mentor
Staten Island, NY

Contents

Scientific Skills and Investigations Handbooks

Big Dipper

Appendices

Features

Hands-On Activity

How Do They Know That?

People in Science

Integrating the Sciences

Real-Life Science

Science and Technology

Web InfoSearch

What are scientific skills?

People are naturally curious. They want to understand the world around them. They want to understand what causes earthquakes and where is the best place to search for useful minerals. The field of science would probably not exist if it were not for human curiosity about the natural world.

People also want to be able to make good guesses about the future. They want to be able to track severe storms such as hurricanes and to find ways to protect their homes against flooding.

Scientists use many skills to explore the world and gather information about it. These skills are called science process skills. Another name for them is science inquiry skills.

Science process skills allow you to think like a scientist. They help you identify problems and answer questions. Sometimes they help you solve problems. More often, they provide some possible answers and lead to more questions. In this book, you will use a variety of science process skills to understand the facts and theories in Earth science.

Science process skills are not only used in science. You compare prices when you shop and you observe what happens to foods when you cook them. You predict what the weather will be by looking at the sky. In fact, science process skills are really everyday life skills that have been adapted for problem solving in science.

▲ **Figure 1** Scientists use science process skills to understand how gravity affects the way crystals grow and materials mix, how caves form and change, how the land is built up and then torn down, and what Earth's place is in the universe.

1 **NAME:** What is the name for the skills scientists use to solve problems?

Contents

1 Observing and Comparing

Making Observations An important part of solving any problem is observing, or using your senses to find out what is going on around you. The five senses are sight, hearing, touch, smell, and taste. When you look at a pebble and feel its smoothness, you are observing. When you observe, you pay close attention to everything that happens around you.

Scientists observe the world in ways that other scientists can repeat. This is a goal of scientific observation. It is expected that when a scientist has made an observation, other people will be able to make the same observation.

2 LIST: What are the five senses?

Comparing and Contrasting Part of observing is comparing and contrasting. When you compare data, you observe the characteristics of several things or events to see how they are alike. When you contrast data, you look for ways that similar things are different from one another.

▲ **Figure 2** River and glacial cut valleys look similar. However, you can see many differences from the valley floor.

3 COMPARE/CONTRAST: How are valleys carved by running water and valleys carved by glaciers similar? How are they different?

Using Tools to Observe Sometimes an object is too small to see with your eyes alone. You need a special tool to help you make observations. One tool that scientists use to observe is the seismograph. A seismograph detects earthquakes by measuring the vibrations of Earth's crust.

▲ **Figure 3** Seismologist checking a seismograph

4 INFER: Besides detecting earthquakes, what other use does a seismograph have?

Hands-On Activity

MAKING OBSERVATIONS

You and a partner will need 2 shoeboxes with lids, 2 rubber bands, and several small objects.

1. Place several small objects into the shoebox. Do not let your partner see what you put into the shoebox.
2. Cover the shoebox with the lid. Put a rubber band around the shoebox to keep the lid on.
3. Exchange shoeboxes with your partner.
4. Gently shake, turn, and rattle the shoebox.
5. Try to describe what is in the shoebox without opening it. Write your descriptions on a sheet of paper.

Practicing Your Skills

6. IDENTIFY: What science process skill did you use?
7. IDENTIFY: Which of your senses was most important to you?
8. ANALYZE: Direct observation is seeing something with your eyes or hearing it with your ears. Indirect observation involves using a model or past experience to make a guess about something. Which kind of observation did you use?

2 Classifying Data

Key Term

data: information you collect when you observe something

Collecting and Classifying Data The information you collect when you observe something is called **data.** The data from an experiment or from observations you have made are first recorded, or written down. Then, they are classified.

When you classify data, you group things together based on how they are alike. This information often comes from making comparisons as you observe. You may classify by size, shape, color, use, or any other important feature. Classifying data helps you recognize and understand the relationships between things. Classification makes studying large groups of things easier. For example, Earth scientists use classification to organize the different types of rocks and minerals.

5 EXPLAIN: How can you classify data?

Hands-On Activity

ORGANIZING ROCKS

You will need 15 pebbles of different colors, textures, and shapes.

1. Lay the pebbles out on a table. Classify the pebbles into two categories based on texture: *Smooth* and *Rough.*
2. Look at the pebbles you classified as smooth. Divide these pebbles into new categories based on similar colors.
3. Repeat Step 2 for the pebbles you classified as rough.

Practicing Your Skills

4. ANALYZE: How did you classify the pebbles? What other ways could you classify the pebbles?
5. EXPLAIN: Why is a classification system useful?

3 Modeling and Simulating

Key Terms

model: tool scientists use to represent an object or process

simulation: computer model that usually shows a process

Modeling Sometimes things are too small to see with your eyes alone. Other times, an object is too large to see. You may need a model to help you examine the object. A **model** is a good way to show what a very small or a very large object looks like. A model can have more details than what may be seen with just your eyes. It can be used to represent a process or an object that is hard to explain with words. A model can be a three-dimensional picture, a drawing, a computer image, or a diagram.

6 DEFINE: What is a model?

Simulating A **simulation** is a kind of model that shows a process. It is often done using a computer. You can use a simulation to predict the outcome of an experiment. Scientists use simulations to study everything from the insides of a volcano to the development of a tornado.

▲ **Figure 4** This student is discovering how volcanoes are created through successive layers of erupted lava.

7 DEFINE: What is a simulation?

4 Measuring

Key Terms

unit: amount used to measure something

meter: basic unit of length or distance

mass: amount of matter in something

gram: basic unit of mass

volume: amount of space an object takes up

liter: basic unit of liquid volume

meniscus: curve at the surface of a liquid in a thin tube

temperature: measure of the amount of heat energy something contains

Two Systems of Measurement When you measure, you compare an unknown value with a known value using standard units. A **unit** is an amount used to measure something. The metric system is an international system of measurement. Examples of metric units are the gram, the kilometer, and the liter. In the United States, the English system and the metric system are both used. Examples of units in the English system are the pound, the foot, and the gallon.

There is also a more modern form of the metric system called SI. The letters *SI* stand for the French words *Système International.* Many of the units in the SI are the same as those in the metric system.

The metric and SI systems are both based on units of 10. This makes them easy to use. Each unit in these systems is ten times greater than the one before it. To show a change in the size of a unit, you add a prefix to the unit. The prefix tells you whether the unit is larger or smaller. For example, a centimeter is ten times bigger than a millimeter.

PREFIXES AND THEIR MEANINGS	
kilo-	one thousand (1,000)
hecto-	one hundred (100)
deca-	ten (10)
deci-	one-tenth (1/10)
centi-	one-hundredth (1/100)
milli-	one-thousandth (1/1,000)

◀ **Figure 5**

8 **IDENTIFY:** What are two measurement systems?

Units of Length Length is the distance from one point to another. In the metric system, the basic unit of length or distance is the **meter.** A meter is about the length from a doorknob to the floor. Longer distances, such as the distances between cities, are measured in kilometers. A kilometer is 1,000 meters. Centimeters and millimeters measure shorter distances. A centimeter is 1/100 of a meter. A millimeter is 1/1,000 of a meter. Figure 6 compares common units of length. It also shows the abbreviation for each unit.

SI/METRIC UNITS OF LENGTH	
1,000 millimeters (mm)	1 meter (m)
100 centimeters (cm)	1 meter
10 decimeters (dm)	1 meter
10 millimeters	1 centimeter
1,000 meters	1 kilometer (km)

▲ **Figure 6**

Length can be measured with a meter stick. A meter stick is 1 m long and is divided into 100 equal lengths by numbered lines. The distance between each of these lines is equal to 1 cm. Each centimeter is divided into ten equal parts. Each one of these parts is equal to 1 mm.

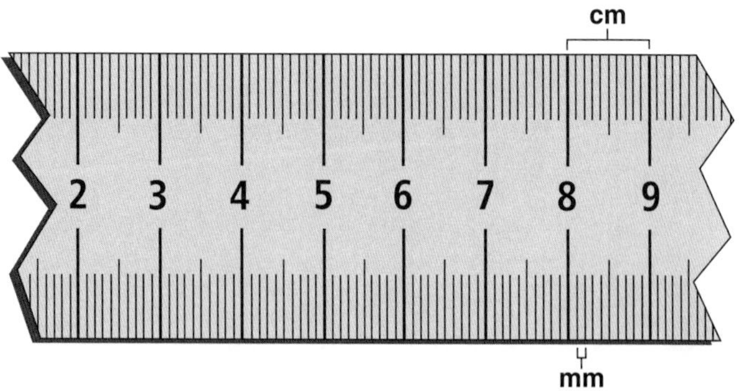

▲ **Figure 7** A meter stick is divided into centimeters and millimeters.

9 **CALCULATE:** How many centimeters are there in 3 m?

Measuring Area Do you know how people find the area of the floor of a room? They measure the length and the width of the room. Then, they multiply the two numbers. You can find the area of any rectangle by multiplying its length by its width. Area is expressed in square units, such as square meters (m^2) or square centimeters (cm^2).

$$\text{Area} = \text{length} \times \text{width}$$

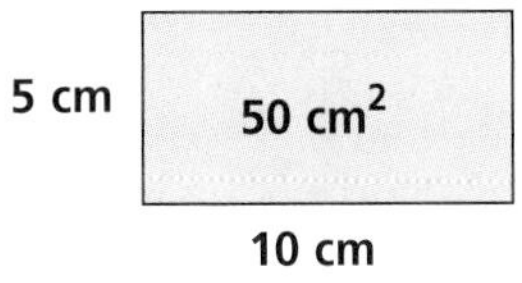

5 cm | 50 cm^2 | 10 cm

◀ **Figure 8** The area of a rectangle equals length times width.

10 CALCULATE: What is the area of a rectangle 2 cm × 3 cm?

Mass and Weight The amount of matter in something is its **mass.** The basic metric unit of mass is called a **gram (g).** A paper clip has about 1 g of mass. Mass is measured with an instrument called a balance. A balance works like a seesaw. It compares an unknown mass with a known mass.

One kind of balance that is commonly used to measure mass is a triple-beam balance. A triple-beam balance has a pan. The object being measured is placed on the pan. The balance also has three beams. Weights, called riders, are moved along each beam until the object on the pan is balanced. Each rider gives a reading in grams. The mass of the object is equal to the total readings of all three riders.

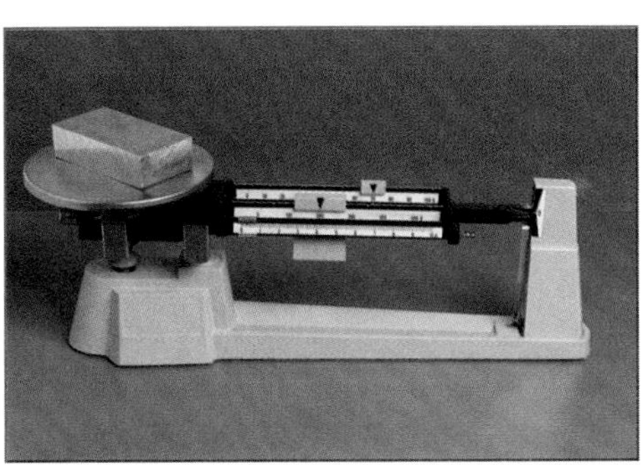

◀ **Figure 9** A triple-beam balance

Mass and weight are related; however, they are not the same. The weight of an object is a measure of Earth's pull of gravity between Earth and that object. Gravity is the force that pulls objects toward the center of Earth. The strength of the pull of gravity between two objects depends on the distance between the objects and how much mass they each contain. So, the weight changes as its distance from the center of Earth changes.

11 IDENTIFY: What instrument is used to measure mass?

Volume The amount of space an object takes up is its **volume.** You can measure the volume of liquids and solids. Liquid volume is usually measured in **liters.** Soft drinks in the United States often come in 2-liter bottles.

A graduated cylinder is used to measure liquid volume. Graduated cylinders are calibrated, or marked off, at regular intervals. Look at Figure 10. It shows a graduated cylinder. On this graduated cylinder, each small line is equal to 0.05 mL. The longer lines mark off every 0.25 mL up to 5.00 mL. However, every graduated cylinder is not calibrated in this manner. They come in different sizes up to 2,000 mL, with different calibrations.

Always read the measurement at eye level. If you are using a glass graduated cylinder, you will need to read the mark on the graduated cylinder closest to the bottom of the meniscus. A **meniscus** is the curve at the surface of a liquid in a thin tube. A plastic graduated cylinder does not show a meniscus.

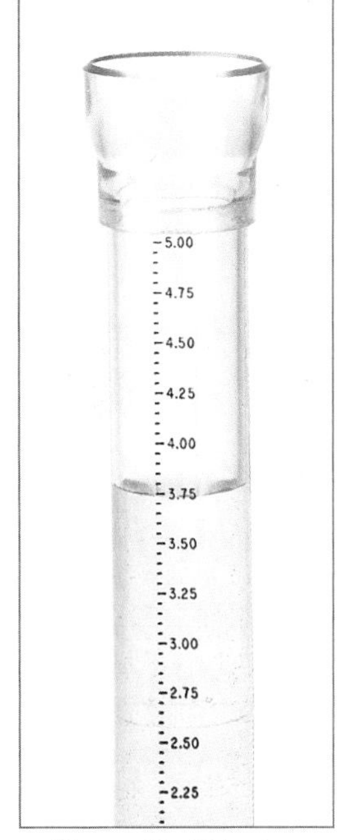

▲ **Figure 10** This glass graduated cylinder shows a meniscus.

The volume of solid objects is often measured in cubic centimeters. One cubic centimeter equals 1 milliliter (mL).

Look at Figure 11. Each side of the cube is 1 cm long. The volume of the cube is 1 cubic centimeter (cm^3). Now, look at the drawing of the box in Figure 12. Its length is 3 cm. Its width is 2 cm. Its height is 2 cm. The volume of the box can be found by multiplying length by width by height. In this case, volume equals $3 \times 2 \times 2$. Therefore, the volume of the box is 12 cm^3.

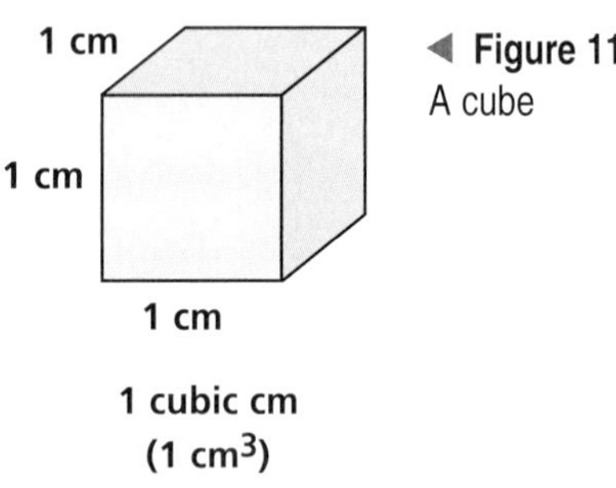

◀ **Figure 11** A cube

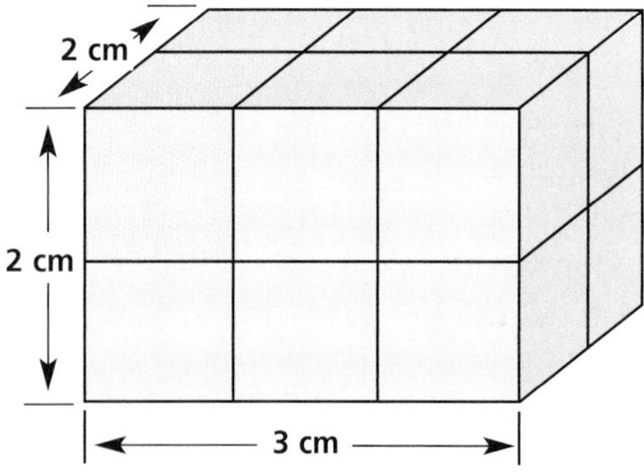

▲ **Figure 12** The volume of a box equals length by width by height.

$$V = L \times W \times H$$

If you have a box that is 10 cm on each side, its volume would be 1,000 cm^3. A liter is the same as 1,000 cm^3. One liter of liquid will fill the box exactly.

CALCULATE: How many milliliters of water would fill a 12-cm^3 box?

Hands-On Activity

CALCULATING AREA AND VOLUME

You will need 3 boxes of different sizes, paper, and a metric ruler.

1. Measure the length, width, and height of each box in centimeters. Record each measurement in your notes.
2. Calculate the volume of each box. Record each volume in your notes.
3. Find the surface area of each box. Record each area in your notes.

Practicing Your Skills

4. **ANALYZE:** Which of the three boxes has the largest volume?
5. **CALCULATE:** How many milliliters of liquid would fill each box?
6. **ANALYZE:** What is the surface area of the largest box?

Temperature **Temperature** is a measure of the amount of heat energy something contains. An instrument that measures temperature is called a thermometer.

Most thermometers are glass tubes. At the bottom of the tube is a wider part, called the bulb. The bulb is filled with liquid. Liquids that are often used include mercury, colored alcohol, or colored water. When heat is added, the liquid expands, or gets larger. It rises in the glass tube. When heat is taken away, the liquid contracts, or gets smaller. The liquid falls in the tube. On the side of the tube is a series of marks. You read the temperature by looking at the mark on the tube where the liquid stops.

Temperature can be measured on three different scales. These scales are the Fahrenheit (F) scale, the Celsius (C) scale, and the Kelvin (K) scale. The Fahrenheit scale is part of the English system of measurement. The Celsius scale is usually used in science. Almost all scientists, even in the United States, use the Celsius scale. Each unit on the Celsius scale is a degree Celsius (°C). The degree Celsius is the metric unit of temperature. Water freezes at 0°C. It boils at 100°C.

Scientists working with very low temperatures use the Kelvin scale. The Kelvin scale is part of the SI measurement system. It begins at absolute zero, or 0K. This number indicates, in theory at least, a total lack of heat.

COMPARING TEMPERATURE SCALES			
	Kelvin	Fahrenheit	Celsius
Boiling point of water	373K	212°F	100°C
Human body temperature	310K	98.6°F	37°C
Freezing point of water	273K	32°F	0°C
Absolute zero	0K	−459.67°F	−273.15°C

▲ **Figure 13**

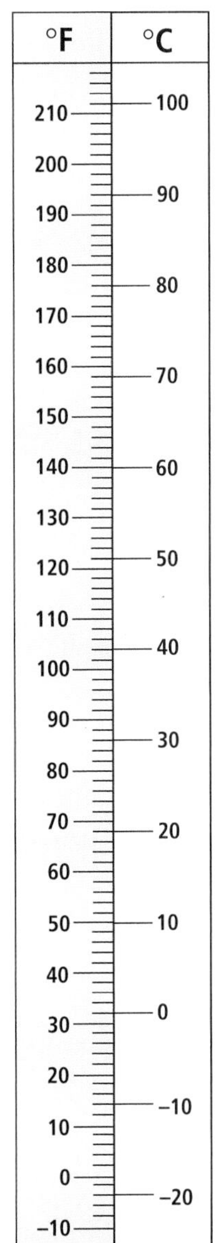

◀ **Figure 14** The Fahrenheit and Celsius scales

13 ▶ **NAME:** What are the three scales used to measure temperature?

Hands-On Activity

READING A THERMOMETER

You will need safety goggles, a lab apron, 2 beakers, a heat source, ice water, a wax pencil, a ruler, and a standard Celsius thermometer.

1. Boil some water in a beaker. ⚠CAUTION: Be very careful when working with heat. Place your thermometer in the beaker. Do not let the thermometer touch the sides or bottom of the beaker. Wait until the mercury rises as far as it will go. Record the temperature.
2. Fill a beaker with ice water. Place the unmarked thermometer into this beaker. Wait until the mercury goes as low as it will go. Record the temperature.

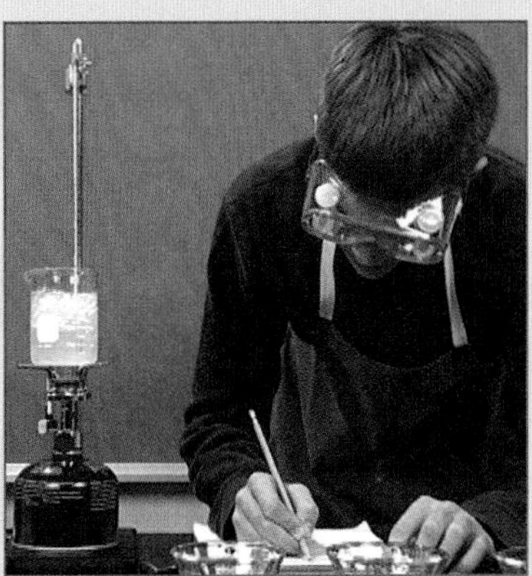

▲ **STEP 1** Record the temperature of the boiling water.

Practicing Your Skills

3. **IDENTIFY:** What is the temperature at which the mercury rose as high as it would go?
4. **IDENTIFY:** What is the temperature at which the mercury went as low as it would go?

Handbook A: Developing Skills

5 Analyzing Data and Communicating Results

Key Term

communication: sharing information

Analyzing Data When you organize information, you put it in a logical order. In scientific experiments, it is important to organize your data. Data collected during an experiment are not very useful unless they are organized and easy to read. It is also important to organize your data if you plan to share the results of your experiment.

Scientists often organize information visually by using data tables, charts, graphs, and diagrams. By using tables, charts, graphs, and diagrams, scientists can display a lot of information in a small space. They also make it easier to compare and interpret data.

Tables are made up of rows and columns. Columns run up and down. Rows run from left to right. Tables usually show numerical data. Information in the table can be arranged in time order. It can also be set up to show patterns or trends. A table showing wind speed can reveal the effects the speed of wind will have on land. Figure 15 shows a table of gases in the atmosphere.

GASES IN THE ATMOSPHERE	
Gas	Percentage
Oxygen	21
Carbon dioxide	0.04
Nitrogen	78
Water vapor, helium, and other gases	0.02
Argon	0.94

▲ **Figure 15**

Graphs, such as bar graphs, line graphs, and circle graphs, often use special coloring, shading, or patterns to represent information. Keys indicate what the special markings represent. Line graphs have horizontal (x) and vertical (y) axes to indicate such things as time and quantities.

14 EXPLAIN: How do tables and graphs help you analyze data?

Sharing Results When you talk to a friend, you are communicating, or sharing information. If you write a letter or a report, you are also communicating but in a different way. Scientists communicate all the time. They communicate to share results, information, and opinions. They write books and magazine or newspaper articles. They may also create Web sites about their work. This is called written **communication.**

Graphs are a visual way to communicate. The circle graph in Figure 16 is showing the same information from Figure 15. The circle graph presents the information in a different way.

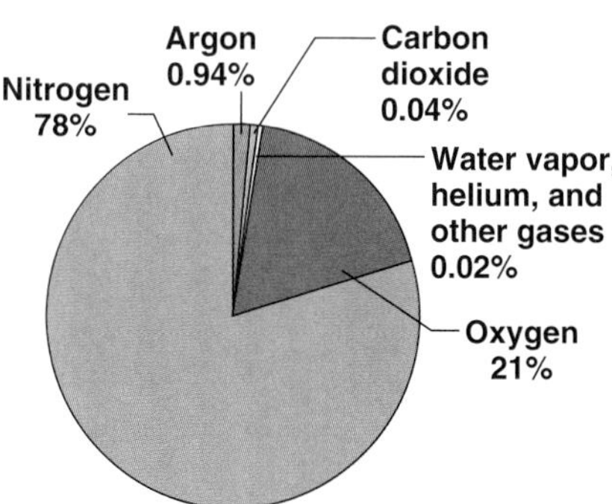

▲ **Figure 16** Circle graphs are a good way to show parts of a whole.

15 LIST: What are some ways to communicate the results of an experiment?

6 Making Predictions

Key Terms

infer: to form a conclusion

predict: to state ahead of time what you think is going to happen

Thinking of Possibilities When you **infer** something, you form a conclusion. This is called making an inference. Your conclusion will usually be based on observations or past experience. You may use logic to form your statement. Your statement might be supported by evidence and perhaps can be tested by an experiment. An inference is not a fact. It is only one possible explanation.

When you **predict,** you state ahead of time what you think will happen. Predictions about future events are based on inferences, evidence, or past experience. The two science process skills of inferring and predicting are very closely related.

16 CONTRAST: What is the difference between inferring and predicting?

How do you conduct a scientific investigation?

By now, you should have a good understanding of the science process skills. These skills are used to solve many science problems. There is also a basic procedure, or plan, that scientists usually follow when conducting investigations. Some people call this procedure the scientific method.

The scientific method is a series of steps that can serve as a guide to solving problems or answering questions. It uses many of the science process skills you know, such as observing and predicting.

Not all experiments use all of the steps in the scientific method. Some experiments follow all of them, but in a different order. In fact, there is no one right scientific method. Each problem is different. Some problems may require steps that another problem would not. However, most investigations will follow the same basic procedure.

1 **DESCRIBE:** What is the scientific method?

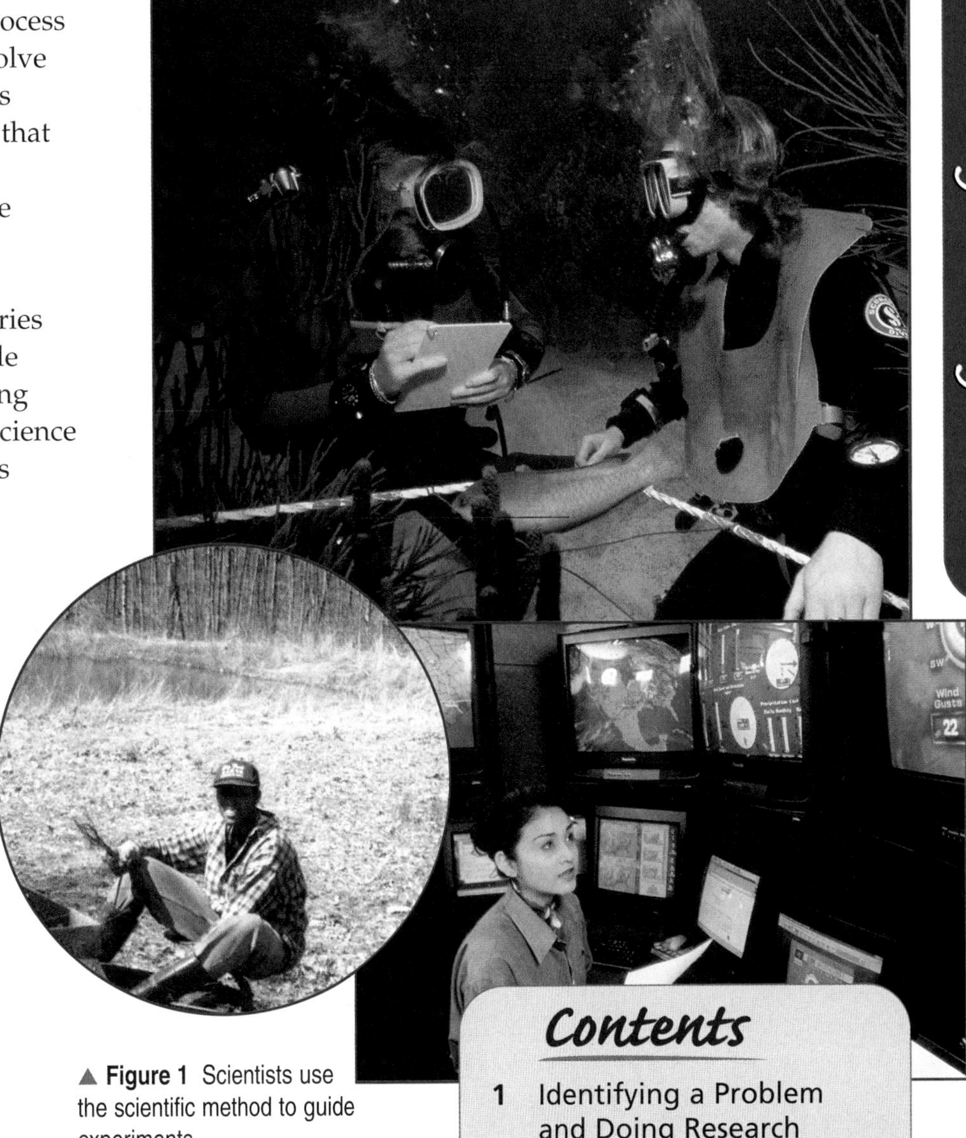

▲ **Figure 1** Scientists use the scientific method to guide experiments.

Contents

1 Identifying a Problem and Doing Research

Starting an Investigation Scientists often state a problem as a question. This is the first step in a scientific investigation. Most experiments begin by asking a scientific question. That is, they ask a question that can be answered by gathering evidence. This question is the reason for the scientific investigation. It also helps determine how the investigation will proceed.

Have you ever done background research for a science project? When you do this kind of research, you are looking for data that others have already obtained on the same subject. You can gather research by reading books, magazines, and newspapers, and by using the Internet to find out what other scientists have done. Doing research is the first step of gathering evidence for a scientific investigation.

 **IDENTIFY:** What is the first step of a scientific investigation?

BUILDING SCIENCE SKILLS

Researching Background Information Suppose you notice that a river running through your town looks brown on some days and clear on others. You also notice that when the river turns brown, it has usually rained the day before. You wonder if rain and the brown color of the river water are related.

To determine if the river water color is related to rainfall, look for information on rivers in encyclopedias, in geology books, and on the Internet. Put your findings in a report.

▲ **Figure 2** Water in river after a heavy rain.

2 Forming a Hypothesis

Key Terms

hypothesis: suggested answer to a question or problem

theory: set of hypotheses that have been supported by testing over and over again

Focusing the Investigation Scientists usually state clearly what they expect to find out in an investigation. This is called stating a hypothesis. A **hypothesis** is a suggested answer to a question or a solution to a problem. Stating a hypothesis helps to keep you focused on the problem and helps you decide what to test.

To form their hypotheses, scientists must think of possible explanations for a set of observations or they must suggest possible answers to a scientific question. One of those explanations becomes the hypothesis. In science, a hypothesis must include something that can be tested.

A hypothesis is more than just a guess. It must consider observations, past experiences, and previous knowledge. It is an inference turned into a statement that can be tested. A set of hypotheses that have been supported by testing over and over again by many scientists is called a **theory.** An example is the theory that explains how living things have evolved, or changed, over time.

A hypothesis can take the form of an "if…then" statement. A well-worded hypothesis is a guide for how to set up and perform an experiment.

3 **DESCRIBE:** How does a scientist form a hypothesis?

BUILDING SCIENCE SKILLS

Developing a Hypothesis If you are testing how river water and rainfall are related, you might write down this hypothesis:

Runoff is one cause of the river water turning brown.

Your hypothesis is incomplete. It is not enough to link water color and rainfall. You need to explain what materials make the river water brown and how rainfall causes those materials to get into the water. Revise the hypothesis above to make it more specific.

3 Designing and Carrying Out an Experiment

Key Terms

variable: anything that can affect the outcome of an experiment

constant: something that does not change

controlled experiment: experiment in which all the conditions except one are kept constant

Testing the Hypothesis Scientists need to plan how to test their hypotheses. This means they must design an experiment. The plan must be a step-by-step procedure. It should include a record of any observations made or measurements taken.

All experiments must take variables into account. A **variable** is anything that can affect the outcome of an experiment. Room temperature, amount of sunlight, and water vapor in the air are just some of the many variables that could affect the outcome of an experiment.

4 **DEFINE:** What is a variable?

Controlling the Experiment One of the variables in an experiment should be what you are testing. This is what you will change during the experiment. All other variables need to remain the same. In this experiment, you will vary the type of earth.

A **constant** is something that does not change. If there are no constants in your experiment, you will not be sure why you got the results you did. An experiment in which all the conditions except one are kept constant is called a **controlled experiment.**

Some experiments have two setups. In one setup, called the control, nothing is changed. In the other setup, the variable being tested is changed. Later, the control group can be compared with the other group to provide useful data.

5 **EXPLAIN:** Explain how a controlled experiment is set up.

Designing the Procedure Suppose you now want to design an experiment to determine what makes river water brown. You have your hypothesis. You decide your procedure is to construct a slightly tilted model of the river, the town, and the land upstream from the town. You will send water down the river and measure the color and clarity of the water. Next, you will create artificial rain and again check the color and clarity of the water.

Does it matter how much rain you add to your model? Does it matter how heavy the rainfall is? Does 3 inches (7.5 cm) of rainfall in 5 minutes have the same effect on your model as 3 inches in 1 hour?

In designing your experiment, you need to identify the variables. The amount of water and the rate at which you apply it to your model are variables that could affect the outcome of your experiment. Another important variable for your experiment is the steepness of the river. To be sure of your results, you will have to conduct your experiment several times. Each time you will alter just one variable while keeping the other variables just the same.

Finally, you should decide on the data you will collect. How will you measure the color and clarity of the water of the river? You might make a color chart that you lower into the river water to see how the sediment in the water changes its color.

The hands-on activity on page 12 is an example of an experiment you might have designed.

◀ **Figure 3** In your experiment, you will elevate the trays with books to test soil runoff.

6 **EXPLAIN:** How do constants and variables affect an experiment?

Hands-On Activity

CARRYING OUT AN EXPERIMENT

You will need 2 styrofoam meat trays from the grocery store, garden soil, grass sod, 2 plastic drinking glasses, 2 books, sprinkling can, scissors, and water. You should wear an apron and safety goggles.

1. Cut a small drain notch from the center of one end of each tray.
   ⚠ **CAUTION:** Be careful when using scissors.
2. Fill one tray with about a 1-inch layer (2.5 cm) of garden soil. Leave 2 inches (5 cm) of the notched end of the tray empty of soil.
3. Fill the second tray with a layer of sod except for 2 inches at the end with the notch.
4. Place the notched end of each tray at the edge of a table so that the trays extend over the edge a short distance.
5. Elevate the other end of the trays with books.
6. Label the cups Soil and Sod.
7. Sprinkle the soil tray with water. Keep sprinkling until the water runs off the surface of the soil and pours out the notch drain. Collect a glass of runoff water.
8. Repeat Step 7 with the sod tray.

Practicing Your Skills

9. **OBSERVE:** How much water did you have to sprinkle on the soil tray in order to collect a full glass?
10. **OBSERVE:** How much water did you have to sprinkle on the sod tray in order to collect a full glass?
11. **COMPARE:** Which glass had the dirtiest water?
12. **EXPLAIN:** What caused the difference in water clarity in the two cups?
13. **INFER:** What would be the best way to reduce soil runoff in rivers?

4 Recording and Analyzing Data

Dealing With Data During an experiment, you must keep careful notes about what you observe. For example, you might need to note how long the rain fell on the trays before water began running off. How fast did the water run off each tray? This is important information that might affect your conclusion.

At the end of an experiment, you will need to study the data to find any patterns. Much of the data you will deal with is written text such as a report or a summary of an experiment. However, scientific information is often a set of numbers or facts presented in other, more visual ways. These visual presentations make the information easier to understand. Tables, charts, and graphs, for instance, help you understand a collection of facts on a topic.

After your data have been organized, you need to ask what the data show. Do they support your hypothesis? Do they show something wrong in your experiment? Do you need to gather more data by performing another experiment?

 **LIST:** What are some ways to display data?

BUILDING SCIENCE SKILLS

Analyzing Data You made the following notes during your experiment. How would you display this information?

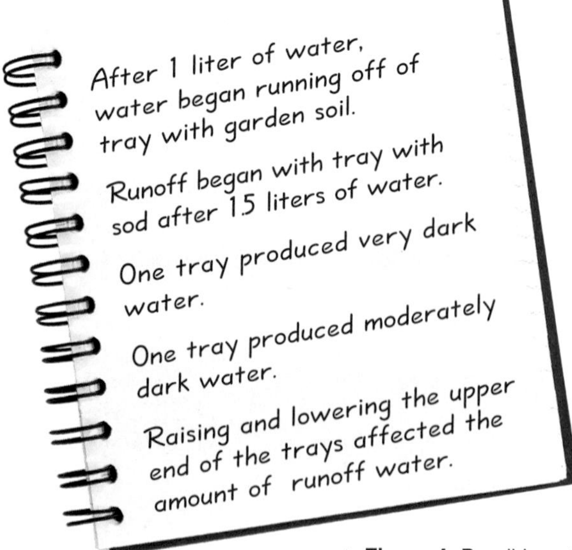

▲ **Figure 4** Possible notes

5 Stating a Conclusion

Drawing Conclusions A conclusion is a statement that sums up what you have learned from an experiment. When you draw a conclusion, you need to decide whether the data you collected supported your hypothesis. You may need to repeat an experiment several times before you can draw any conclusions from it. Conclusions often lead you to ask new questions and plan new experiments to answer them.

8 **EXPLAIN:** Why might it be necessary to repeat an experiment?

BUILDING SCIENCE SKILLS

Stating a Conclusion Review your hypothesis statement regarding the effect of surface material on rainwater runoff. Then, review the data you obtained during the experiment.

- Was your hypothesis correct? Use your observations to support your answer.
- Which surface reduced soil runoff better?

▲ **Figure 5** Throughout this program, you may use forms like these to organize your lab reports.

6 Writing a Report

Communicating Results Scientists keep careful written records of their observations and findings. These records are used to create a lab report. Lab reports are a form of written communication. They explain what happened in the experiment. A good lab report should be written so that anyone reading it can duplicate the experiment. It should contain the following information:

- A title
- A purpose
- Background information
- Your hypothesis
- Materials used
- Your step-by-step procedure
- Your observations
- Your recorded data
- Your analysis of the data
- Your conclusions

Your conclusions should relate back to the questions you asked in the "purpose" section of your report. Also, the report should not have any experimental errors that might have caused unexpected results. For example, did you follow the steps in the correct order? Did an unexpected variable interfere with your results? Was your equipment clean and in good working order? This explanation of possible errors should also be part of your conclusions.

9 **EXPLAIN:** Why is it important to explain possible errors in your lab report?

BUILDING SCIENCE SKILLS

Writing a Lab Report Write a lab report to communicate to other scientists your discoveries about soil runoff. Your lab report should include a title, your hypothesis statement, a list of materials you used, the procedure, your observations, and your conclusions. Try to include one table of data in your report.

LAB SAFETY

Working in a science laboratory can be both exciting and meaningful. However, you must always be aware of safety precautions when carrying out experiments. There are a few basic rules that should be followed in any science laboratory:

- Read all instructions carefully before the start of an experiment. Follow all instructions exactly and in the correct order.
- Check your equipment to make sure it is clean and working properly.
- Never taste, smell, or touch any substance in the lab that you are not told to do so. Never eat or drink anything in the lab. Do not chew gum.
- Never work alone. Tell a teacher at once if an accident occurs.

Experiments that use chemicals or heat can be dangerous. The following list of rules and symbols will help you avoid accidents. There are also rules about what to do if an accident does occur. Here are some rules to remember when working in a lab:

1. Do not use glass that is chipped or metal objects with broken edges. Do not try to clean up broken glassware yourself. Notify your teacher if a piece of glassware is broken.

2. Do not use electrical cords with loose plugs or frayed ends. Do not let electrical cords cross in front of working areas. Do not use electrical equipment near water.

3. Be very careful when using sharp objects such as scissors, knives, or tweezers. Always cut in a direction away from your body.

4. Be careful when you are using a heat source. Use proper equipment, such as tongs or a ringstand, when handling hot objects.

5. Confine loose clothing and hair when working with an open flame. Be sure you know the location of the nearest fire extinguisher. Never reach across an open flame.

6. Be careful when working with poisonous or toxic substances. Never mix chemicals without directions from your teacher. Remove any long jewelry that might hang down and end up in chemicals. Avoid touching your eyes or mouth when working with chemicals.

7. Use extreme care when working with acids and bases. Never mix acids and bases without direction from your teacher. Never smell anything directly. Use caution when handling chemicals that produce fumes.

8. Wear safety goggles, especially when working with an open flame, chemicals, and any liquids.

9. Wear lab aprons when working with substances of any sort, especially chemicals.

10. Use caution when handling or collecting plants. Some plants can be harmful if they are touched or eaten.

11. Use caution when handling live animals. Some animals can injure you or spread disease. Handle all live animals as humanely as possible.

12. Dispose of all equipment and materials properly. Keep your work area clean at all times.

13. Always wash your hands thoroughly with soap and water after handling chemicals or live organisms.

14. Follow the ⚠ CAUTION and safety symbols you see used throughout this book when doing labs or other activities.

Chapter 1 The Motions of Earth, the Sun, and the Moon

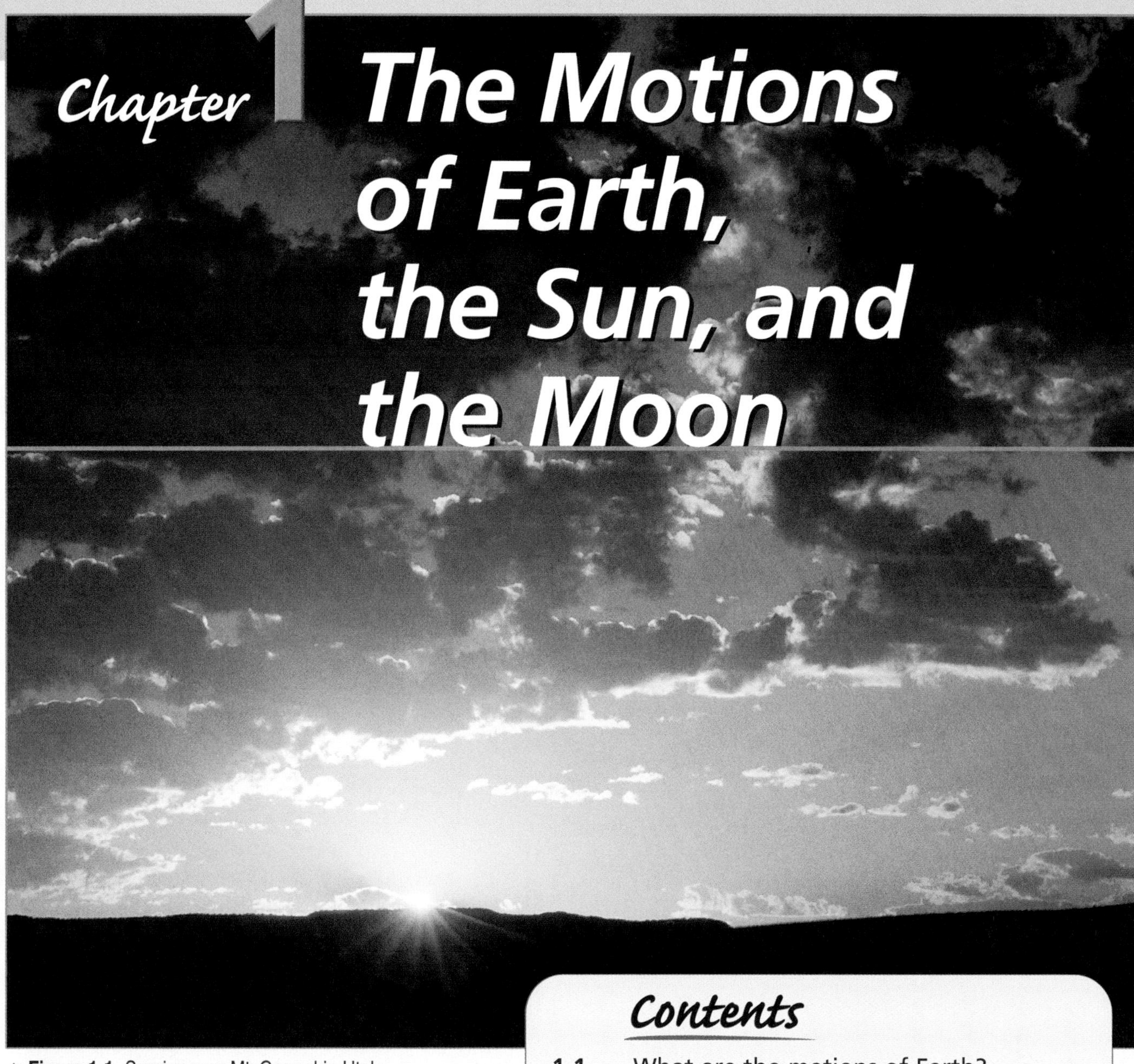

▲ **Figure 1-1** Sunrise over Mt. Carmel in Utah

Contents

The passing of a single day can be seen by watching the Sun in the sky. The Sun appears each morning in the east. This is sunrise. During the daytime, the Sun appears to move westward across the sky. Finally, at sunset, it disappears below the western horizon. This is what we call a day. A few hours later, the Sun seems to rise again in the east to begin a new day. However, the Sun never actually rises or sets. It is just an illusion.

▶ How do you think the motions of Earth makes it seem as if the Sun is moving across the sky?

1-1 What are the motions of Earth?

Modeling Day and Night
HANDS-ON ACTIVITY

1. Push a wooden stick through a plastic foam ball. Mark a line of dots around the ball.
2. Place the stick upright in modeling clay. Tilt it at about a 20° angle. Turn on a flashlight or desk lamp and darken the room.
3. Point the angled stick toward the light source. Rotate it and observe.
4. Move the ball so that the stick points away from the light source and observe.

THINK ABOUT IT: What happens to the light when it hits the ball? What do you observe when you rotate the ball on its stick?

Objective
Explain Earth's motions.

Key Terms
revolution (rehv-uh-LOO-shuhn)**:** movement of a planet or other body orbiting another body

axis (AK-sihs)**:** imaginary line through the center of a planet or other body around which that body spins

rotation (roh-TAY-shuhn)**:** spinning of a planet or other body on its axis

Revolution Although you cannot feel it, Earth is always moving. It moves in an orbit around the Sun. This movement is called **revolution.** One complete revolution around the Sun takes 365 1/4 days, or one year. Earth's path as it goes around the Sun is called its orbit. As Earth travels around the Sun, Earth's orbit forms a slightly flattened circle, or oval, shape.

1 **DESCRIBE:** What is the motion of Earth around the Sun called?

Rotation Besides revolving, Earth also spins on its axis. An **axis** is an imaginary line through the center of a planet or other body around which that body spins. Earth's axis is tilted at an angle of 23 1/2° relative to an imaginary line drawn perpendicular to its orbit. The North Pole of Earth always points toward Polaris, the North Star.

The spinning of a planet or other body on its axis is called **rotation.** Our planet rotates once every 24 hours. This gives us a daily cycle of daylight and darkness, or day and night. The side of Earth's surface that faces the Sun has daylight. The side that faces away from the Sun has darkness. At any moment, half of Earth is experiencing daylight. The other half is experiencing darkness.

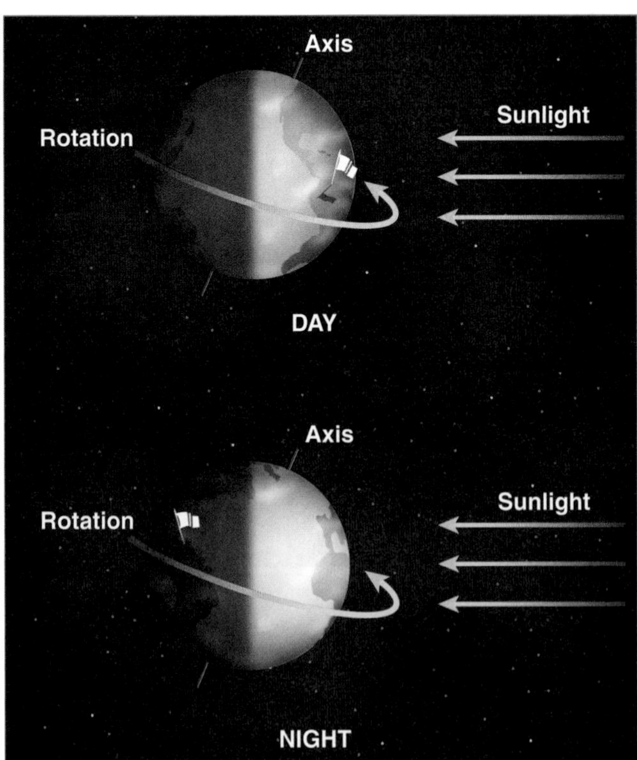

▲ **Figure 1-2** Earth rotating on its axis causes day and night.

2 **IDENTIFY:** What is the motion of Earth on its axis called?

Sunrise and Sunset When viewed from the North Pole, Earth rotates on its axis from west to east. This makes the Sun appear to rise in the east and set in the west. As Earth rotates, the Sun seems to move across the sky from east to west. This is called the Sun's apparent motion.

 **RELATE:** In which direction does Earth rotate?

✓ CHECKING CONCEPTS

1. How long does it take Earth to make one complete revolution around the Sun?
2. What causes the change from day to night?
3. Why does the Sun appear to rise in the east?
4. At what angle is Earth's axis tilted?

THINKING CRITICALLY

5. **CONTRAST:** How is rotation different from revolution?
6. **DESCRIBE:** What is the shape of Earth's orbit?
7. **PREDICT:** What would happen if Earth did not rotate?
8. **INFER:** Like the Sun, the Moon seems to rise in the east and set in the west. Why?

Web InfoSearch

The 24-Hour Day Since ancient times, people have had an interest in measuring and recording the passage of time. The ancient Egyptians were the first to use a 24-hour day. Their system was based on observing a series of 36 stars called decan stars. The decan stars rise and set in the sky every 40 to 60 minutes.

SEARCH: Use the Internet to find out more about decan stars. What are they? How did they lead the Egyptians to create the 24-hour day? Start your search at www.conceptsandchallenges.com. Some key search words are **decan stars, Egyptian astronomy,** and **ancient calendars.**

How Do They Know That?

EARTH ROTATES ON ITS AXIS

A pendulum is a weight that swings freely back and forth. It can be used to show that Earth rotates.

French physicist Jean Bernard Leon Foucault (1819–1868) provided proof of Earth's rotation with a pendulum. Using an early camera, he photographed the Sun. The camera took pictures on a light-sensitive plate. Leaving the camera focused on the Sun for some time, Foucault showed that the Sun's position relative to Earth changed. He invented a pendulum-driven device to keep the camera in line with the Sun. However, he noticed that his pendulum tended to swing in the direction from which it was first released. If he tried to turn it, it always returned to its original path. From this experiment, he concluded that Earth was rotating.

▲ **Figure 1-3** Foucault's pendulum

Foucault set up a demonstration to prove his conclusion. He released a giant ball over a pile of sand. The ball scratched a straight line in the sand. Over the course of the day, that line shifted again and again to the right. Eventually, it came full circle.

Thinking Critically What did it mean that the pendulum was not changing course?

1-2 What are time zones?

Objectives

Use standard time zones to compare times around the world. Identify eight U.S. time zones.

Key Terms

solar noon: time of day when the Sun is highest in the sky

standard time: system whereby all places within a time zone all have the same time

International Date Line: boundary formed where the first and twenty-fourth time zones meet

Solar Time The Sun can be used to tell time. Using the Sun to measure time is called solar time. When the Sun is highest in the sky, the time is **solar noon.** Because Earth rotates, different places have solar noon at different times. For example, when it is solar noon in Philadelphia, it is 4 minutes after solar noon in New York and 17 minutes after solar noon in Boston.

1 **HYPOTHESIZE:** What is a problem that is likely to arise using solar time?

Standard Time Even though clocks allowed people to keep track of time, there was still a problem. Each region set its own time, and there was no way to coordinate between regions. This problem grew when railroads were built and people traveled more. A system was needed on which to base a train schedule. This system would also help travelers schedule meetings in other towns.

In 1884, an international agreement was reached that divided Earth's surface into 24 time zones. Each of these time zones was to be 15° of longitude wide. All places within a time zone would have the same time. This time was called **standard time.**

2 **DESCRIBE:** What is standard time?

U.S. Time Zones The United States has eight time zones. These are Eastern Standard, Central Standard, Mountain Standard, Pacific Standard, Alaska Standard, Hawaiian Standard, Samoan Standard, and Atlantic Standard.

As you move west, the time in each zone is one hour earlier than in the previous time zone. As a result, when it is noon in New York, it is 11:00 A.M. in Chicago.

Look at Figure 1-4. Notice that time zones do not have straight boundaries. The boundaries were drawn this way to keep whole states or large neighboring cities in the same time zone.

3 **CALCULATE:** If it is 12:00 noon in California, what time is it in Virginia?

World Time Zones There are 24 standard time zones and 24 hours in a day. The first time zone is on one side of the boundary called the **International Date Line.** The twenty-fourth time zone is on the other side. As you cross over the International Date Line, you either gain or lose 24 hours. If you were to travel west, you would have to move your calendar ahead one full day when you crossed the International Date Line.

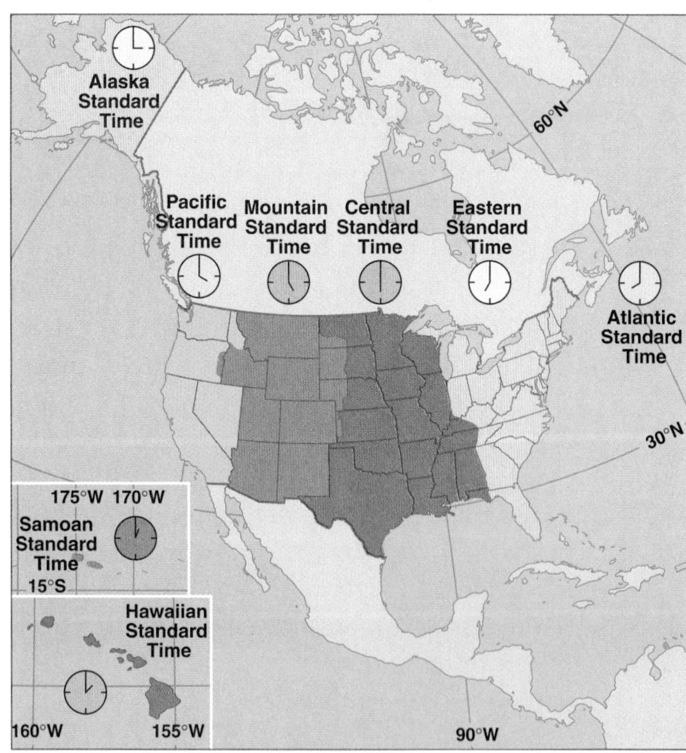

▲ **Figure 1-4** Time zones of the United States

4 **INFER:** What happens to the date if you cross the International Date Line going east?

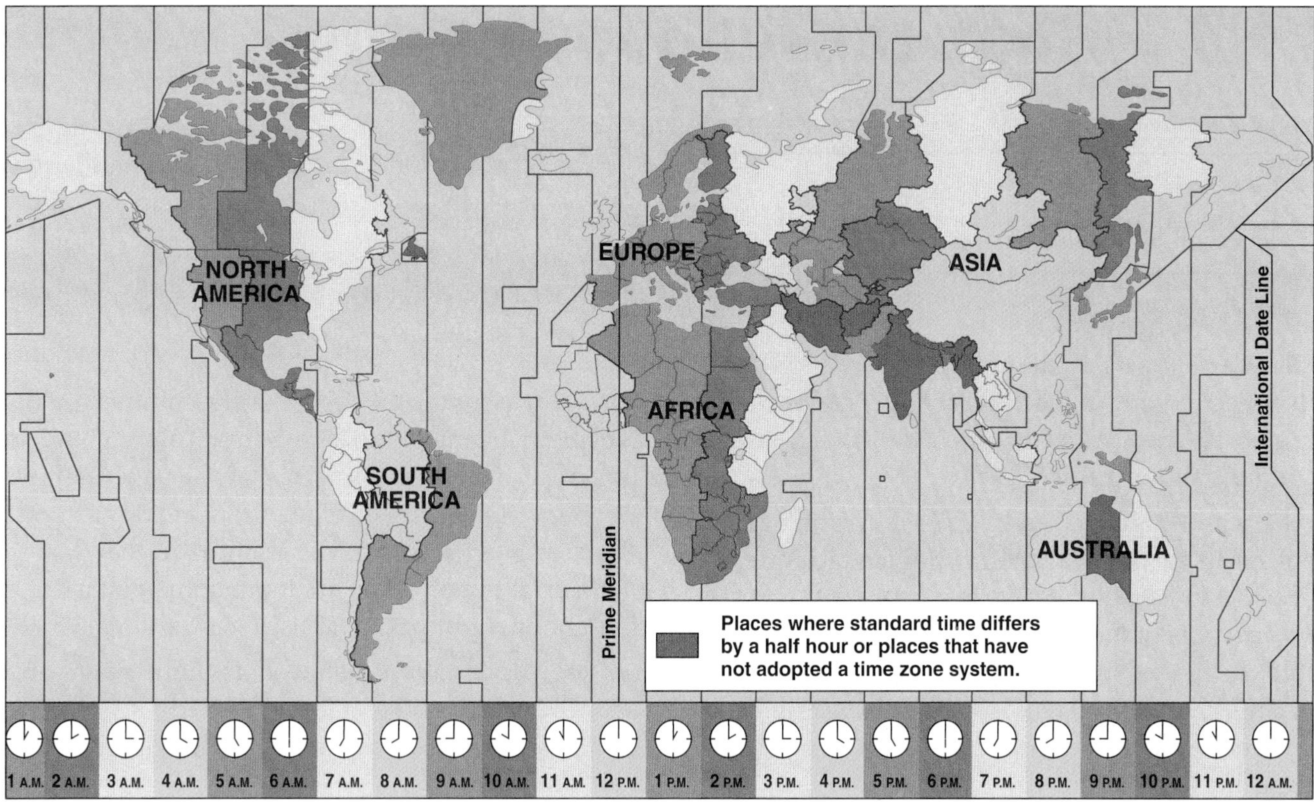

▲ **Figure 1-5** Time zones around the world

CHECKING CONCEPTS

1. There are __________ time zones in the world.
2. Using the Sun to measure time is __________.
3. The 48 states in the continental United States have __________ time zones.
4. If you cross the International Date Line going east, you would __________ 24 hours.
5. As you travel west, you move the clock __________ one hour for each time zone.

THINKING CRITICALLY

Use Figures 1-4, 1-5, and Appendix G in this book to help you answer the following questions.

6. **IDENTIFY:** In which time zone is Texas located?
7. **ANALYZE:** If it is 3:00 P.M. in Florida, what time is it in Oregon?
8. **CALCULATE:** Suppose you leave California at 12:00 noon Pacific Standard Time and take a six-hour plane trip to Boston. When you land in Boston, what would the time be there?
9. **IDENTIFY:** In which time zone do you live?
10. **ANALYZE:** Earth rotates from west to east. Would a town to your west have solar noon before or after you? Explain.

Web InfoSearch

Jet Lag Jet lag is a term given to the tired feeling people get when they travel across three or more time zones. Jet lag occurs because your body is adjusted to the time zone where you live, and not adjusted to the time zone to which you have just traveled. It is easier for your body to adjust to a longer day traveling west than to a shorter day traveling east. For this reason, jet lag usually affects people who are flying east more than it affects people who are flying west.

SEARCH: Use the Internet to find out more about jet lag. How does it affect choice of flying times? What methods are there for overcoming the effects of jet lag? Start your search at www.conceptsandchallenges.com. Some key search words are **time zone, jet lag,** and **avoiding jet lag.**

1-3 What causes the seasons?

Objective

Explain what causes the change of seasons.

Why the Seasons Change As you learned earlier, Earth's axis is tilted at 23 1/2°. The North Pole of Earth points toward Polaris, the North Star. The axis always points in the same direction as Earth moves in its orbit.

The seasons are caused by a combination of the tilt of Earth's axis and Earth's movement around the Sun. At one point in Earth's orbit of the Sun, the North Pole of Earth is tilted toward the Sun. Six months later, the North Pole is tilted away from the Sun. This change in position changes the angle at which the Sun's rays strike Earth's surface and is responsible for the change of seasons.

When the North Pole is tilted toward the Sun, the Northern Hemisphere receives the Sun's rays almost directly. The more direct the rays are, the better that part of Earth's surface is heated.

The tilt of Earth's axis also causes the total number of daylight hours to change. When the North Pole is tilted toward the Sun, the Northern Hemisphere has more hours of daylight than it does of darkness.

The combination of more direct rays and longer days warms the Northern Hemisphere. It causes summer in that region.

1 **DESCRIBE:** What combination of factors causes the change of seasons?

Opposite Seasons When it is summer in the Northern Hemisphere, the Southern Hemisphere tilts away from the Sun. The rays it receives from the Sun are less direct. They are spread out more. There are also fewer daylight hours in that part of the world. In fact, there are more hours of darkness than of daylight.

The combination of fewer daylight hours and less direct rays cause that part of Earth's surface to cool. The lower temperatures cause winter in that part of the world.

The Northern and Southern hemispheres have opposite seasons. Look at Figure 1-6. Notice that when the Northern Hemisphere is tilted away from the Sun, it has winter.

At the same time it is winter in the Northern Hemisphere, the Southern Hemisphere is tilted toward the Sun and has summer. When summer comes to the Northern Hemisphere, it is winter in the Southern Hemisphere.

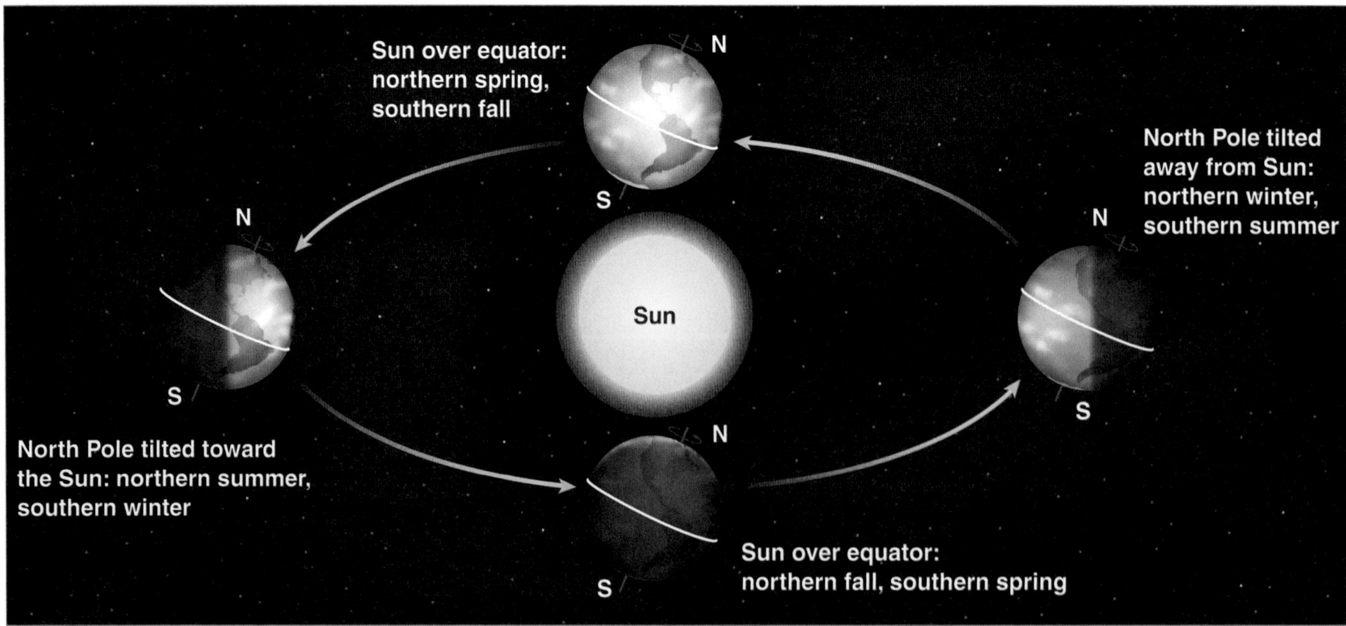

▲ **Figure 1-6** The seasons are caused by Earth's tilt and its revolution around the Sun.

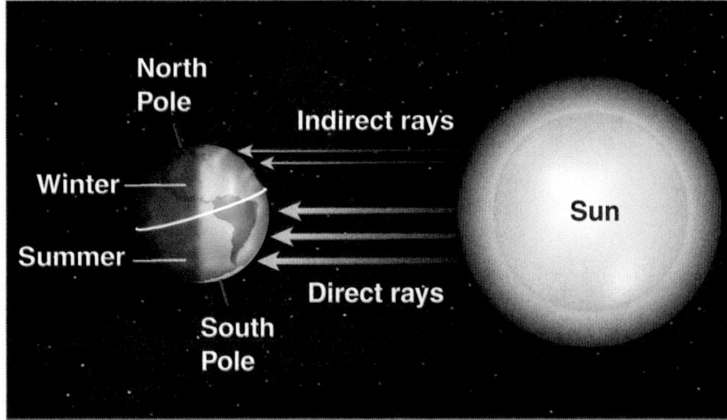

▲ **Figure 1-7** December in New York City

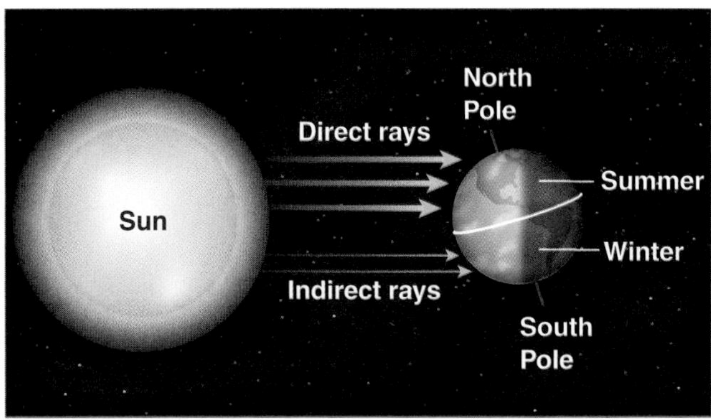

▲ **Figure 1-8** June in Australia

 **IDENTIFY:** If it is summer in the Northern Hemisphere, what season is it in the Southern Hemisphere?

 CHECKING CONCEPTS

1. The North Pole points __________ the Sun during the summer in the Northern Hemisphere.
2. Seasons are caused by the __________ of Earth's axis.

THINKING CRITICALLY

3. **ANALYZE:** If it is summer at the North Pole, what season is it at the South Pole?
4. **INFER:** Why do you think direct sunlight produces more heat than indirect sunlight?

BUILDING MATH SKILLS

Measuring Light from the Sun strikes Earth's surface at different angles. Angles are measured in degrees. A full circle has 360°. When the Sun is directly overhead, near the equator, it is at an angle of 90° to Earth's surface. A 90° angle is called a right angle. It is one-fourth of a circle. When the Sun is near the horizon, it is at an angle of 0° to Earth's surface. Earth's axis is tilted at an angle of $23\frac{1}{2}$°. About what fraction of a right angle is this?

Hands-On Activity

MODELING DIRECT AND INDIRECT RAYS

You will need a flashlight and graph paper.

1. Hold a flashlight about 20 cm above a sheet of graph paper. Shine the flashlight straight down. On the paper, trace around the outer edge of light. Count how many boxes are inside the circle you made. Record the number.
2. Tilt the flashlight, making sure you keep it at the same height. Again, trace around the edge of the light. Count the number of boxes inside this. Record the number.

▲ **STEP 2** Again trace around the outline of light made by the flashlight.

Practicing Your Skills

3. **OBSERVE:** **a.** Which light rays were spread out over a larger area, the direct rays or the slanted rays? **b.** Which rays were brighter, the direct rays or the slanted rays?
4. **HYPOTHESIZE:** Which rays do you think heat better, direct rays or slanted rays?
5. **CONCLUDE:** When do you think Earth's surface in the Northern Hemisphere gets the more direct rays of the Sun, in the summer or in the winter? Explain.

1-4 What are the solstices and equinoxes?

Objective

Define solstice and equinox.

Key Terms

perihelion (per-uh-HEE-lee-uhn)**:** point in a planet's orbit at which it is closest to the Sun

aphelion (uh-FEE-lee-uhn)**:** point in a planet's orbit at which it is farthest from the Sun

solstice (SAHL-stihs)**:** day of the year the Sun reaches its highest or lowest point in the sky

equinox (EE-kwih-nahks)**:** day the Sun shines directly on the equator

Near and Far During the year, the distance between Earth and the Sun changes. Earth is at **perihelion,** or closest to the Sun, in early January. Earth and the Sun are then about 147 million km apart. The Northern Hemisphere has winter. In early July, Earth is at **aphelion,** or its farthest point from the Sun. This distance is about 152 million km. Yet, this is summer in the Northern Hemisphere. The seasons do not depend on how far Earth is from the Sun.

1 NAME: During which season is the Northern Hemisphere closest to the Sun?

The Solstices The beginning of the summer and winter seasons is marked by a day called a solstice. The word **solstice** means "Sun stop."

In the Northern Hemisphere, the first day of summer is on or about June 21. The Sun seems to travel in its highest path across the sky. This day is called the summer solstice. On this day, Earth is very close to aphelion. The North Pole has 24 hours of daylight. At the same time, the South Pole points away from the Sun. The South Pole has 24 hours of darkness. Winter begins on this date in the Southern Hemisphere.

▲ **Figure 1-10** The period of daylight reaches a full 24 hours at the polar zones in summer. This phenomenon is known as the midnight Sun.

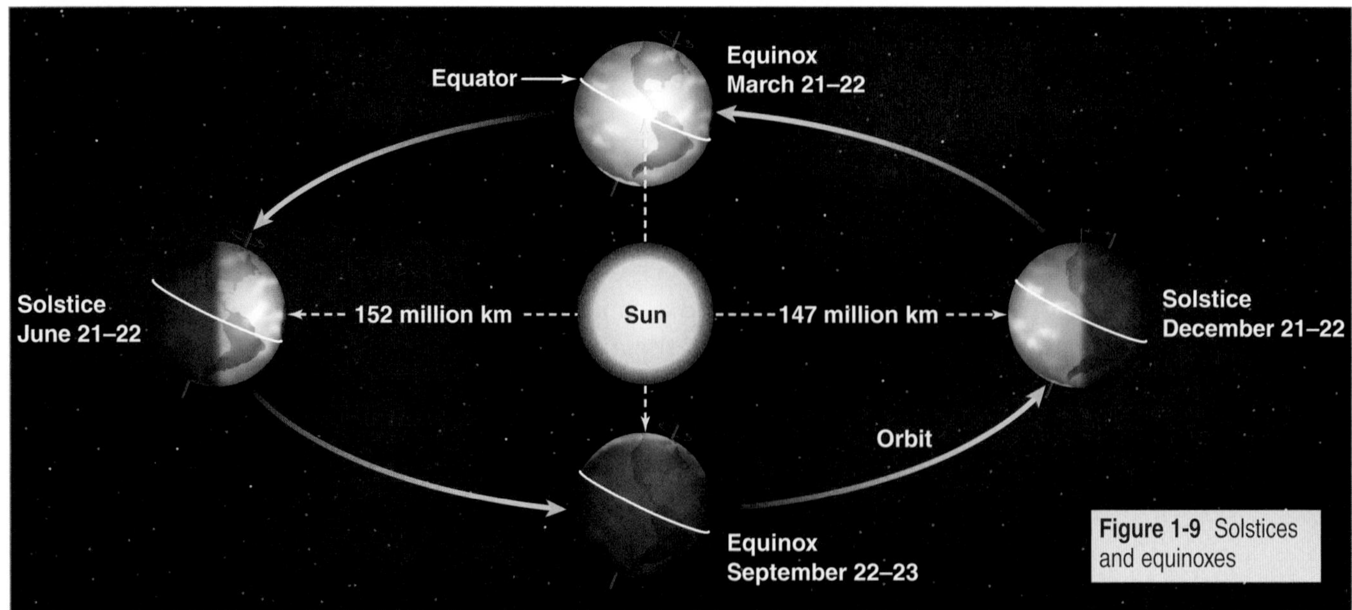

Figure 1-9 Solstices and equinoxes

The first day of winter in the Northern Hemisphere is on or about December 21. This day is called the winter solstice. On the winter solstice, Earth is very close to perihelion. The North Pole points away from the Sun. The Sun seems to follow its lowest path across the sky. On this day, the South Pole has 24 hours of daylight.

IDENTIFY: What day marks the first day of winter in the Southern Hemisphere?

The Equinoxes Because of the tilt of Earth's axis, the Sun's position relative to Earth's equator is constantly changing. Most of the time, the Sun is north or south of the equator at solar noon. Two times during the year, the Sun is directly over the equator at solar noon. These are the **equinoxes.** The equinoxes mark the beginning of the spring and fall seasons. The spring, or vernal, equinox occurs around March 21. The fall, or autumnal, equinox occurs around September 21. During an equinox, there are 12 hours of darkness and 12 hours of daylight everywhere on Earth.

NAME: On which days of the year does the North Pole have 12 hours of daylight and 12 hours of night?

CHECKING CONCEPTS

1. What is a day with 12 hours of daylight and 12 hours of darkness called?
2. What date marks the beginning of winter in the Northern Hemisphere?
3. Are the days longer or shorter in the Northern Hemisphere right after the autumnal equinox?
4. *Equinox* means "equal night." How many hours of daylight and darkness are there during the fall and spring equinoxes?

THINKING CRITICALLY

5. **DESCRIBE:** What is winter like in your area? Explain why.
6. **HYPOTHESIZE:** On the winter solstice, the North Pole has 24 hours of darkness. How would this affect your life that day if you lived there?

BUILDING READING SKILLS

Using Prefixes The prefix *equi-* means "equal." Find five words in the dictionary that contain this prefix. Write down these words and their definitions on a sheet of paper. Circle the part of the definition that relates to the prefix.

How Do They Know That?

PREDICTING THE CHANGE OF SEASONS

Ancient peoples made calendars based on astronomical events that occurred the same time each year. Some of these calendars were monuments. One such monument is called Stonehenge.

Stonehenge stands on a plain in Salisbury, England. It was built around 1848 B.C. The monument is made of huge blocks of sandstone 4 m high. They form a circle 30 m across. Inside the circle, there are two horseshoe-shaped sets of stones. A flat block of sandstone 5 m long rests inside the inner horseshoe. About 73 m away from the flat sandstone block is a stone marker.

▲ **Figure 1-11** Stonehenge is a giant calendar that predicts solstices and equinoxes.

Stonehenge is a giant calendar that can predict the change of seasons. It can also predict the solstices and equinoxes. A shadow is cast by the stone marker onto the flat sandstone block. This marks the direction in which the Sun rises and sets on the longest day of the year, the summer solstice.

Thinking Critically What might ancient peoples have needed calendars for?

Integrating Life Science

THE Big IDEA

How does the change of seasons affect animal behavior?

Does the weather in your town change with the seasons? If so, you probably respond to this by wearing different clothing and participating in different activities. Animals respond to environmental changes, too. Some shed thick coats to prepare for warm summer weather. Others store food to prepare for the time cold weather makes food scarce. Animals that migrate take more drastic actions. They leave their homes and travel thousands of miles in search of better living conditions for the season. Many breed in their winter homes.

California gray whales are migratory animals. During the summer and early fall, the whales live in the cold waters of the Chukchi and Bering seas. In late fall, they migrate southward. They travel more than 8,000 km to the calm, warm waters of Baja California. In the shallow waters of their winter home, the whales breed and produce young. In the late spring, they return to their Arctic summer home.

Monarch butterflies migrate in the same general direction as California gray whales. The butterflies spend the summer in the northern United States. In the fall, they migrate to the California coast, Mexico, and Florida.

Of all migrating animals, Arctic terns travel the greatest distance. These birds spend the summer breeding in northern Canada. In the fall, they travel more than 17,600 km southward to their Antarctic winter home. The arrival of spring triggers a return trip northward.

Look at the illustrations and photos that appear on these two pages. Then, follow the directions in the Science Log to find out more about "the big idea." ✦

BERING SEA

California Gray Whales

During their southward journey in fall, California gray whales travel along the West Coast. For this reason, whale watching is a popular fall activity in California.

PACIFIC OCEAN

WRITING ACTIVITY

Science Log

Choose a migrating animal. You may choose one that is mentioned here or another one that you know about. Write a report about the different environments in which the animal you have chosen lives. Tell why it migrates as well as where it migrates to. Start your search for information at www.conceptsandchallenges.com.

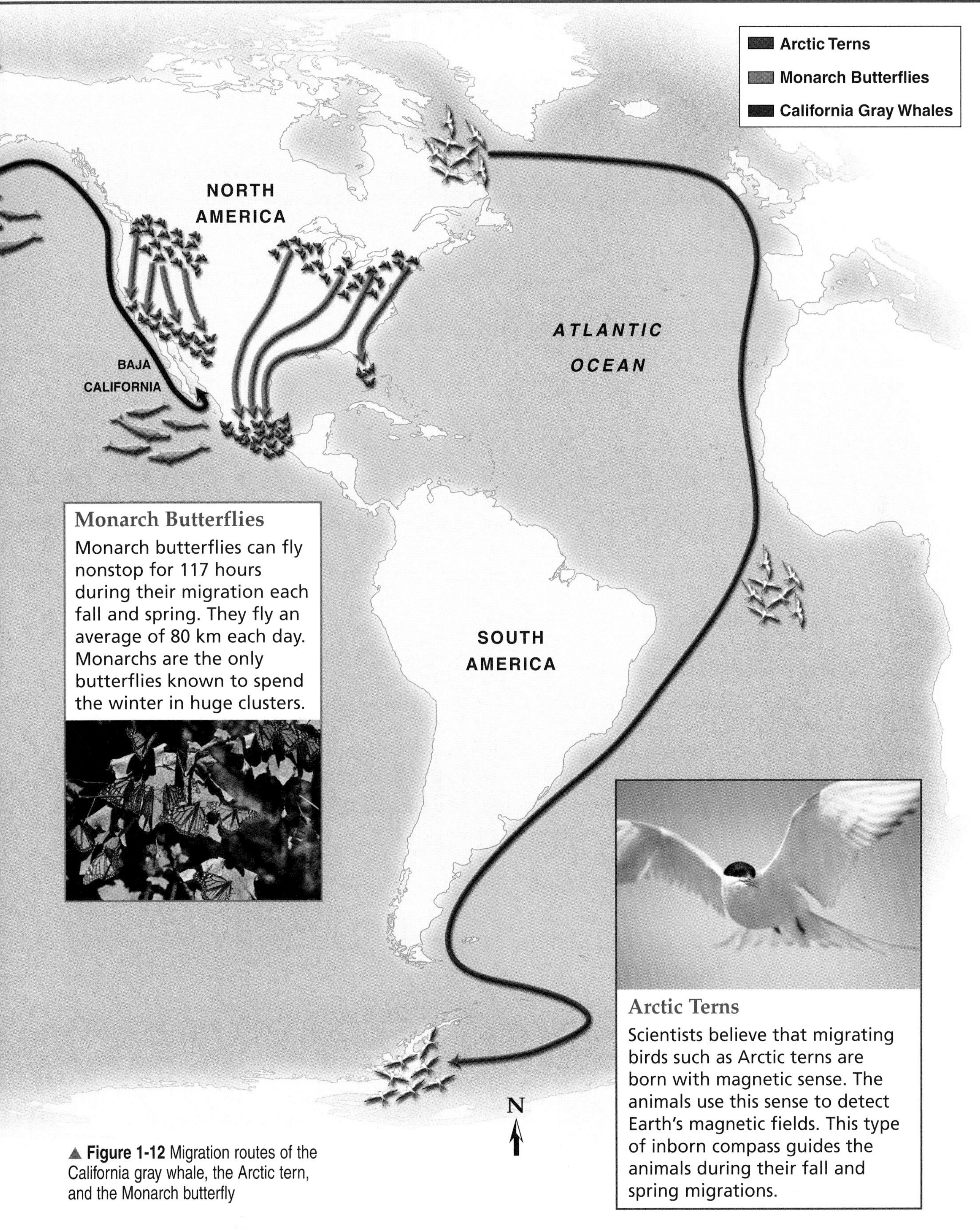

Monarch Butterflies

Monarch butterflies can fly nonstop for 117 hours during their migration each fall and spring. They fly an average of 80 km each day. Monarchs are the only butterflies known to spend the winter in huge clusters.

Arctic Terns

Scientists believe that migrating birds such as Arctic terns are born with magnetic sense. The animals use this sense to detect Earth's magnetic fields. This type of inborn compass guides the animals during their fall and spring migrations.

▲ **Figure 1-12** Migration routes of the California gray whale, the Arctic tern, and the Monarch butterfly

1-5 What are the motions of the Moon?

Objectives

Describe and identify two motions of the Moon. Explain how the Moon's motions affect the tides.

Key Terms

apogee (AP-uh-jee)**:** point at which the Moon is farthest from Earth

perigee (PER-uh-jee)**:** point at which the Moon is closest to Earth

spring tide: tide that is higher or lower than a normal tide

neap tide: tide that is not as high or as low as a normal tide

Rotation and Revolution Earth and its Moon travel together around the Sun. In addition, the Moon orbits Earth. Its journey around Earth takes about a month. The Moon also rotates on its axis.

The Moon rotates more slowly on its axis than Earth does. It takes the Moon $27\frac{1}{3}$ days to rotate once on its axis. The Moon revolves around Earth at a speed of about 3,500 km/h. It takes the Moon $27\frac{1}{3}$ days to make one complete revolution around Earth. This is the same time it takes the Moon to rotate. All of these motions are constantly changing the relative positions of the Sun, Earth, and Moon and how the Moon appears to us in the sky.

1 CALCULATE: How many kilometers does the Moon travel around Earth in one day?

▼ **Figure 1-13** The revolution and rotation of the Moon

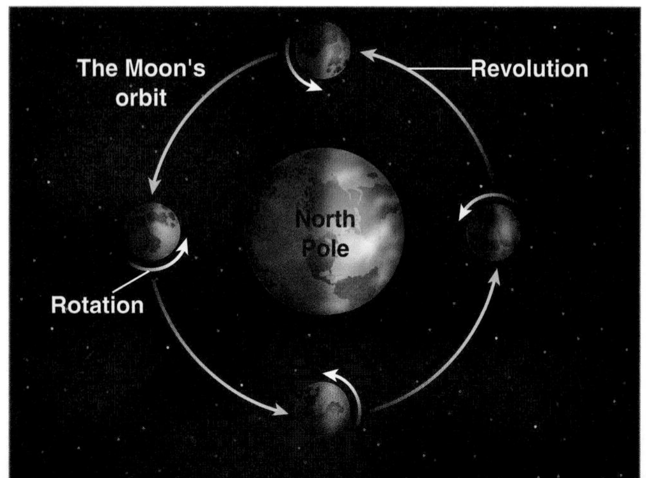

Apogee and Perigee When the Moon is farthest from Earth, it is at **apogee.** The distance from the Moon to Earth at apogee varies from about 405,000 to 407,000 km.

When the Moon is closest to Earth, it is at **perigee.** At perigee, the distance from the Moon to Earth varies from about 360,000 to about 370,000 km. This change in distance has an effect on Earth's tides, among other things.

 INFER: Why do the distances between Earth and the Moon change?

Moon's Gravity and Tides At certain times in the Moon's orbit of Earth, the Sun and the Moon are lined up in their orbits. The combined gravitational pull of the Sun and the Moon results in higher high tides and lower low tides on Earth. Therefore, the daily tidal range is greatest at these times. During these periods, which occur in a regular cycle twice a month, the tides become what are called **spring tides.**

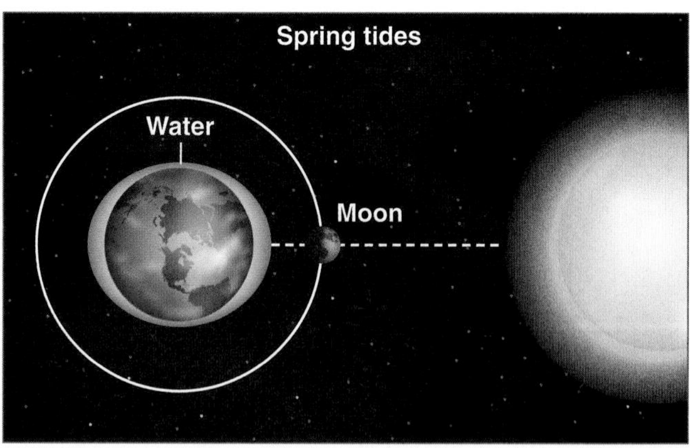

▲ **Figure 1-14** Spring tides

At certain times of the year, in between the spring tides, the Sun and the Moon pull at right angles to each other in relation to Earth. Because the Sun and the Moon pull at right angles to each other, their gravity forces do not combine or act together on Earth's oceans. Instead, they pull against each other. As a result, the daily tidal range is small. Tides that occur during this time are called **neap tides.**

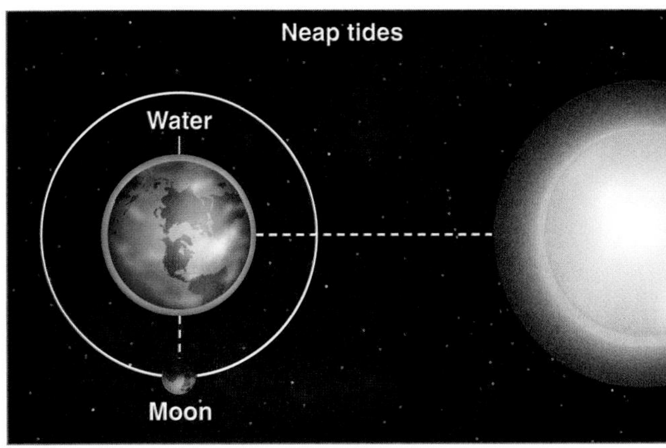

▲ **Figure 1-15** Neap tides

 **INFER:** How often do spring and neap tides occur?

Moonrise Like the Sun, the Moon appears to rise in the east and set in the west. As the Moon revolves around Earth, Earth must go through more than one rotation to "catch up" with the Moon. Earth must rotate 24 hours and 50 minutes to bring the Moon back into view. As a result, the Moon comes into view at moonrise about 50 minutes later each day.

 **EXPLAIN:** Why does the Moon rise about 50 minutes later each day?

✓ CHECKING CONCEPTS

1. How long does it take the Moon to make one complete revolution around Earth?
2. What causes the tides?
3. Why does the Moon not always rise at the same time?

THINKING CRITICALLY

4. **EXPLAIN:** Why does the Moon appear to rise in the east and set in the west?
5. **ANALYZE:** How many times does the Moon rotate during one revolution around Earth?
6. **CALCULATE:** If the Moon rose at 6:45 P.M. on Tuesday, at about what time will it rise on Thursday?

BUILDING READING SKILLS

Using Prefixes The prefix *peri-* means "around," "surrounding," or "close." Perigee is when the Moon is closest to Earth. Using a dictionary, find five other words that contain this prefix. Explain how the prefix relates to the meaning of each word.

People in Science

ASTRONAUT

▲ **Figure 1-16** Astronauts collect lunar samples from the Moon's surface.

The first person to travel in space was a Soviet air force pilot named Yuri Gargarin. His one orbit around Earth in April 1961 took less than two hours. American astronauts first flew in space in the *Mercury* and *Gemini* missions. However, it was the dramatic landing of American *Apollo* astronauts on the Moon in July 1969 that really marked the beginning of a human presence in space.

An astronaut travels and works in space. The word *astronaut* usually refers to a person involved in the American space program. Astronauts help design and test spacecraft and other space equipment. While in space, they operate their spacecraft and analyze any problems that arise. They also carry out experiments in space. Astronauts work for the National Aeronautics and Space Administration, or NASA. Many are also military officers. To be an astronaut, you need a background in mathematics and science. Most astronauts have advanced degrees. Astronauts who are pilots also have many hours of flight experience.

Thinking Critically Which Earth science specialists might want to be astronauts?

1-6 What are the phases of the Moon?

Objective

Identify the different phases of the Moon.

Key Terms

phases (FAYZ-uhz)**:** changing shapes of the Moon

crescent (KREHS-uhnt) **phase:** phase when less than half the Moon is visible

gibbous (GIHB-uhs) **phase:** phase when more than half the Moon is visible

Phases of the Moon From Earth, the Moon sometimes looks round. Other times, it looks like a thin sliver. The Moon appears to change shape because of the way it reflects light from the Sun. The changing shapes of the Moon are called **phases.** These phases depend on the positions of the Sun, the Moon, and Earth.

1 **IDENTIFY:** Why does the Moon appear to change shape?

Waxing Phases Look at Figure 1-17. When the side of the Moon facing Earth is dark, it appears as if there is no Moon at all. This is called a new Moon. As the Moon revolves around Earth, a small part of it becomes visible. As the visible part of it increases, the Moon is said to be waxing. The first phase is called the waxing **crescent phase.** During the crescent phase, less than half of the Moon is visible. When the Moon has moved one-quarter of the way around Earth, it enters the first quarter phase. This means that half of the side of the Moon facing Earth is visible.

As the Moon continues in its orbit, more and more of the side facing Earth becomes visible. This is called the waxing **gibbous phase.** During the gibbous phase, more than half of the Moon is visible. Finally, the Moon completes half of its trip around Earth. The whole side facing Earth is visible. This is the full Moon.

2 **DEFINE:** What is the Moon's gibbous phase?

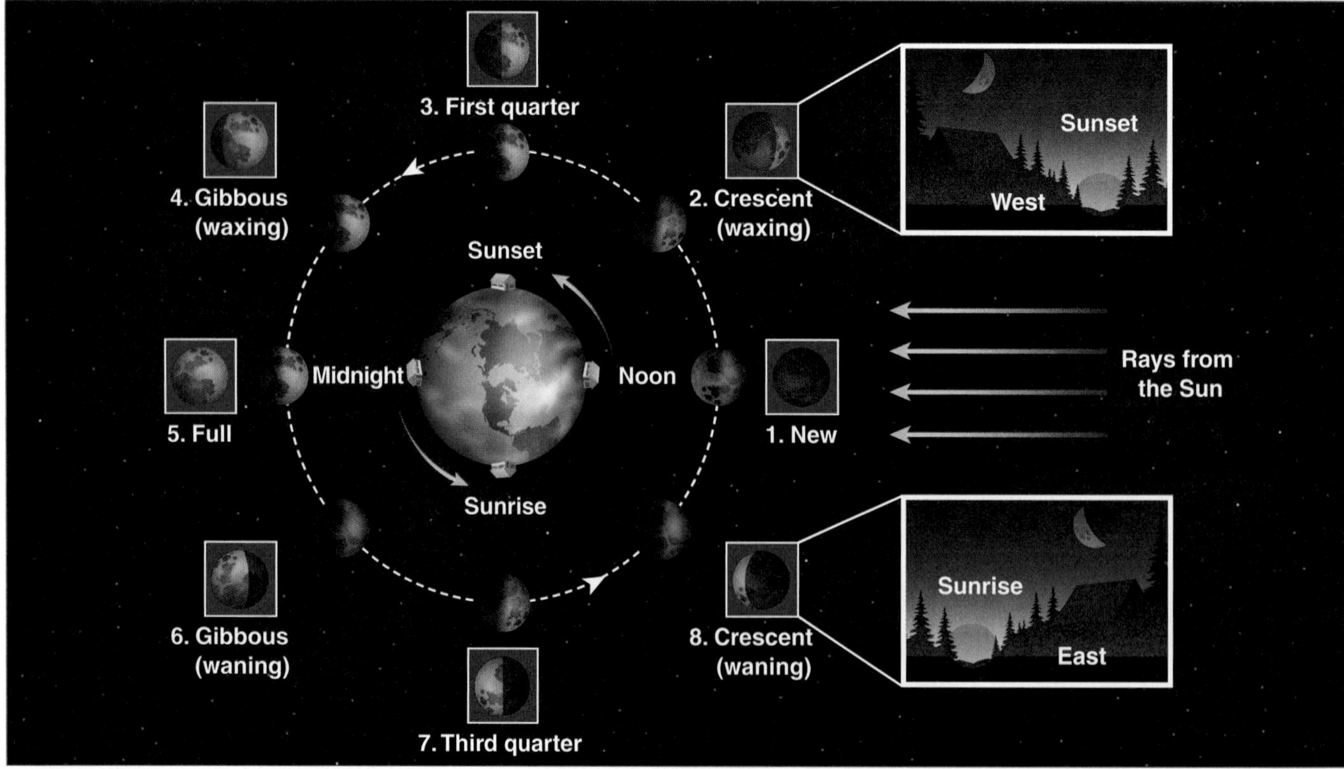

▲ **Figure 1-17** The phases of the Moon

Waning Phases As the Moon continues to move around Earth, less and less of the surface becomes visible. The Moon is waning. After the full Moon, the Moon enters the waning gibbous phase. At the last quarter phase, only half of the Moon's surface facing Earth is visible. The last phase of the Moon is the waning crescent phase.

The Moon takes 29 1/2 days to go through all of its phases. This is a little longer than the time it takes for one revolution of the Moon around Earth. The reason for this is that as the Moon orbits Earth, the two bodies are also moving around the Sun. The Moon must travel a little farther to get directly between Earth and the Sun.

COMPARE: When do the waxing and waning crescent phases of the Moon take place?

CHECKING CONCEPTS

1. The Moon reflects light from the __________.
2. The phases of the Moon depend on the positions of Earth, __________, and the Sun.
3. During the __________ phase of the Moon, half of the side of the Moon facing Earth is visible.
4. When the Moon has finished half of its revolution around Earth, the Moon is called a __________ Moon.
5. The Moon goes through all of its phases in __________ days.

THINKING CRITICALLY

6. **CONTRAST:** How do the crescent phase and the quarter phase of the Moon differ?
7. **PREDICT:** What would the Moon look like if it did not reflect light from the Sun?
8. **SEQUENCE:** List the eight phases of the Moon in order, beginning with the new Moon.

BUILDING SCIENCE SKILLS

Comparing The time period between one full Moon and the next is called a lunar month. On a calendar, identify each of the Moon's phases for the next two months. How does the length of the lunar month compare to the length of the calendar month?

Integrating Physical Science

TOPICS: radiation, light

HOW THE MOON IS LIT

Light travels in a straight line. Usually, it cannot go through an object. When light strikes an object, it may be totally absorbed, in which case it appears black. If the light is totally or partially reflected, then the object can appear white. Different colors of light might also be partially absorbed, with only some of them being reflected. The object will then appear in the reflected color.

We see the Moon because some of the light from the Sun is reflected off of the Moon rather than absorbed. The Moon appears white in the sky. Unlike stars, the Moon makes no light of its own. If it were not for the Sun, we would not be able to see the Moon. As the Moon revolves around Earth, the Sun's light strikes the Moon at different angles. This makes the Moon appear to change shape as viewed from Earth. We call this feature of the Moon "going through phases."

Thinking Critically Could we see the Moon if it absorbed all of the light instead of reflecting some of it?

▲ **Figure 1-18** The crescent phase of the Moon

LAB ACTIVITY

Modeling the Phases of the Moon

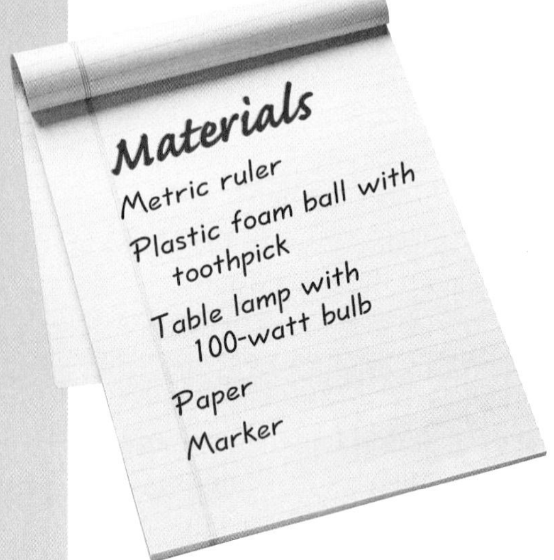

Materials
Metric ruler
Plastic foam ball with toothpick
Table lamp with 100-watt bulb
Paper
Marker

BACKGROUND

Moonshine is actually light from the Sun reflecting off the Moon's surface. When viewed from Earth on different nights throughout the month, the Moon appears to have different shapes. These shapes are called phases.

PURPOSE

In this activity, you will investigate why the Moon has phases.

PROCEDURE

1. Work with a partner in a darkened room. Place the lamp on a shelf or bookcase so that the bulb is about 120 cm above the floor. The bulb represents the Sun, the ball is the Moon, and your head is Earth.

2. Sit facing the lamp and hold the ball level with the bulb, between you and the lamp. Have your partner stand behind you and draw three circles to represent the Sun, Moon, and Earth in this setup.

3. Now have your partner shade in the part of the Moon that is not lighted by the Sun. Label this drawing Position 1.

4. Turn your body and the Moon about 45 degrees to the left. With the Moon in this position, have your partner draw the shape of the lighted part of the Moon that can be seen from Earth. Label this drawing Position 2.

▲ **STEP 2** The ball should be held level with the bulb, between you and the lamp.

▲ **STEP 4** Turn your body and the Moon about 45 degrees to the left.

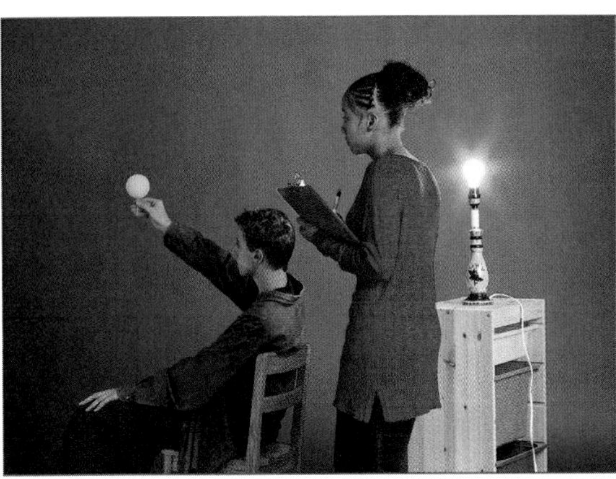

▲ **STEP 5** Turn your body and the Moon another 45 degrees.

5. Turn your body and the Moon to the left another 45 degrees and repeat Step 4. Label this drawing Position 3.

6. Continue turning the ball in the same direction, 45 degrees at a time, until you come back to your original position. Have your partner draw and label the Moon shape at each position.

7. Copy the chart in Figure 1-19. Using the information from your partner's diagrams, draw each phase of the Moon in its appropriate section in the chart.

Moon's Phases			
New	First quarter	First half	Three-quarters
Full	Three-quarters	Last half	Last quarter

▲ **Figure 1-19** Use a copy of this chart to organize your diagrams.

CONCLUSIONS

1. **OBSERVE:** In what position is the Moon when it is in its first quarter phase?
2. **OBSERVE:** What position of the Moon is opposite its new Moon phase?
3. **ANALYZE:** Why does the Moon have phases?
4. **INFER:** What happens when the Moon is directly between Earth and the Sun?

1-7 What causes an eclipse of the Moon?

Objectives

Describe a lunar eclipse. Distinguish between a total and a partial lunar eclipse.

Key Terms

umbra (UHM-bruh)**:** center or dark part of a shadow

penumbra (pih-NUHM-bruh)**:** light part of a shadow

lunar eclipse (ih-KLIHPS)**:** passing of the Moon through Earth's shadow

Casting Shadows When you walk outside on a sunny day, you can see your shadow. A shadow is formed when an object blocks a light source. A shadow has two parts. The center of a shadow is very dark. The dark part of a shadow is called the **umbra.** Around the outside of a shadow, you will see a lighter part. The light part of a shadow is called the **penumbra.**

People and objects are not the only things that can cast shadows. Earth, the Moon, and other bodies in space also cast shadows.

1 IDENTIFY: What are the two parts of a shadow?

Eclipse of the Moon As the Moon revolves around Earth, it usually passes above or below Earth's shadow. Sometimes the Moon passes directly through Earth's shadow. As a result, sunlight is blocked from reaching the Moon. When the sunlight is blocked from the Moon, a **lunar eclipse** occurs. A lunar eclipse can occur only during the full-Moon phase.

2 DEFINE: What is a lunar eclipse?

Total or Partial Eclipses Sometimes the Moon moves entirely into Earth's umbra. When this happens, all of the Sun's light is blocked. The entire face of the Moon darkens. This is called a total lunar eclipse.

Sometimes, only part of the Moon moves into Earth's umbra. Sunlight can still reach the Moon. As a result, only part of the Moon darkens. This is called a partial lunar eclipse.

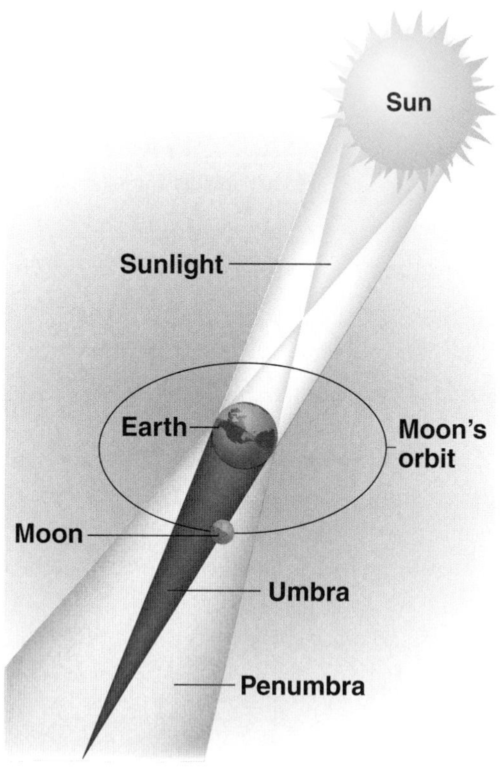

▲ **Figure 1-20** A partial lunar eclipse

Total lunar eclipses are rare. Also, they do not occur at regular intervals. They may occur as often as six months apart or as much as $2\frac{1}{2}$ years apart.

▲ **Figure 1-21** A partial lunar eclipse

3 DESCRIBE: How does the Moon look during a total lunar eclipse?

✓ CHECKING CONCEPTS

1. The dark part of a shadow is the __________.
2. A lunar eclipse occurs when Earth is between the __________ and the Moon.
3. A __________ lunar eclipse occurs when part of the Moon is in Earth's penumbra.
4. During a __________ lunar eclipse, all of the Moon is dark.

THINKING CRITICALLY

5. **HYPOTHESIZE:** When would a partial lunar eclipse be difficult to see?
6. **INFER:** Can a lunar eclipse occur during the quarter-Moon phase? Why or why not?
7. **INFER:** Can Earth's shadow have only an umbra and not a penumbra? Explain your answer.

INTERPRETING VISUALS

Use Figure 1-22 to answer the following questions.

8. **EXPLAIN:** The Moon in Figure 1-22 is in a total eclipse. What would happen if the Moon were to move into the penumbra?
9. **HYPOTHESIZE:** If Earth and the Moon were closer to the Sun, how would the size of the umbra change?
10. **EXPLAIN:** Why can a lunar eclipse only occur during a full Moon?

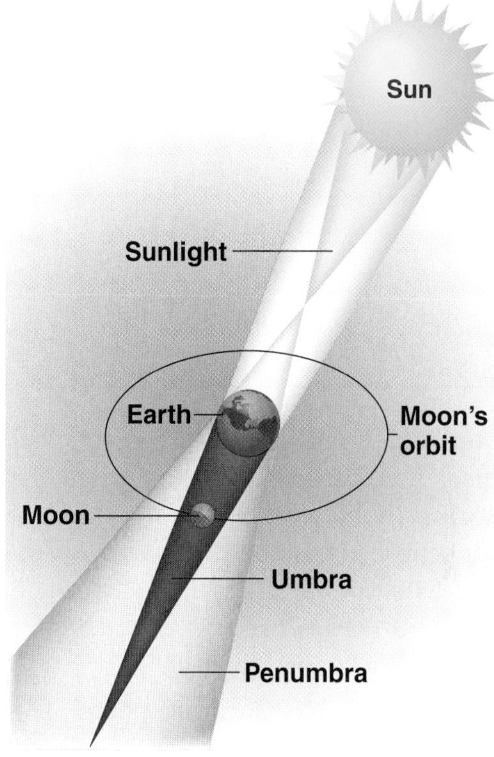

▲ **Figure 1-22** A total lunar eclipse

Hands-On Activity

MODELING LUNAR ECLIPSES

You will need tracing paper, a ruler, and a pencil.

1. Figure 1-23 shows the Moon in three different positions as it revolves around Earth. Copy the diagram onto a sheet of paper.
2. Indicate on your diagram which position represents a total eclipse, which represents a partial eclipse, and which represents no eclipse of the Moon.

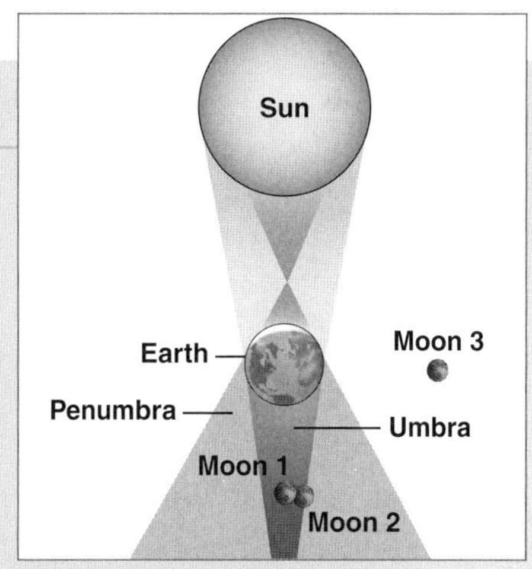

▲ **Figure 1-23** The Moon revolving around Earth

Practicing Your Skill

3. **ANALYZE:** Does Position 1 represent a total eclipse, a partial eclipse, or no eclipse of the Moon? Explain.
4. **ANALYZE:** Does Position 2 represent a total eclipse, a partial eclipse, or no eclipse of the Moon? Explain.
5. **ANALYZE:** Does Position 3 represent a total eclipse, a partial eclipse, or no eclipse of the Moon? Explain.
6. **MODEL:** Draw a model of a total eclipse of the Moon.

1-8 What causes an eclipse of the Sun?

Objective

Explain how a solar eclipse occurs.

Key Terms

solar eclipse: passing of the Moon between Earth and the Sun

corona (kuh-ROH-nuh)**:** outer layer of the Sun's atmosphere

Casting Shadows An eclipse of the Sun is called a **solar eclipse.** A solar eclipse occurs when the Moon passes directly between Earth and the Sun. During a solar eclipse, the Moon casts a shadow on Earth. Figure 1-24 shows a solar eclipse. During a solar eclipse the Sun looks like it is covered by a black circle. This circle is the Moon.

Like Earth, the Sun has an atmosphere. The outer layer of the Sun's atmosphere is called the **corona.** The corona is like a halo around the Sun. Usually, the corona cannot be seen from Earth because the Sun itself is so bright. During a solar eclipse, however, most of the Sun's surface is blacked out. As a result, the corona can be seen from Earth.

1 **DEFINE:** What is a solar eclipse?

Kinds of Solar Eclipses Like lunar eclipses, solar eclipses can either be total or partial. A total solar eclipse occurs when the entire face of the Sun is blocked by the Moon. Only the outer atmosphere of the Sun still shows. A partial solar eclipse happens when only part of the Sun's face is blocked.

▲ **Figure 1-24** A total solar eclipse

2 **DESCRIBE:** What causes a total solar eclipse?

Viewing Solar Eclipses Look at Figure 1-25 below. When the Moon's umbra touches Earth, people within it see a total solar eclipse.

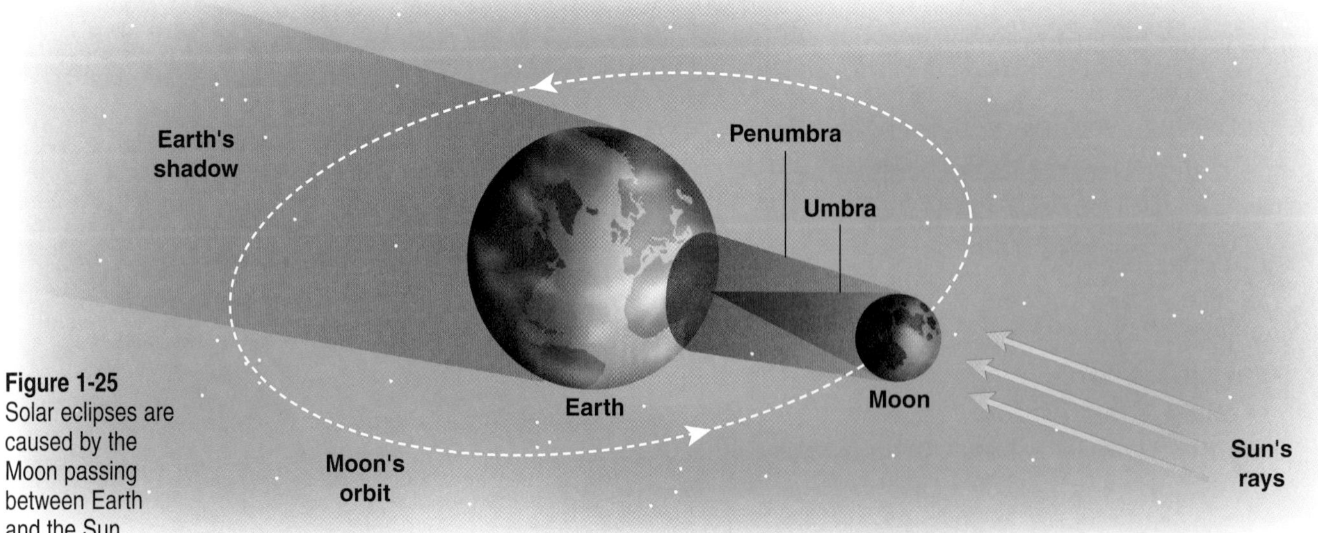

Figure 1-25 Solar eclipses are caused by the Moon passing between Earth and the Sun.

The umbra of the Moon is very small. Therefore, a total solar eclipse is visible from only a small area of Earth. People who are in the Moon's penumbra see a partial solar eclipse.

The penumbra of the Moon's shadow is much larger than the umbra. As a result, a partial solar eclipse can be seen over a larger area of Earth than a total solar eclipse can. Partial solar eclipses are seen more often than total solar eclipses.

IDENTIFY: Which kind of solar eclipse is seen more often, a total or a partial solar eclipse?

✓ CHECKING CONCEPTS

1. When does a solar eclipse occur?
2. What is a partial eclipse of the Sun?
3. What happens when the Moon's umbra touches Earth?
4. Which part of the Moon's shadow is the largest?

THINKING CRITICALLY

Use Figure 1-25 to answer the following questions.

5. **ANALYZE:** What part of the Moon's shadow are you in if you see a total solar eclipse?
6. **EXPLAIN:** What can people outside the area of a total solar eclipse see?
7. **COMPARE:** How are total eclipses of the Moon and the Sun similar?
8. **INFER:** Why is a partial solar eclipse seen more often than a total solar eclipse?

HEALTH AND SAFETY TIP

Never look directly at the Sun, especially during a total solar eclipse. Doing this can cause permanent eye damage. Some people use a special filter to view the Sun. However, poorly made filters can also cause eye damage. The best way to watch a solar eclipse is with a pinhole box. Go to www.conceptsandchallenges.com to learn how to make one. Use the key search words **pinhole box.**

How Do They Know That?

PREDICTING SOLAR ECLIPSES

People have always been fascinated by solar eclipses. In some cultures, solar eclipses were connected with superstition, mystery, and fear. Some ancient cultures thought the darkened sky caused by a solar eclipse was a sign of the displeasure of certain spirits. The ancient Chinese thought that solar eclipses happened when a dragon in the sky tried to swallow the Sun.

Descriptions of solar eclipses have been found dating back many centuries. In Babylon, a record of solar eclipses was kept from 747 B.C. on. In China, 36 solar eclipses were recorded between 720 B.C. and 495 B.C. Scientists have calculated the exact dates of many past solar eclipses. The records of eclipses in ancient writings have been used to pinpoint the dates of historical events.

▲ **Figure 1-26** This moment during a solar eclipse is known as the diamond ring effect. Can you see why?

Today, scientists can accurately predict solar eclipses. This is important in the study of the Sun and the Moon.

Thinking Critically Why do you think solar eclipses were once feared?

Chapter 1 Challenges

Chapter Summary

Lessons 1-1 and 1-2

- **Revolution** and **rotation** are movements of Earth. Earth's rotation causes day and night. The number of daylight hours changes because Earth's **axis** is tilted.
- The Sun appears to rise in the east and set in the west because of Earth's rotation. When the Sun is highest in the sky, the time is **solar noon.**
- Earth is divided into 24 time zones. There are eight **standard time** zones in the United States. As you cross the **International Date Line,** you either gain or lose one full day.

Lesson 1-3

- The seasons are caused by Earth's tilt and orbit around the Sun. The Northern and Southern hemispheres have opposite seasons.

Lesson 1-4

- During the year, the distance between Earth and the Sun varies.
- **Solstices** and **equinoxes** mark the changes in seasons. The North Pole tilts toward the Sun on the summer solstice. The North Pole tilts away from the Sun on the winter solstice. The Sun shines directly on the equator during the vernal and autumnal equinoxes.

Lesson 1-5

- The Moon revolves around Earth in the same way Earth revolves around the Sun. The Moon rotates once every 27 1/3 days.
- **Apogee** and **perigee** describe the Moon's position in relation to Earth.
- The motions of the Moon cause changes in tides. Two kinds of tides are **spring tides** and **neap tides.**

Lesson 1-6

- The Moon has waxing and waning **phases.**

Lessons 1-7 and 1-8

- The **umbra** and the **penumbra** are the two parts of a shadow.
- A **lunar eclipse** occurs when the Moon passes through Earth's shadow. A **solar eclipse** occurs when the Moon passes between Earth and the Sun. Eclipses can be partial or total.

Key Term Challenges

aphelion (p. 22)
apogee (p. 26)
axis (p. 16)
corona (p. 34)
crescent phase (p. 28)
equinox (p. 22)
gibbous phase (p. 28)
International Date Line (p. 18)
lunar eclipse (p. 32)
neap tide (p. 26)
penumbra (p. 32)
perigee (p. 26)
perihelion (p. 22)
phases (p. 28)
revolution (p. 16)
rotation (p. 16)
solar eclipse (p. 34)
solar noon (p. 18)
solstice (p. 22)
spring tide (p. 26)
standard time (p. 18)
umbra (p. 32)

MATCHING **Write the Key Term from above that best matches each description.**

1. time when the Sun is highest in the sky
2. changing shapes of the Moon
3. daily tidal range is the largest
4. imaginary line through the center of a planet or other body on which that body spins
5. passing of the Moon through Earth's shadow
6. movement of Earth on its axis
7. movement of Earth in its orbit
8. point in its orbit when Earth is farthest from the Sun

IDENTIFYING WORD RELATIONSHIPS **Explain how the words in each pair are related. Write your answers in complete sentences.**

9. rotation, revolution
10. International Date Line, meridian
11. equinox, solstice
12. apogee, perigee
13. penumbra, umbra
14. crescent phase, gibbous phase
15. solar eclipse, lunar eclipse

Content Challenges TEST PREP

FILL IN **Write the term or phrase that best completes each statement.**

1. When viewed from the North Pole, Earth rotates on its axis from __________.
2. Earth's axis is tilted at an angle of __________.
3. Because of Earth's tilted axis, the North Pole of Earth always points toward __________.
4. In the Northern Hemisphere, the summer solstice occurs on __________.
5. During an equinox, the number of daylight hours and nighttime hours are __________.
6. The continental United States has __________ standard time zones.
7. The Moon takes __________ days to make one complete revolution around Earth.
8. The Moon takes __________ days to make one complete rotation on its axis.
9. As the visible part of the Moon decreases, the Moon is __________.
10. The waxing crescent phase of the Moon occurs __________ the full Moon.
11. When the daily tide range is largest, this is called a __________ tide.
12. When the daily tide range is smallest, this is called a __________ tide.
13. Because Earth rotates, the Sun appears to set in the __________.
14. Earth is closest to the Sun during the month of __________.
15. The darkest center part of a shadow is called the __________.

TRUE/FALSE **Write *true* if the statement is true. If the statement is false, change the underlined term or phrase to make the statement true.**

16. The change from day to night is caused by Earth's <u>revolution</u>.
17. The number of daylight hours is not equal all year because of Earth's <u>tilted axis</u>.
18. The change in seasons is caused by Earth's <u>rotation</u>.
19. In the Southern Hemisphere, the first day of summer is <u>June 21</u>.
20. The vernal equinox marks the first day of <u>spring</u>.
21. Earth is divided into <u>24</u> time zones, each 15° of longitude wide.
22. As you move <u>east</u>, each time zone is one hour earlier than the previous time zone.
23. When the Moon is <u>closest</u> to Earth, it is at apogee.
24. The Moon rises 50 minutes <u>earlier</u> each day.
25. As the part of the Moon that is visible increases, the Moon is <u>waxing</u>.
26. The Moon appears to <u>change shape</u> because of the way it reflects light from the Sun.
27. During a total lunar eclipse, the entire face of the <u>Moon</u> is darkened.
28. When the Moon moves entirely into Earth's umbra, people within see a <u>solar</u> eclipse.
29. The difference between high tide and low tide is greatest during <u>spring</u> tides.
30. The Sun is farthest from Earth at <u>perihelion</u>.

Concept Challenges TEST PREP

WRITTEN RESPONSE **Answer each of the following questions in complete sentences.**

1. CALCULATE: If the Moon rises at 6:30 P.M. on Thursday, what time will it rise on Friday? Explain your answer.
2. COMPARE: How does the number of days between one full Moon and the next compare to how long it takes the Moon to revolve once around Earth?
3. HYPOTHESIZE: Gravitational attraction decreases with distance. Is the Moon's gravitational attraction to Earth stronger at apogee or perigee? Explain.
4. COMPARE: How does the number of time zones on Earth compare with the number of hours in a day?
5. CONTRAST: How do the position of the Sun, the Moon, and Earth during a solar eclipse differ from their positions during a lunar eclipse?
6. INFER: How do the tides on Earth change during the Moon's apogee and perigee?

INTERPRETING VISUALS **Use Figure 1-27 below to answer the following questions.**

7. Which phase of the Moon does the picture labeled *A* represent?
8. Which phase of the Moon does the picture labeled C represent?
9. Which phase of the Moon does the picture labeled *F* represent?
10. Which phase of the Moon is not shown?
11. Why is the phase of the Moon labeled *E* called a waning phase?
12. Which phase of the Moon follows a full Moon?
13. How long does it take the Moon to go from one new Moon phase to the next new Moon phase?
14. Name the phases of the Moon in the correct order, beginning with the one labeled *A*.
15. What causes the Moon to change phases?

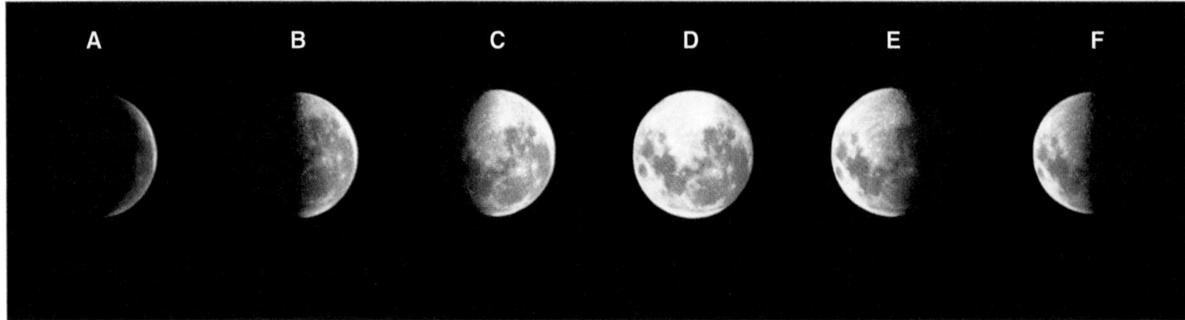

▲ **Figure 1-27** Phases of the Moon

Chapter 2 The Exploration of Space

▲ **Figure 2-1** The space shuttle lifts off from its launch pad in Cape Canaveral, Florida.

The space shuttle is made up of an orbiter, a fuel tank, and booster rockets. The orbiter carries the crew and cargo into space and lands back on Earth like an airplane. The space shuttle is the world's first reusable spacecraft. It can fly missions and return home, then return to space later for more missions. The first shuttle mission, with the orbiter *Columbia*, was launched on April 12, 1981.

▶What do you think are the advantages in having a reusable spacecraft system?

Contents

2-1 What is astronomy?

Calculating the Length of a Light Year

HANDS-ON ACTIVITY

1. Light travels about 300,000 km per second. How many kilometers does light travel per minute? Write this number down.
2. How many kilometers does light travel per hour? Multiply your number from Step 1 by 60. Write this number down.
3. How many kilometers does light travel in a day? Multiply the number you got in Step 2 by 24. Write this number down.
4. Multiply the number you got in Step 3 by 365, for the number of days in a year. This will give you the distance in kilometers that light travels in one year.

THINK ABOUT IT: Why would knowing the speed of light be important to astronomers?

Objective

Explain what is meant by astronomy.

Key Terms

astronomy (uh-STRAHN-uh-mee)**:** study of stars, planets, and other objects in space

solar system: Sun and all the bodies that orbit it

Ancient Astronomy People have wondered about the skies for thousands of years. The study of space and all the objects in it is called **astronomy.** Astronomy is one of the oldest sciences. Ancient records predicting eclipses of the Sun date back to the first century B.C.

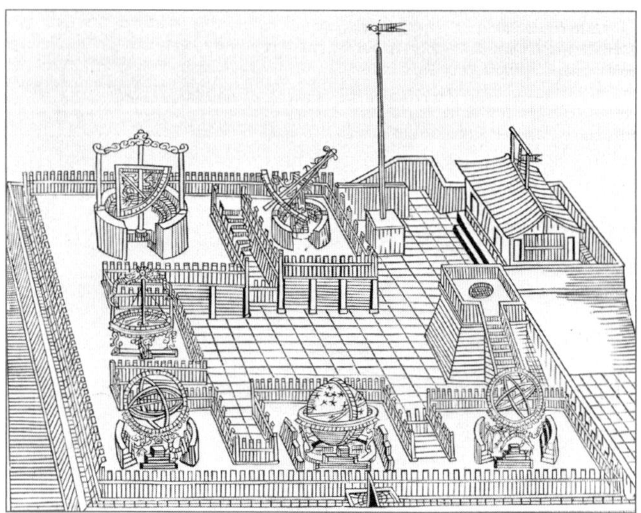

▲ **Figure 2-2** Ancient astronomers studied the skies from observatories like the one shown here.

The planets Mercury, Venus, Mars, Jupiter, and Saturn were all known more than 5,000 years ago. No new planets were found until 1781, when Uranus was discovered.

 LIST: Which planets did the ancients know?

Uses of Astronomy Ancient peoples solved many problems using astronomy. Most ancient societies depended on the changing of the seasons. Farmers had to know when to plant their crops. Astronomers were able to predict the coming of spring for them. Sailors, too, used the positions of the stars to navigate at sea.

 EXPLAIN: How did the ancients use astronomy?

Modern Astronomy Ancient astronomers made observations using only their eyes. Over time, new tools helped astronomers to see farther into space. In 1609, the Italian scientist Galileo (gal-uh-LAY-oh) Galilei used a simple telescope to look at the Moon and other objects. Today, astronomers use telescopes, satellites, and space probes to observe the planets and study stars many trillions of kilometers from Earth.

What do modern astronomers study? They study the universe. The universe is everything that exists. Astronomers called planetologists study the solar system. The **solar system** includes the Sun and all of the bodies in space that orbit it. Astronomers called cosmologists study how the universe began and how it will end.

▲ **Figure 2-3** Telescopes help astronomers study objects in space.

 **DESCRIBE:** What are two kinds of astronomers?

CHECKING CONCEPTS

1. Five thousand years ago, there were __________ known planets, not including Earth.
2. Sailors found their way using the __________.
3. The universe is __________ that exists.
4. Ancient astronomers made observations using only their __________.
5. Astronomers called __________ study how the universe began.
6. The first astronomer to use a telescope to view the Moon was __________.

THINKING CRITICALLY

7. **INFER:** Early astronomers observed that the planets changed their positions in the night sky. However, the stars kept the same positions. Why did sailors use the stars and not the planets to find their way at sea?

BUILDING READING SKILLS

Vocabulary On a sheet of paper, list the names of the following stars: Vega, Sirius, Aldebaran, Polaris, Algol, Capella, Betelgeuse, and Proxima Centauri. Find out what each name means in its original language. Write the meaning and identify the original language next to each name. Also, find out how the names are pronounced.

How Do They Know That?

EARLY IDEAS ABOUT EARTH

Astronomy is an ancient science. Records dating back to before 2000 B.C. show that there was a calendar based on movements of the Sun and Moon. At that time, most people believed Earth was flat, with the stars inside a giant sphere that moved around Earth.

In the sixth century B.C., Pythagoras (pih-THAG-uh-ruhs), a Greek mathematician, challenged the view that Earth was flat. He noted that the masts of ships disappeared below the horizon. He also saw that Earth's shadow on the Moon during a lunar eclipse was curved. From these observations, Pythagoras reasoned that Earth must be round. In the fourth century B.C., the Greek philosopher Aristotle (AR-ihs-taht-uhl) claimed that Earth was at the center of the universe. This claim went mostly unchallenged for almost 2,000 years. Then, in the early sixteenth century, the Polish mathematician Nicolaus Copernicus (koh-PUHR-nih-kuhs) suggested that the Sun, not Earth, was the center of the solar system. Later observations by Tycho Brahe, Johannes Kepler, Galileo, and Sir Isaac Newton supported Copernicus. This was the beginning of modern astronomy.

▲ **Figure 2-4** Nicolaus Copernicus

Thinking Critically What change in thinking led to modern astronomy?

2-2 How is space explored?

Objective

Explain how space exploration helps scientists learn about Earth and the universe.

Key Term

galaxy (GAL-uhk-see)**:** huge collection of stars, gas, and dust that travel together through space

Answers from Space

The Space Age really began in 1957 with the launch of the Russian satellite *Sputnik*. A year later, the United States launched *Explorer 1*. Since then, humankind has sent spacecraft all around the solar system and people to the Moon. Scientists hope that these missions will answer questions about the universe. They want to know, for example, how the solar system formed and whether intelligent life exists elsewhere in the universe.

▲ **Figure 2-5** *Explorer 1* was the first U.S. spacecraft to be successfully launched.

1 INFER: Why do scientists explore space?

How the Universe Formed Space exploration may provide clues as to how the universe was formed. Scientists think that the universe began about 15 billion years ago in a huge explosion called the Big Bang.

Soon after the Big Bang, galaxies began to form. A **galaxy** is a huge collection of stars, gas, and dust that travels together through space as one body. The most distant galaxies were probably formed soon after the Big Bang.

2 DEFINE: What are galaxies?

Hubble Space Telescope Astronomers are learning more about the universe by using a telescope that is orbiting Earth. The Hubble Space Telescope was launched into space in 1990. It is named after the American astronomer Edwin Hubble. This telescope has observed and taken pictures of many of the planets and distant galaxies that are hard or even impossible to see clearly from Earth.

When the Hubble began operating in space, it did not work properly. Images from deep space were blurry. The problem was corrected several years later during a mission of the space shuttle *Endeavour*.

3 INFER: How can the Hubble Space Telescope see so far into space?

◄ **Figure 2-6** The Hubble Space Telescope is shown here orbiting Earth. It has provided images of many galaxies, such as the Large Magellanic Cloud, seen above.

CHECKING CONCEPTS

1. Space exploration really began in the year __________.
2. Scientists think that the universe began about __________ years ago.
3. The explosion that scientists think might have started the universe is called the __________.
4. The __________ Telescope, which orbits Earth, is able to see very distant galaxies.
5. The space shuttle __________ fixed the Hubble's imaging problem.

THINKING CRITICALLY

6. **HYPOTHESIZE:** How might traveling deeper into space help scientists answer some of their questions about space?
7. **INFER:** Why is it easier for telescopes in orbit to view stars?
8. **CONCLUDE:** How has the Hubble Space Telescope increased our knowledge of space?

Web InfoSearch

Astrolabes The most common astronomical instrument until about 1650 was the astrolabe. It was used to observe the altitude of stars and to guide sailors. The Greek astronomer Hipparchus probably made the first one.

▲ **Figure 2-7** Astrolabe from the seventeenth century

Astrolabes were often made of brass. The Adler Planetarium and Astronomy Museum in Chicago has the largest collection of astrolabes in North America.

SEARCH: Use the Internet to find out more about astrolabes. Are they still being made today? Start your search at www.conceptsandchallenges.com. Some key search words are **astrolabe instrument,** and **Hipparchus astrolabe.**

Real-Life Science

SPINOFFS FROM SPACE

How can space exploration help people on Earth? It produces spinoffs. A spinoff is a benefit or product that results from an unrelated activity or process.

Sending spacecraft into space is very costly. One way to save costs is by developing smaller, lighter equipment. Smaller radios, computers, and televisions made for use in space travel are now used on Earth. Many foods sent into space with the astronauts are freeze-dried to make them lighter and last longer. Many of these foods are available in supermarkets today. Lightweight, fireproof, durable clothing, nonstick cookware, and sunglasses that adjust to changes in light are all spinoffs from space.

▲ **Figure 2-8** Improvements in fireproof clothing are a spinoff from space exploration.

Other spinoffs help us recover from illnesses. Doctors on Earth need to check on astronauts in space. To meet this need, scientists developed tiny monitoring, recording, and transmitting devices now used on Earth.

Thinking Critically Why is freeze-dried food good for any type of travel?

2-3 How does a refracting telescope work?

Objective

Explain how a refracting telescope works.

Key Terms

refracting (rih-FRAKT-ing) **telescope:** telescope that uses convex lenses to produce an enlarged image

convex (kahn-VEHKS) **lens:** lens that is thicker in the middle than it is at the edges

Galileo's Telescope Galileo was the first person to look at objects in space through a telescope. Have you ever looked through a telescope? If you have, you know that a telescope makes faraway objects appear much nearer than they are. If you look at the Moon through a telescope, you can see many features on its surface that you cannot see with your eyes alone. Galileo looked at the Moon soon after the telescope was invented. He was the first person to see that the Moon's surface is not smooth. Galileo saw craters, plains, and hills on the Moon.

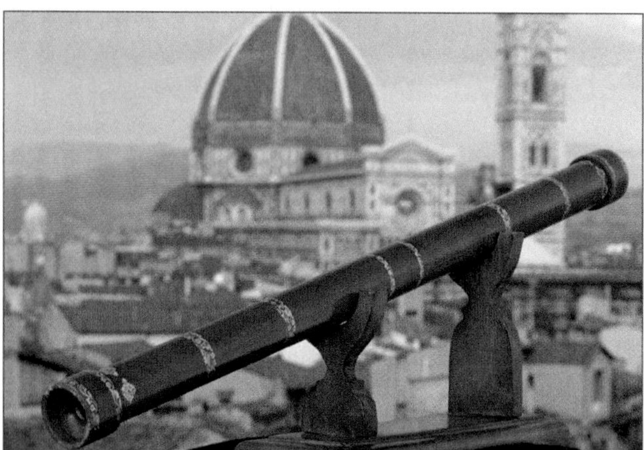

▲ **Figure 2-9** Galileo's telescope, with Italy in the background

1 **NAME:** What features did Galileo see on the surface of the Moon?

Refracting Telescopes Galileo used a **refracting telescope.** It consisted of a tube with two lenses inside. A lens is a piece of glass or plastic that refracts, or bends, light.

The telescope shown in Figure 2-10 is a simple refracting telescope. The lenses in a refracting telescope are convex lenses. **Convex lenses** are lenses that bulge outward. They are thicker in the middle than they are at the edges.

When light passes through a convex lens, the light appears to bend inward, as shown in Figure 2-10. The light produces an image that is larger than the image you would see with your eyes alone.

2 **DESCRIBE:** What kinds of lenses are used in a refracting telescope?

How the Lenses Work Each of the convex lenses in a refracting telescope has a special job to do. The lens at the far end of the tube is called the objective lens. The objective lens collects light and brings the image into focus. The lens at the other end of the tube is called the eyepiece. This lens enlarges, or magnifies, the image formed by the objective lens.

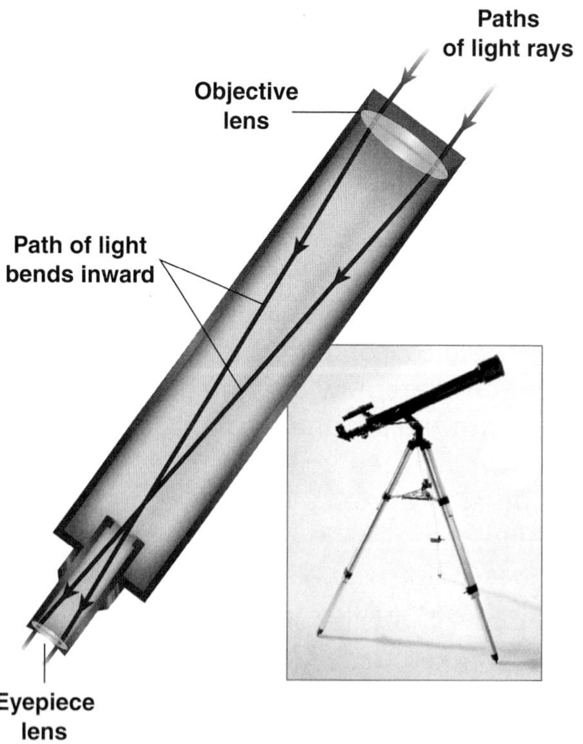

▲ **Figure 2-10** A simple refracting telescope

The objective lens and the eyepiece lens work together. They can produce a sharp, clear image of a distant object.

NAME: What are the two lenses in a refracting telescope called?

CHECKING CONCEPTS

1. A telescope makes the Moon appear ___________.
2. Galileo saw ___________, hills, and plains on the Moon.
3. The ___________ in a refracting telescope contains two convex lenses.
4. A convex lens appears to bend, or ___________, light.
5. The lenses in a refracting telescope are ___________ lenses.
6. The two lenses that are used in a refracting telescope are the objective lens and the ___________ lens.

THINKING CRITICALLY

7. **COMPARE:** Which surface features of the Moon are also found on Earth?
8. **INFER:** Why does the image that is formed by a telescope appear to be nearer than the object really is?
9. **HYPOTHESIZE:** If light did not bend when it was passed through a lens, would the refracting telescope still work? Why or why not?

BUILDING SCIENCE SKILLS

Observing Many objects that you use every day contain convex lenses. Make a list of common objects that contain convex lenses. List as many of them as you can. Briefly describe how the lenses are used in these objects. Hint: What part of your body has a convex lens?

Hands-On Activity

MAKING A SIMPLE TELESCOPE

You will need 2 convex lenses or magnifying glasses.

1. Look at a distant object through a convex lens.
2. Move the lens back and forth slowly. Stop when you see the object clearly through the lens.
3. Without moving the first lens, hold a second convex lens close to your eye.
4. Move the second lens back and forth slowly. Stop when you can see the distant object clearly through both lenses.

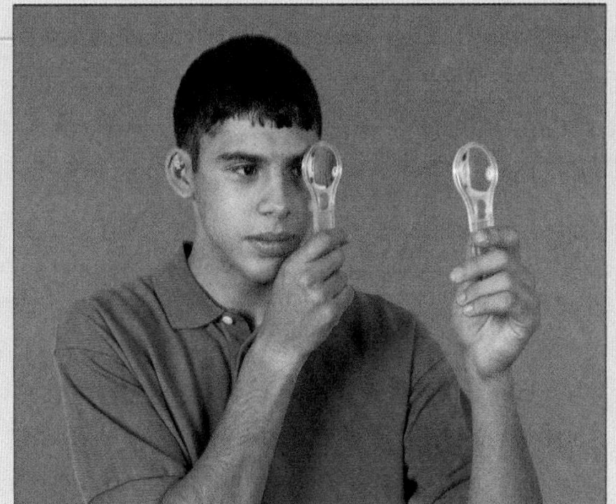

▲ **STEP 4** The distant object should show clearly through both lenses.

Practicing Your Skills

5. **IDENTIFY:** What part of a telescope does the first lens represent?
6. **OBSERVE:** How does the image appear through the first lens?
7. **IDENTIFY:** What part of a telescope does the second lens represent?
8. **OBSERVE:** How does the image appear when you look through both lenses?
9. **ANALYZE:** Would a telescope with a large objective lens be better than one with a small objective lens? Explain.

2-4 How does a reflecting telescope work?

Modeling the Way Light Travels

HANDS-ON ACTIVITY

1. Cut three 15-by-15-cm cards from cardboard. On each card, in the middle of one side, cut a 2-by-2-cm notch. Use modeling clay to place the cards about 10-cm apart. Line up the notches so they are in a straight line with each other.
2. Shine a flashlight behind the cards. Use the modeling clay to hold up a large index card at the other end of the row of cards.
3. Darken the room. Observe any light on the index card.
4. Move the cards so that the notches are not in a straight line. Observe the light on the index card.

THINK ABOUT IT: When did light appear on the index card? What does this tell you about how light travels?

Objectives

Explain how a reflecting telescope works. Compare it with a refracting telescope.

Key Terms

reflecting (rih-FLEHKT-ing) **telescope:** telescope that uses a concave mirror to collect light

concave mirror: mirror that curves inward

Using Mirrors to See A refracting telescope uses lenses to collect light. A **reflecting telescope** uses a mirror. This mirror is a **concave mirror.** It curves inward. In a reflecting telescope, the mirror collects light from distant objects and focuses it to form an image.

1 **DEFINE:** What is a reflecting telescope?

Newton's Telescope In 1668, Isaac Newton, an English scientist, made the first reflecting telescope. He used a concave mirror to collect the light and a convex lens as an eyepiece to magnify the image. He also used a flat mirror to reflect light from the concave mirror to one side. This prevented the eyepiece from blocking the incoming light.

Some reflecting telescopes have the eyepiece to one side of the telescope tube. A camera can then be attached to it to take pictures.

▲ **Figure 2-11** Newton uses his reflecting telescope.

2 **EXPLAIN:** Why is the eyepiece that is used in a reflecting telescope sometimes found on one side of the tube?

Modern Reflecting Telescopes Modern reflecting telescopes have very large mirrors. The Hale Telescope on Mount Palomar in California has a mirror 5 m across.

The twin Keck telescopes that sit on the summit of Mauna Kea in Hawaii have 36 mirrors that together measure about 10 m across. This gives a light-collecting area almost half the size of a tennis court. Composite telescopes are being developed today that will have mirrors of up to 16 m across.

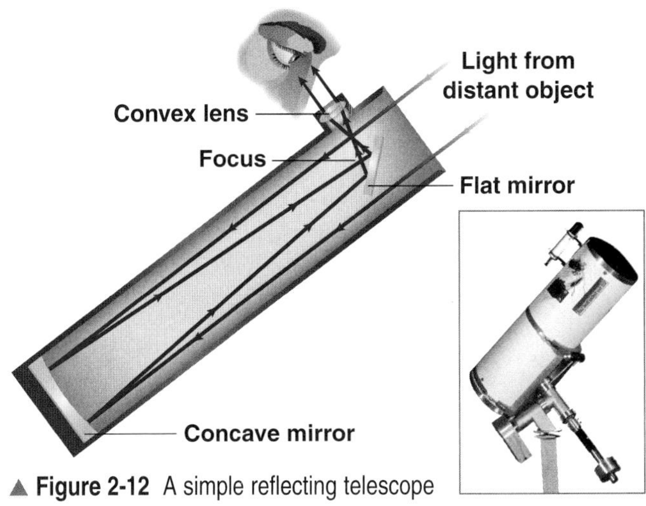

▲ **Figure 2-12** A simple reflecting telescope

EXPLAIN: What are modern reflecting telescopes like?

CHECKING CONCEPTS

1. What kind of telescope uses a mirror to collect and focus light?
2. Who made the first reflecting telescope?
3. What kind of lens is used as an eyepiece in a reflecting telescope?
4. Where is a reflecting telescope's eyepiece sometimes found?
5. Where are two modern reflecting telescopes with very large mirrors found?

THINKING CRITICALLY

6. **CONTRAST:** How do refracting and reflecting telescopes differ?
7. **ANALYZE:** Why is a reflecting telescope with a large concave mirror better than a reflecting telescope with a small mirror?
8. **INFER:** What would the pictures taken by a reflecting telescope be used for?

BUILDING SCIENCE SKILLS

Researching An observatory is a building or group of buildings with large telescopes. Find out what kinds of telescopes are used in the following observatories: Kitt Peak, Mauna Kea, Yerkes, and Mount Wilson. Write a report.

Integrating Environmental Science

TOPICS: pollution, overdevelopment

LIGHT POLLUTION

Because of street lights, the night sky near cities and towns is never very dark. This is true even when there is no Moon showing and clouds hide the stars. The lights reflect off of water droplets and other particles in the air. So much light makes it difficult for astronomers to observe stars and other objects using optical telescopes. Astronomers call this interference light pollution.

Street lamps cause a large percentage of light pollution. Businesses that leave on electric signs all night contribute, too. Many people keep lights on around their homes for safety and security. All of these lights brighten the nighttime sky and make viewing difficult. They can also upset the natural cycles of plants and animals in the area. Fewer lights, shields on streetlights that direct light down, and lights that are activated only when needed can all help to reduce light pollution.

Thinking Critically What could you do to cut down on light pollution?

▲ **Figure 2-13** Satellite photos from 20 years ago (top) and today (bottom).

2-5 What is a radio telescope?

Objective

Explain how a radio telescope works.

Key Term

radio telescope: telescope that can receive radio waves from sources in space

Star Search Stars are usually not visible during the day. They are there, but you cannot see them because of the Sun.

The Sun is also a star. It is the star closest to Earth. The bright light of the Sun outshines the dimmer light from the distant stars. On rainy nights, clouds hide the light from the stars. Not even a refracting or reflecting telescope can help you see the stars on a cloudy night.

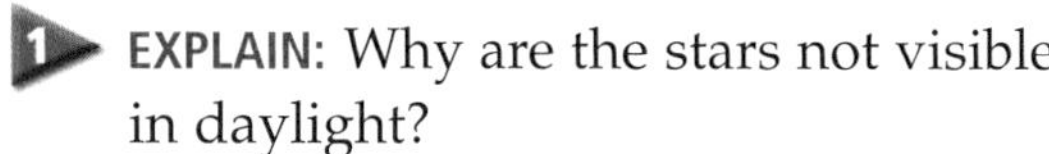

1 **EXPLAIN:** Why are the stars not visible in daylight?

Radio Waves from Space Stars not only send out visible light. They also send out all forms of electromagnetic radiation.

A **radio telescope** can receive radio waves from space. It can find stars during the day or when there are clouds.

In 1932, an American engineer, Karl Jansky, heard the first radio signals from space. He found that the radio waves were coming from the center of our galaxy, the Milky Way Galaxy.

In 1937, Grote Reber built a radio telescope with a 9.5-m reflector dish, or antenna. With this, Reber was able to make the first radio map of the Milky Way Galaxy.

The antenna of a radio telescope works like a mirror does in a reflecting telescope. The antenna collects and focuses radio waves given off by stars and other objects in space. The radio waves are transmitted to a receiver. An astronomer can actually "listen" to the stars this way.

2 **COMPARE:** How is a radio telescope like a reflecting telescope?

Advantages of Radio Telescopes There are three main advantages to using radio telescopes. First, a radio telescope can detect some objects that refracting and reflecting telescopes cannot see. Many objects in the universe give off strong radio waves but very little visible light.

Second, a radio telescope can be used in any kind of weather. Radio waves can travel through clouds in Earth's atmosphere. Reflecting or refracting telescopes cannot be used on very cloudy nights.

Third, a radio telescope can be used during the day, when stars other than the Sun are not visible. Reflecting or refracting telescopes can only be used at night, when the Sun's light does not drown out the light from other, more distant stars.

3 **EXPLAIN:** How is a radio telescope able to function on a cloudy night?

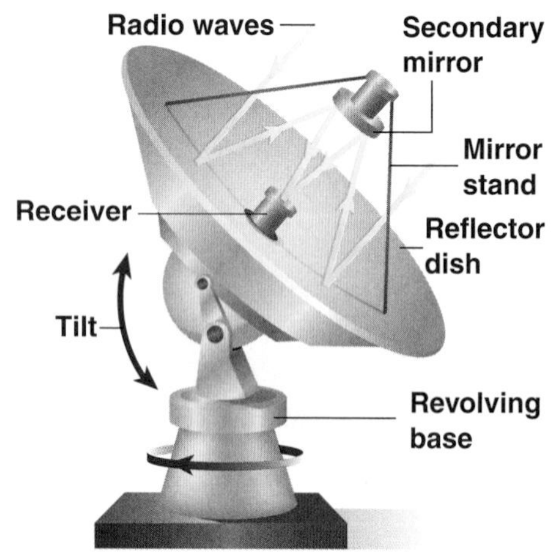

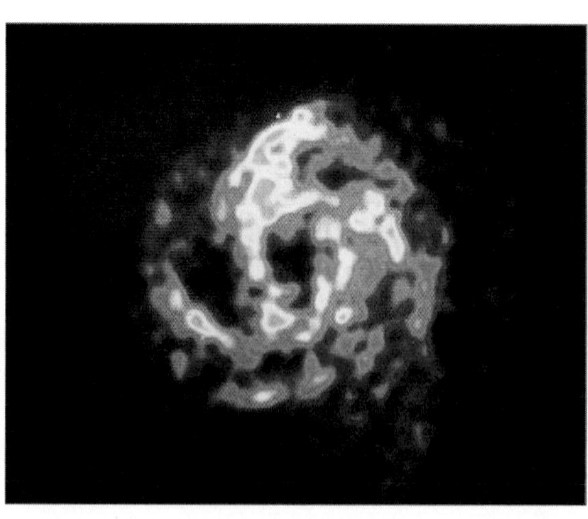

◀ **Figure 2-14** Left: the antenna system of a radio telescope. Right: A false-color image produced by a radio telescope.

✓ CHECKING CONCEPTS

1. The star closest to Earth is ____________.
2. You cannot see stars on a ____________ night.
3. A ____________ telescope can be used during the day.
4. The first radio map of the Milky Way Galaxy was made by ____________.
5. The ____________ of a radio telescope works like the mirror of a reflecting telescope.

THINKING CRITICALLY

6. **CONTRAST:** How do radio telescopes differ from reflecting and refracting telescopes?
7. **LIST:** What are three advantages of radio telescopes over optical telescopes?
8. **INFER:** How do you think astronomers can identify that a sound picked up by a radio telescope is from space?

Web InfoSearch

Interferometry A radio interferometer is two or more radio telescopes linked electronically. This greatly increases their power. Radio interferometers, such as the Very Large Array, can make much more detailed pictures than single radio telescopes can.

▲ **Figure 2-15** The Very Large Array

SEARCH: Use the Internet to find out more about this. Where is the Very Large Array found? What is it used for? Start your search at www.conceptsandchallenges.com. Some key search words are **radio telescope, interferometer,** and **Very Large Array radio telescope.**

Science and Technology

THE SEARCH FOR LIFE ELSEWHERE

Exobiology is a branch of biology that deals with the search for life, including intelligent life, outside of the solar system. In the 1950s, American scientists realized that radio signals could come from or be sent across the galaxy. They were, therefore, perfect for communicating with aliens, should any be talking or listening.

▲ **Figure 2-16** The radio telescope at Arecibo in Puerto Rico

Project SETI (Search for Extraterrestrial Life) was formed in 1959 to listen for radio signals. In 1974, the radio telescope at Arecibo in Puerto Rico sent the first human message to the stars. It was made up of 1,679 on-off pulses aimed 25,000 light years away, at a cluster of stars known as M13.

SETI was canceled in 1992 without having received any alien signals. However, in 1995, a new program was formed called Project Phoenix. Based in Greenbank, West Virginia, Phoenix uses radio telescopes from all over the world to listen for artificial radio signals from space.

Thinking Critically If you could contact an alien, what would you tell it about Earth?

Integrating Physical Science

THE Big IDEA

How do telescopes detect electromagnetic waves in space?

A rainbow shows the colors of the visible spectrum. Each color of the visible spectrum forms from light rays that have a particular wavelength. Violet has the shortest wavelength of the visible spectrum. Red has the longest wavelength.

Rays of light can have wavelengths shorter than violet and longer than red. We cannot see light at these wavelengths with our unaided eyes. However, special telescopes and other instruments are able to detect this light. Using these tools, scientists know that the visible spectrum is just one small part of the entire electromagnetic spectrum.

Astronomers use the invisible parts of the electromagnetic spectrum to study light rays with shorter or longer wavelengths than those of the visible spectrum. Using these tools, astronomers have gathered a great deal of information about distant stars and galaxies.

Note that infrared light, microwaves, and radio waves all have wavelengths longer than the colors of the visible spectrum. These invisible parts of the electromagnetic spectrum are used in everyday life. Microwaves cook foods. Infrared light keeps foods warm. Radio waves broadcast movies and music around the world. Ultraviolet light, X-rays, and gamma rays all have wavelengths shorter than the colors of the visible spectrum. Tanning booths use ultraviolet rays to darken the skin. X-rays take pictures of bones and teeth. Gamma rays can kill cancer cells.

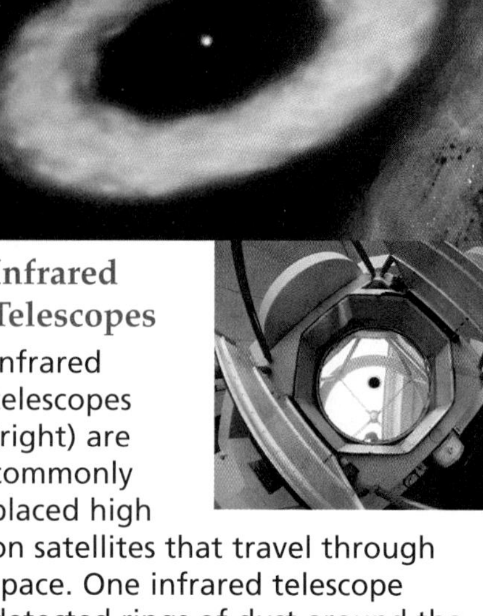

Infrared Telescopes

Infrared telescopes (right) are commonly placed high on satellites that travel through space. One infrared telescope detected rings of dust around the star Vega (shown above) and other nearby stars. Scientists believe these rings might be newly forming solar systems.

Gamma Ray Telescopes

The Compton Gamma Ray Observatory (above right) spent four years in space compiling an image of the Milky Way. The halo effect shown (above left) was made by gamma rays emitted from space.

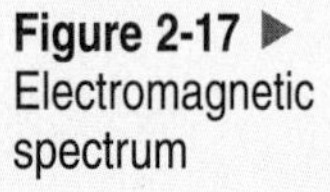

Figure 2-17 ▶ Electromagnetic spectrum

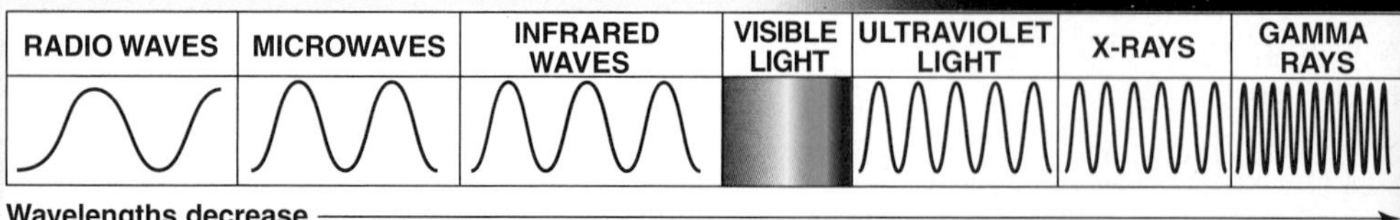

Look at the illustrations that appear on these two pages. Then, follow the directions in the Science Log to learn more about "the big idea." ✦

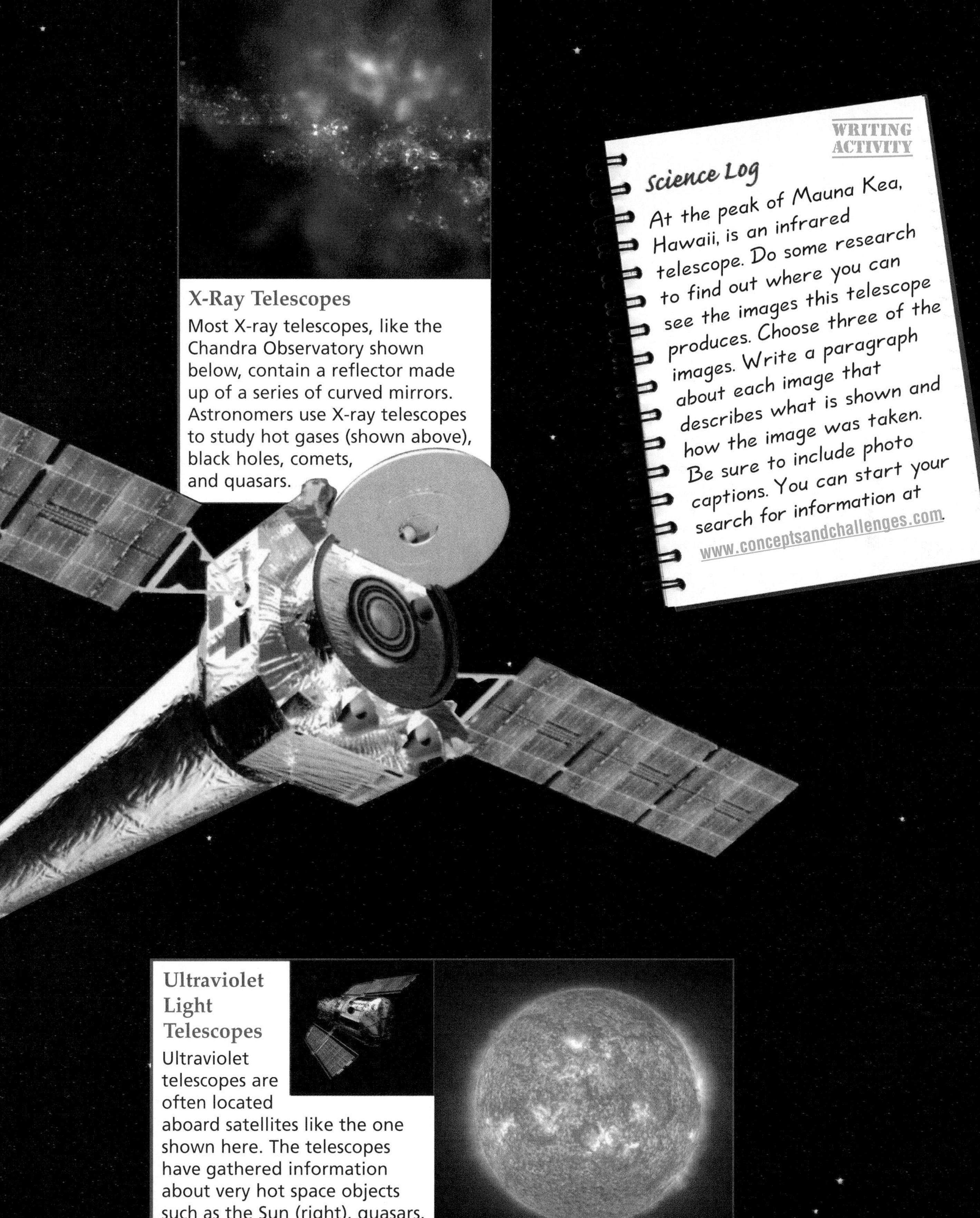

X-Ray Telescopes

Most X-ray telescopes, like the Chandra Observatory shown below, contain a reflector made up of a series of curved mirrors. Astronomers use X-ray telescopes to study hot gases (shown above), black holes, comets, and quasars.

WRITING ACTIVITY

Science Log

At the peak of Mauna Kea, Hawaii, is an infrared telescope. Do some research to find out where you can see the images this telescope produces. Choose three of the images. Write a paragraph about each image that describes what is shown and how the image was taken. Be sure to include photo captions. You can start your search for information at www.conceptsandchallenges.com.

Ultraviolet Light Telescopes

Ultraviolet telescopes are often located aboard satellites like the one shown here. The telescopes have gathered information about very hot space objects such as the Sun (right), quasars, and white dwarfs.

2-6 How do astronomers measure distance?

Objective

Identify two methods astronomers use to measure distances in space.

Key Terms

light year: unit of measurement equal to about 10 trillion km

parallax (PAR-uh-laks)**:** apparent change in the position of a distant object when seen from two different places

astronomical (as-truh-NAHM-ih-kuhl) **unit (AU):** unit of measurement based on the Sun's distance from Earth and equal to about 150 million km

Measuring Distance Most distances on Earth can be measured in meters or kilometers. How would you measure the distance from Earth to the stars? You might try to use kilometers. However, astronomers have found that the distances to stars are so great that the numbers are too large to work with easily.

For example, the star called Proxima Centauri (PRAHK-suh-muh sen-TAW-ree) is the closest star, other than the Sun, to Earth. Proxima Centauri is 40,000,000,000,000 km from Earth. As you can see, this is a very large number. Astronomers had to create special units to measure distances in space.

1 EXPLAIN: Why did scientists create special units to measure distances in space?

Light Years Astronomers often measure the distance to an object in space using light years. A **light year** is equal to the distance light travels in one year.

Light travels through space at a speed of about 300,000 km per second. A light year is equal to almost 10 trillion km. Light from the Sun reaches Earth in a little more than 8 minutes. Light from the North Star, Polaris, reaches Earth in about 700 years.

2 INTERPRET: How far, in light years, is Polaris from Earth?

Parallax Astronomers can use parallax to find out distances to the closer stars. **Parallax** is the apparent change in the position of a distant object when seen from two different places.

Figure 2-18 shows how a nearby star seems to move against a background of more distant stars. By measuring how much the nearby star appears to move, astronomers can calculate how far away the star actually is. Nearby stars have a larger angle of parallax than distant stars do.

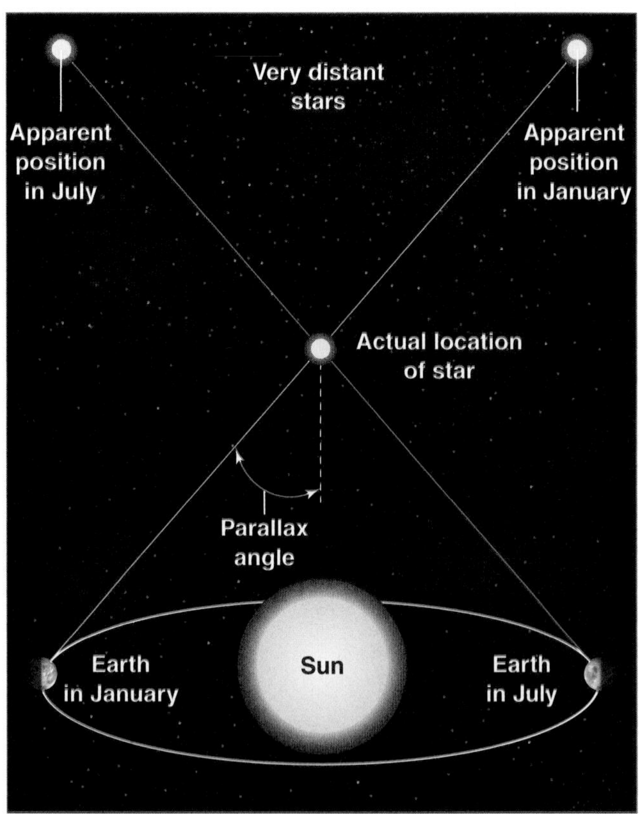

▲ **Figure 2-18** Parallax

Astronomical Units Although it varies, the average distance from Earth to the Sun is about 150 million km. Astronomers call this distance an astronomical unit. One **astronomical unit**, or 1 AU, is equal to 150 million km. An astronomical unit can also be used to measure distances in space, especially distances between the planets in the solar system. Figure 2-19 shows the distances of the planets from the Sun in astronomical units.

DISTANCES OF PLANETS FROM THE SUN			
Planet	**Distance**	**Planet**	**Distance**
Mercury	0.4 AU	Saturn	9.5 AU
Venus	0.7 AU	Uranus	19.2 AU
Earth	1.0 AU	Neptune	30.1 AU
Mars	1.5 AU	Pluto	39.4 AU
Jupiter	5.2 AU		

▲ **Figure 2-19**

 **OBSERVE:** In astronomical units, how far from the Sun is Venus?

CHECKING CONCEPTS

1. Why do astronomers not measure the distances to stars in kilometers?
2. What is the name of the star, other than the Sun, closest to Earth?
3. What is the average distance from Earth to the Sun in kilometers?
4. What is an astronomical unit?
5. What is the speed of light in space?
6. What is a light year?

THINKING CRITICALLY

7. **CALCULATE:** Convert each of the distances shown in Figure 2-19 into kilometers.
8. **SEQUENCE:** Put the planets in order based on distance to each other, from greatest distance to least distance.

BUILDING MATH SKILLS

Calculating One light year is equal to the distance light travels in one Earth year, or 10 trillion km. The diameter of Earth is only 13,000 km. The star known as Alpha Centauri is 4.4 light years away. Figure out how many Earths would have to be placed side by side to reach Alpha Centauri. Procyon is 11.4 light years away. How many Earths would be needed to reach the star known as Procyon?

Hands-On Activity

OBSERVING PARALLAX

You will need three sheets of continuous-feed computer paper, a metric ruler, a drinking straw, and tape.

1. Remove one of the side edges from the computer paper. Tape this strip horizontally to the wall.
2. Tape the straw upright on a metric ruler at the 15-cm mark.
3. Stand about 3 m from the wall. Hold the ruler level with the floor. Close your left eye and line up the straw with the left end of the paper strip.
4. Open your left eye and close your right eye. Count the number of holes the straw appears to move along the strip.
5. Move the straw to the ruler's 30-cm mark and repeat Steps 3 and 4.

▲ **STEP 3** Close your left eye and line up the straw with the left end of the paper strip.

Practicing Your Skills

6. **IDENTIFY:** What does the strip of paper with the holes represent?
7. **OBSERVE:** **a.** At the 15-cm mark, how many holes did the straw appear to move? **b.** How many did it move at the 30-cm mark?
8. **ANALYZE:** Why does the straw appear to change position?
9. **COMPARE:** Which has a greater parallax, a nearby star or a faraway star? Why?

2-7 How does a rocket work?

Objective

Describe how a rocket works.

Key Term

thrust: forward force produced in a rocket engine

Newton's Third Law of Motion The Chinese invented rockets almost 800 years ago. They used them for fireworks and weapons.

To understand how a rocket works, you must know Newton's third law of motion. This law says that for every action, there is an equal and opposite reaction. For example, suppose you are sitting in a rowboat on a lake. You throw a rock into the lake. This is the action. At the same time, the rowboat moves backward slightly. This is the reaction.

1 **STATE:** What is Newton's third law of motion?

Rocket Engines The force that pushes a rocket forward is called **thrust.** The greater the thrust, the higher and faster the rocket will travel. What causes thrust? Fuel is burned inside a rocket engine. The fuel can be a solid or a liquid. As the fuel burns, inside the engine hot gases are produced that begin to rapidly expand. The expanding gases create pressure inside of the engine. This pressure forces the hot gases out of the back of the rocket. This is the action force. The rocket moves forward, in the opposite direction. This is called the thrust, or reaction force.

▲ **Figure 2-20** The *Saturn V* rocket was much more powerful than earlier rockets. It was used to launch the *Apollo* astronauts to the Moon.

2 **DEFINE:** What is thrust?

Escaping Earth's Gravity A lot of thrust is needed for a rocket to escape Earth's gravity. To get into Earth orbit, a rocket must reach a speed of more than 40,000 km/h. Large amounts of fuel are needed to produce enough thrust to reach this speed.

Rocket engines need oxygen to burn fuel. In space, there is no air to supply the oxygen. Rockets must carry their own.

As a rocket moves farther away from Earth, the pull of Earth's gravity on the rocket becomes weaker. Once the rocket is in space, there is little to slow it down. The rocket does not need to burn fuel to keep moving. It keeps moving in the same direction at a constant speed. Fuel is needed in space only to change the rocket's speed or direction.

Figure 2-21
A rocket uses thrust to move forward.

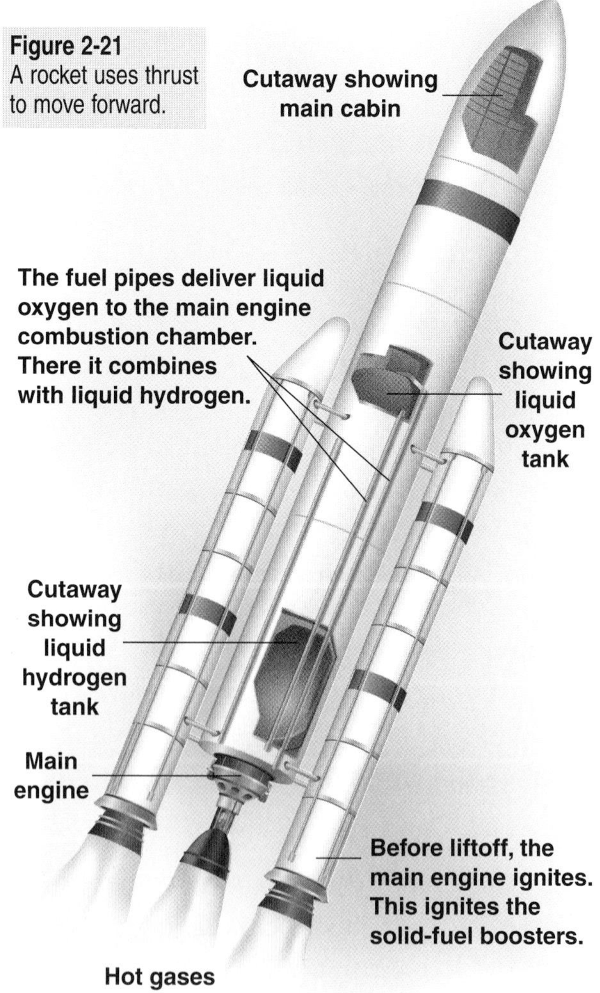
Cutaway showing main cabin
The fuel pipes deliver liquid oxygen to the main engine combustion chamber. There it combines with liquid hydrogen.
Cutaway showing liquid oxygen tank
Cutaway showing liquid hydrogen tank
Main engine
Before liftoff, the main engine ignites. This ignites the solid-fuel boosters.
Hot gases

3 **EXPLAIN:** Why must rockets carry oxygen?

CHECKING CONCEPTS

1. Rockets were invented by the __________ people.
2. Newton's third law of motion says that for every action, there is an equal and __________ reaction.
3. The force that pushes a rocket forward is called __________.
4. Rocket fuel needs __________ to burn.
5. As a rocket moves farther away from Earth, the pull of gravity becomes __________.

THINKING CRITICALLY

6. **ANALYZE:** What is fuel needed for in space?
7. **PREDICT:** Could a rocket traveling at a speed of 10,000 km/h get into space? Explain.
8. **INFER:** Why is thrust also known as the reaction force?
9. **EXPLAIN:** Why does a rocket not need to burn fuel to keep moving once it is in space?

BUILDING MATH SKILLS

Calculating Thrust is a force. The unit of force in the metric system is the newton (N). One newton (1 N) is equal to 4.5 lb. Below is a list of rockets and their thrusts at launch. The thrust is given in pounds. Convert each thrust into newtons. Then, list the rockets in order, from least thrust to greatest thrust.

Delta	205,000 lb
Saturn V	7,570,000 lb
Mercury-Atlas	367,000 lb
Space shuttle	6,925,000 lb
Vanguard	28,000 lb

For example:

$$1 \text{ N} = 4.5 \text{ lb}$$

$$105{,}000 \text{ lb} \div 4.5 \text{ lb/N} = 23{,}333 \text{ N}$$

Hands-On Activity

DEMONSTRATING ACTION AND REACTION FORCES

You will need about 3 m of fishing line, a 3-cm piece of a drinking straw, tape, a balloon, and a twist tie.

1. Inflate a balloon. Close the end with a twist tie.
2. Thread the fishing line through the straw. Tape the straw across the top of the balloon.
3. Tie one end of the string to a chair. Hold the other end.
4. Move away from the chair. Hold the string tight. Remove the twist tie from the balloon and observe what happens.

▲ **STEP 2** Tape the straw to the balloon after you thread the fishing line through it.

Practicing Your Skills

5. **EXPLAIN:** What happened to the air in the balloon when you removed the twist tie?
6. **OBSERVE:** Where did the balloon go?
7. **INFER:** In which direction did the air from the balloon move?
8. **IDENTIFY:** **a.** What was the action force? **b.** What was the reaction force?

LAB ACTIVITY
Modeling Newton's Third Law of Motion

Materials
Safety goggles,
35-mm film canister
with inner-locking cap,
sheet of paper,
cellophane tape,
scissors, fizzing
antacid tablet, water,
tablespoon

BACKGROUND

The only way to reach space is to ride a rocket. The force driving most rockets is produced when rocket fuel burns. Hot gases shoot out from the engines of the rocket, and the rocket travels upward into space. However, not all rockets have to burn fuel to work. Thrust can be produced in many ways.

PURPOSE

In this activity, you will construct and fly a rocket.

PROCEDURE  

1. Copy the chart in Figure 2-22.
2. Using half a sheet of paper, roll and tape a snug tube around a film canister. Make sure the cap end of the canister sticks out 12 mm. Tape the tube to the canister.
3. Cut out and tape rocket fins to the lower end of the tube. The fins can be of any shape. Make three or four fins. Cut out a half-circle of paper. Roll it into a nose cone. **CAUTION** ⚠ Be careful when using scissors.
4. Tape the nose cone to the upper end of the tube. Your rocket is now ready. Draw a diagram of the rocket in your chart.
5. Put on your safety goggles. Take your rocket to a launch site. Put a tablespoon of water inside the canister. Drop in one half of an antacid tablet that fizzes when dropped into water.

▲ **STEP 2** Roll the paper around the film canister.

▲ **STEP 3** Tape rocket fins to the lower end of the tube. Prepare a nose cone.

▲ **STEP 5** Drop half of your antacid tablet into the canister.

▲ **STEP 6** Set your rocket on the launch pad and step away.

6. Quickly snap the film canister cap in place. Set the rocket right side up on the launch pad and step away. Record your observations in your chart.

Diagram of your rocket	How well did your rocket perform?
Diagram of someone else's rocket	How well did that rocket perform?

▲ **Figure 2-22** Draw a diagram of your rocket and someone else's rocket. Record your observations.

CONCLUSIONS

1. **OBSERVE:** How high did your rocket go?
2. **OBSERVE:** Did any other rockets fly higher than yours?
3. **ANALYZE:** What do you think made some rockets fly higher than others?
4. **COMPARE:** Write a report comparing the two rockets you observed. Say why you think one worked better than the other.

2-8 What is the space shuttle?

Objective

Explain how the space shuttle works.

A Reusable Spaceship In the 1960s and 1970s, all spaceflights were made with spacecraft that could be used only once. This was very expensive and wasteful. The National Aeronautics and Space Administration (NASA) decided to build a spacecraft that could go into space and return to Earth many times. This new kind of spacecraft was known as the Space Transportation System, or the space shuttle.

1 INFER: How was the space shuttle an improvement over earlier spacecraft?

Design of the Shuttle The space shuttle has three main parts. Two of the parts are needed to get the shuttle into space. These are the solid-fuel booster rockets and the liquid-fuel tank. The third part is the shuttle orbiter. The orbiter is the only part that stays in space after launch.

How does the shuttle get into orbit? At launch, both the booster rockets and the orbiter's rocket engines are fired. After launch, the boosters separate from the orbiter. They fall back into the ocean and can be hauled out to be used again.

The large liquid-fuel tank provides fuel for the orbiter's engines. The tank drops away before the orbiter reaches orbit. It is not reusable.

Once the orbiter is in space, the engines are turned off. They are fired again to change the orbiter's speed and direction when it is ready to return to Earth. When its mission is over, the orbiter glides to a landing on a runway.

◀ **Figure 2-24** The orbiter uses a parachute to help slow its speed upon landing.

2 LIST: What are the three main parts of the space shuttle?

Uses of the Shuttle The shuttle's cargo bay is designed to carry between 10,000 and 50,000 kg of equipment into orbit. The weight depends partly on the shuttle's altitude in space. Satellites and space probes can be launched from the shuttle.

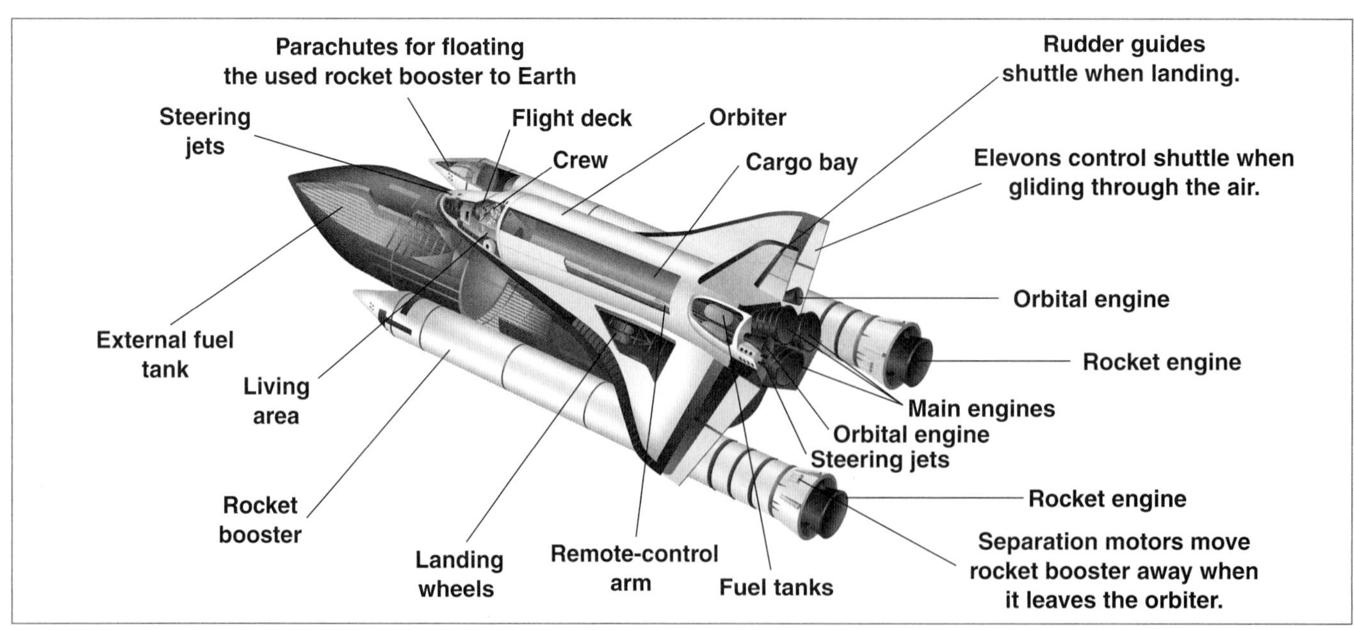

▲ **Figure 2-23** The space shuttle

Shuttle astronauts can repair satellites in orbit. Satellites can also be returned to Earth for repair.

The shuttle will sometime carry a flying laboratory called Spacelab in its cargo bay. In this laboratory, a variety of science experiments are performed. The shuttle is also used to ferry people and supplies into space.

▲ **Figure 2-25** Spacelab is used for experiments aboard the space shuttle.

NAME: What is the laboratory carried by the shuttle called?

 CHECKING CONCEPTS

1. Another name for the space shuttle is ___________.
2. The shuttle orbiter lands like an airplane on a ___________.
3. Satellites are carried in the shuttle's ___________.
4. Spacelab is a flying ___________.

THINKING CRITICALLY

5. **ANALYZE:** How is the space shuttle useful to people on Earth?
6. **INFER:** Why is it important for the boosters to be separated from the orbiter before going into orbit?

INTERPRETING VISUALS

Use Figure 2-23 to answer the following questions.

7. **IDENTIFY:** How many main parts does the space shuttle have?
8. **INFER:** What part of the shuttle actually goes into space?
9. **ANALYZE:** How does the design of the shuttle make it a kind of space plane?

Science and Technology

THE NATIONAL AERONAUTICS AND SPACE ADMINISTRATION

The National Aeronautics and Space Administration, or NASA, started operations in 1958. NASA is a government agency that supports research. It also develops vehicles and programs for exploring Earth's atmosphere and space.

Over the years, NASA has achieved many technological breakthroughs. Project Mercury, NASA's first major project, proved that technology could help humans to survive in space. The *Apollo* missions put people on the Moon.

Space shuttles today are helping to build the International Space Station. Spacecraft are being sent to Mars and beyond. The Hubble Space Telescope takes pictures of the solar system and the stars beyond. Satellites are being launched into space for many different purposes. NASA technology has also been used to improve our health. *Apollo* technologies led to computerized aerial tomography, or CAT scans, and better kidney dialysis machines. Space shuttle technologies led to a new pump used in artificial hearts.

▲ **Figure 2-26** Technicians work on a mirror for a NASA space telescope.

Thinking Critically What types of vehicles has NASA built?

2-9 What are satellites and space probes?

Objective

Explain how artificial satellites and space probes are used to explore space.

Key Terms

satellite (SAT-uhl-eyet)**:** natural or artificial object orbiting a body in space

orbit: curved path of one object around another object in space

Artificial Satellites

A **satellite** is any object, natural or artificial, that follows a curved path around another object in space. The curved path of the object is its **orbit.**

▲ **Figure 2-27**
An *Intelsat VI* satellite

For thousands of years, astronomers were only able to study the skies from the surface of Earth. Then, on October 4, 1957, the Space Age began. On that day, the Soviet Union launched the first artificial satellite. It was called *Sputnik. Sputnik* circled Earth every 96 minutes.

Most satellites are launched into one of four main orbits. Nearly circular orbits are usually about 250 km above Earth's surface. Polar orbits are usually about 800 km high.

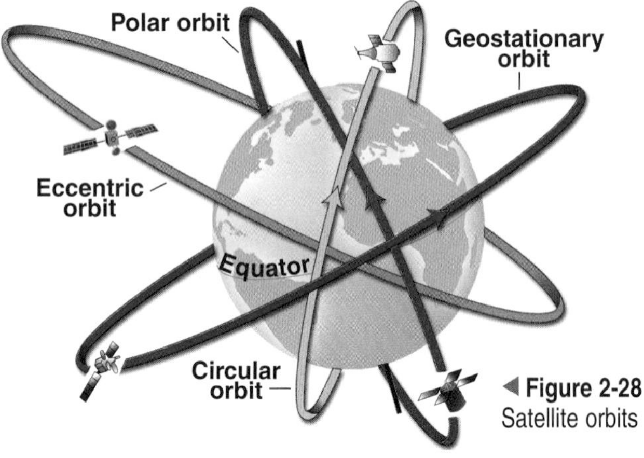

◀ **Figure 2-28**
Satellite orbits

The height of a highly elliptical, or eccentric, orbit depends on where the satellite is in its orbit. A geostationary orbit is 36,000 km above Earth's surface. A satellite in geostationary orbit stays above the same spot on Earth. This is because it travels at the same speed as the planet rotates.

1 NAME: What is the curved path of a satellite called?

Uses of Satellites Since *Sputnik*, thousands of artificial satellites have been placed in orbit around Earth. These collect information about Earth, the Sun, the stars, other planets, comets, and other bodies in the solar system.

For example, the Global Positioning System (GPS) is a radio navigation system of about 24 satellites operating in circular orbits. GPS is a guidance service provided by the U. S. Air Force Space Command unit.

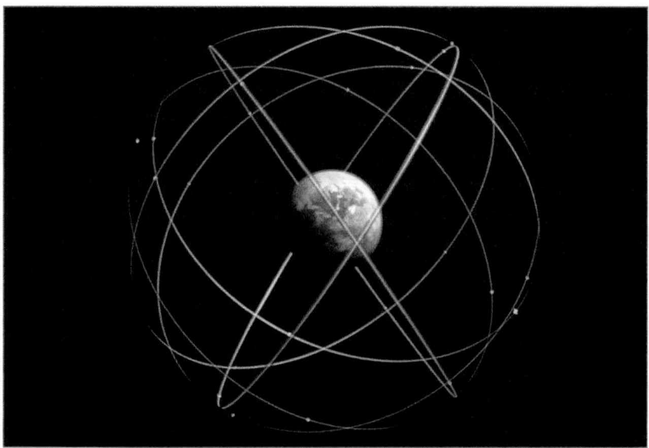

▲ **Figure 2-29** The 24 GPS satellites circle Earth using six different orbits.

The system relays positions on Earth's surface in degrees of latitude and longitude. GPS receivers with computers have improved surveying techniques. Surveyors are now able to monitor changes of Earth's crust caused by tectonic motion. Meteorologists are able to use GPS signals to measure the temperature and water content of the atmosphere. Geologists can accurately map changes in the Greenland ice sheet to help them understand climate changes.

Computers are essential in turning satellite data or measurements into meaningful information. For example, computers help meteorologists translate weather satellite data into current temperatures, pressures, humidity readings, and wind speeds. This information is used to create a weather report.

 **DESCRIBE:** What are satellites used for?

Space Probes Astronauts have been sent to the Moon to explore it and have returned safely to Earth. Space can also be explored by space probes, which do not carry people. In fact, many kinds of space exploration are best done with space probes. Space probes can go places that would be too far or too dangerous for astronauts to travel to.

For example, part of the *Galileo* space probe sent to Jupiter entered its atmosphere in 1995. It radioed important information to Earth before being destroyed by high temperatures and pressure. *Cassini*, launched in 1997, will reach Saturn in 2004. It is scheduled to orbit the planet and its moons for four years.

▲ **Figure 2-30** The *Cassini* probe will explore Saturn from orbit when it gets there, in the year 2004.

Space probes are usually sent on one-way missions. They do not return to Earth. Some space probes to the outer planets, such as *Voyagers 1* and *2*, have even been sent out of the solar system.

The *Voyager* space probes were launched in 1977. In 1989, *Voyager 2* became the first spacecraft from Earth to reach Neptune. Both space probes sent back stunning images of all the giant planets.

Scientists believe that *Voyager 2* will continue traveling for thousands of years. They hope to continue receiving signals from both space probes until at least the year 2020.

 **IDENTIFY:** What are two planets that have been visited by space probes?

✓ CHECKING CONCEPTS

1. What is a satellite?
2. What was *Sputnik*?
3. What was the first space probe to reach Neptune?
4. What will *Cassini* do when it gets to Saturn?

THINKING CRITICALLY

5. **NAME:** What are two advantages that space probes have over spaceships and human crews?
6. **INFER:** *Telstar* was one of the first artificial satellites. It was launched in 1962. *Telstar* was a communications satellite. What do you think was the function of *Telstar?*
7. **INFER:** How does GPS help ships and aircraft?

BUILDING SCIENCE SKILLS

Classifying Below is a list of some important artificial satellites. Find out the function of each. Then, classify each according to its function. On a piece of paper, write the words *Communications Satellite*, *Weather Satellite*, *Navigation Satellite*, and *Scientific Satellite*. Place each satellite under its correct heading.

Early Bird	*Explorer I*	*Intelsat*	*Tiros*
Echo	*Landsat*	*Nimbus*	*Transit*

◀ **Figure 2-31** *Tiros*

2-10 How are space stations used?

Objective

Explain the role of space stations.

Space Stations Artificial satellites and space probes are very useful in space exploration. They can gather information and send it back to scientists on Earth. The scientists do not have to leave Earth. Sometimes, however, scientists prefer to make their observations directly. In a space station, scientists can live and work in space for long periods of time.

1 EXPLAIN: What is a space station useful for?

Early Space Stations In 1971, the former Soviet Union launched the first space station, *Salyut* ("salute"). The first U.S. space station, *Skylab*, was launched in 1973. It was about the size of a small house. Three teams of astronauts visited *Skylab*. Eventually, *Salyut* and *Skylab* wandered from their orbits, causing them to fall to Earth. They had shown, though, that people could safely live and work in space.

▲ **Figure 2-32** *Skylab* was the first U.S. space station.

The former Soviet Union later constructed in space their second space station, called *Mir* ("Peace"). The first part of *Mir* was launched in 1986. Some cosmonauts stayed on *Mir* for more than a year, setting new records. *Mir* fell out of orbit and back to Earth in 2001.

2 NAME: What was the first U.S. space station?

The International Space Station The United States and Russia launched the first parts of a new space station, called the International Space Station, or ISS, in 1998. Other countries are involved in this project as well. The ISS may be complete by 2006. Many parts have already been carried into orbit by space shuttles or other rockets.

People have been working and living on the ISS since the year 2000. They use the space shuttle to travel to and from Earth. The completed ISS will have laboratories, living quarters, docking bays for shuttles, and solar panels for energy. It will also have a satellite repair shop.

▲ **Figure 2-33** The International Space Station (ISS) is scheduled to be finished by the year 2006.

3 DESCRIBE: What are some parts of the ISS?

Living in Space Astronauts on the ISS must live and work in conditions that are very different from those on Earth. Life-support systems on board must provide oxygen and remove carbon dioxide. The air has to be pressurized. Food and water must be supplied from Earth. The water must be recycled.

Because of the very low gravity in space, the body does not have to work as hard in space as it does on Earth. Muscles tend to weaken. Therefore, exercise is essential to keep the astronaut's bodies in shape. Also, sleeping areas in space must have straps to prevent astronauts from floating off. Eye shades must be worn because the Sun rises and sets every hour and a half on a spacecraft in near-Earth orbit.

HYPOTHESIZE: What are some other problems astronauts might have living in space?

CHECKING CONCEPTS

1. In a __________, scientists can live and work in space.
2. The first space station was called __________.
3. Parts for the ISS are carried into orbit mostly by the __________.
4. The ISS will be used to repair __________.

THINKING CRITICALLY

5. **INFER:** Astronauts living on a space station have to adjust to the weightlessness of space. Ordinary chores are often more complicated than they are on Earth. Identify three things that you do every day on Earth, such as take a shower, that might be very difficult to do on a space station.

DESIGNING AN EXPERIMENT

Design an experiment to solve the following problem. Include a hypothesis, variables, a procedure with materials, and a type of data to study. Also, tell how you would record your data.

PROBLEM: Earth's climate may be getting warmer partly because of the burning of fossil fuels. This could melt polar ice caps and create new deserts. How can scientists study this problem from the ISS?

People in Science

AEROSPACE WORKER

Space probes, satellites, and space stations are manufactured by the aerospace industry. This industry employs about 1 million workers. About half of the people in the aerospace industry actually work on putting spacecraft together. Many inspectors check the quality of each job as it is completed.

Because the aerospace industry uses the latest technologies, many aerospace workers have a background in science and engineering. The aerospace industry also employs lawyers, accountants, and clerical workers. If you are a high school graduate and a graduate of a technical school or college, you might want to find a job in the aerospace industry.

▲ **Figure 2-34** Many aerospace workers help assemble rockets.

Thinking Critically Why is it important to have many inspectors checking spacecraft?

Chapter 2 Challenges

Chapter Summary

Lessons 2-1 and 2-2

- **Astronomy** helped ancient societies solve practical problems. Modern astronomers use telescopes, satellites, and space probes to study the **solar system** and the rest of the universe.

Lessons 2-3 and 2-4

- Galileo used an early **refracting telescope** to look at the Moon. A refracting telescope uses two **convex lenses.**
- A **reflecting telescope** usually uses a **concave mirror** to collect light. Newton made the first reflecting telescope.

Lesson 2-5

- A **radio telescope** picks up radio waves from objects in space.

Lessons 2-6 and 2-7

- **Light years** are used to measure distances in space. One light year is the distance light travels in one year, or about 10 trillion km.
- One **astronomical unit,** the distance from Earth to the Sun, is equal to 150 million km.
- Newton's third law of motion explains how rockets work. **Thrust** pushes a rocket forward.
- Rocket engines carry oxygen to burn fuel in space for changing speed or direction.

Lesson 2-8

- The space shuttle is reusable. Both the booster rockets and the liquid-fuel tank drop off before the orbiter reaches space. The orbiter returns to Earth and lands on a runway.
- The shuttle has many uses, including the launching and repairing of satellites.

Lessons 2-9 and 2-10

- Thousands of artificial **satellites** are in **orbit** today around Earth.
- Space probes can go to dangerous places. They can be sent on one-way missions.
- A space station allows scientists to live and work in space for long periods of time.
- The ISS is being built in orbit from parts carried by space shuttles. It has a full-time research laboratory and satellite repair station.

Key Term Challenges

astronomical unit (p. 52)
astronomy (p. 40)
concave mirror (p. 46)
convex lens (p. 44)
galaxy (p. 42)
light year (p. 52)
orbit (p. 60)
parallax (p. 52)
radio telescope (p. 48)
reflecting telescope (p. 46)
refracting telescope (p. 44)
satellite (p. 60)
solar system (p. 40)
thrust (p. 54)

MATCHING Write the Key Term from above that best matches each description.

1. curved path of an object around another object
2. force that pushes a rocket forward
3. distance of 150 million km
4. mirror that curves inward
5. lens thicker in the middle than at its edges
6. large system of stars
7. the Sun and all the bodies that circle the Sun
8. natural or artificial object that orbits a body in space

FILL IN Write the Key Term from above that best completes each statement.

9. The study of stars, planets, and other bodies in space is called ___________.
10. A telescope that uses two convex lenses to produce an enlarged image of an object is a ___________.
11. A telescope that is used to study radio waves coming from space is a ___________.
12. A unit of distance equal to 10 trillion km is the ___________.
13. A telescope that uses mirrors to form an image is a ___________.
14. An apparent change in the position of a distant object when seen from two different places is called ___________.
15. To measure distances to the planets, astronomers usually use ___________.

Content Challenges TEST PREP

MULTIPLE CHOICE Write the letter of the term or phrase that best completes each sentence.

1. The first artificial satellite launched into space was
   a. *Apollo.*
   b. *Voyager.*
   c. *Telstar.*
   d. *Sputnik.*
2. A concave mirror
   a. curves inward.
   b. curves outward.
   c. is flat.
   d. curves inward and outward.
3. The telescope used by Newton was a
   a. refracting telescope.
   b. reflecting telescope.
   c. radio telescope.
   d. scanning telescope.
4. The closest star to Earth, other than the Sun, is
   a. Io.
   b. Proxima Centauri.
   c. Polaris.
   d. *Voyager.*
5. An astronomical unit is equal to the distance from
   a. Earth to the Moon.
   b. the Sun to the Moon.
   c. Earth to the Sun.
   d. Earth to Pluto.
6. To get into space, a rocket must reach a speed of more than
   a. 3,000 km/h.
   b. 4,000 km/h.
   c. 30,000 km/h.
   d. 40,000 km/h.
7. The space station that is currently in orbit is called the
   a. space shuttle.
   b. *Saturn V.*
   c. *Apollo.*
   d. ISS.
8. Muscles can weaken in space because of the
   a. high temperatures.
   b. low air pressure.
   c. low gravity.
   d. change of diet.

TRUE/FALSE Write *true* if the statement is true. If the statement is false, change the underlined term to make the statement true.

9. The first <u>artificial</u> satellite was launched in 1957.
10. Scientists think that the universe began when a huge explosion called the <u>Big Bang</u> occurred.
11. The telescope used by Galileo was a <u>radio</u> telescope.
12. The first person to study the surface of the Moon with a telescope was <u>Newton</u>.
13. The lens in a refracting telescope that collects light and focuses the image is the <u>objective</u> lens.
14. A telescope that uses mirrors instead of lenses is a <u>refracting</u> telescope.
15. Stars can be studied on a cloudy night with a <u>radio</u> telescope.
16. The *Galileo* space probe is studying the atmosphere of <u>Earth</u>.
17. The only part of a space shuttle that goes into space is the <u>liquid-fuel tank</u>.
18. Newton's <u>third</u> law of motion states that for every action, there is an equal and opposite reaction.

Concept Challenges TEST PREP

WRITTEN RESPONSE Answer each of the following questions in complete sentences.

1. **EXPLAIN:** Why is space exploration important?
2. **CONTRAST:** What is the difference between a refracting telescope and a reflecting telescope?
3. **INFER:** What are the advantages of unmanned space probes?
4. **EXPLAIN:** How do scientists use parallax to calculate the distances to stars?
5. **EXPLAIN:** How does Newton's third law of motion describe how a rocket works?
6. **ANALYZE:** What is the advantage of the space shuttle over earlier spacecraft?
7. **INFER:** How are space probes able to travel to the outer reaches of our solar system without a huge fuel reserve?
8. **INFER:** Before the discovery of the planet Uranus, no planets had been discovered for 5,000 years. Why did it take such a long time for astronomers to discover Uranus?
9. **ANALYZE:** If you were an astronomer today, what types of tools could you use to explore space?
10. **INFER:** How many natural satellites orbit Earth?
11. **CALCULATE:** One astronomical unit is equal to 150 million km. One light year is equal to 10 trillion km. How many astronomical units are in one light year?

INTERPRETING VISUALS Use Figure 2-35 to answer each of the following questions.

12. Which of these star systems is closest to Earth?
13. Which of these star systems is farthest from Earth?
14. How many stars are in the Alpha Centauri star system?
15. Can you tell from this chart how close these stars are to each other? Explain your answer.
16. How could two stars that are about the same distance from Earth be far apart from each other?

NEAREST STARS AND STAR SYSTEMS

Name of Star or Star System	Distance (in light years)
Alpha Centauri A, B, C	4.4
Barnard's Star	5.9
Lalande 21185	8.3
Sirius A, B	8.6
Ross 154	9.7
Epsilon Eridani	10.5
HD 217987	10.7
Ross 128	10.9
61 Cygni A, B	11.4
Procyon	11.4

▲ Figure 2-35

Chapter 3 The Solar System

▲ **Figure 3-1** Saturn's majestic rings, shown here in false colors, were first seen by Galileo in 1610.

Saturn is the second largest planet in our solar system. Its beautiful rings make it the easiest planet to recognize. Like Jupiter, Saturn is a huge ball made mostly of gas. It is surrounded by clouds. Saturn is ten times farther from the Sun than Earth is. To the naked eye, it looks bright yellow. Computers often enhance the images taken of Saturn using false colors. This allows its atmosphere and its many individual rings to be seen.

▶ What do you think Saturn's rings might be made of?

Contents

3-1 What is the solar system?

Objectives

Name the planets that make up the solar system. Describe how they are grouped.

Key Terms

solar system: Sun and all the objects that orbit the Sun

nebula (NEHB-yuh-luh)**:** cloud of gas and dust in space

orbit: curved path of one object around another object in space

Formation of the Solar System The **solar system** is the Sun and all the objects that orbit it. Scientists are not sure how the solar system formed. However, several theories have been developed. One popular theory states that the solar system formed from a spinning cloud of gas and dust called a **nebula.**

Scientists think that gravity caused the nebula to shrink, or contract, to form the Sun. After the Sun formed, the leftover gas and dust in the nebula formed the other objects in the solar system. This took many millions of years.

The Sun contains more than 99.8 percent of the mass in our solar system. The planets make up most of the rest of the mass.

1 **DEFINE:** What is a nebula?

The Sun's Family The Sun has a "family" of nine planets, more than 90 moons, and countless chunks of debris made of rock, ice, and gas. Together, these objects fill a volume of space about 10 trillion km in diameter. Almost all of this space is surrounded by one or more sphere-shaped clouds of comets.

Ancient peoples observed that the planets changed their positions among the stars. The planets seemed to wander in the sky. The word *planet* comes from a Greek word meaning "wanderer."

Earth is one of the nine planets in the solar system. Like the other planets, Earth moves in a curved path around the Sun. This path is the planet's **orbit.** All of the planets orbit the Sun in the same direction.

EXPLAIN: Why were the planets called wanderers?

The Inner and Outer Planets The nine planets are often divided into the inner planets and the outer planets. Mercury, Venus, Earth, and Mars are the inner planets. They are all fairly small and rocky.

The outer planets are the gas giants Jupiter, Saturn, Uranus, and Neptune. Pluto is also an outer planet. However, like the inner planets, Pluto is small and rocky. The inner and outer planets are separated by the Asteroid Belt, which contains billions of smaller rocks.

CLASSIFY: Which are the inner planets?

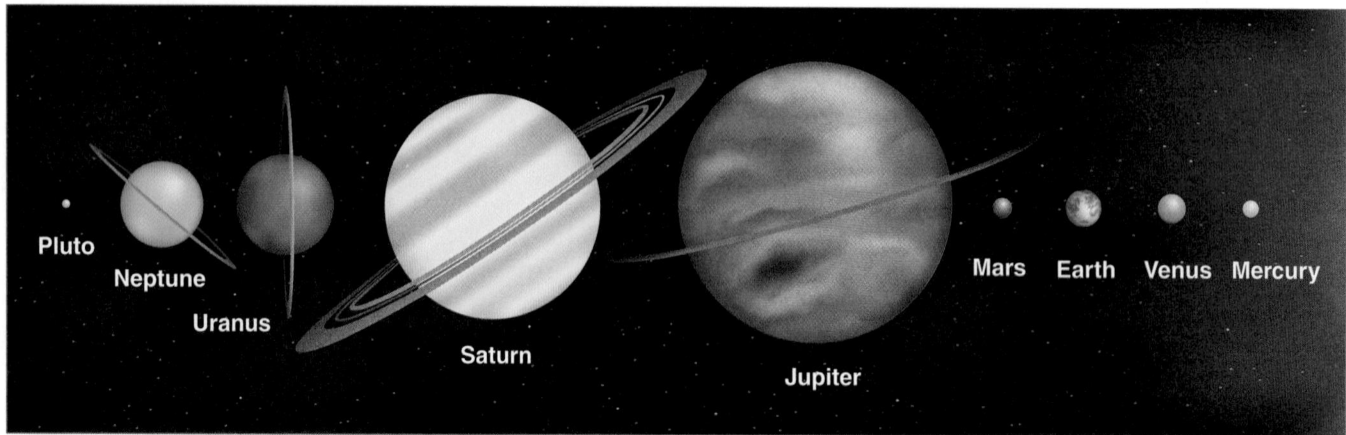

▲ **Figure 3-2** The solar system contains nine planets. They are divided into the inner planets and the outer planets.

✓ CHECKING CONCEPTS

1. The solar system may have formed from a ___________.
2. The solar system contains ___________ planets.
3. A nebula is a ___________.
4. The path of a planet around the Sun is the planet's ___________.
5. The planets can be divided into two groups, the inner planets and the ___________ planets.
6. The ___________ separates the inner and outer planets.

THINKING CRITICALLY

7. **SEQUENCE:** List the planets in order from nearest to the Sun to farthest from the Sun.
8. **HYPOTHESIZE:** Why is the solar system often referred to as the Sun's "family"?

BUILDING SCIENCE SKILLS

Researching As seen from Earth, some planets seem to have unusual motions in their orbits. For example, early astronomers were puzzled to discover that for part of the year Mars and some other planets seemed to move backward in their orbits compared with the movements of Earth. Do research to find out why Mars and some other planets seem to sometimes exhibit these "retrograde" motions. Draw a diagram of these motions and write a report explaining them.

◀ **Figure 3-3** Mars, along with some other planets, exhibits retrograde motion.

How Do They Know That?

PLANETS BEYOND THE SOLAR SYSTEM

Are there planets going around other suns? Are there other solar systems?

It isn't easy to find planets around other suns. Planets are very small compared with stars and usually have less than one-billionth the brightness. Still, it is possible to find planets orbiting other stars. Jupiter is the largest planet in our solar system. The Hubble Space Telescope or other more powerful telescopes now being built may someday be able to detect planets around other stars if they are at least as large as Jupiter.

Planets have a gravitational effect on stars the same way that stars have a gravitational effect on planets. Planets cause a star to wobble. Telescopes can detect this wobble. Using this method, a planet was discovered in orbit around the star 51 Pegasi in 1995. Since then, many more "extrasolar" planets have been discovered.

FIRST TEN EXTRASOLAR PLANETS DISCOVERED

Name of Parent Star	Star's Distance From Sun (In Light Years)	Year Found	Minimum Mass of Planet (Earth = 1)
51 Pegasi	50	1995	150
55 Cancri	44	1996	270
47 Ursae Majoris	46	1996	890
Tau Böötis	49	1996	1,230
Upsilon Andromedae	54	1996	220
70 Virginis	59	1996	2,100
16 Cygni B	72	1996	480
Rho Coronae Borealis	55	1997	350
Gliese 876	15	1998	670
14 Herculis	55	1998	1,050

▲ **Figure 3-4**

Thinking Critically Why are planets that orbit other stars called extrasolar planets?

3-2 What do we know about orbits?

Objective

Describe the shape of Earth's orbit.

Key Terms

ellipse (eh-LIPS)**:** flattened circle or oval

perihelion (per-uh-HEE-lee-uhn)**:** point in a planet's orbit at which it is closest to the Sun

aphelion (uh-FEE-lee-uhn)**:** point in a planet's orbit at which it is farthest from the Sun

Gravity Every object in the universe pulls on every other object. This pull is the force of gravity, or gravitational attraction. There is gravitational attraction between all objects in the universe. For example, there is gravitational attraction between the Sun and the planets. This gravitational attraction pulls the planets toward the Sun as they move through space. Instead of flying off into space, the planets move in orbits around the Sun. Gravity also pulls all objects on Earth toward the center of the planet.

1 STATE: What force pulls all nearby objects toward the center of Earth?

Earth's Orbit A circle is perfectly round. All lines drawn from the center of the circle to its rim are the same length. An **ellipse** looks like a flattened circle or oval. Lines drawn from the center to different points on its rim are different lengths.

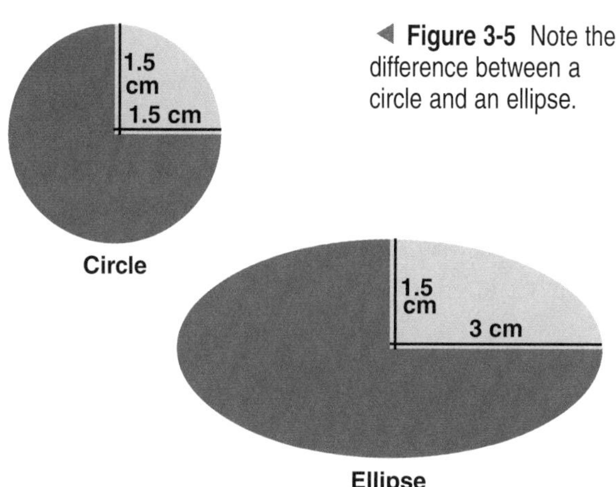

◀ **Figure 3-5** Note the difference between a circle and an ellipse.

Earth and all the other planets travel around the Sun in elliptical orbits. This means that the planet is not always the same distance from the Sun. In January, for example, Earth reaches its perihelion. **Perihelion** is the point at which a planet is closest to the Sun. Earth is about 147 million km from the Sun at perihelion. In July, Earth reaches its aphelion. **Aphelion** is the point at which a planet is farthest from the Sun. Earth is 152 million km from the Sun at aphelion.

2 DESCRIBE: What is the shape of Earth's orbit?

Orbital Velocity The speed at which a planet travels in its orbit is called its orbital velocity. The closer a planet is to the Sun, the greater is its orbital velocity. A planet moves fastest at perihelion. It moves slowest at aphelion.

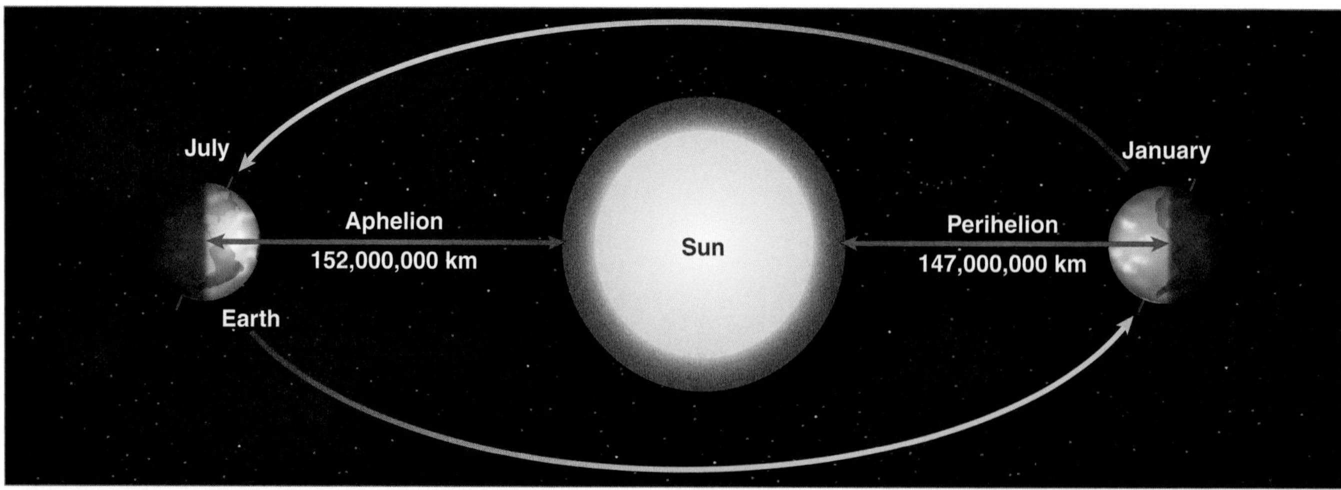

▲ **Figure 3-6** Earth travels in an elliptical orbit around the Sun. It is closer to the Sun at perihelion than at aphelion.

The closer two objects are to each other, the greater the gravitational attraction between them. As a planet gets closer to the Sun, the gravitational attraction between the planet and the Sun increases. As a result, the planet moves faster in its orbit.

As a planet moves farther from the Sun, the gravitational attraction between the planet and the Sun decreases. The planet slows down. This is why a planet moves fastest at perihelion and slowest at aphelion. The difference in gravitational attraction also explains why the planets closer to the Sun move faster than those farther from the Sun.

STATE: When does Earth move fastest in its orbit?

CHECKING CONCEPTS

1. An ellipse has an __________ shape.
2. Earth's path around the Sun is its __________.
3. Earth moves in an __________ orbit.
4. The point at which Earth is closest to the Sun is __________.
5. A planet's speed in its orbit is its __________.

THINKING CRITICALLY

6. **HYPOTHESIZE:** The planets are different distances from the Sun. Mercury is closest to the Sun. Pluto is usually farthest from the Sun. Which of the two planets has the greater orbital velocity? Explain.

INTERPRETING VISUALS

Use Figure 3-6 to answer the following questions.

7. **ANALYZE:** What month is it when Earth is closest to the Sun?
8. **ANALYZE:** What month is it when Earth is farthest from the Sun?
9. **CALCULATE:** How much farther from the Sun is Earth at aphelion than at perihelion?

Hands-On Activity

DRAWING THE SHAPE OF EARTH'S ORBIT

You will need paper, cardboard, two pushpins, string, a pencil, and a metric ruler.

1. Place a sheet of paper on the cardboard. Draw a horizontal line 4 cm long across the paper.
2. Stick a pushpin through the paper and cardboard at each end of the line. Draw a circle around one of the pushpins. Label it *Sun*.
3. Tie the ends of a piece of string together to make a loop about 12 cm long. Place the loop around both pushpins.
4. Hold a pencil point inside of and against the string. Move the pencil around the loop, marking the paper.

▲ **STEP 4** Hold your pencil inside of the string and move it around.

Practicing Your Skills

5. **INFER:** What shape did you draw?
6. **IDENTIFY:** Label the perihelion and the aphelion on your drawing.
7. **IDENTIFY:** Label the distances to aphelion and perihelion.
8. **IDENTIFY:** Label the months Earth reaches aphelion and perihelion.

 *Integrating Physical Science*

THE Big IDEA

What keeps the planets and moons in orbit?

When you throw a ball, you give it a forward motion. At the same time, gravity pulls the ball toward the center of Earth. As a result, the ball has two motions. It has a forward and a downward motion. These two motions cause the ball to follow a curved path.

Suppose that you tied a string around the ball and swung the ball around your head. You would feel an outward pull on the string. If you were to let go of the string, the ball would fly away from you. However, as long as you hold onto the string, the ball will keep moving in a curved path around your head. This curved path is the ball's "orbit."

The motion of the planets around the Sun is similar to the motion of the ball. The planets, which are in motion, keep moving forward in a straight line. However, there is also a force pulling them inward, toward the Sun. This is the force of gravity. Together, gravity and forward motion help determine a planet's orbital motion.

When you hear the word *gravity*, you probably think of the force that pulls objects toward Earth. However, gravity is not limited to our planet. It happens in space, too. Every object in space pulls on every other object. That means that gravity occurs between the Sun and each planet. This attraction toward the Sun keeps the planets from spinning off into space. Gravity also keeps moons orbiting planets.

Look at the illustrations that appear on these two pages. Then, follow the directions in the Science Log to learn more about "the big idea." ✦

Pluto

The smallest planet of the solar system, Pluto is usually the farthest planet from the Sun. Moving at a rate of 4.8 km/s, it completes one revolution of the Sun every 90,700 Earth days.

Uranus

Uranus completes one revolution around the Sun every 30,685 Earth days. It moves at an average speed of 6.4 km/s.

WRITING ACTIVITY

Science Log

Technology has given us new tools for learning about the solar system. Find out some new information about a planet or read about a new tool scientists are using to study the planets. Write a news article that sums up the discovery. Start your search for information at www.conceptsandchallenges.com.

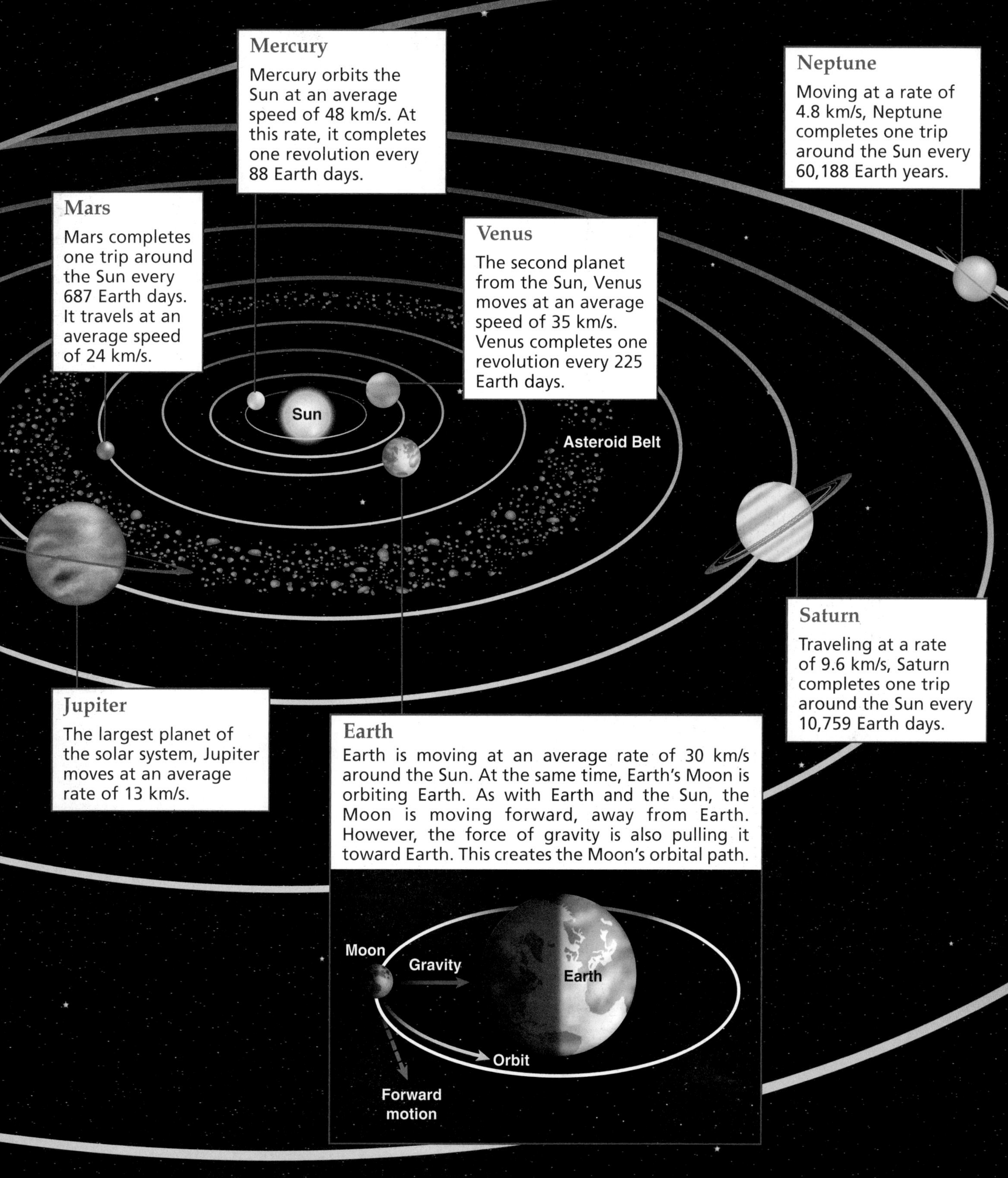

Mercury
Mercury orbits the Sun at an average speed of 48 km/s. At this rate, it completes one revolution every 88 Earth days.
Neptune
Moving at a rate of 4.8 km/s, Neptune completes one trip around the Sun every 60,188 Earth years.
Mars
Mars completes one trip around the Sun every 687 Earth days. It travels at an average speed of 24 km/s.
Venus
The second planet from the Sun, Venus moves at an average speed of 35 km/s. Venus completes one revolution every 225 Earth days.
Sun
Asteroid Belt
Saturn
Traveling at a rate of 9.6 km/s, Saturn completes one trip around the Sun every 10,759 Earth days.
Jupiter
The largest planet of the solar system, Jupiter moves at an average rate of 13 km/s.
Earth
Earth is moving at an average rate of 30 km/s around the Sun. At the same time, Earth's Moon is orbiting Earth. As with Earth and the Sun, the Moon is moving forward, away from Earth. However, the force of gravity is also pulling it toward Earth. This creates the Moon's orbital path.
Moon
Gravity
Earth
Orbit
Forward motion

Figure 3-7 The solar system

3-3 What do we know about Earth's Moon?

Objective

Describe some features of the Moon.

Key Terms

mare (MAH-ray), *pl.* **maria:** broad, flat plain on the Moon's surface

crater (KRAYT-uhr)**:** round hole on the Moon's surface

Moon Landing On July 20, 1969, an American astronaut, Neil Armstrong, Jr., stepped onto the surface of the Moon. He was the first human to do so. He and his crew had traveled 384,000 km from Earth to the Moon. The trip took five days. Since 1969, 17 astronauts have been to the Moon and returned to Earth. *Apollo 17* in 1972 was the last mission to send astronauts to the Moon.

▲ **Figure 3-8** Astronauts walked on the Moon for the first time in 1969.

 **STATE:** When did the first person walk on the Moon?

Moon Facts Earth has only one natural satellite, called the Moon. The Moon is much smaller than Earth. It has a diameter of about 3,400 km. Because the Moon has less mass than Earth does, its gravity is less than Earth's gravity.

The gravity on the Moon's surface is only one-sixth as strong as the gravity on Earth. The Moon's weaker gravity means that you can jump much higher on the Moon than you can on Earth.

The Moon has no liquid water, and it has no atmosphere. Temperatures on the Moon can range from over 100°C to below –200°C. Astronauts need to wear space suits to survive on the Moon.

 **NAME:** What are three important facts about the Moon?

The Moon's Surface Galileo saw and named the three main types of features on the Moon's surface. He named the smooth, dark areas that he saw **maria.** The word *maria* means "seas" in Latin. The first astronauts to step foot on the Moon landed in the Sea of Tranquility. Today, scientists know that the Moon's maria are not seas but broad, flat plains. Galileo also saw light areas on the Moon. These light areas are mountains, or highlands. Some mountains on the Moon are higher than the highest mountains on Earth.

▲ **Figure 3-9** The Moon has no water to drink and no air to breathe. Visitors must bring their own supplies.

The third feature Galileo saw on the Moon's surface were its many **craters.** Large objects striking the Moon's surface caused most of the craters. Erupting volcanoes may have caused the rest.

▲ **Figure 3-10** Craters on the Moon

IDENTIFY: Who named the main features on the Moon's surface?

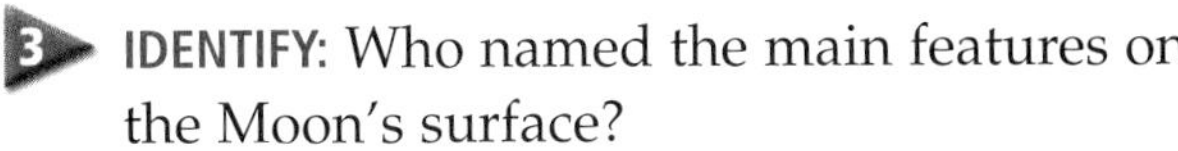

CHECKING CONCEPTS

1. The distance from Earth to the Moon is __________ km.
2. The Moon has a __________ of 3,400 km.
3. The word *maria* means __________ .
4. Three features on the Moon's surface are maria, __________, and highlands.

THINKING CRITICALLY

5. CALCULATE: How much would a 120-lb person weigh on the Moon?
6. CALCULATE: How much would you weigh on the Moon?
7. INFER: Astronauts left their footprints on the Moon's surface. These footprints may remain unchanged for millions of years. Why?
8. ANALYZE: Why did the astronauts who walked on the Moon have to wear boots with lead weights in them?

BUILDING SCIENCE SKILLS

Observing Many features on the Moon are visible to the unaided eye. Others can be seen clearly through binoculars. Observe a full Moon. First use only your eyes. Then use binoculars. Compare how well you are able to see certain features with your unaided eyes and with binoculars. Make a drawing of the features you were able to identify and label those features.

Hands-On Activity

MODELING CRATER FORMATIONS

You will need a shoebox, plaster of Paris, a metric ruler, and three rocks of different sizes.

1. Mix the plaster of Paris according to the directions. Make enough to fill the shoebox one-third of the way up.
2. Pour the plaster of Paris into the shoebox. Just before the plaster hardens, drop one of the rocks into the box from a height of 25 cm. Then, drop the other rocks from the same height.
3. Remove the rocks and drop them from a height of 10 cm.
4. Remove the rocks and let the plaster of Paris harden. Measure the rocks and craters in as many ways as you can.

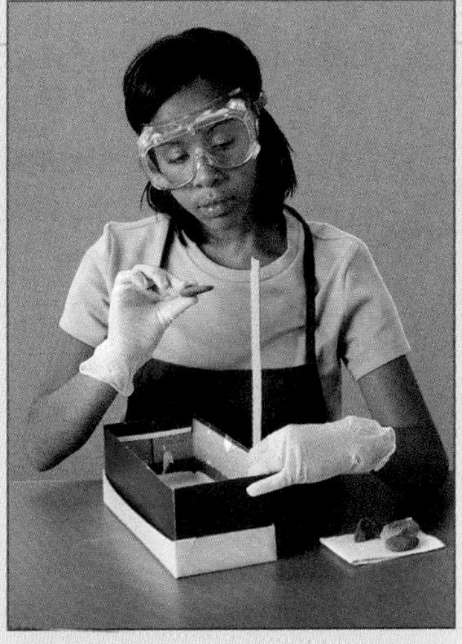

▲ **STEP 3** Drop the rocks a second time from a lower height.

Practicing Your Skills

5. EXPLAIN: What do the rocks represent?
6. COMPARE: Which rock made the deepest crater? Which rock made the widest crater?
7. APPLY: How do you think craters were formed on the Moon?

3-4 What are the other moons in the solar system?

Objective

Compare the moons of the different planets in the solar system.

Key Term

satellite (SAT-uhl-eyet)**:** natural or artificial object orbiting another body in space

Natural Satellites A **satellite** is any natural or artificial object that orbits another object in space. People have observed the only natural satellite of Earth, the Moon, since ancient times.

For thousands of years, Earth was believed to be the only planet in the solar system to have a moon. Then, in 1610, Galileo discovered four of the moons of Jupiter. Today, astronomers know that seven of the planets (Earth, Mars, Jupiter, Saturn, Uranus, Neptune, and Pluto) have moons.

Until the late 1970s, almost all of the known moons had been discovered using Earth-based telescopes. Then, two space probes, called *Voyager 1* and *Voyager 2*, traveled beyond the Asteroid Belt to the outer planets. They sent back to Earth the first detailed, close-up photographs of the many moons that orbited Jupiter, Saturn, Uranus, and Neptune. Together, *Voyagers 1* and *2* discovered at least 35 new moons.

1 **DESCRIBE:** What planets have natural satellites?

Moons of the Inner Planets Mercury and Venus are the only planets in the solar system without at least one moon. Earth, like Pluto, has only one moon.

Mars has two moons, named Deimos and Phobos. These were discovered in 1877. They are made of dark, carbon-rich rock. Because of their makeup, both reflect very little light from their surface. Both moons are small and lumpy. Deimos has a peanut shape. Both moons also have many craters. One crater on Phobos is 5 km across.

Both moons orbit close to Mars. Phobos takes less than a Martian day to go once around the planet. Deimos takes a little more than a day.

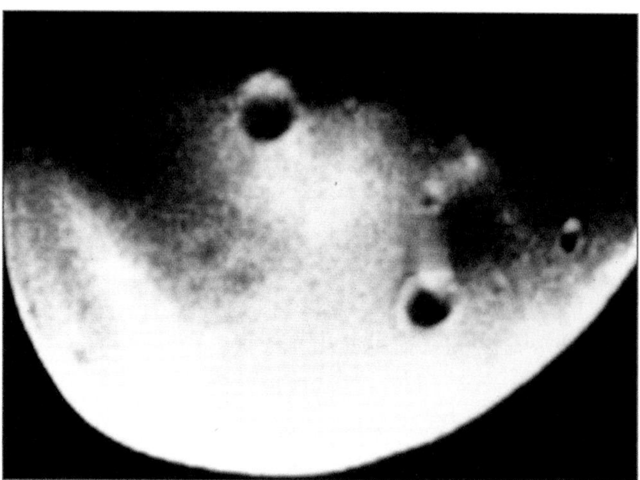

▲ **Figure 3-11** Mars' moon Deimos is shaped like a peanut.

2 **IDENTIFY:** Which of the inner planets have one or more moons?

Moons of the Outer Planets Jupiter has at least 28 known moons. Jupiter and its moons have been described as a mini-solar system.

Jupiter's moons are very varied. Some are rocky. Others are icy. The four moons first viewed by Galileo are often referred to as the Galilean moons. They are the largest of Jupiter's moons.

The Galilean moons travel around Jupiter in a nearly circular orbit, almost exactly around the planet's equator. It is possible to track the movements and positions of these moons using a good pair of binoculars.

The Galilean moons played an important role in the history of astronomy. When their orbits were first observed, it was proven that not everything in space revolved around Earth.

In 1995, a space probe, appropriately named *Galileo*, arrived at Jupiter to study the Galilean moons. The largest Galilean moon is Ganymede, followed by Callisto, Io, and Europa. Ganymede is the largest moon in the solar system, with a diameter of 5,268 km. Callisto has a dark, icy surface with many white craters. Impacts from asteroids and other bodies probably exposed clean ice beneath the dirtier top layer. Io has active volcanoes on it. Europa is covered with ice that may have liquid water below the surface.

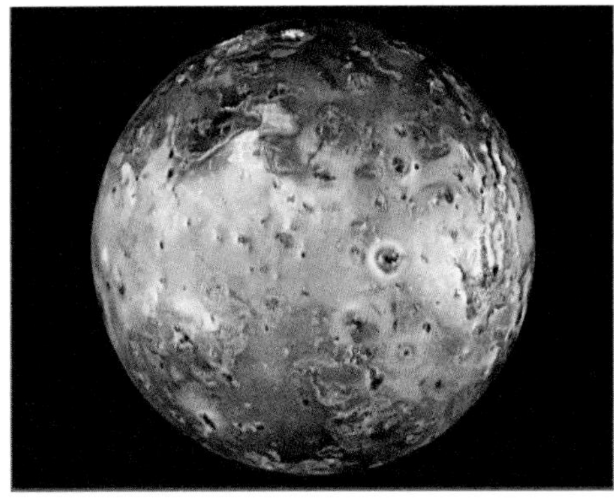

◀ **Figure 3-12** Io is a large, volcanically active moon of Jupiter.

Saturn has 30 known moons. Five of these moons are very large. Saturn's largest moon is Titan. Titan is the second largest moon in the solar system.

Huygens is a probe being sent to Titan by the European Space Agency. It will arrive there in 2004, as part of the *Cassini* mission to Saturn. It will parachute toward the surface and report on conditions beneath the moon's orange clouds.

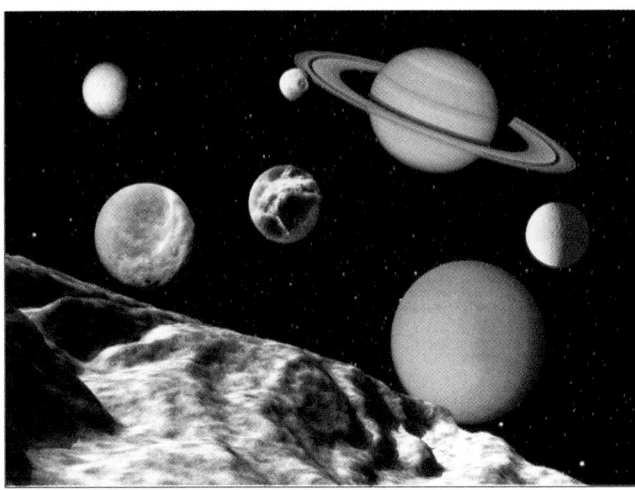

▲ **Figure 3-13** This is an artist's concept of Saturn and six of its moons as seen from a seventh moon.

Uranus has 21 known moons. Titania is the largest, with Oberon second. The moons of Uranus are very varied. Some have deep canyons and long scars on their surface. Others have large, smooth areas between areas riddled with craters. Miranda may have more types of landforms than any other body in the solar system. Ten of Uranus's moons were discovered by *Voyager 2* in 1986.

Neptune has eight known moons. Only two are visible from Earth. These are Triton and Nereid. Triton, the larger of the two, orbits in the opposite direction from the rest of Neptune's moons. It has the coldest surface in the solar system, at –235°C. Scientists think Triton is covered with frozen nitrogen and methane.

Like Earth, Pluto has only one moon. Pluto's moon is called Charon. It was discovered in 1978. Its surface is probably covered with water ice and impact craters. One theory suggests that Charon is a piece of ice that was knocked off Pluto when another object collided with it. No probes have yet been sent to Pluto or Charon.

 **IDENTIFY:** Which outer planet has the most moons?

✓ CHECKING CONCEPTS

Match each planet with its correct moon.

1. Jupiter	**a.** Charon
2. Mars	**b.** Triton
3. Uranus	**c.** Io
4. Pluto	**d.** Titania
5. Neptune	**e.** Titan
6. Saturn	**f.** Phobos

THINKING CRITICALLY

7. SEQUENCE: List the planets in order from the one with the most moons to the ones with the fewest. Include planets that have no moons.

8. INFER: Why are the four largest moons of Jupiter called the Galilean moons?

BUILDING SCIENCE SKILLS

Researching The names given to moons are chosen by the International Astronomical Union. Newly discovered moons are numbered first, with the year they are discovered, then named later. The names chosen come from many different sources. For example, recently discovered moons of Uranus were named after characters in the plays of Shakespeare. Choose the moons of one planet. Find the source of each moon's name. Write a report of your findings.

LAB ACTIVITY
Looking Back in Time

Materials
Safety goggles
2 Plastic petri dishes
Dry sandbox sand
Dropper bottle
Water
Pictures of craters on the Moon

BACKGROUND

The solar system has more than 90 moons. Meteorite impacts have altered the terrain of most of these moons by creating craters. Many moons, such as Earth's Moon and Jupiter's Callisto, are heavily pitted with meteor craters. If a plain on the surface of a moon has craters, it is likely that the plain formed first and was later altered by impacts. The number of impacts helps scientists estimate the age of the plain. If the plain has very few or no craters, it probably formed very recently. If the plain is heavily cratered, the plain is probably ancient. Scientists can often determine the sequence of when the impacts occurred that created the craters. They do this by looking for overlapping craters.

▲ **STEP 1** Fill the petri dish with sand and the dropper bottle with water.

PURPOSE

In this activity, you will create a moon with many craters on its surface and infer its history.

PROCEDURE 

1. Put on your safety goggles. Fill one petri dish almost to the top with sand. Fill the dropper bottle with water.

2. Copy the chart in Figure 3-14. Hold the dropper bottle about 25 cm above the dish and squeeze out a drop of water. Observe what happens when the water strikes the surface of the sand. Record your observations in your chart.

3. For the next minute, squeeze a drop from the bottle every second. Move around the dish as you release the drops every second. Have some drops fall by themselves. Have other drops fall on top of each other or close together. Observe the raindrop pattern you produced on the sand. Record your observations.

4. Trade your dish for a dish made by another group. Try to determine the sequence in which the craters were made. Record your observations.

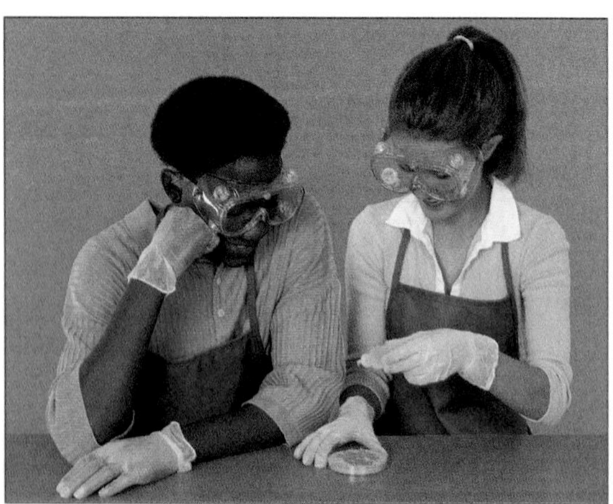

▲ **STEP 3** Move your dish around as you squeeze out drops of water from the bottle.

5. In your chart draw a picture of the dish with circles to represent the craters. Look at the overlapping craters. Mark older craters with the number 1. Mark newer craters with the numbers 2, 3, and so on.

6. Fill a second petri dish with sand. Use your thumb to make a large crater in the center.

7. Squeeze drops from the bottle in and around the big crater. Observe and record what happens.

8. Look at pictures of the craters on the Moon. Can you tell which craters are younger and which are older? Note down your comments below the chart.

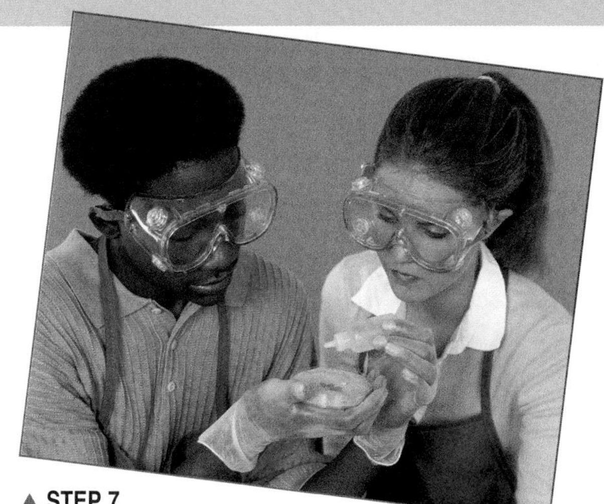

▲ **STEP 7**
Squeeze drops of water around the large crater you made with your thumb.

Step	What You Observe	Written Description
1		
2		
3		

▲ **Figure 3-14** Use a copy of this chart to write down your observations and draw your pictures.

CONCLUSIONS

1. **OBSERVE:** What happened when the first drop of water hit the sand?

2. **ANALYZE:** How can you tell which crater is newer when two craters overlap?

3. **OBSERVE:** What happened to the large crater you created with your thumb when it was hit with more drops of water?

4. **ANALYZE:** What is the difference between an old crater and a young one?

5. **INFER:** How do craters tell scientists if the surface of a moon is very young or very old?

3-5 What do we know about Mercury, Venus, and Earth?

Objective

Identify the basic features of the three innermost planets.

Mercury Mercury is the planet closest to the Sun. Of all the planets, Mercury travels the fastest around the Sun. However, it rotates slowly on its axis. This dry, rocky planet has no atmosphere. Temperatures on Mercury range from 430°C during daylight hours to –170°C during Mercury's night. Because Mercury is so close to the Sun, astronomers cannot see it easily from Earth. However, astronomers learned a lot when, in 1974, the space probe *Mariner 10* visited Mercury and sent back photographs. In the 1990s, radar was used to study Mercury's surface. We now know that the surface of Mercury is covered with craters.

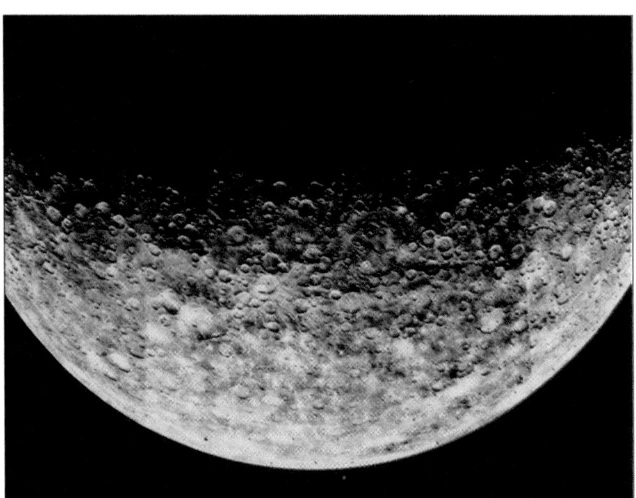

▲ **Figure 3-15** Mercury is very similar to Earth's Moon. It has no atmosphere, and its surface is covered with impact craters.

1 **DESCRIBE:** What is Mercury like?

Venus The planet Venus is similar to Earth in size, mass, and density. However, Venus is a very hostile world. Its average temperature is higher than the average temperature of any other known planet. The air pressure on Venus is 90 times more crushing than that of Earth's air at sea level.

Astronomers think these conditions are related to Venus's carbon dioxide atmosphere and thick clouds of sulfuric acid. From Earth, we can only see Venus's cloudtops.

▲ **Figure 3-16** The pressure on the surface of Venus, seen here, is equal to that of the pressure on Earth deep down in the ocean.

Venus has retrograde rotation. This means that it spins slowly in the opposite direction from most of the other planets.

Many space probes have orbited Venus or landed on it. These probes have revealed smooth plains, mountains, and valleys. Like the Moon, Venus goes through phases. We see only varying amounts of its sunlit side.

2 **INFER:** Why was Venus once called Earth's twin?

Earth The third planet from the Sun and the fifth largest in the solar system is Earth. Earth is the only planet known to have oceans of liquid water. It is also the only planet known to support life. Life occurs on Earth because of moderate temperatures, an atmosphere containing oxygen, and liquid water.

Earth has a magnetic field around it because of the iron in its core. Electrically charged particles from the Sun, mostly electrons and protons, bounce around in the atmosphere above Earth. They are trapped in Earth's magnetic field.

Occasionally, some of these particles escape from the magnetic field and rain down on Earth. They strike atoms and molecules that are in the upper atmosphere and cause them to glow. In the Northern Hemisphere, this glow is known as the aurora borealis, or the northern lights. In the Southern Hemisphere, it is the aurora australis, or southern lights.

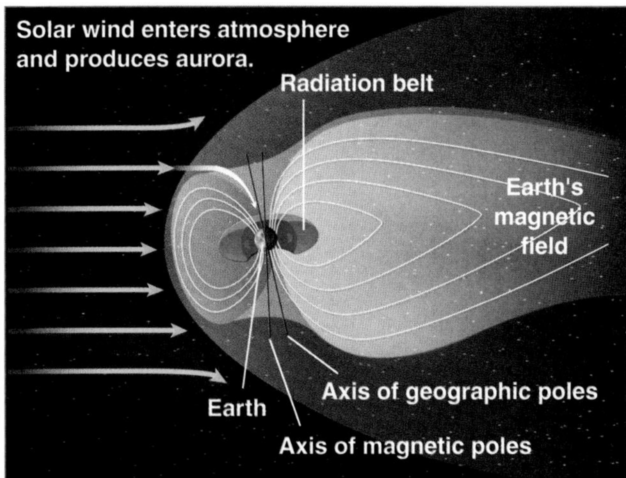

▲ **Figure 3-17** Charged particles from the Sun are trapped in Earth's magnetic field.

 LIST: What conditions make life on Earth possible?

CHECKING CONCEPTS

1. What are the three innermost planets?
2. What does the surface of Mercury look like?
3. What gas in the atmosphere makes the surface of Venus so hot?
4. Which inner planet has liquid water?

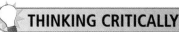

THINKING CRITICALLY

5. COMPARE: How is the surface of Mercury similar to the surface of Earth's Moon?
6. ANALYZE: Venus has rocks similar to basalt. On Earth, these rocks are usually found near volcanoes. What does this suggest?

Web InfoSearch

More About Venus Sunlight striking the surface of a planet warms the ground. This releases heat radiation. Like glass in a greenhouse, the atmosphere traps some of the heat. In some places, such as on Venus, the heat keeps building up. This is called a runaway greenhouse.

SEARCH: Use the Internet to find out what the temperature is on Venus and why. Could Earth someday become like Venus? How could it? Start your search at www.conceptsandchallenges.com. Use the key search words **runaway greenhouse effect, Venus, planet profile,** and **carbon dioxide.**

Integrating Life Science

TOPICS: origin of life, molecular biology

HOW LIFE ON EARTH BEGAN

Nobody knows for sure how life on Earth began. Scientists think they know when it happened—about 3.5 billion years ago.

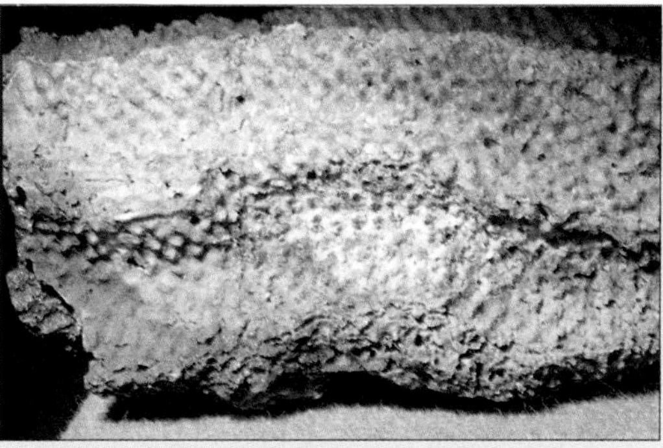

▲ **Figure 3-18** Stromatolites (above) are among the oldest fossils. They were formed in sedimentary rock by blue-green algae.

Many scientists think that the first living things were certain molecules, or strings of atoms. These molecules floated in water, alongside billions of unattached atoms. As these molecules bumped into other molecules, they traded atoms. Eventually, a chain of atoms came together that could actually make copies of itself using the free-floating atoms.

How can a chain of atoms make copies of itself? It happens all the time, right inside your body. It is how your body grows. Molecules inside your body grab onto atoms to create more molecules. When molecules first did this billions of years ago, they began to show some of the characteristics of living things.

Over time, life forms that were especially good at making copies of themselves outnumbered other life forms. These life forms were our very distant ancestors.

Thinking Critically What parts of your body can make copies of themselves?

3-6 What do we know about Mars?

Seeing Mars in 3-D

HANDS-ON ACTIVITY

1. Make a viewer by cutting out two eyeholes from a rectangle of stiff paper. The holes should match your eye positions.
2. Tape a piece of red filter over one hole. Tape a piece of blue filter over the other hole.
3. Hold the viewer in front of your eyes so that your right eye looks through the blue filter and your left eye looks through the red filter. Examine pictures of Mars's surface taken by the *Pathfinder* mission supplied by your teacher.

THINK ABOUT IT: Why might scientists find 3-D pictures useful for studying Mars?

Objective

Describe features on the planet Mars.

Key Term

rift: valley caused by a crack in the crust of a planet

The Red Planet Mars is the fourth planet from the Sun. Its orbit period is 687 days. Its rate of rotation is 24 hours and 37 minutes. Therefore, the lengths of a day on Mars and on Earth are almost the same. Mars has seasons similar to Earth's seasons because of the similar tilt of its axis. However, Mars is half the diameter of Earth. Its surface is reddish in color. Mars has volcanoes, valleys, polar ice caps, craters, and river channels. It has a thin carbon dioxide atmosphere.

The air pressure on Mars is about the same as the air pressure on Earth at an altitude of 35 km. Except for some icy spots at the poles, no water is visible on the Martian surface. Mars is a dry world. It can be colder than Antarctica in winter and as warm as a spring day in the American Midwest.

1 **CONTRAST:** How do Mars and Earth differ?

The Martian Surface Many space probes, including two *Viking* landers, have studied Mars. Photographs show that the surface has many craters and is covered with loose rocks. Winds of up to 100 km/h raise giant dust storms that cover the planet. Scientists think that Mars probably once had rivers or lakes on its surface.

2 **IDENTIFY:** What spacecraft visited Mars?

▲ **Figure 3-19** The surface of Mars was photographed by the *Viking* lander. It showed a landscape with rocks scattered all around.

Giant Volcanoes and Canyons The largest known volcano in the solar system is called Olympus Mons. Olympus Mons is found on Mars. It is 27 km high. Had Olympus Mons formed on Earth, it would not have been nearly as high. This is because Earth's gravity is stronger. At the summit of the volcano is a large crater. Mars has many other large volcanoes. Mars also has a large **rift,** or crack, in its crust that forms a complex canyon system. The canyon, called Vallis Marineris, stretches 4,000 km. On Earth, this canyon would reach across the United States.

3 EXPLAIN: Why are volcanoes on Mars much larger than volcanoes on Earth?

Water on Mars Scientists have used robot spacecraft to search for water on Mars. Finding water could mean that Mars has life. There is some water ice at the Martian south pole. There are also many dry channels on Mars that look like they were carved by running water. Where is the water today? It may be frozen beneath the surface or have boiled away in the thin atmosphere.

4 INFER: Where might water be on Mars?

✓ CHECKING CONCEPTS

1. What causes the huge dust storms on Mars?
2. How are Mars and Earth similar?
3. How do the Vallis Marineris on Mars and the Grand Canyon on Earth compare in size?
4. Why do we think water might exist on Mars?

THINKING CRITICALLY

5. INFER: If Mars once had water, what might have happened to it?
6. APPLY: Could humans live on Mars? How?

Web InfoSearch

Martian Canals In 1877, an Italian astronomer said that he had seen "channels" on Mars. This word became "canals" when the report was translated into English. Some people, including the astronomer Percival Lowell, assumed that the canals must have been built by Martians.

SEARCH: Use the Internet to find out more about the "canals" on Mars. Do they exist? Start your search for information at www.conceptsandchallenges.com. Use the key search words **Martian canals, Mars canals Lowell,** and **Percival Lowell.**

Integrating Life Science

TOPICS: bacteria, fossils

FOSSILS FROM MARS?

In 1984, a meteorite was found in Antarctica that scientists think came from Mars. Like other planets, Mars has been struck by asteroids often in its past. Mars was struck by one such asteroid about 16 million years ago. Pieces of the surface broke off and went flying into space. Eventually, a meteorite from this asteroid strike fell to Earth.

▲ **Figure 3-20** Possible bacteria fossils (right) were found on an Antarctic ice sheet similar to the one shown above.

Some scientists studying the rock found unusual, rodlike structures in it. They suggested that these tiny structures might be bacteria fossils. If the rodlike structures are from Mars, it could mean that life existed on Mars many years ago. However, these structures might have become part of the meteorite as it fell through the atmosphere to Earth.

Thinking Critically What evidence of possible life was in the meteorite?

3-7 What are asteroids and meteoroids?

Objective

Compare asteroids, meteoroids, meteors, and meteorites.

Key Terms

asteroid (AS-tuhr-oid)**:** large chunk of rock or metal that orbits the Sun

meteoroid (MEET-ee-uhr-oid)**:** small piece of rock or metal that travels through space

meteor (MEET-ee-uhr)**:** rock or metal that enters Earth's atmosphere

meteorite (MEET-ee-uhr-yt)**:** piece of rock or metal that falls on a planet or moon's surface

Asteroids There is a large gap in the solar system between the orbits of Mars and Jupiter. For many years, astronomers thought the gap must contain a planet. They searched the gap but did not find the missing planet. Then, in 1801, an Italian astronomer spotted a tiny dot of light that orbited the Sun, like the planets. The astronomer had discovered the first asteroid. Ceres, as it was named, is 940 km across.

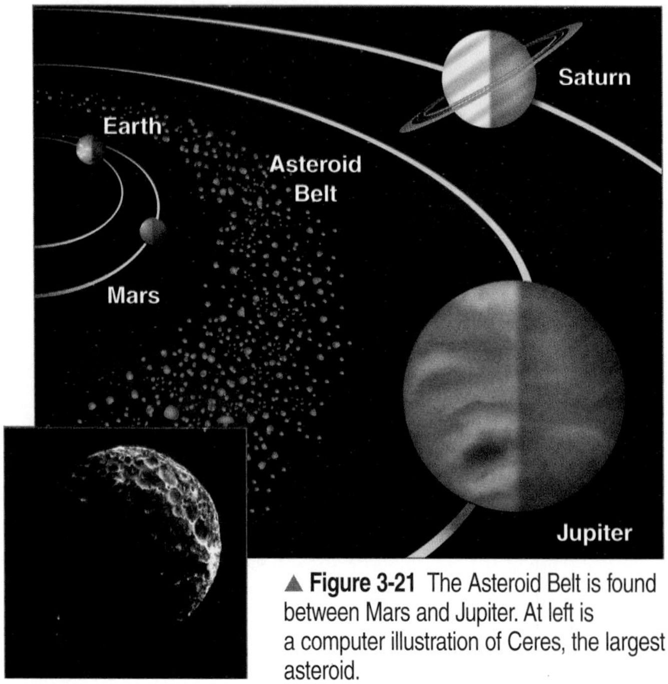

▲ **Figure 3-21** The Asteroid Belt is found between Mars and Jupiter. At left is a computer illustration of Ceres, the largest asteroid.

Ceres and other **asteroids** are leftover debris from the formation of the solar system. They are made up of pieces of rock or metal or a combination of rock and metal. Today, thousands of asteroids are known. Most orbit the Sun in the so-called Asteroid Belt between Mars and Jupiter.

1 **LOCATE:** Where is the Asteroid Belt?

Meteoroids Asteroids can collide, breaking off small pieces from both asteroids. These pieces, called **meteoroids,** scatter around the solar system. Most pieces are smaller than a sand grain. If a meteoroid enters a planet's atmosphere, friction will cause all or some of the meteoroid to burn. A bright streak will then be seen in the sky. Meteoroids that produce that bright streak are called **meteors.** Large pieces of meteoroids that reach a planet's surface are called **meteorites.** A crater can result from the impact.

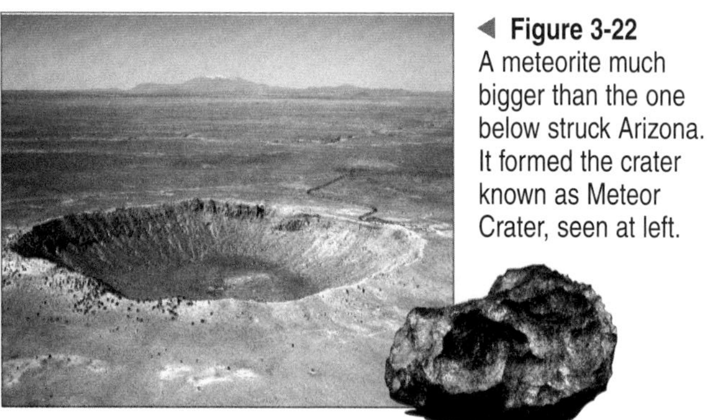

◀ **Figure 3-22** A meteorite much bigger than the one below struck Arizona. It formed the crater known as Meteor Crater, seen at left.

2 **NAME:** What is a meteoroid that enters Earth's atmosphere called?

Meteor Showers Sometimes many meteor flashes will be seen in a night. These displays are called meteor showers. The meteoroids that fall in meteor showers are tiny dust-sized particles from comets. Comets travel in long orbits that regularly take them close to the Sun. As a comet approaches the Sun, some of the ice in it melts. This releases trapped dust particles. When Earth passes through the dust left by a passing comet, the dust burns up in the atmosphere. A meteor shower occurs.

3 **EXPLAIN:** How are meteor showers produced?

Meteorites on Earth Over 30,000 meteorites have been found on Earth's surface. However, most meteorites fall into the sea. Some meteorites have crashed through the roofs of houses and slammed into cars. Fortunately, these events are very rare.

Once in a while, a large meteorite strikes Earth's surface. One such impact took place in Arizona 50,000 years ago. A 1-km-wide crater, shown in Figure 3-22, was produced when the meteorite struck.

The best place to look for meteorites today is in Antarctica. When meteorites fall on ice, they are easy to see. Some four-billion-year-old meteorites have been found there.

4 IDENTIFY: Where are meteorites easy to spot?

CHECKING CONCEPTS

1. Where are meteoroids found?
2. What is a meteoroid?
3. How big are the particles in a meteor shower?
4. Where do most meteorites land on Earth?
5. What particles are burned up in meteor showers?

THINKING CRITICALLY

6. CONTRAST: How are meteoroids, meteorites, and meteors different?
7. INFER: How might the surface of a meteorite look after going through Earth's atmosphere?

Web InfoSearch

How the Moon Formed One thing scientists wanted to learn from the *Apollo* program was how the Moon was created. Moon rocks provided scientists with important clues. Today, some scientists believe that the early Earth was struck by a very large object, very likely an asteroid. Some of the debris from the collision flew off into space. Eventually, this debris came together to become the Moon.

SEARCH: Use the Internet to find out what evidence led scientists to this theory. Go to www.conceptsandchallenges.com to begin your search. Some key search words are **Moon rocks** and **asteroids.**

Real-Life Science

NEAR-EARTH OBJECTS

Not all asteroids are in the Asteroid Belt. Thousands cross or come close to Earth's orbit every year. These are named near-Earth objects (NEOs). About 170 NEOs are considered a possible danger to Earth. These objects are all being monitored by several groups.

About 65 million years ago, an asteroid about 10 km wide struck Earth. The huge crater it is believed to have formed, called Chicxulub, is found in the Gulf of Mexico and on Mexico's Yucatán peninsula. This is the impact that many scientists now think might have ended the rule of the dinosaurs. However, there is no known NEO that is currently a serious threat to Earth.

▲ **Figure 3-23** Artist's concept of an asteroid hitting Earth

What if such an object should appear? Can anything be done to stop a catastrophe? Some people have suggested blowing the object up with a nuclear bomb. However, this might create many small pieces that could strike with the same deadly force. It would be better to nudge the asteroid in another direction. However, no one knows exactly how to do this yet.

Thinking Critically How might you force an asteroid to change direction?

3-8 What do we know about Jupiter and Saturn?

Objective

Identify some features of Jupiter and Saturn.

A Gas Giant Jupiter is the largest planet in the solar system. It is the fifth planet out from the Sun. Because of its size, Jupiter can be seen without a telescope. Its mass is twice that of all the other planets combined. Jupiter has a diameter of 143,000 km. Earth's diameter is less than 13,000 km.

Jupiter is a gas giant with a rocky core. It is made up mostly of the light gases hydrogen and helium. Its density is only one-fourth that of Earth's. Colorful bands of clouds cover the entire planet.

All of the gas giants, including Jupiter, have rings around them. These rings are made up of small particles of dust and ice. Each particle is a tiny satellite. The rings circle the planet around the equator. A thin, faint ring around Jupiter was discovered by *Voyager 1* in 1979.

▲ **Figure 3-24** The planet Jupiter (upper right) is big enough to hold more than 1,300 Earths. The other objects in the picture are four of Jupiter's moons.

1 **NAME:** What two gases make up most of Jupiter?

The Great Red Spot The largest and best-known feature of Jupiter is its Great Red Spot. Astronomers believe this is a huge storm, similar to a cyclone. It was probably created by steam and ammonia rising from the atmosphere below Jupiter's cloudtops.

In 1994, Jupiter was hit by comet Shoemaker-Levy 9. The comet was pulled apart by Jupiter's gravity. Twenty-one pieces crashed into the thick atmosphere of Jupiter. Astronomers studied the impacts to learn more about Jupiter's atmosphere.

▲ **Figure 3-25** The Great Red Spot is a huge storm on Jupiter.

2 **DESCRIBE:** What is the Great Red Spot?

The Ringed Planet The second largest planet in the solar system and the sixth out from the Sun is Saturn. The diameter of Saturn is about 121,000 km.

Like Jupiter, Saturn is a gas giant made up mostly of hydrogen and helium. Saturn has colorful bands of clouds like Jupiter. However, Saturn is less dense than Jupiter is. It is even less dense than water.

Saturn's rings are its most distinctive feature. Galileo thought they were ears or handles when he saw them through his telescope. There are three main rings. Many thousands of smaller rings orbit inside the main rings. There is a large gap between two rings called the Cassini division. The *Cassini* probe will study Saturn's rings in the year 2004.

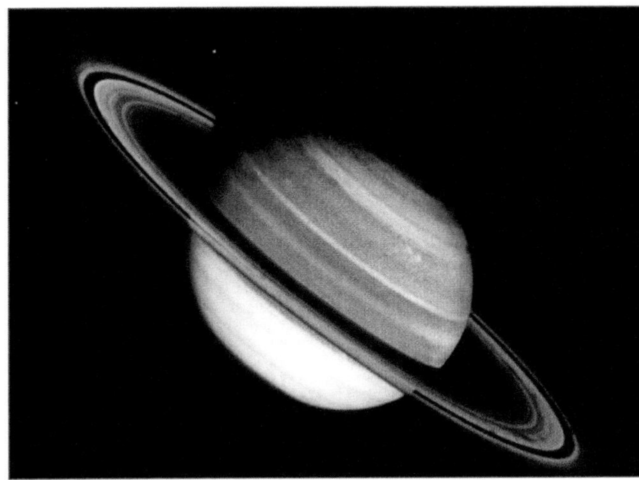

▲ **Figure 3-26** The orange bands in this picture are really clouds racing from east to west around Saturn.

 IDENTIFY: What is Saturn mostly made up of?

✓ CHECKING CONCEPTS

1. The largest planet in our solar system is ___________.
2. The second largest planet in our solar system is ___________.
3. Jupiter's mass is more than ___________ the mass of the other planets put together.
4. Jupiter is made up mostly of ___________ and helium.
5. The Great Red Spot is caused by steam and ___________ rising into Jupiter's atmosphere.

THINKING CRITICALLY

6. COMPARE: What are two ways in which Jupiter and Saturn are alike?
7. INFER: What make Jupiter and Saturn gas giants?

BUILDING SCIENCE SKILLS

Researching and Modeling Two small moons of Saturn, Pandora and Prometheus, orbit on either side of what is called the F ring. These moons are known as shepherds. *Pioneer 11* first saw them in 1979. Find out what these moons do and how they do it. Report your findings. Then, draw a sketch of Saturn's ring system and label the shepherd moons and the F ring.

Science and Technology

PROBING THE SECRETS OF JUPITER

The *Voyagers* gave us incredible images of Jupiter and its moons as they flew by. Then, in December 1995, the space probe *Galileo* went into orbit around Jupiter. This began a lengthy and still ongoing scientific exploration of Jupiter and its moons.

▲ **Figure 3-27** The *Galileo* space probe

Galileo's first task involved separating a smaller probe and releasing it. This probe, slowed by a parachute, fell through Jupiter's atmosphere. Instruments on the probe measured the amounts of gases. Scientists found much less helium and water vapor than they had expected. They were also surprised to learn that the winds grew stronger instead of weaker as the probe descended.

Galileo also provided new information about Jupiter's largest moons. For example, it appears that sections of ice covering Europa are moving away from each other. This movement might be caused by water beneath the ice. Another surprising discovery was a magnetic field around Ganymede.

Thinking Critically Why might finding water on Europa be exciting to scientists?

3-9 What do we know about Uranus, Neptune, and Pluto?

Objective

Identify some features of Uranus, Neptune, and Pluto.

Uranus The seventh planet from the Sun and the third largest planet in the solar system is Uranus. The diameter of Uranus is about 51,000 km.

In 1781, Uranus became the first planet to be discovered by using a telescope. Very little was known about Uranus until 1986, when the *Voyager 2* space probe flew past it. *Voyager 2* sent back many images and discovered ten new moons.

Uranus is made mostly of hydrogen and helium. The blue-green color of the clouds shows that the atmosphere also contains methane.

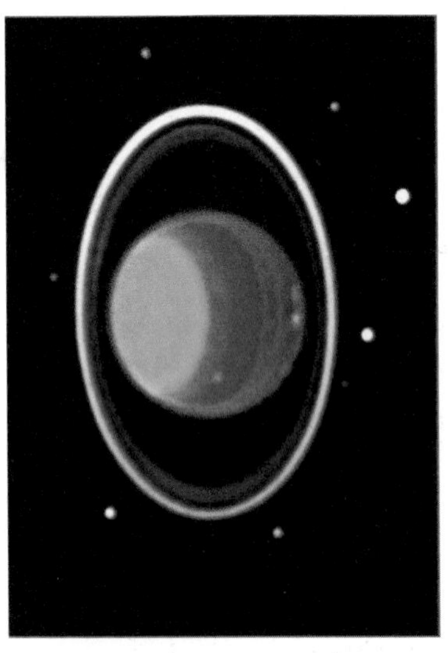

◄ **Figure 3-28** Uranus may have collided with another large body early in its history and been knocked over. This image was taken by an infrared camera. The planet's real color is blue-green, and its ring is very thin.

Oddly, the axis of Uranus is horizontal. The planet appears to be lying on its side. Its poles point toward the Sun. This unusual tilt may have been caused by a collision with another planet-size body early in its history.

Uranus spins fast and has a very strong magnetic field. It also has a faint ring.

1 LIST: What are three gases found in the atmosphere of Uranus?

Neptune The eighth planet from the Sun is Neptune. Neptune is similar to Uranus in size and mass. Its diameter is about 49,500 km, and it also has a faint ring around its equator. Neptune is so far from the Sun that it takes 165 Earth years to revolve once around it.

Neptune was discovered in 1845. It was the last planet to be visited by *Voyager 2*. Photographs taken by *Voyager 2* show that Neptune has a Great Dark Spot, similar to Jupiter's Great Red Spot. Neptune is also a gas giant. Its upper atmosphere is made mostly of clouds of frozen methane, which gives the planet its blue-green color. The lower atmosphere contains mostly hydrogen and helium. Neptune is the windiest planet. Winds can blow east to west at over 1,500 km/h.

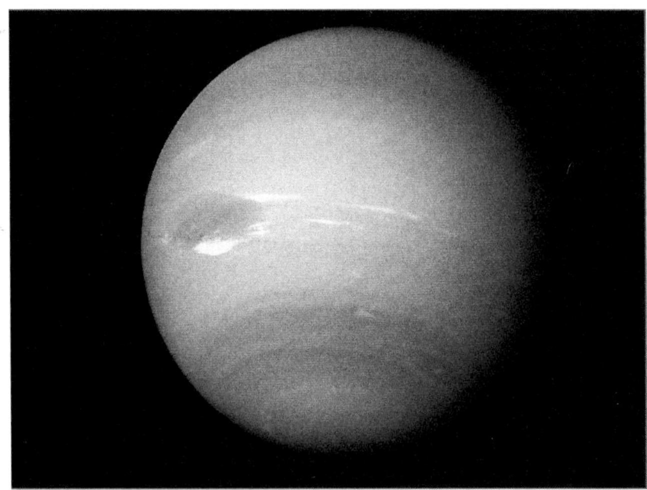

▲ **Figure 3-29** Through a telescope, Neptune is blue-green and shows few features.

2 IDENTIFY: When was Neptune discovered?

Pluto Pluto is the smallest planet in the solar system. It has a diameter of only about 2,300 km. Pluto was discovered by the American astronomer Clyde Tombaugh in 1930.

▲ **Figure 3-30** From Pluto's orbit, the Sun, seen on the left in this artist's conception, looks very small.

Pluto is usually the farthest planet from the Sun. However, its unusual orbit sometimes brings it inside the orbit of Neptune.

Pluto is an icy planet with a rocky core. It has methane ice on its surface. Pluto has not yet been visited by a space probe.

 **EXPLAIN:** Why is Pluto not always the farthest planet from the Sun?

The Kuiper Belt Between Neptune and the outer regions of the solar system is the Kuiper Belt. This belt was discovered in 1992. It was named after the Dutch astronomer who suggested that it might exist. The Kuiper Belt contains about 70,000 rocks or ice fragments, possibly from a planet that failed to form. About 100 of these rocks or bits of ice have been discovered. Many scientists think that Pluto and its moon Charon are Kuiper Belt objects.

 **EXPLAIN:** What kinds of objects are in the Kuiper Belt?

CHECKING CONCEPTS

1. What is the most unusual feature of Uranus?
2. How is Neptune similar to Uranus?
3. How long does Neptune take to complete one orbit around the Sun?
4. Which was the last planet *Voyager 2* visited?

THINKING CRITICALLY

5. **HYPOTHESIZE:** Pluto may have once been a moon of Neptune. What might have caused Pluto to go into its own orbit?

Web InfoSearch

Neptune's Wobble A century ago, astronomers thought they observed a strange wobble in Neptune's orbit. Many thought the wobble was caused by a distant, unseen planet. Today, we know that the wobble does not exist at all.

SEARCH: Use the Internet to find out more about this. How did the search for another gas giant lead to the discovery of Pluto? Start your search at www.conceptsandchallenges.com. Some key search words are **Clyde Tombaugh, discovery of Pluto,** and **Pluto Charon.**

People in Science

JET PROPULSION LAB WORKER

The Jet Propulsion Laboratory (JPL) in Pasadena is run by the California Institute of Technology for NASA. Since 1960, it has been involved in exploring the solar system using space probes. Today, it serves as command center for missions such as *Voyager, Magellan,* and *Galileo.*

JPL employs many scientists, engineers, and technicians. They are involved in the launching and tracking of satellites as well as space probes. The satellites study the oceans, the ozone, and other physical features of Earth. Scientists at JPL constantly analyze the data sent back to Earth. They must also check that the instruments are working and try to fix them remotely if they are not. JPL instruments also scan the skies for near-Earth objects that might collide with Earth. Most JPL scientists have a strong background in science and mathematics.

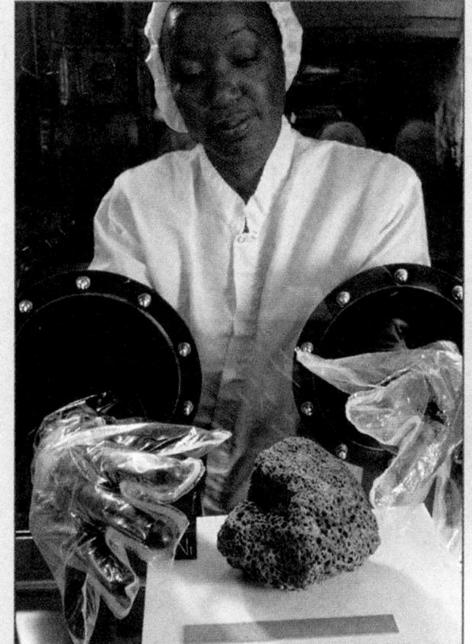

▲ **Figure 3-31** A Jet Propulsion Lab scientist is examining a volcanic Moon rock.

Thinking Critically What are some activities engineers at JPL might take part in?

3-10 What is a comet?

Making a Scale Model of a Comet

HANDS-ON ACTIVITY

1. Using a pen, put a dot in the center of a 5-inch paper plate. This dot represents a comet's nucleus. Glue a cotton ball to the plate to cover the dot. The cotton ball represents the comet's coma.
2. Attach five streamers to the back of the plate with tape. The streamers represent the comet's tail. Make sure all the streamers face in the same direction.
3. Compare your comet with a whole peppercorn or a small pea, which can represent Earth.
4. Compare your comet with a 10-inch paper plate, which can represent the Sun.

THINK ABOUT IT: How does your comet model compare to the size of Earth? How does it compare to the size of the Sun?

Objectives

Define comet and identify the features of a comet.

Key Terms

comet: lump of ice, frozen gas, and dust that orbits the Sun

nucleus: head or solid part of a comet

coma: gas cloud that surrounds the nucleus of a comet

tail: long, ribbonlike trail of comet dust and gas

Comet Parts Like planets and asteroids, comets are also members of the solar system. A **comet** is a lump of ice, frozen gas, and dust that orbits the Sun. Comets orbit the Sun in very long ellipses that often take them beyond the orbit of Pluto.

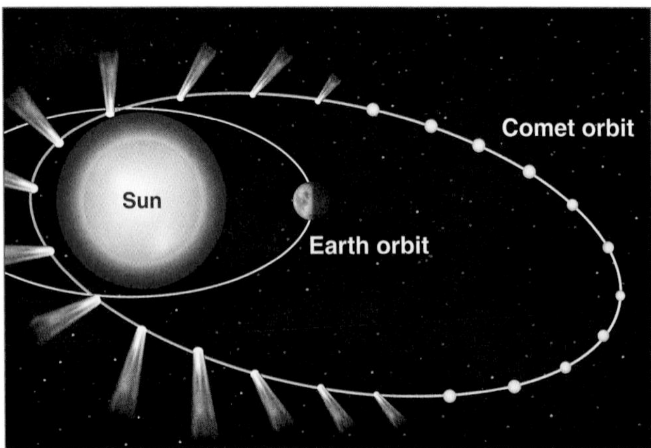

▲ **Figure 3-32** A comet's orbit typically takes it near the Sun and then back to the outer reaches of the solar system.

A comet has three parts. The core, or **nucleus,** is basically a dirty ice ball. It is made of water ice, frozen gas, and dust. The cloud of gas that surrounds the nucleus is called the **coma.** Stretching out from the coma is one or more **tails.** A stream of particles coming from the Sun pushes the tail or tails away from the center of the solar system.

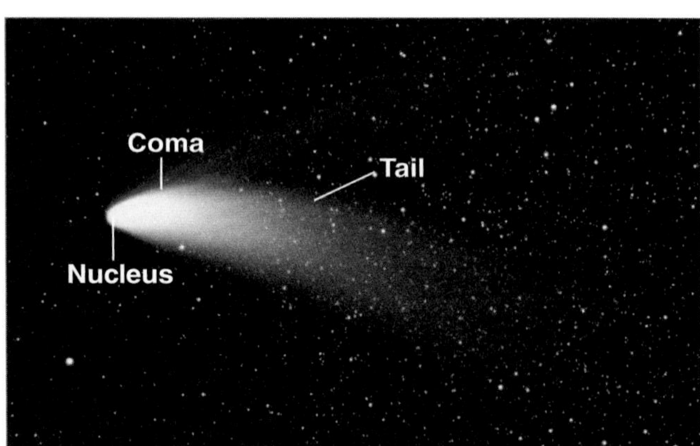

▲ **Figure 3-33** The structure of a comet

1 **DESCRIBE:** What are comets made of?

Ghostly Travelers Comets travel in deep space, where it is very cold. For most of their trip around the Sun, they are invisible. As a comet approaches the Sun, it begins to warm up. Some of the ice begins to melt. Gas and dust are released from the nucleus and spread out to form the coma. Soon, the tail begins to form. Tails can stretch out for millions of kilometers.

From Earth, a comet looks like a ghostly patch in the sky. It suddenly appears one night as sunlight begins reflecting off it.

Over time, the coma expands, and the tail stretches out into space. After rounding the Sun, the comet moves back into deep space and disappears from view.

2 ▶ **EXPLAIN:** What causes a comet's tail to grow?

Where Comets Come From Astronomers think that many comets come from the Oort Cloud. This cloud, named after the Dutch astronomer Jan Oort, is far beyond Pluto's orbit. The Oort Cloud may contain trillions of inactive comets. A second cloud of comets or cometlike material called the Kuiper Belt exists beyond the orbit of Neptune.

Comets were formed billions of years ago when the solar system was young. After the Sun formed, gas and dust surrounding the new Sun formed into small pieces of ice, rock, and metal. These pieces eventually stuck together to form larger objects. The largest bodies became planets and moons. The smaller bodies became asteroids and comets.

3 ▶ **INFER:** What materials became comets?

CHECKING CONCEPTS

1. The parts of a comet are the nucleus, the coma, and the __________.
2. Comets orbit the Sun in long, __________ orbits.
3. The Oort Cloud is found outside the orbit of __________.
4. The heaviest materials, such as rock and __________, formed the planets, moons, comets, and asteroids.

THINKING CRITICALLY

5. **INFER:** Why are scientists interested in comets?
6. **INFER:** What happens to the size of the nucleus of a comet each time it orbits the Sun?

DESIGNING AN EXPERIMENT

Design an experiment to solve the following problem. Include a hypothesis, variables, a procedure with materials, and a type of data to study. Be sure to also include a way to record your data.

PROBLEM: Astronomers believe that the nucleus of a comet begins melting as the comet nears the Sun. Design an experiment that will prove this. Your experiment will be carried on a spacecraft that will travel with the comet as it orbits the Sun.

How Do They Know That?

PREDICTING COMETS

Scientists know that comets are coming days or months before they become visible to the naked eye. The comets appear in the sky right where scientists predict they will be. How do they do that?

▲ **Figure 3-34** Halley's comet as seen in 1960.

Most comets travel around the Sun many times before they melt or leave the solar system. British astronomer Sir Edmund Halley was the first person to predict a comet's return, in 1758. The comet was later named after him.

Old comets, ones that have passed by the Sun before, are easy to predict. Today, comet orbits are calculated by computers. To find new comets, astronomers take pictures of the same regions of the night sky several days apart. If one of the stars in the first picture is in a different place in the second picture, it could be a comet. Powerful telescopes are then trained on the object. Eventually, astronomers identify it as a comet or some other object like an asteroid. If it is a comet, it will begin releasing gas as it nears the Sun.

Thinking Critically Why do comets become visible as they get closer to the Sun?

Chapter 3 Challenges

Chapter Summary

Lessons 3-1 and 3-2

- The **solar system** may have formed from a spinning cloud of gases and dust called a **nebula.** There are nine planets in the solar system. The planets can be divided into inner and outer planets.
- An **ellipse** has an oval shape. Most planets travel around the Sun in elliptical **orbits.**
- Earth's orbital velocity is greatest at **perihelion** and least at **aphelion.**

Lesson 3-3

- The Moon is Earth's only natural **satellite.** Humans first landed on it in 1969. There is no air or water on the Moon. The Moon has **maria,** highlands, and **craters.**

Lessons 3-4 and 3-5

- Mercury and Venus have no moons. Mars has 2, Jupiter has at least 28, Saturn 30, Uranus 21, Neptune 8, and Pluto 1.
- Mercury is the closest planet to the Sun. It has many craters. Venus has a blanket of sulfuric acid clouds. Earth supports life.

Lessons 3-6 and 3-7

- Mars is reddish. It might have had running water in the past.
- **Asteroids** orbit the Sun in a belt between Mars and Jupiter. Space objects called **meteoroids** may enter Earth's atmosphere. If they burn up, they are called **meteors.** If they strike Earth's surface, they are **meteorites.**

Lessons 3-8 and 3-9

- Jupiter is the largest, most massive planet. It is a gas giant. Its Great Red Spot is a huge storm. Saturn is the least dense planet and has distinctive rings. Rings are particles of ice and dust that orbit a planet around its equator.
- Uranus is a gas giant that appears to be lying on its side. Neptune, also a gas giant, has an upper atmosphere of frozen methane.
- Tiny Pluto sometimes orbits inside Neptune's orbit.

Lesson 3-10

- **Comets** are dirty ice balls. They have long, elliptical orbits.

Key Term Challenges

aphelion (p. 70)
asteroid (p. 84)
coma (p. 90)
comet (p. 90)
crater (p. 74)
ellipse (p. 70)
mare (p. 74)
meteor (p. 84)
meteorite (p. 84)
meteoroid (p. 84)
nebula (p. 68)
nucleus (p. 90)
orbit (p. 68)
perihelion (p. 70)
rift (p. 82)
satellite (p. 76)
solar system (p. 68)
tail (p. 90)

MATCHING Write the Key Term from above that best matches each description.

1. curved path of one object around another object in space
2. flattened circle, or oval
3. lump of dust and ice that orbits the Sun and has a gaseous tail
4. natural or artificial object orbiting another body in space
5. cloud of gas and dust in space
6. valley caused by a crack in the crust of a planet
7. rock or metal that enters Earth's atmosphere from space
8. head or solid part of a comet
9. Sun and all the objects that orbit the Sun
10. point in a planet's orbit at which the planet is farthest from the Sun

APPLYING DEFINITIONS Explain the difference between the words in each pair. Write your answers in complete sentences.

11. asteroid, meteoroid
12. meteor, meteorite
13. aphelion, perihelion
14. craters, maria
15. nebula, solar system
16. satellite, moon

Content Challenges TEST PREP

MULTIPLE CHOICE Write the letter of the term or phrase that best completes each statement.

1. The planet closest in size to Earth is
   - **a.** Venus.
   - **b.** Mercury.
   - **c.** Pluto.
   - **d.** Jupiter.

2. The Great Red Spot is the best known feature of
   - **a.** Pluto.
   - **b.** Neptune.
   - **c.** Uranus.
   - **d.** Jupiter.

3. The planet that usually is the farthest from the Sun is
   - **a.** Pluto.
   - **b.** Neptune.
   - **c.** Uranus.
   - **d.** Jupiter.

4. The only planets in the solar system without at least one moon are
   - **a.** Jupiter and Pluto.
   - **b.** Earth and Venus.
   - **c.** Jupiter and Mercury.
   - **d.** Mercury and Venus.

5. American astronauts first set foot on the Moon in
   - **a.** 1957.
   - **b.** 1969.
   - **c.** 1972.
   - **d.** 1975.

6. Earth is closest to the Sun in
   - **a.** July.
   - **b.** September.
   - **c.** March.
   - **d.** January.

7. Pluto's orbit sometimes takes it inside the orbit of
   - **a.** Uranus.
   - **b.** Saturn.
   - **c.** Neptune.
   - **d.** Mars.

8. The light-colored areas on the Moon are
   - **a.** mountains.
   - **b.** rivers.
   - **c.** plains.
   - **d.** oceans.

9. The first planet to be discovered by using a telescope was
   - **a.** Pluto.
   - **b.** Uranus.
   - **c.** Mars.
   - **d.** Mercury.

TRUE/FALSE Write *true* if the statement is true. If the statement is false, change the underlined term to make the statement true.

10. Some scientists think that a nebula <u>expanded</u> to form the solar system.
11. The <u>core</u> of a comet is made of dust and ice.
12. Earth moves <u>fastest</u> at perihelion.
13. The largest planet in the solar system is <u>Neptune</u>.
14. Earth has only one <u>ring</u>.
15. <u>Uranus</u> is tipped on its side.
16. The region between Mars and Jupiter is called the <u>Meteoroid</u> Belt.
17. Saturn's density is <u>less</u> than the density of Jupiter and even water.
18. The first asteroid found was named <u>Ceres</u>.

Concept Challenges TEST PREP

WRITTEN RESPONSE **Answer each of the following questions in complete sentences.**

1. INFER: Why is the term *wanderer* inaccurate for describing a planet?
2. INFER: Why do rocks on the Moon not weather or erode like rocks on Earth do?
3. ANALYZE: In what ways is Pluto more similar to the inner planets than it is to the outer planets?
4. HYPOTHESIZE: What are some reasons astronauts may go back to the Moon?
5. INFER: Why are scientists looking for water on Mars?
6. ANALYZE: Why was Galileo's discovery of four moons orbiting Jupiter important to the history of astronomy?
7. EXPLAIN: How can a comet passing through Earth's orbit cause a meteor shower?
8. INFER: Why does a comet's tail always point away from the Sun?
9. EXPLAIN: Why does Earth's orbital velocity change as it orbits the Sun?
10. COMPARE/CONTRAST: How are the inner planets and outer planets alike and how are they different?

INTERPRETING VISUALS **Use Figure 3-35 to answer each of the following questions.**

11. How many moons does Neptune have?
12. What is the only outer planet without any rings?
13. What planet has the most known moons?
14. Do any of the inner planets have rings?

PLANETS, MOONS, AND RINGS		
Planets	Number of Known Moons	Rings
Mercury	0	No
Venus	0	No
Earth	1	No
Mars	2	No
Jupiter	28	Yes
Saturn	30	Yes
Uranus	21	Yes
Neptune	8	Yes
Pluto	1	No

▲ Figure 3-35

Chapter 4 The Sun and Other Stars

▲ **Figure 4-1** The Eagle Nebula is also known to astronomers as M16.

These dark structures may look like cave formations or undersea coral. However, they are actually columns of cool hydrogen gas and dust in a nebula. Nebulae are the birthplaces of new stars. The Eagle Nebula, seen here, is 7,000 light years away. The tallest column (left) is about one light year tall. This picture was taken with a camera on the Hubble Space Telescope. The image reveals the various elements that make up the matter in the nebula.

▶ What do you think are some of the elements that make up stars?

Contents

4-1 How are stars formed?

Objectives

Describe how stars form. Name some characteristics of stars.

Key Terms

star: ball of gases that gives off light and heat

nebula (NEHB-yuh-luh)**:** cloud of gas and dust in space

protostar: dense material in the center of a nebula that is about to become a star

binary stars: two stars that revolve around each other

star cluster: large group of stars that travel together through space

Tiny Points of Light The Sun is a star. A **star** is a big ball of gases that gives off heat and light. The Sun is only one of billions of stars that make up our galaxy, and there are billions of galaxies. Between the stars and galaxies are vast stretches of nearly empty space.

On a clear night, you can see thousands of stars in the sky. Most of these look to us like tiny points of light. This is because they are so far away. Most stars appear white to the naked eye. However, a closer look reveals that stars come in different colors. For example, Rigel is a blue star. Betelgeuse (BEET-uhl-jooz) is red. The Sun, of course, is yellow. Stars also show a huge range in size, brightness, and surface temperature. How large and massive a star is determine what will eventually happen to it.

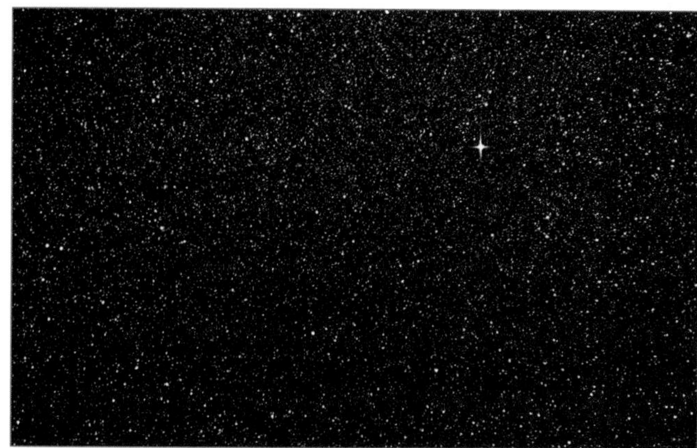

▲ **Figure 4-2** The Sun is only one of billions of stars. However, the naked eye sees only a few thousand stars.

Different stars have different elements. Most stars are made up of the gases hydrogen and helium. Other elements often found in stars include sodium, calcium, and iron. The most common element in stars is hydrogen. All of these elements are found in varying amounts in stars.

1 NAME: What is the most common element in stars?

Formation of Stars A star forms from a cloud of gas and dust in space called a **nebula.** Gravity causes the nebula to contract and start spinning. This flattens the nebula into a disk. Material at the center of the disk forms a **protostar.**

As the nebula continues to contract, temperature and pressure build. Eventually, nuclear reactions begin, and the protostar starts to give off light and heat. A new star is born.

2 NAME: What is the first stage in star formation?

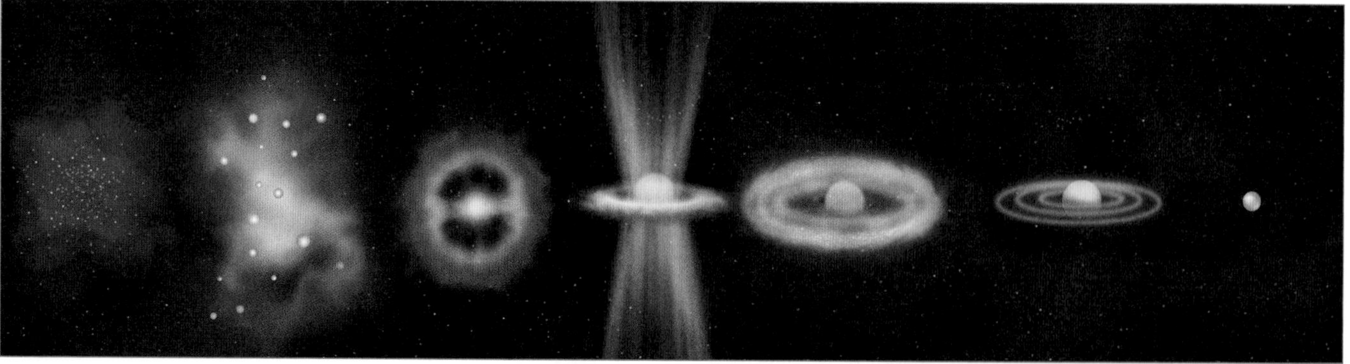

▲ **Figure 4-3** A star begins as a cloud of gas and dust that forms into a protostar. When it begins to give off light and heat, the protostar has become a true star.

Double Stars and Star Clusters Unlike the Sun, most stars are double, or binary, stars. **Binary stars** are pairs of stars that travel through space together and revolve around each other.

Some stars are part of multiple-star systems. They contain three or more stars. Many stars move through space in large groups called **star clusters.** Some clusters are globular, or round, in shape. Others are open, or loosely arranged.

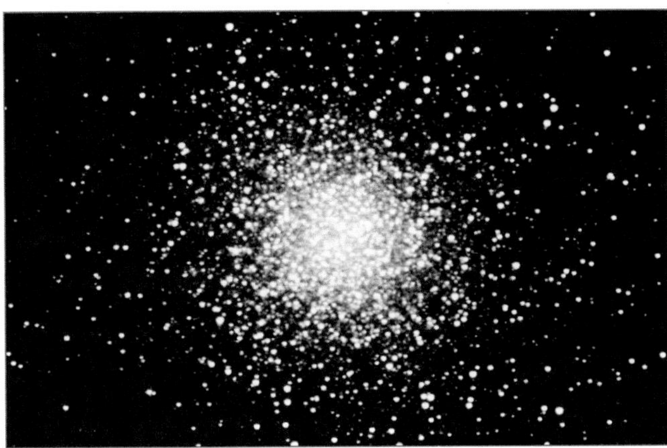

▲ **Figure 4-4** A globular cluster can contain millions of stars.

 DEFINE: What are binary stars?

CHECKING CONCEPTS

1. What is the star closest to Earth?
2. What two gases make up most stars?
3. What is a nebula?
4. What causes a spinning nebula to contract?
5. What two shapes do star clusters form?

THINKING CRITICALLY

6. **SEQUENCE:** What are the stages in the formation of a star?
7. **INFER:** Why are rounded clusters called globular clusters?

BUILDING SCIENCE SKILLS

Classifying Stars are grouped according to color, or spectral classes. The letters *O*, *B*, *A*, *F*, *G*, *K*, and *M* each represent spectral classes. Blue stars are in spectral class O or B. Red stars are M stars. Do some research on the following stars: Canopus, Arcturus, Sirius, Rigel, the Sun, Betelgeuse, Altair, and Capella. Then, put them in their correct spectral class.

Science and Technology

OBSERVATORIES

Most professional astronomers today work at observatories. Instead of using just their eyes to look through telescopes, they use sensitive electronic cameras to build up an exposure over many minutes or hours. Then, computers analyze the data. Astronomers study the pictures and the computer data.

Most observatories use reflecting telescopes with large mirrors. The Special Astrophysical Observatory in Russia has a mirror 6 m in diameter. However, large mirrors often sag under their own weight, blurring the image. This has led scientists to build reflecting telescopes that use many small mirrors acting as one. The Keck Telescope at Mauna Kea, Hawaii, has a mirror made of 36 thin glass segments. Together, these segments make a mirror 10 m in diameter.

▲ **Figure 4-5** Kitt Peak National Observatory

Many observatories in the United States, such as Palomar near San Diego, California, are run by cities or nonprofit groups. Kitt Peak National Observatory, near Tucson, Arizona, is the largest U.S. observatory.

Thinking Critically What activities are conducted inside observatories?

4-2 How is spectroscopy used to study stars?

Objective

Describe how astronomers use spectroscopy to study stars.

Key Terms

spectrum: pattern of different colors of light coming from an object

spectrograph (SPEHK-truh-graf)**:** device that measures the spectrum of an object

spectroscopy (spehk-TRUH-skohp-ee)**:** study of light coming from objects in space

Colors of Starlight White light is really a mixture of different colors of light. When you aim a beam of white light at a prism, the prism separates or spreads out the light into its colors. This pattern of colors is called a **spectrum.**

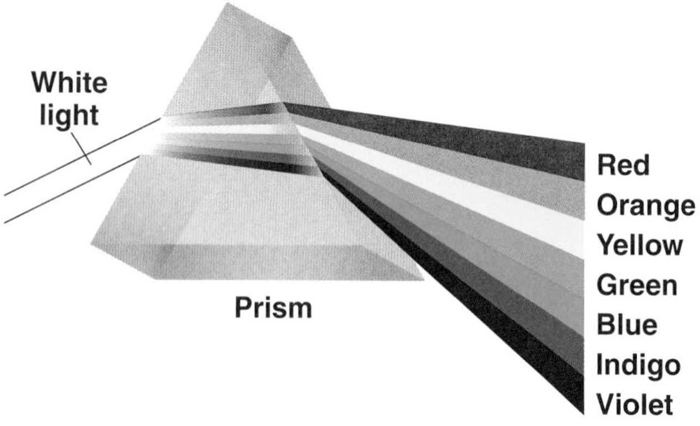

▲ **Figure 4-6** A prism breaks up white light into a spectrum.

The spectrum of white light contains red, orange, yellow, green, blue, indigo, and violet. These are the colors you see in a rainbow.

Astronomers learn about stars by studying their light. They use a **spectrograph,** which contains a prism that separates light from the star into bands of colors. The spectrograph also contains a camera to focus the spectrum and record it on photographic or electronic film. The study of light coming from objects in space is called **spectroscopy.**

 **DEFINE:** What is a spectrum?

Color and Composition A spectrum reveals the chemical makeup of a star. Stars are very hot. When elements are heated enough, they give off light. Each element gives off its own spectrum of light. Astronomers can study this spectrum to find out what elements make up the star.

 **EXPLAIN:** What does a spectrum reveal?

Color and Temperature The surface temperature of a star is related to its color. Stars come in different colors. Blue stars are the hottest, at around 29,000°C to 40,000°C. Red stars, at around 2,100°C to 3,200°C, are the coolest. A yellow star, like our Sun, is about 6,000°C. Scientists are able to determine the approximate temperature of a star from its spectrum.

 **APPLY:** If a star is medium hot, what would be its color?

Hydrogen

Helium

◀ **Figure 4-7** The spectra for hydrogen and helium.

✓ CHECKING CONCEPTS

1. Different colors of light make up a __________.
2. When an element is __________, it gives off a spectrum of light.
3. Each __________ in a star gives off its own spectrum.
4. The __________ of a star is related to its color.
5. The hottest stars are the color __________.

THINKING CRITICALLY

6. ANALYZE: A star has a very high surface temperature. What color does this star appear?
7. CALCULATE: What is the difference in degrees Centigrade between the hottest stars and the coolest stars?

Web InfoSearch

The Doppler Effect Have you ever noticed that a siren moving toward you sounds different from one moving away from you? This is known as a Doppler effect. Both sound and light waves are affected by the Doppler effect.

SEARCH: Use the Internet to find out more about the Doppler effect. How is it important in astronomy? What are red-shift and blue-shift? How can scientists find out how fast an object is moving from its Doppler effect? Begin your search at www.conceptsandchallenges.com. Some key search words are **Doppler effect astronomy, Doppler red shift,** and **Doppler blue shift.**

Hands-On Activity

MAKING A SPECTROSCOPE

You can use a spectroscope to separate white light into a band of colors. You will need a cardboard tube, a diffraction grating, a sheet of black construction paper, scissors, tape, a light bulb, and colored crayons.

1. Tape a diffraction grating to one end of a cardboard tube.
2. Cut a thin slit in the center of a sheet of black construction paper. ⚠ CAUTION: Be careful when using scissors.
3. Cover the other end of the cardboard tube with the sheet of black paper. Use tape to hold the paper in place.
4. Hold the end of the tube with the diffraction grating up to your eye. Look through the tube at a light bulb. Slowly turn the tube until you see a spectrum. Draw the spectrum.
5. Use your spectroscope to look at other light sources, such as a fluorescent tube. ⚠ CAUTION: Do not look at the Sun with your spectroscope.

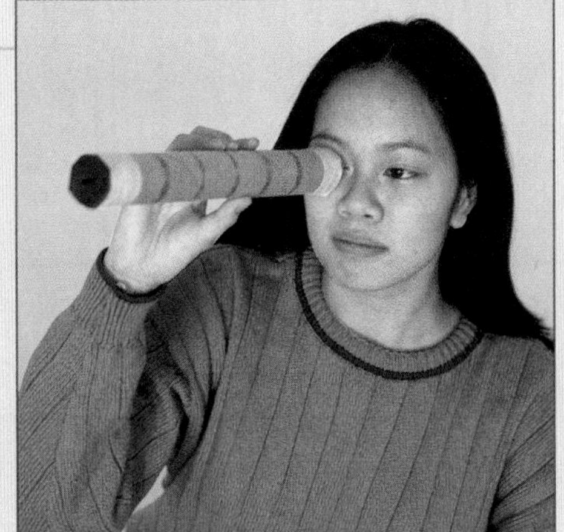

▲ **STEP 4** Look through your tube at a light bulb.

Practicing Your Skills

6. DESCRIBE: What does a spectroscope do?
7. COMPARE: **a.** Were the spectra from different light sources the same or different? **b.** How can you explain the similarities or differences of the spectra?

4-3 What is magnitude?

Objective

Compare apparent magnitude and absolute magnitude.

Key Term

magnitude (MAG-nuh-tood): way to measure a star's brightness

Brightness of Stars Without a telescope, you can see about 2,000 stars in the night sky. Some stars appear brighter than others. One way to measure a star's brightness is by **magnitude.**

How bright a star appears to us depends on its temperature, size, and distance from Earth. A hot star is usually brighter than a cool star. A large star is usually brighter than a small star. The closer a star is to Earth, the brighter it usually appears to us.

1 NAME: What is the measure of a star's brightness called?

Apparent Magnitude The brightness of a star as seen from Earth is called the star's apparent magnitude. Planets can be classified this way, too, although they shine only with reflected light.

Astronomers have developed a scale for apparent magnitude. On this scale, a star with a low number appears brighter than a star with a high number. Bright stars usually have an apparent magnitude of 1. These are called first-magnitude stars. Very bright stars can have negative magnitudes. The dimmest stars you can see without a telescope are sixth-magnitude stars. You can see the magnitudes of some stars and other bodies in Figure 4-8 below.

2 COMPARE: Which appears brighter, a third-magnitude star or a sixth-magnitude star?

Absolute Magnitude Astronomers can also find the absolute magnitude of a star. The absolute magnitude of a star is its actual brightness. Absolute magnitude describes how bright a star would appear to us if all the stars were the same distance from Earth.

▼ **Figure 4-8** Comparison of apparent magnitudes

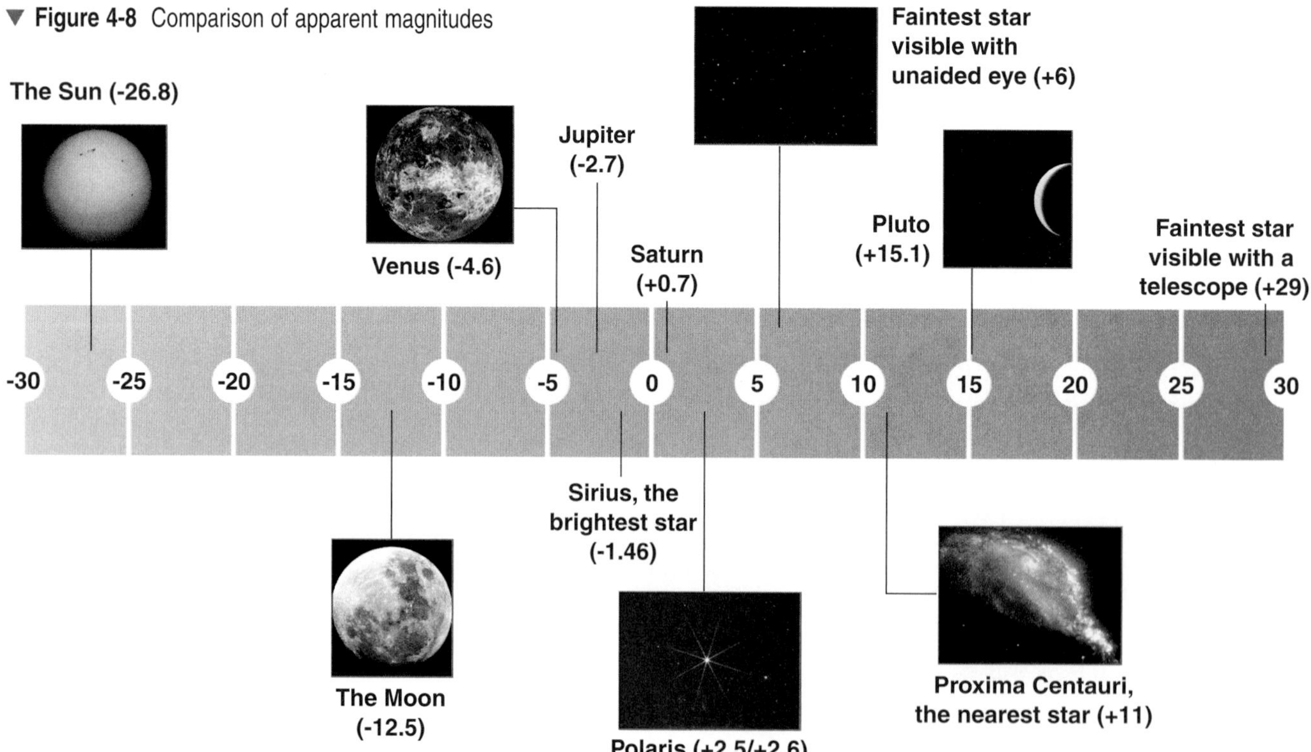

For example, the Sun appears very bright to us because it is so near Earth. If the Sun were farther away, it would not appear as bright to us. A dim star that is close to Earth may appear brighter than a bright star that is far away. All stars have both an apparent magnitude and an absolute magnitude.

 **DESCRIBE:** What is absolute magnitude?

CHECKING CONCEPTS

1. Magnitude is a measure of a star's ___________.
2. Magnitude depends on a particular star's size, ___________, and distance from Earth.
3. A fourth-magnitude star appears ___________ than a first-magnitude star.
4. The brightness of a star as seen from Earth is its ___________ magnitude.
5. The actual brightness of a star is its ___________ magnitude.

THINKING CRITICALLY

6. **HYPOTHESIZE:** Two stars have the same absolute magnitude but different apparent magnitudes. Explain how this can be true.
7. **COMPARE:** The Sun is the star closest to Earth. It has an absolute magnitude of 5.4. The star Altair has an absolute magnitude of 2.2. Which star is really brighter? Explain.

BUILDING MATH SKILLS

Calculating First-magnitude stars are about 2.512 times brighter than second-magnitude stars. These are about 2.512 times brighter than third-magnitude stars, and so on. Using this information, you can figure out how faint a star is compared to some other star. If two stars are five magnitudes apart, you would multiply 2.512 to the fifth power (2.512^5) to get 100. This means that a first-magnitude star is 100 times brighter than a sixth-magnitude star. Use this formula and a calculator to compare a star with a magnitude of 25 to a star with a magnitude of 5.

Hands-On Activity

OBSERVING MAGNITUDE

You will need one large flashlight and one small flashlight.

1. Work in groups of three.
2. Have one partner hold a large flashlight and another partner hold a small flashlight. Have both partners stand the same distance away from you and turn on their flashlights.
3. Compare the brightness of the two flashlights.
4. Now, have the person holding the small flashlight move closer to you. Compare the brightness of the two lights.

▲ **STEP 2** Have your partners stand the same distance away from you and turn on their flashlights.

Practicing Your Skills

5. **COMPARE:** **a.** When they were the same distance away, which appeared brighter, the large flashlight or the small flashlight? **b.** Which had the greater apparent magnitude? **c.** Which had the greater absolute magnitude?
6. **OBSERVE:** **a.** What happened when the small flashlight was moved closer? **b.** Which had the greater apparent magnitude? **c.** Which had the greater absolute magnitude?

4-4 How are stars classified?

Objective

Explain how the Hertzsprung-Russell diagram is used to classify stars.

Key Terms

main sequence star: star that falls within a long, narrow, diagonal band across the H-R diagram

red giant: large, bright star that is fairly cool

supergiant: very large and very bright star

white dwarf: very small, hot star

The H-R Diagram In the early 1900s, astronomers Ejnar Hertzsprung and Henry Russell each made a separate but similar discovery about stars. They found that there is a relationship between a star's absolute magnitude and its surface temperature and color. Together, Hertzprung and Russell developed a chart called the Hertzsprung-Russell, or H-R, diagram. The H-R diagram shows that the brightness of most stars increases as the star's surface temperature increases.

1 DESCRIBE: What does the H-R diagram show?

Main Sequence Stars A star's position on the H-R diagram depends on its absolute magnitude and its surface temperature, or color. Temperature is in degrees Kelvin (K). Suppose that a star has a blue color and a low absolute magnitude. This star would be placed in the upper left corner of the diagram. A red star with a high absolute magnitude would appear in the lower right corner. Most stars fall in a narrow diagonal band that runs from the upper left to the lower right corner of the diagram. Stars that fall in this band are called **main sequence stars.** The Sun and most stars that you can see at night are main sequence stars.

2 CLASSIFY: What kind of star is the Sun on an H-R diagram?

Other Stars Some stars do not fall within the main sequence. They may be bright but not very hot. Many of these stars are red, orange, or yellow in color. Because they are not very hot, they should not be very bright. However, because these stars are very large, they give off a great deal of light. They have large absolute magnitudes. These stars are called **red giants.** Red giants appear in the upper right corner of an H-R diagram.

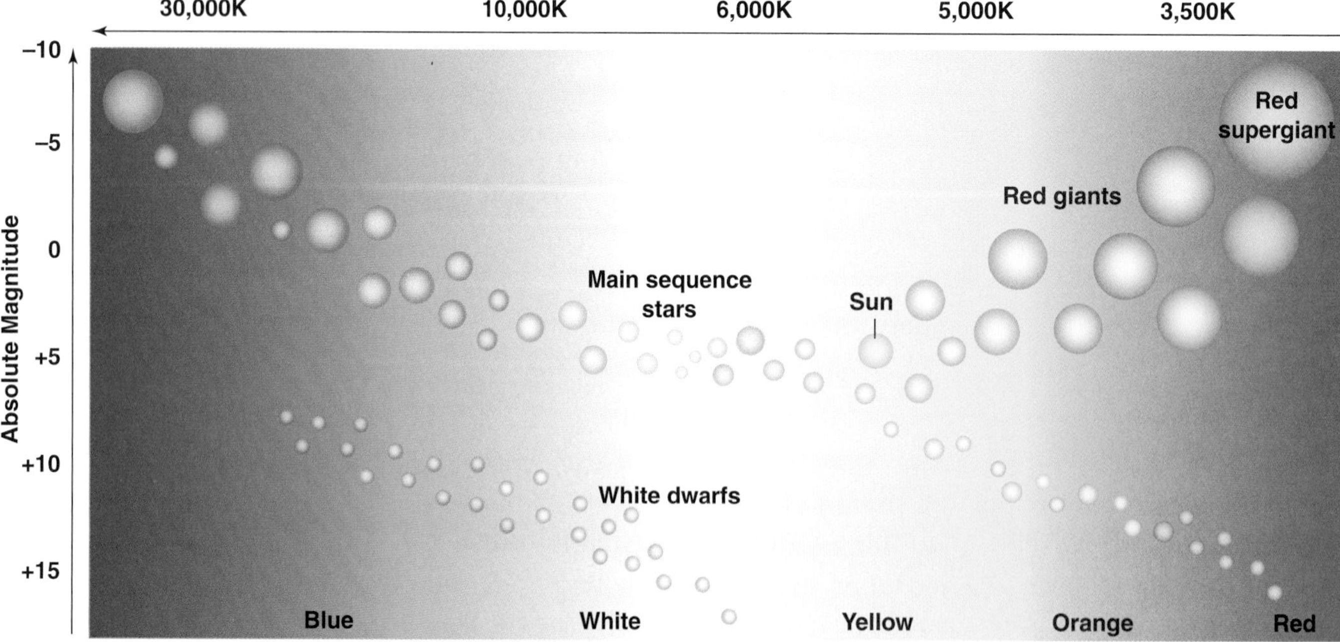

▲ Figure 4-9 An H-R diagram shows the relationship between the brightness of stars and their surface temperatures.

Some stars are even larger and brighter than red giants. These stars are called **supergiants.**

Other stars that fall outside of the main sequence are hot but very small. These stars are blue or white. They are called **white dwarfs.** White dwarfs are found in the lower part of an H-R diagram, below the main sequence stars.

 DEFINE: What are white dwarfs?

CHECKING CONCEPTS

1. The H-R diagram shows the relationship between __________ magnitude and temperature.
2. The Sun is a __________ sequence star.
3. A very large, bright star is a red __________.
4. Red giants are found in the upper __________ of an H-R diagram.
5. White dwarfs are small, __________ stars.

THINKING CRITICALLY

Use Figure 4-9 to answer the following questions.

6. COMPARE: Which star has a higher absolute magnitude, a red giant or a white dwarf?
7. COMPARE: Which star has a greater surface temperature, a red giant or a white dwarf?
8. ANALYZE: What is the average surface temperature of a white dwarf?
9. IDENTIFY: What stars are even larger than red giants?

BUILDING MATH SKILLS

Graphing Create a line graph that shows where each kind of star appears on the H-R diagram. Plot the absolute magnitude along the vertical axis. Plot the temperature along the horizontal axis. Label each point with the kind of star it represents. Do the points form a pattern? Write a few sentences describing how the pattern formed compares to the pattern in Figure 4-9.

How Do They Know That?

DISTANCES TO THE STARS

How do astronomers measure distances to stars? The distance of close stars can be found by observing the star's parallax. Parallax is based on how the star seems to shift position over time. However the distances to stars that are very far away seemed almost impossible to measure. Then, an American astronomer discovered a way to find the distances to stars in other galaxies.

▲ **Figure 4-10** Henrietta Swan Leavitt used Cepheid stars to show that a star's brightness is related to its distance.

Henrietta Swan Leavitt (1868–1921) was born in Lancaster, Massachusetts. She graduated from what is now Radcliffe College and soon went to work at the Harvard Observatory. She was studying a kind of star called a Cepheid (SEHF-ee-id) variable. A Cepheid variable is a star that changes its brightness in a regular pattern over a set period of time.

In 1912, Leavitt identified 25 Cepheid variables in a nearby galaxy. She observed the period of each star, or how long the star took to go from bright to dim and back to bright again. She showed that the longer the period of a star is, the brighter the star. A star's brightness is related to its distance. Astronomers used this relationship to calculate the distance to faraway stars.

Thinking Critically Why do you think parallax is not useful for measuring all stars?

4-5 What is a star's life cycle?

Objective

Describe the stages in the life cycle of a star.

Key Terms

nova: explosion where the outer layers of a star are blown off

supernova: violent explosion where a star is blown apart

Life Cycle of a Star Stars change over time. This is called a life cycle. A star's complete life cycle takes many millions of years. As time passes, the star changes its mass into energy. The energy is given off as light and heat. Eventually, most of the mass is used up, and the star dies. By studying many different stars, astronomers have learned how stars change during their life cycle.

1 **EXPLAIN:** Where does a star's energy come from?

Protostar to Giant Stars are formed from nebulae. Gravity pulls the dust and the gas in the nebula together, forming a protostar. If the protostar becomes hot enough, nuclear reactions start to take place. In these reactions, hydrogen is changed into helium. Large amounts of energy are produced. These reactions turn the protostar into a star.

Now the star is on the main sequence. During this stage, hydrogen at the star's center continues to change into helium. When this process ends, small stars will stop shining and contract to become white dwarfs. Larger stars, however, will start new nuclear reactions that turn helium into carbon. The energy produced by these reactions expands the star and makes it cooler. It is now a red giant.

2 **DESCRIBE:** What is the main sequence stage?

Death of a Star The next stage in a star's life cycle depends on the star's mass. A medium-sized star loses mass and begins to contract. It becomes a white dwarf. For a brief time, the white dwarf becomes very hot. Then it begins to cool and becomes fainter and fainter with time. The end stage of a white dwarf is thought to be a small, cold, dark object called a black dwarf.

Sometimes, before it becomes a black dwarf, a white dwarf will blow off its outer layers in huge, bright explosion. This explosion is called a **nova.** A very massive star may blow itself apart in a **supernova.** During a supernova, or right after it, the star may collapse to become a neutron star or a black hole.

3 **DESCRIBE:** What happens when a medium-sized star runs out of hydrogen?

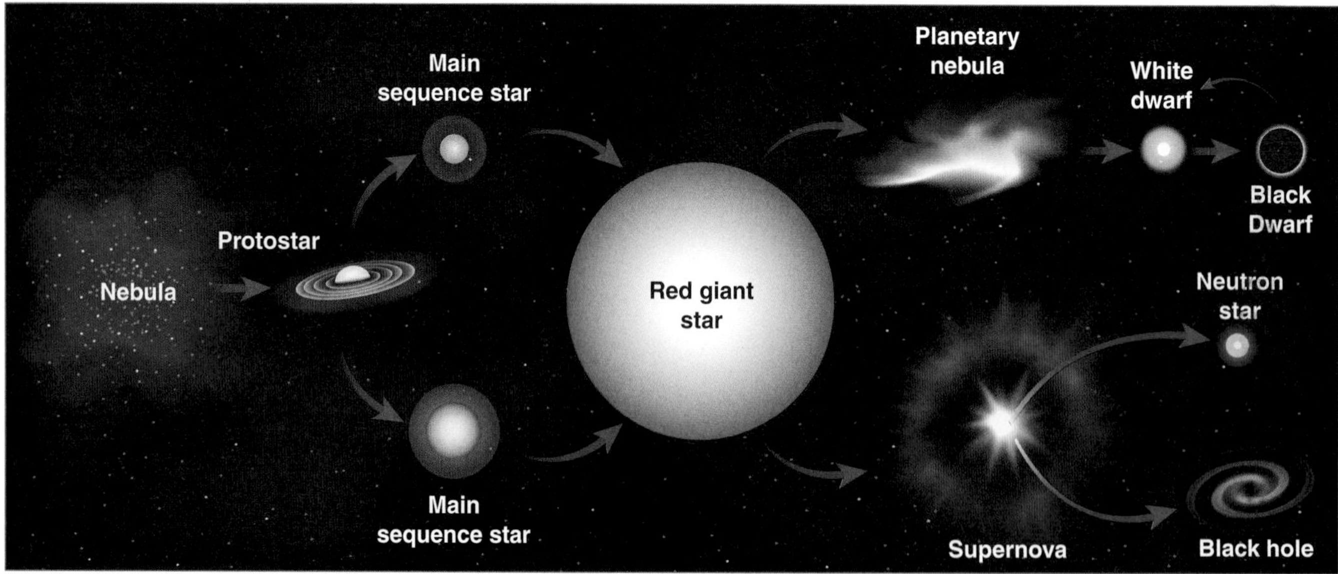

▲ **Figure 4-11** The life cycle of a star

Supernova 1987A On February 24, 1987, a supernova was seen in the Large Magellanic Cloud. This is more than 160,000 light years from Earth. The so-called Supernova 1987A was the first to be seen by the naked eye from Earth in almost 400 years. Astronomers studied the light coming from the supernova as it slowly dimmed. Viewing the supernova helped them to learn more about the evolution of stars.

4 **INFER:** What was the likely energy source of Supernova 1987A?

CHECKING CONCEPTS

1. A star changes __________ into energy.
2. The __________ stage is the briefest in a star's life cycle.
3. A main sequence star becomes a red giant or __________ when __________.
4. A white dwarf may blow off its outer shell in an explosion called a __________.
5. A supernova may occur in a very __________ star.

THINKING CRITICALLY

Use Figure 4-11 to complete the following exercise.

6. **SEQUENCE:** A flowchart shows a sequence of events. Create a flowchart showing the stages in the life cycle of a star. Begin with a protostar.

Web InfoSearch

Tycho Brahe Tycho Brahe was a 16th-century Danish astronomer. After studying law all day, he would go out at night to observe the stars. Brahe found that most of the astronomical information of the time was not accurate. He decided to devote his life to making accurate observations of the stars.

SEARCH: Use the Internet to find out more about Tycho Brahe's achievements. What did the king of Denmark give Brahe and why? Start your search at www.conceptsandchallenges.com. Key search words are **Tycho Brahe, Brahe King Denmark,** and **Tycho Brahe biography.**

How Do They Know That?

PULSARS

After a very massive star explodes, its core collapses. This collapse squeezes protons and electrons together until they become neutrons. This is how a neutron star is formed.

Neutron stars are incredibly dense. One teaspoonful of neutron star material would weigh over 2 billion tons. As they rotate, neutron stars send out radio waves and light that reach Earth in pulses. This is how pulsars got their name. Pulsars spin like the light atop a lighthouse. They emit radio or light waves or both that appear and then disappear in a regular pattern. The radio waves can be detected using a radio telescope.

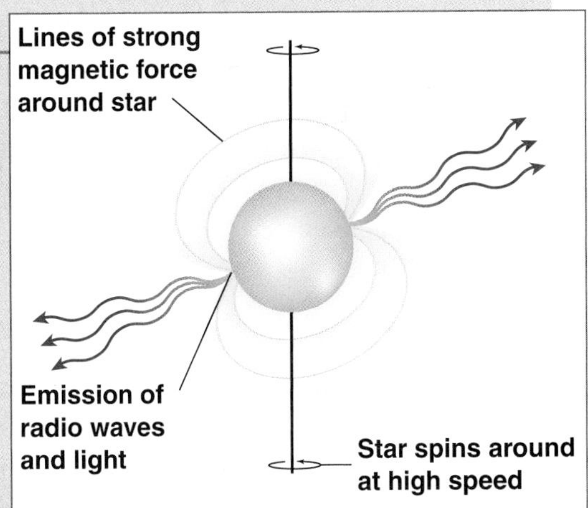

▲ **Figure 4-12** A pulsar spins like a light on a lighthouse.

The pulse of a pulsar tells us how fast the pulsar is spinning. The fastest pulsars discovered so far spin about 642 times per second. Some pulsars spin much more slowly, only once every few seconds.

Pulsars were first discovered in 1967 by Anthony Hewish and his graduate student, Jocelyn Bell. Hewish later received a Nobel Prize for identifying pulsars as a new class of stars.

Thinking Critically How did neutron stars get their name?

4-6 What kind of star is the Sun?

Objective

Describe the parts of the Sun.

Key Terms

core: center of the Sun

photosphere (FOHT-oh-sfeer)**:** inner layer of the Sun's atmosphere

chromosphere (KROH-muh-sfeer)**:** layer of the Sun's atmosphere above the photosphere

corona (kuh-ROH-nuh)**:** outer layer of the Sun's atmosphere

Structure of the Sun The Sun is one of about 100 billion stars in our part of the universe. However, it is the only one close enough for us to study in detail. The Sun is an average star in size, mass, and temperature. Its diameter is 1,400,000 km. Because the Sun is made mostly of gases, it has no distinct boundaries. However, it has two main parts. These parts are the core and the atmosphere.

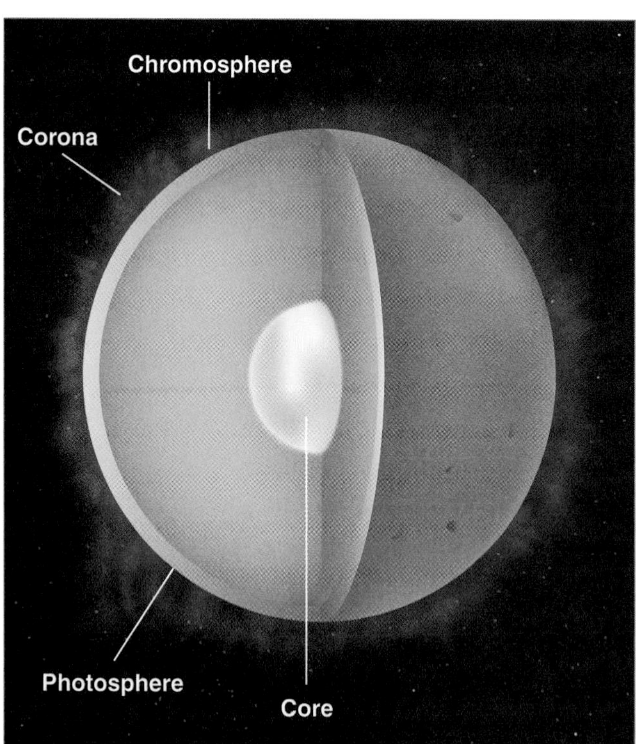

▲ **Figure 4-13** The atmosphere of the Sun is made up of the photosphere, the chromosphere, and the corona.

1 NAME: What are the two main parts of the Sun?

The Sun's Core The center and hottest part of the Sun is the **core.** The core makes up about 10 percent of the Sun's diameter. It is where the Sun's energy is produced. The temperature of the core is about 15,000,000°C.

 **IDENTIFY:** Where is the Sun's core?

The Sun's Atmosphere Since the Sun is made up almost entirely of gas, its atmosphere takes up most of its volume. There are three thin layers at the outer edge of the atmosphere. One layer is the **photosphere,** or light sphere. The photosphere is the visible surface of the Sun. The gas in the photosphere glows and gives off light.

Above the photosphere lies another layer of the atmosphere, called the **chromosphere,** or "color sphere." This part of the Sun gives off a weak red glow that can be seen only under special conditions, such as during a solar eclipse. The chromosphere extends for thousands of kilometers.

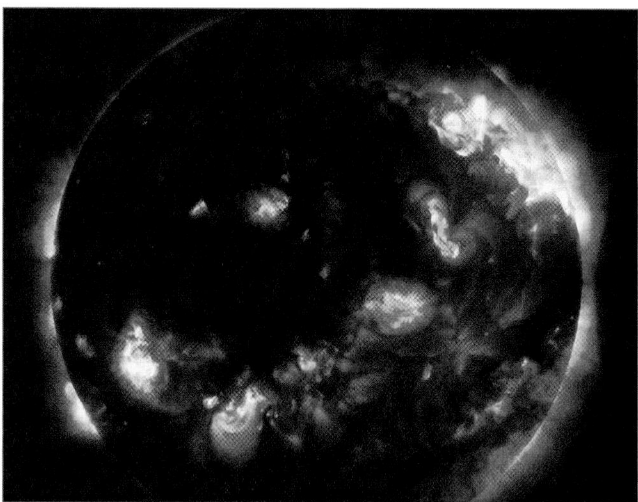

▲ **Figure 4-14** The chromosphere is seen more clearly in this photograph of the Sun taken by a special telescope.

The **corona** is the outermost layer of the Sun's atmosphere. This envelope of gases normally extends 1 million km from the Sun. It produces a glow about half as bright as a full Moon. The temperature of the corona is about 1,500,000°C. Like the chromosphere, the corona can usually be seen only during a solar eclipse.

 **LIST:** What are three layers of the Sun's atmosphere?

✓ CHECKING CONCEPTS

1. What is at the center of the Sun?
2. What is the approximate temperature of the Sun's core?
3. Which part of the Sun is the source of the Sun's energy?
4. How many layers make up the Sun's atmosphere?
5. Which layers of the Sun's atmosphere can be seen only during a solar eclipse?

THINKING CRITICALLY

6. **DESCRIBE:** What is the basic structure of the Sun?
7. **COMPARE:** Which is the hottest part of the Sun?
8. **INFER:** Why is the part of the Sun you named in Question 7 the hottest?
9. **ANALYZE:** The word *corona* comes from a Latin word meaning "crown." Why do you think the outer layer of the Sun is called the corona?

HEALTH AND SAFETY TIP

Earth's atmosphere filters out most of the harmful rays the Sun produces. However, some of the rays that get through can be harmful. For example, the Sun is far too bright to look at directly without damaging your eyes. Astronomers use special telescopes to study the surface of the Sun. Also, you know that sunlight can cause sunburn and can damage skin. Some kinds of skin cancer are caused by overexposure to the Sun. You should always take care to protect your skin and your eyes from overexposure to sunlight.

Hands-On Activity

OBSERVING THE SUN

You will need a ring stand, a clamp, a 20- by 28-cm sheet of cardboard, binoculars, and a sheet of white paper.

1. Clamp a pair of binoculars to a ring stand.
2. Cut a hole in the cardboard so that it fits over one eyepiece; the other eyepiece is covered. Tape the cardboard on securely.
3. Point the binoculars toward the Sun. ⚠ CAUTION: Never look directly at the Sun. Looking directly at the Sun could damage your eyes.
4. Hold the sheet of white paper a short distance from the eyepiece. An image of the Sun should appear on the sheet of white paper. Move the paper back and forth until your image of the Sun comes into sharp focus.
5. Quickly trace your image of the Sun onto the paper. Then, move the paper away to prevent scorching it. ⚠ CAUTION: If you hold the paper there for too long, it may ignite. Be sure to quickly remove it and the binoculars after you have drawn your image.

▲ **STEP 4** Hold the paper a short distance from the eyepiece and look for an image of the Sun on it.

Practicing Your Skills

6. **IDENTIFY:** When you look at your image of the Sun, what layer are you are seeing?
7. **INFER:** Why do you think you cannot see the other layers of the Sun's atmosphere?
8. **INFER:** Why is this a good method to use to observe a solar eclipse?

4-7 What is the surface of the Sun like?

Objective

Describe sunspots, solar flares, and prominences.

Key Terms

sunspot: dark, cool area on the Sun's surface

prominence (PRAHM-uh-nuhns)**:** stream of gas that shoots high above the Sun's surface

solar flare: eruption of electrically charged particles from the surface of the Sun

Sunspots Some areas on the surface of the Sun are cooler than the areas around them. The gases in these cooler areas do not shine as brightly as the areas around them. As a result, these areas appear dark. The dark, cooler areas on the Sun's surface are called **sunspots.** Sunspots usually appear to move in groups across the Sun in the same direction. The appearance of movement is caused by the spinning of the Sun on its axis. Sunspots may last for days or even months.

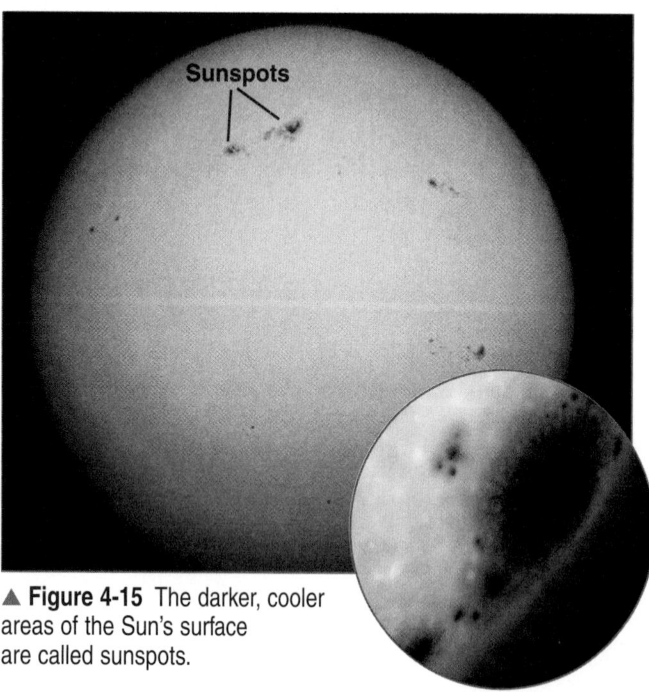

▲ **Figure 4-15** The darker, cooler areas of the Sun's surface are called sunspots.

1 **EXPLAIN:** Why do sunspots all appear to move in the same direction?

Prominences Streams of flaming gas shoot out from the surface of the Sun. These streams of gas are called **prominences.**

Prominences most often form in the chromosphere or photosphere. They can reach many thousands of kilometers above the Sun's surface. Then, they fall back into the Sun, forming huge arches. Prominences are best seen during a solar eclipse. They can last for weeks or months.

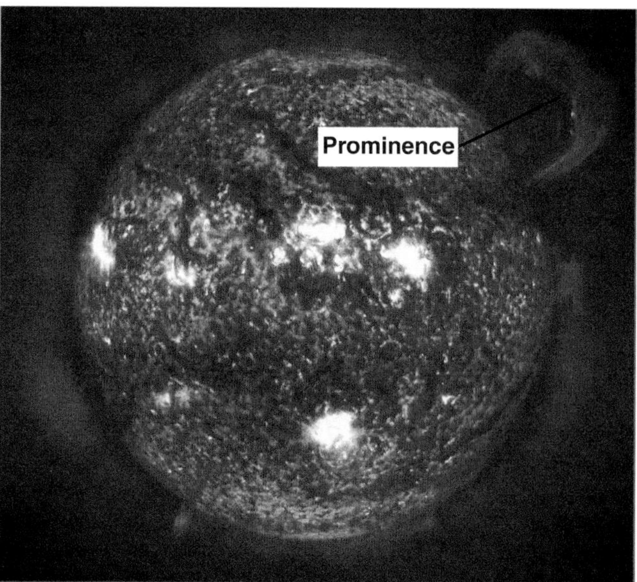

▲ **Figure 4-16** Prominences form in the chromosphere or photosphere.

2 **DEFINE:** What are prominences?

Solar Flares Energy sometimes builds up in the Sun's atmosphere. This buildup of energy usually happens near a group of sunspots. If the energy is given off suddenly, a **solar flare** is formed.

Solar flares usually do not last for more than an hour. Some may last for only a few minutes. In that time, though, they release enormous amounts of energy.

Solar flares send streams of electrically charged particles out into space. When these particles reach Earth's surface, they can cause electrical outages and disrupt communications. Solar flares are also the cause of the auroras, also called the northern and southern lights, on Earth.

▲ **Figure 4-17** Solar flares send streams of charged particles out into space.

 **DESCRIBE:** How do solar flares affect Earth?

CHECKING CONCEPTS

1. Sunspots appear dark because they are ___________ than surrounding areas.
2. Streams of gas from the surface of the Sun are ___________.
3. Solar flares release streams of ___________ particles.

THINKING CRITICALLY

4. **MODEL:** Draw and label a picture of the Sun. Show all of the features of the Sun that were discussed.

Web InfoSearch

Sunspots and Ice Ages Astronomers have found that sunspot activity seems to build up and decrease in an 11-year cycle. This cycle has been linked to climate changes on Earth. For example, the Little Ice Age of the 1600s has been associated with a long period of low sunspot activity.

SEARCH: Use the Internet to find out more about sunspots. Why do they move across the Sun in an 11-year cycle? Could magnetic activity be a part of it? If so, how? Start your search for information at www.conceptsandchallenges.com. Some key search words are **sunspots, sunspots magnetic,** and **sunspot ice ages.**

Integrating Physical Science

TOPICS: magnetism, solar energy, ions

THE SOLAR WIND

Electrons and charged particles called ions move off the surface of the Sun. They slip through gaps in the magnetic fields of the Sun's corona and travel through space in all directions. This movement of charged particles through space is called the solar wind. It is not related to the air that blows across Earth's surface.

The ions heading toward Earth are drawn to Earth's magnetic poles. As the solar wind passes Earth, the charged particles that are moving at very high speeds may interact with the magnetic field of Earth. Once in Earth's atmosphere, they react with the oxygen and nitrogen atoms there. This reaction causes the light shows in the sky known as the auroras, or the northern and southern lights.

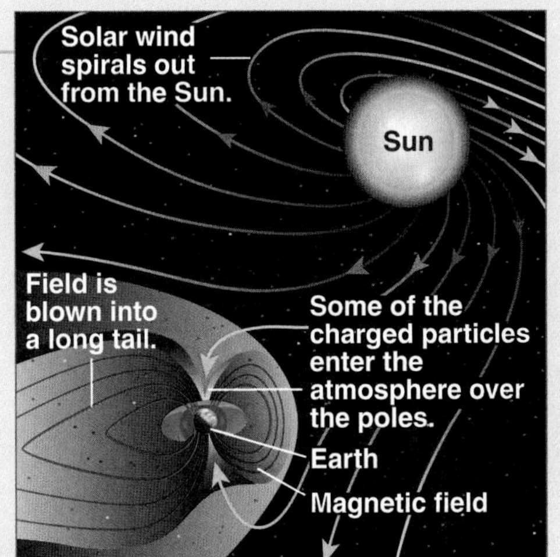
Solar wind spirals out from the Sun.
Sun
Field is blown into a long tail.
Some of the charged particles enter the atmosphere over the poles.
Earth
Magnetic field

▲ **Figure 4-18** The solar wind spirals out from the Sun and enters the atmosphere over the poles.

The tail of a comet also shows evidence of the solar wind. The solar wind sweeps the gases evaporating from the comet nucleus into a tail. Because of the solar wind, a comet's tail always points away from the Sun.

Thinking Critically Why do you think ions are drawn toward the magnetic poles of Earth?

4-8 How does the Sun produce energy?

Objective

Describe the process by which energy is produced in the Sun.

Key Terms

nucleus (NOO-klee-uhs): center, or core, of an atom

fusion (FYOO-zhuhn): reaction in which atomic nuclei combine to form larger nuclei

Solar Energy The Sun gives off energy in many forms, including heat and light. Where does this energy come from? You know that burning produces heat and light. However, burning does not produce the heat and the light of the Sun. The Sun produces energy by nuclear reactions. The **nucleus** is the center of an atom. In a nuclear reaction, the nuclei of atoms are changed.

1 DESCRIBE: What kind of reaction produces the heat and the light of the Sun?

Nuclear Fusion The Sun is about 71 percent hydrogen and 27 percent helium. Other elements make up the remaining 2 percent. Deep inside the Sun, the temperature is more than 15,000,000°C. At these high temperatures, the nuclei of hydrogen atoms combine, or fuse. This kind of reaction is called hydrogen **fusion.** In this reaction, four hydrogen nuclei combine to form one helium nucleus. The mass of a helium nucleus is less than the mass of all four hydrogen nuclei put together. The missing mass has been changed into energy.

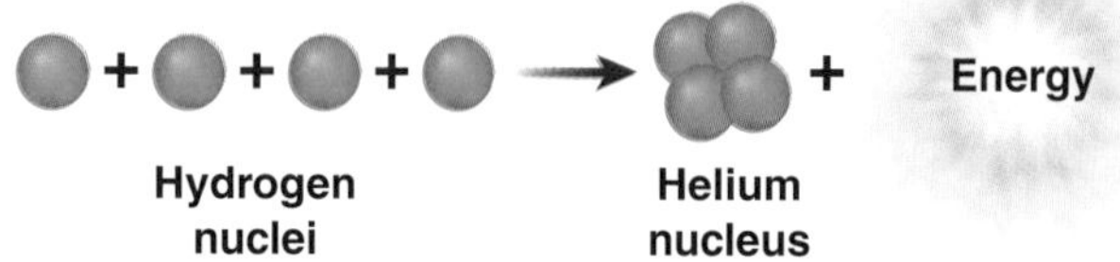

▲ **Figure 4-19** Hydrogen fusion

2 EXPLAIN: What happens in a fusion reaction?

Matter and Energy Albert Einstein helped explain how the Sun produces its energy. Einstein said that matter could be changed into energy. His equation, $E = mc^2$, explains how a small amount of matter can be changed into a large amount of energy. In this equation, E is energy, m is mass, or the amount of matter, and c is the speed of light. The speed of light is 300,000 km/s. Astronomers have used Einstein's equation to calculate how much energy the Sun produces.

▲ **Figure 4-20** Albert Einstein

3 STATE: What is Einstein's equation?

Fusion Energy Fusion energy is one possible alternative source of nuclear energy. Fusion reactors may someday be a source of economical, clean, and safe energy. Hydrogen atoms can be combined in a fusion reaction to produce helium plus a great deal of energy. Because water contains hydrogen, the oceans could be an almost unlimited source of fusion energy.

▲ **Figure 4-21** The Tokamak fusion test reactor in Princeton, New Jersey

Extremely high temperatures and pressures are needed for fusion reactions to take place. Scientists are experimenting with different ways to bring about these reactions.

One experimental fusion reactor uses a magnetic trap, or "magnetic bottle," to hold the fusion reaction. It also uses high-powered laser beams.

IDENTIFY: What would be the main fuel for fusion reactors?

✓ CHECKING CONCEPTS

1. What are two forms of solar energy?
2. What is the core of an atom called?
3. What two elements make up 98 percent of the Sun?
4. What happens to the missing mass in a hydrogen fusion reaction?
5. What does *E* stand for in Einstein's equation?

THINKING CRITICALLY

6. **INFER:** Why are the nuclear reactions that take place in the Sun called fusion reactions?
7. **ANALYZE:** Explain how $E = mc^2$ shows that a small amount of matter can be changed into a very large amount of energy.

INTERPRETING VISUALS

Ordinary hydrogen nuclei contain one proton. Heavy hydrogen nuclei contain one proton and one neutron. Two pairs of heavy hydrogen nuclei fuse with two stray protons to form two light helium nuclei. These then fuse to form one ordinary helium nucleus. This reaction releases two protons, or ordinary hydrogen nuclei, and energy. Use Figure 4-22 to answer the following questions.

8. **IDENTIFY:** What kinds of atoms are produced during the Sun's fusion reactions?
9. **ANALYZE:** What symbol in the diagram represents the energy released?

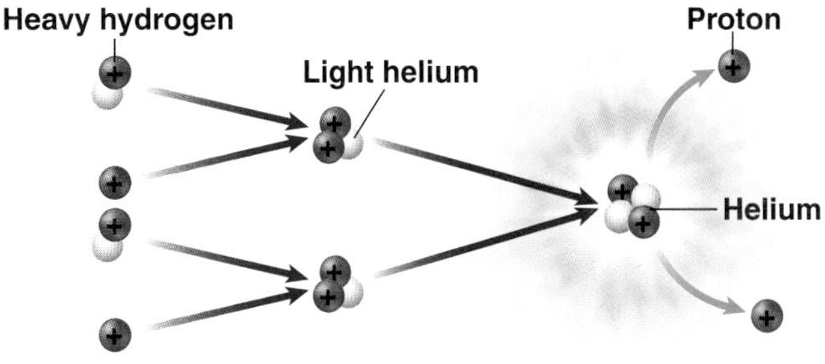

▲ **Figure 4-22** Fusion

Integrating Life Science

TOPICS: photosynthesis, food chain

FOOD FROM THE SUN

The Sun's energy reaches Earth as heat and light. This energy causes water on Earth to evaporate and rise into the air. The water then falls to Earth as rain. Rain helps plants to grow. Plants use sunlight to make food. Without rain and sunlight, plants would die. People and other animals could not survive.

▲ **Figure 4-23** All animals depend on photosynthesis for food.

The foodmaking process in green plants is called photosynthesis. The plants take in carbon dioxide and water. Sunlight supplies the energy needed by plants to make food. Some of the food is then used by the plants. The rest is stored. People and other animals use the stored food in plants when they eat the plants. Animals that eat other animals are taking in the energy from plants stored in the cells of the animals that are eaten.

During photosynthesis, plants give off oxygen. The oxygen goes into the air. People, other animals, and plants need oxygen to survive. Not all animals breathe air, but they do respire and get their oxygen this way. Without plants covering Earth and releasing oxygen, animals could not breathe.

Thinking Critically How is the oxygen produced by plants a kind of food animals must take in to survive?

4-9 What are constellations?

Objectives

Explain what constellations are. Name some familiar constellations.

Key Term

constellation (kahn-stuh-LAY-shuhn)**:** group of stars that form a pattern in the sky

Star Patterns When you look at the night sky, you can see many stars. Some of these stars seem to form patterns. These patterns are called **constellations.**

Ancient peoples thought they could see animals and people in constellations. They named the constellations and made up stories about them. Today, astronomers recognize 88 constellations. Constellations are often used to locate individual stars.

Stars seem to move slowly across the sky. Different constellations and star groups appear overhead at different times of the year. The constellations visible in the Northern Hemisphere are different from those visible in the Southern Hemisphere. However, the stars are relatively stationary. It is the movements of Earth that are making it look like the stars are changing position in the sky.

1 DEFINE: What is a constellation?

Orion the Hunter In the Northern Hemisphere, Orion the Hunter is a constellation seen in the evening sky from November to March. It rises in the east.

Three bright stars make up Orion's belt. Betelgeuse, a red giant star, is under Orion's arm. Rigel, a giant blue-white star, is in Orion's knee.

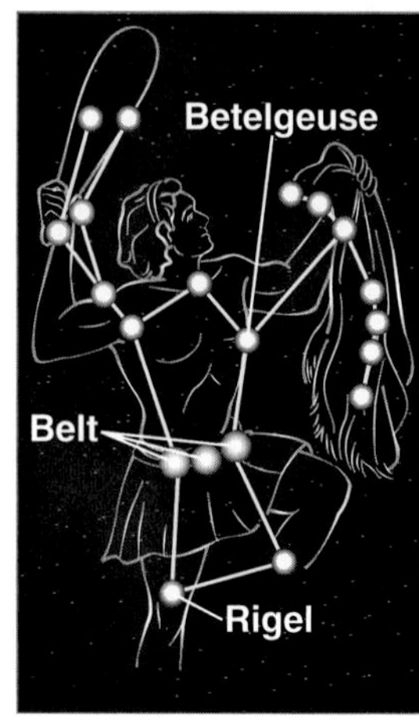

▲ **Figure 4-25** Orion

2 NAME: What are two stars in Orion?

The Bear Constellations One of the easiest constellations to find in the northern sky is Ursa Major. Its name means "big bear."

Ancient peoples thought they could see the shape of a large bear in the constellation. The Big Dipper is part of Ursa Major. It is made up of seven stars, three in the handle, four in the cup. Two bright stars in the cup of the Big Dipper are called the pointers. They point to Polaris, which is also known as the North Star.

Ursa Minor, meaning "little bear," is another constellation in the northern sky. Ursa Minor is also called the Little Dipper. Polaris is the first star in the handle of the Little Dipper.

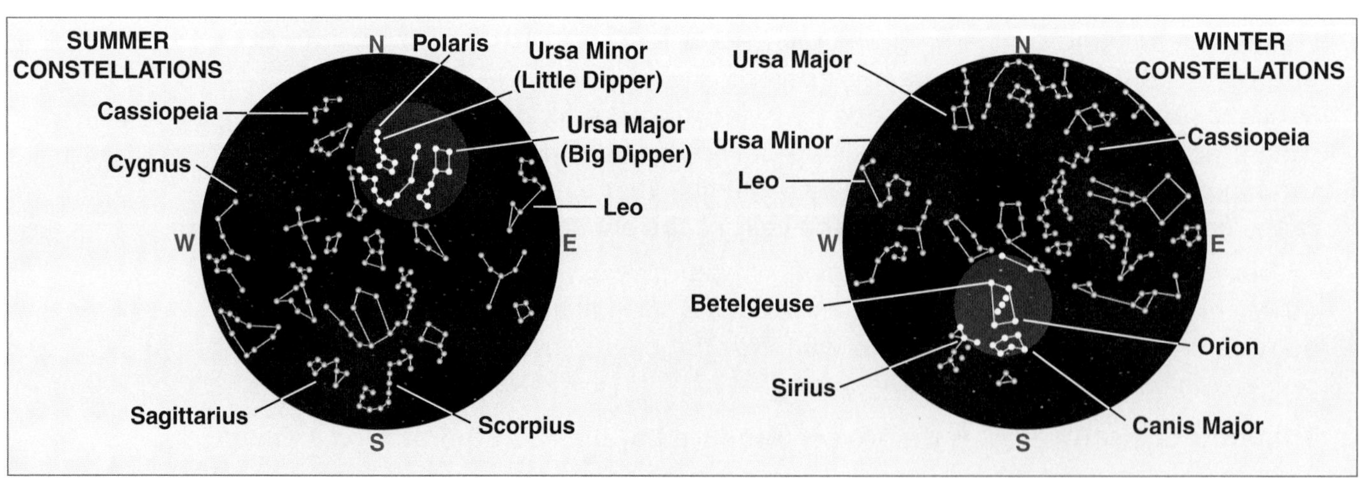

▲ **Figure 4-24** The summer and winter skies in the Northern Hemisphere

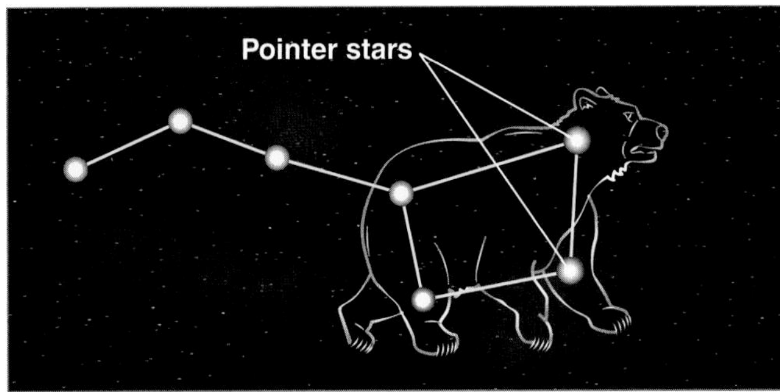

▲ **Figure 4-26** The Big Dipper is in the constellation Ursa Major.

 **NAME:** What does the name Ursa Major mean?

CHECKING CONCEPTS

1. What are patterns of stars called?
2. How many constellations are there?
3. What is the Big Dipper?
4. What is the name of the North Star?
5. What is the name of the red star in Orion?

THINKING CRITICALLY

6. **INFER:** Why are the two bright stars in the cup of the Big Dipper called the pointers?
7. **INFER:** Although other stars appear to rotate in the night sky, Polaris does not seem to change position over the North Pole. Why do you think this is?
8. **ANALYZE:** Why do stars in constellations appear close even though they may be very far apart?

BUILDING SCIENCE SKILLS

Researching The zodiac is a band of constellations that lie along the ecliptic. Over a year's time, the Sun seems to trace a path in the sky along the ecliptic. What is the ecliptic? How many different constellations make up the zodiac? Do research on one of the constellations. What is the story behind it? Write your findings in a report.

Real-Life Science

IDENTIFYING THE CONSTELLATIONS

The oldest known astronomical texts were written by the ancient Sumerians. They recorded the names of constellations still known today as the lion, the bull, and the scorpion. The ancient Greek and Chinese peoples had different names for some of the same constellations. The ancient Egyptians named about 25 constellations, including the crocodile and the hippopotamus.

Astronomers continued naming the constellations right up until the twentieth century. In 1930, an official listing of 88 constellations was published by the International Astronomical Union. One of these is Leo the Lion.

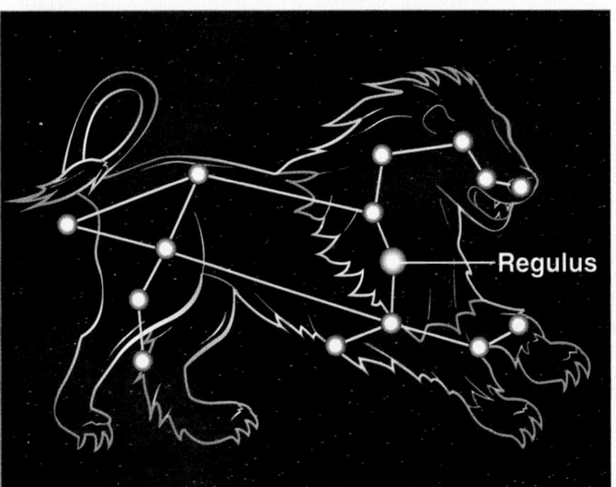

▲ **Figure 4-27** The constellation called Leo is in the zodiac between Cancer and Virgo. Its brightest star is called Regulus.

To find the constellations, go out on a dark night and scan the sky. If you do not already know geographical directions in your area, learn them. This will help you use the sky charts published in books and magazines. To orient yourself, try to find the brightest stars and identify them. They can help you locate other star groups.

Orion is one of the easiest constellations to see in the winter sky. Look for Betelgeuse and Rigel. The three stars in Orion's belt point to Sirius in Canis Major (the Dog Star) and Aldebaran in Taurus, the bull constellation.

Thinking Critically How could you find out geographical directions in your area?

4-10 What are galaxies?

Objective

Describe the three main types of galaxies.

Key Terms

galaxy (GAL-uhk-see)**:** huge collection of stars, gas, and dust that travel together through space

elliptical galaxy: galaxy shaped like a ball or slightly flattened ball

irregular galaxy: galaxy with no definite shape

spiral galaxy: galaxy shaped like a flattened disk with spiral arms

Galaxies Stars appear as small points of light. Among these points of light, you can also see some fuzzy patches. Some of these patches are nebulae, or clouds of gas and dust. Others are galaxies. A **galaxy** is a huge collection of stars, gas, and dust that travel together through space. Using the newest telescopes, astronomers can see billions of galaxies. Galaxies are the building blocks of the universe.

Galaxies have different shapes. Astronomers classify, or group, galaxies based on shape. There are three kinds of galaxies: elliptical, irregular, and spiral.

1 DEFINE: What are galaxies?

Elliptical and Irregular Galaxies Some galaxies have rounded shapes. These galaxies are known as **elliptical galaxies.** Elliptical galaxies can also look like slightly flattened balls. The stars in an elliptical galaxy are usually older than the stars in other kinds of galaxies. Elliptical galaxies are larger than irregular galaxies but smaller than spiral galaxies.

Galaxies with no regular shape are called **irregular galaxies.** Irregular galaxies are smaller and fainter than elliptical and spiral galaxies. They may be the most common kind of galaxy.

 COMPARE: Which is more common, an elliptical galaxy or an irregular galaxy?

Spiral Galaxies **Spiral galaxies** are shaped like flattened disks. They usually have one or more spiral arms that branch out from their centers. One type of spiral galaxy is called the barred spiral. The arms of barred spirals branch out from the end of a short bar made up of stars and gas.

 DESCRIBE: What special feature do spiral galaxies have?

The Milky Way Galaxy All the stars you can see in the night sky with your unaided eye are part of our home galaxy, called the Milky Way Galaxy. Our solar system is in the Milky Way Galaxy.

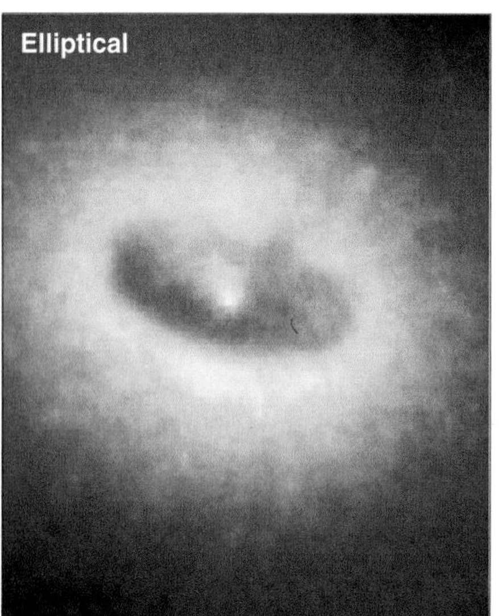

▲ **Figure 4-28** Galaxies come in three basic shapes: elliptical, irregular, and spiral.

The Milky Way Galaxy is part of a group of more than 20 other galaxies. Together, these galaxies are known as the Local Group.

The Milky Way Galaxy is a spiral galaxy. It contains about 100,000 billion stars. At its center is a huge bulge of stars about 10,000 light years across. The distance from edge to edge of the spiral arms is about 100,000 light years. The Sun is in a spiral arm about two-thirds of the way from the center of the Milky Way Galaxy.

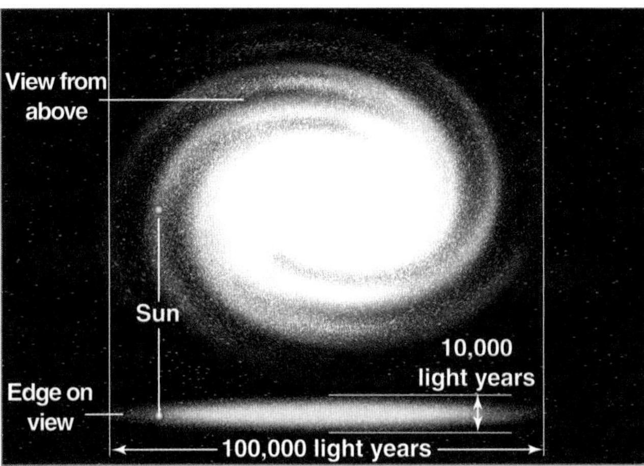

▲ **Figure 4-29** The Milky Way Galaxy

4 CLASSIFY: What kind of galaxy is the Milky Way Galaxy?

The Milky Way Band There is a band of stars stretching across the sky. Ancient peoples called this band the Milky Way. They thought it looked like a river of milk. When you look at the Milky Way band of stars, you are seeing the flattened disk of the Milky Way Galaxy, where the spiral arms lie.

▲ **Figure 4-30** Part of the Milky Way band of stars in the sky

5 IDENTIFY: What is the Milky Way band?

Galactic Neighbors Most galaxies are millions of light years from Earth. For example, the great spiral galaxy in the constellation Andromeda, seen on the far right in Figure 4-28, is 2 million light years away. The Andromeda Galaxy is much larger than our own galaxy. You can see it without a telescope.

The closest galaxies to Earth are the Large Magellanic Cloud and the Small Magellanic Cloud. These irregular galaxies are 160,000 and 200,000 light years away, respectively.

6 IDENTIFY: Which galaxies are closest to the Milky Way Galaxy?

CHECKING CONCEPTS

1. Galaxies are made up of billions of ___________.
2. Astronomers classify galaxies on the basis of their ___________.
3. There are ___________ main types of galaxies.
4. The oldest stars are found in ___________ galaxies.
5. Stretching across the sky is the ___________ band of stars.

THINKING CRITICALLY

6. LIST: What are the three main types of galaxies?
7. CALCULATE: If all the galaxies in the Local Group have about the same number of stars, about how many stars are in the Local Group?

INTERPRETING VISUALS

Use Figure 4-31 to complete the following exercise.

8. CLASSIFY: Classify each of the galaxies shown as spiral, elliptical, or irregular.

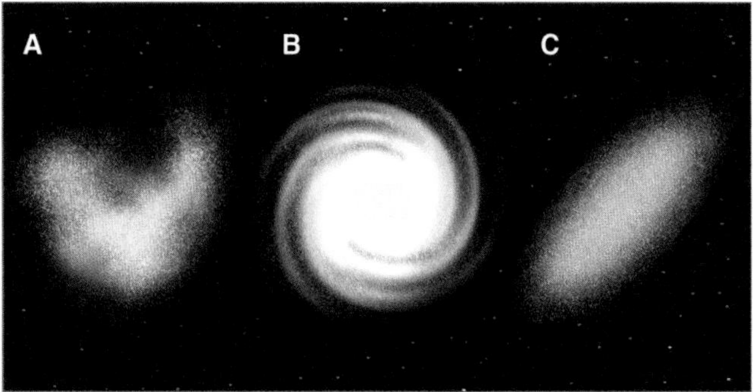

▲ **Figure 4-31**

LAB ACTIVITY
Counting Galaxies

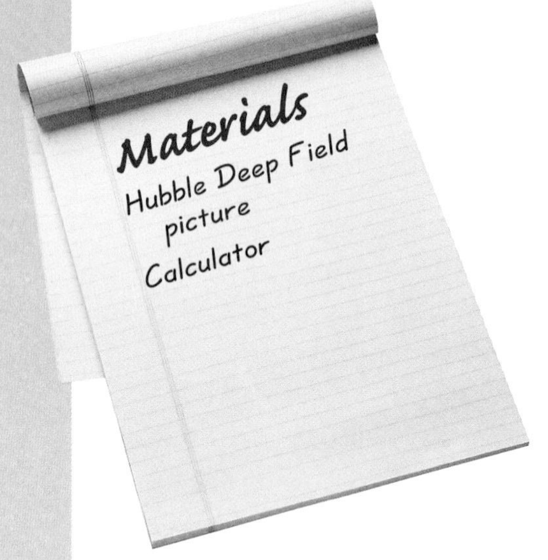

BACKGROUND

The universe is very large. It has a vast number of galaxies that are each home to billions of stars like our Sun. The Hubble Deep Field picture represents only a tiny part of the whole sky. More than 30 million of these pictures would be needed to cover the entire sky.

PURPOSE

In this activity, you will estimate how many galaxies are found in a tiny fragment of the sky.

PROCEDURE

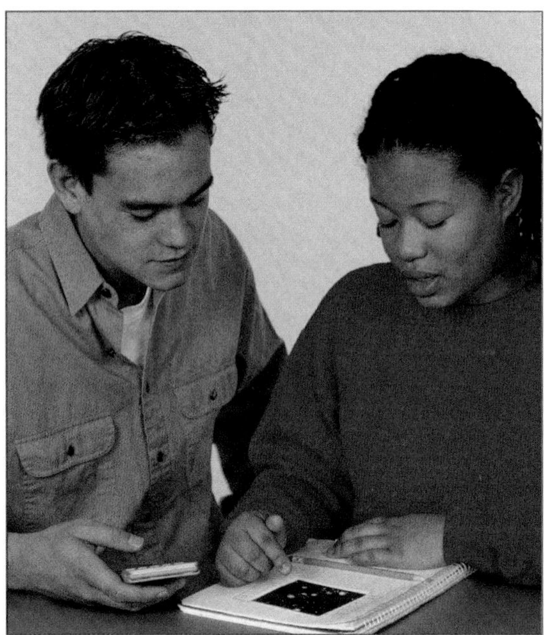

STEP 1 Examine the picture given to you by your teacher.

1. Your teacher will divide you into four groups. Examine the picture given to your group by your teacher. It was taken by the Hubble Space Telescope.

2. Copy the chart in Figure 4-33. Then, count the number of galaxies in your picture and record the number in your chart.

3. Your picture is a part of a larger picture. The larger picture is four times the size of your picture. The other groups are looking at the other three parts. How many galaxies do you think the entire picture contains? Estimate how many and record this number in your chart.

4. Trade the number of galaxies you counted in your picture with numbers arrived at by the groups that are counting the other three pictures. Record the numbers in your chart.

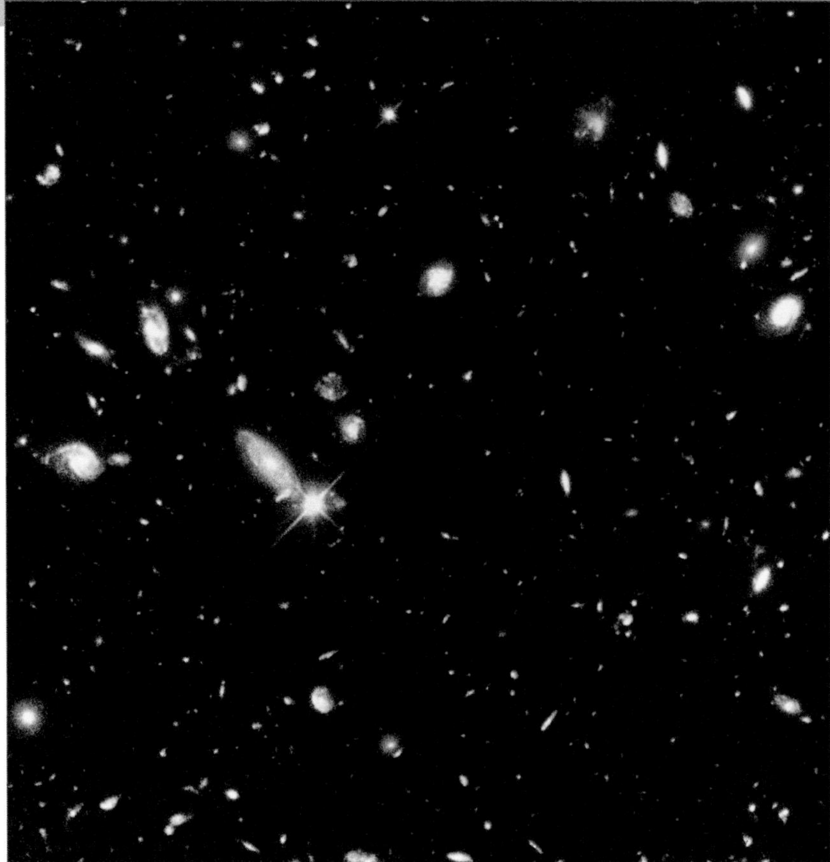

▲ **Figure 4-32** The Hubble Deep Field image

My Data Chart	
Number of galaxies in your picture	
Estimate the total number of galaxies. (Your number times 4.)	
Number of galaxies in group 2's picture	
Number of galaxies in group 3's picture	
Number of galaxies in group 4's picture	
Total of all pictures	

▲ **Figure 4-33** Use a copy of this chart to record your calculations.

CONCLUSIONS

1. **OBSERVE:** How many galaxies did you count?
2. **ESTIMATE:** How many galaxies are there in the total picture?
3. **COMPARE:** How did your estimate compare with the actual count when you totaled the counts from the four groups?
4. **INFER:** For what other things might you use this estimating technique?

4-11 What else do we know about the universe?

Modeling the Expanding Universe

HANDS-ON ACTIVITY

1. Partially inflate a round balloon. Twist the opening and hold it shut with a paper clip or a rubber band.
2. With a marking pen, draw four dots on the surface of the balloon in a square pattern. Label them *A*, *B*, *C*, *D*.
3. Using a string, measure the distance between each of the four dots (*A* to *B*, *A* to *C*, *A* to *D*, *B* to *C*, *B* to *D*, and *C* to *D*). Hold the string next to a ruler and record each measurement in a table.
4. Inflate the balloon to its fullest and tie the end.
5. Repeat your measurements and record the distances.

THINK ABOUT IT: What happened to the distances between the dots as you inflated the balloon? Did some dots move farther apart than others did? Why? Suppose the balloon represents the universe. How does this activity show what is happening to the universe and to the galaxies in it?

Objective

Describe some unusual features of the universe.

Key Terms

Big Bang: explosion that may have begun the universe many billions of years ago

black hole: massive star that has collapsed and whose gravity is so powerful that it pulls in everything, even light

quasar: continuous burst of brilliant light and enormous energy from a very massive black hole

How Big Is the Universe The universe is everything, including the Sun, its solar system, and the many billions of stars in all the galaxies. It is everything that exists in space, even space itself. The distances between stars and galaxies are vast. If you could travel at the speed of light (300,000 km/s), it would take you more than 10 billion years to cross the part of space astronomers can see with their telescopes.

1 EXPLAIN: What does the universe include?

The Big Bang Scientists think that the entire universe was once contained in a single, very hot, very dense point. Between 10 and 15 billion years ago, a huge explosion caused it to start expanding rapidly. This explosion is called the **Big Bang.**

As the universe expanded, it cooled. Atoms and molecules formed. Gradually, the atoms and molecules collected into the objects that make up today's universe, which is still expanding.

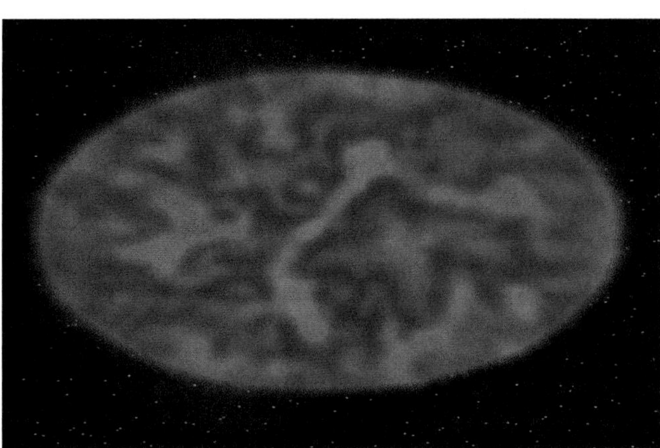

▲ **Figure 4-34** The radio waves caused by the Big Bang are represented in this picture by the pink ripples. These waves can still be detected today.

2 EXPLAIN: What is the Big Bang?

Black Holes and Quasars The universe is filled with many strange objects. For example, a black hole can form when a very massive star collapses in on itself. A **black hole** is an object so dense that nothing pulled into it by gravity can come out.

A black hole appears black because not even light can escape from its surface. All of the matter at the center of a black hole is squeezed into an infinitely tiny point.

Black holes are often found at the centers of galaxies. These black holes can be millions of times heavier than stars. When matter falls into these extremely massive black holes, tremendous bursts of light and energy are released. Astronomers call these bursts **quasars.** Quasars glow brighter than the light of a thousand galaxies.

ANALYZE: How are black holes and quasars related?

Colliding Galaxies The whole universe is in motion. Planets swirl around stars. Stars swirl around galaxies. Galaxies spread out into deep space. Sometimes two or more galaxies approach each other like colliding cars. The distance between stars is so great that the two galaxies pass right through each other like ghosts. However, gravity will sometimes pull galaxies like these together. They form into a single, bigger galaxy.

EXPLAIN: How can galaxies merge?

CHECKING CONCEPTS

1. About how many stars are in the universe?
2. What happens when stars fall into a black hole?
3. What are colliding galaxies?
4. How long ago did the universe form?

THINKING CRITICALLY

5. **EXPLAIN:** Why are the galaxies moving outward?
6. **INFER:** Do you think the galaxies will continue to move outward?
7. **ANALYZE:** If you had a spaceship that could travel at the speed of light, could you visit another galaxy?

DESIGNING AN EXPERIMENT

Design an experiment to solve the following problem. Include a hypothesis, variables, a procedure with materials, a type of data to study, and a way to record your data.

PROBLEM: The gravity field near a black hole is very strong. Any matter that gets near the black hole is sucked in by its powerful gravity. Design an experiment that models what might happen to matter as it passes near a black hole. Will it fall straight in or spiral around it first? Indicate why you chose one or the other.

Integrating Physical Science

TOPICS: forces, waves

GRAVITATIONAL WAVES

▲ **Figure 4-35** A gravitational wave spreads out a little like ripples in a pond.

Energy travels freely across the universe. We only see light waves, but scientific instruments can see radio waves, X-rays, ultraviolet light, and other forms of radiation. The energy in gravity also travels across the universe. Unless you are very close to an object, the gravity, or the attraction, you feel from it is very faint. Very massive objects have a stronger gravitational attraction than less massive objects do.

If all objects in the universe stayed still, the attraction of gravity would remain the same at all times. However, stars and galaxies do not stand still. When they move, they are believed to produce ripples in the gravitational field that travel across the universe as gravity waves. The waves would spread out in a manner similar to the water waves in a pond when a pebble is thrown in. However, instead of just moving across a flat surface like the pond waves, gravity waves would likely move in all directions.

Thinking Critically How could gravitational attraction cause waves?

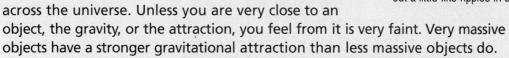

Integrating Mathematics

THE Big IDEA

How can we estimate the size of the universe?

The universe has been expanding since the Big Bang. It is not expanding into anything, however. Instead, space itself is stretching out, and carrying the galaxies with it. The American astronomer Edwin Hubble was the first to present this idea. In 1929, he showed that the galaxies were rushing away from each other.

Hubble studied the brightness of a class of stars known as Cepheid stars. Using these stars, he was able to measure how far away certain galaxies were. He was also able to figure out how fast the galaxies were moving by examining their red shift. Hubble discovered that the galaxies closest to us are moving slower than the galaxies farther away. He also discovered that a galaxy's speed, or velocity (V), is directly related to its distance (D) from us. This relationship can be expressed using a number called the Hubble constant (H).

Knowing that the universe is expanding is very useful to astronomers. By measuring the velocity of a distant galaxy, they can determine its distance. Since the universe must be large enough to hold every galaxy, astronomers can use the most distant galaxies known to estimate the size of the universe.

However, astronomers have discovered that it is very difficult to give an exact value for Hubble's constant. This number could be as low as 15 and as high as 30 km/s/mly (kilometers per second per million light years). Unless we can determine this value exactly, we can only give a range of possible sizes for the universe.

Look at the photos on these two pages. Then, follow the directions in the Science Log to learn more about "the big idea." ✦

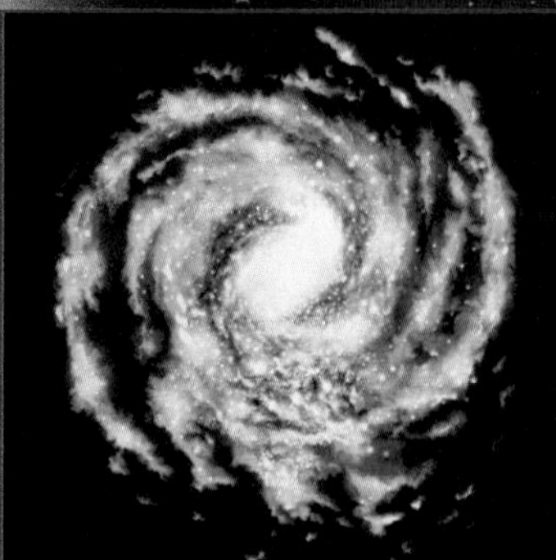

The Milky Way
Earth and the other planets of our solar system are located about 50,000 light years from the center of the Milky Way Galaxy, on one of its spiral arms.

The Small Magellanic Cloud
About 200,000 light years from Earth lies the Small Magellanic Cloud. By the 1920s, astronomers had realized that this fuzzy cloud of light was actually a distant galaxy.

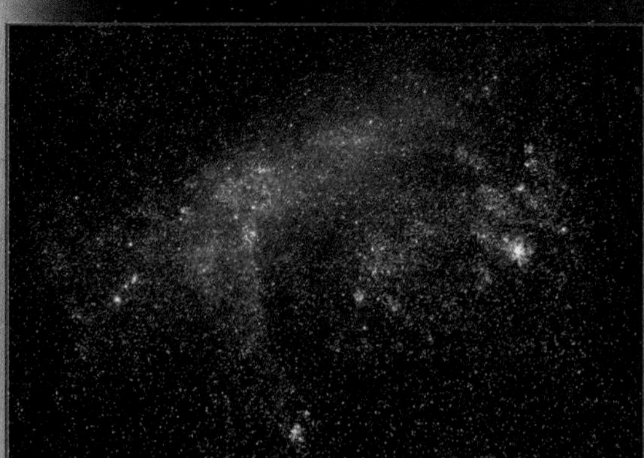

The Large Magellanic Cloud
The Large Magellanic Cloud is an irregular galaxy visible only in the Southern Hemisphere. It is named after Portuguese explorer Ferdinand Magellan. Magellan's crew were the first Europeans to describe this cluster of stars that is more than 160,000 light years from Earth.

Andromeda

The Andromeda Galaxy is the most distant galaxy that can be seen from Earth without a telescope. This spiral galaxy lies about 2 million light years from Earth.

With the **Big Bang** explosion, the universe was created and began to expand outward.

WRITING ACTIVITY

Science Log

How would you like to take a trip through the universe and visit other parts of the Milky Way Galaxy, the neighboring Magellanic Clouds, and other places? You can! To get started on your trip, go to www.conceptsandchallenges.com. After you complete your trip, write a story for a travel magazine. Tell others how to prepare for the trip and what to look for on the way.

DO THE MATH!

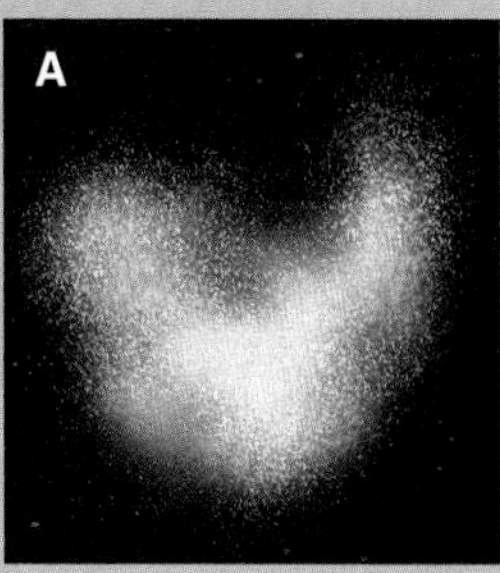

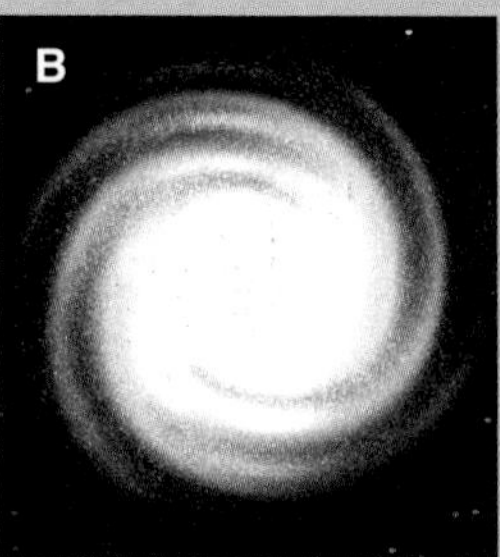

▲ **Figure 4-36**

The two galaxies shown in Figure 4-36 appear to be the same size. They are not. One is simply farther away. You can tell which galaxy is bigger than the other by measuring how far each galaxy is from Earth.

STEP 1 Use the following formula to determine each galaxy's distance:

$$D = \frac{V}{H}$$

Distance (D) is equal to the velocity (V) of the galaxy divided by the Hubble constant. (H). Velocity, or speed, is measured in kilometers per second (km/s). Let Hubble's constant here be as 20 km/sec/mly.

STEP 2 Find out how far Galaxy A is from Earth. The velocity for Galaxy A is 1,000 km/s.

Galaxy A:

$$D = \frac{1{,}000 \text{ km/s}}{20 \text{ km/s/mly}} = \underline{\hspace{2cm}} \text{ mly}$$

STEP 3 Find out how far Galaxy B is from Earth. The velocity for Galaxy B is 4,000 km/s.

Galaxy B:

$$D = \underline{\hspace{2cm}} = \underline{\hspace{2cm}} \text{ mly}$$

So, which galaxy is farther from Earth, A or B? Explain your choice.

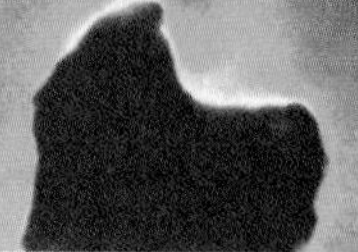

Chapter 4 Challenges

Chapter Summary

Lesson 4-1

- Most stars are hot, glowing balls of hydrogen and helium gases. The Sun is one of many billions of stars. A star forms from a **protostar** in a cloudy **nebula.**

Lessons 4-2 and 4-3

- **Spectroscopy** is the study of light from objects in space. A **spectrum** helps us identify a star's elements.
- The measure of a star's brightness is its **magnitude.** There is apparent magnitude and absolute magnitude.

Lessons 4-4 and 4-5

- An H-R diagram shows how a star's absolute magnitude is related to its surface temperature.
- Most stars, like the Sun, are **main sequence stars** on the H-R diagram.
- **Red giants** and **supergiants** are huge, bright stars. **White dwarfs** are small, hot stars.
- Stars begin life as protostars. Then, they enter the main sequence stage. Small and medium-sized stars become white dwarfs, then black dwarfs. Very massive stars explode as **supernovas** and become neutron stars or black holes.

Lessons 4-6, 4-7, and 4-8

- The Sun has a **core** and an atmosphere. The Sun's atmosphere consists of the **photosphere,** the **chromosphere,** and the **corona.**
- **Sunspots** are dark, cooler areas on the Sun's surface. **Prominences** are streams of gas that arch above the Sun's surface. **Solar flares** send out energy and charged particles.
- The Sun has nuclear reactions called **fusion.** During fusion, hydrogen atoms combine to form helium.

Lessons 4-9, 4-10, and 4-11

- **Constellations** are groups of stars that form patterns in the sky.
- **Galaxies** are **elliptical, irregular,** or **spiral** in shape. The Milky Way Galaxy is a spiral galaxy.
- The Milky Way band of stars is in the Milky Way Galaxy.
- The universe is all that exists. **Black holes** pull in even light. **Quasars** emit tremendous energy.

Key Term Challenges

Big Bang (p. 118)
binary stars (p. 96)
black hole (p. 118)
chromosphere (p. 106)
constellation (p. 112)
core (p. 106)
corona (p. 106)
elliptical galaxy (p. 114)
fusion (p. 110)
galaxy (p. 114)
irregular galaxy (p. 114)
magnitude (p. 100)
main sequence star (p. 102)
nebula (p. 96)
nova (p. 104)
nucleus (p. 110)
photosphere (p. 106)
prominence (p. 108)
protostar (p. 96)
quasar (p. 118)
red giant (p. 102)
solar flare (p. 108)
spectrograph (p. 98)
spectroscopy (p. 98)
spectrum (p. 98)
spiral galaxy (p. 114)
star (p. 96)
star cluster (p. 96)
sunspot (p. 108)
supergiant (p. 102)
supernova (p. 104)
white dwarf (p. 102)

MATCHING **Write the Key Term from above that best matches each description.**

1. inner layer of the Sun's atmosphere
2. grouping of stars that form a pattern in the sky
3. cloud of dust and gas in space
4. measure of a star's brightness
5. dark, cooler areas on the Sun's surface
6. large group of stars in a galaxy
7. very small, hot star
8. center, or core, of an atom
9. device that measures the spectrum of an object
10. galaxy with no definite shape

IDENTIFYING WORD RELATIONSHIPS **Explain how the words in each pair are related. Write your answers in complete sentences.**

11. nova, supernova
12. star, protostar
13. binary star, star cluster
14. red giant, white dwarf
15. elliptical galaxy, spiral galaxy

Content Challenges TEST PREP

MULTIPLE CHOICE **Write the letter of the term or phrase that best completes each statement.**

1. The Sun is only one of billions of
   a. nebulas.
   b. stars.
   c. galaxies.
   d. constellations.

2. In Einstein's equation, $E = mc^2$, c is
   a. energy.
   b. mass.
   c. the speed of light.
   d. the amount of matter.

3. The Milky Way Galaxy is
   a. a spiral galaxy.
   b. an elliptical galaxy.
   c. an irregular galaxy.
   d. a spherical galaxy.

4. The hottest stars are
   a. red.
   b. blue.
   c. yellow.
   d. orange.

5. The Sun's energy is produced in the
   a. corona.
   b. photosphere.
   c. chromosphere.
   d. core.

6. Supernova 1987A occurred in
   a. the Milky Way Galaxy.
   b. the Large Magellanic Cloud.
   c. the Andromeda Galaxy.
   d. the star cluster M13.

7. The actual brightness of a star is its
   a. apparent magnitude.
   b. first-magnitude.
   c. sixth-magnitude.
   d. absolute magnitude.

8. The spinning of the Sun on its axis causes
   a. solar flares.
   b. sunspot movement.
   c. prominences.
   d. fusion.

9. The outermost layer of the Sun's atmosphere is the
   a. photosphere.
   b. chromosphere.
   c. corona.
   d. core.

10. Betelgeuse is a star found in
    a. the Big Dipper.
    b. the Little Dipper.
    c. Ursa Major.
    d. Orion.

TRUE/FALSE **Write *true* if the statement is true. If the statement is false, change the underlined term to make the statement true.**

11. The gravity of a black <u>dwarf</u> is so great that nothing can escape.
12. The main features of the universe are <u>galaxies</u>.
13. The most common element in most stars is <u>helium</u>.
14. Sunspots are dark, <u>cooler</u> areas on the surface of the Sun.
15. The brightness of most stars increases as the star's surface temperature <u>decreases</u>.
16. The Sun and all the planets in the solar system are in the <u>Milky Way Galaxy</u>.
17. Each <u>element</u> gives off its own spectrum of light.
18. To separate white light into the colors of the rainbow, scientists can use a <u>prism</u>.
19. Galaxies with no regular shape are called <u>elliptical</u> galaxies.
20. Streams of gas shooting from the Sun's surface are called <u>prominences</u>.

Concept Challenges TEST PREP

WRITTEN RESPONSE **Answer each of the following questions in complete sentences.**

1. COMPARE: How is a nova similar to a supernova?
2. EXPLAIN: What happens to material in the center of a nebula?
3. INFER: What forces cause streams of gases to shoot high above the Sun's surface?
4. INFER: What holds the stars together in a galaxy?
5. INFER: How does the Sun produce energy?
6. ANALYZE: Where are the electrically charged particles that stream out from the Sun created?
7. CONTRAST: What is the difference between a red giant star and a supergiant star?
8. INFER: Which is the densest part of the Sun?
9. ANALYZE: How do astronomers find out the chemical makeup of a star?
10. INFER: What is meant by the "birth" and "death" of a star?
11. INFER: Why can fossil fuels be called "stored sunlight"?
12. ANALYZE: Why is an old main sequence star made up of a larger percentage of helium than a young main sequence star?

INTERPRETING VISUALS **Use Figure 4-37 to answer the following questions.**

13. What is the center part of the Sun called?
14. What three layers make up the Sun's atmosphere?
15. What is the temperature of the corona?
16. About how many degrees Celsius hotter is the chromosphere than the photosphere?

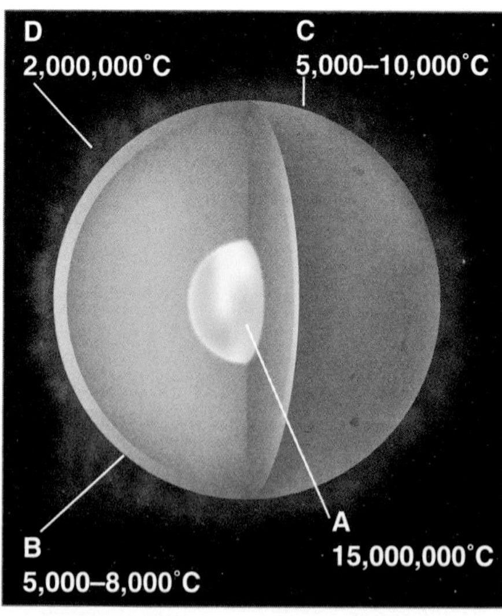

▲ Figure 4-37

Appendix A Metric System

The Metric System and SI Units

The metric system is an international system of measurement based on units of ten. More than 90% of the nations of the world use the metric system. In the United States, both the English system and the metric system are used.

The *Système International*, or SI, has been used as the international measurement system since 1960. The SI is a modernized version of the metric system. Like the metric system, the SI is a decimal system based on units of ten. When you want to change from one unit in the metric system to another unit, you multiply or divide by a multiple of ten.

- When you change from a smaller unit to a larger unit, you divide.
- When you change from a larger unit to a smaller unit, you multiply.

METRIC UNITS		
LENGTH	SYMBOL	RELATIONSHIP
kilometer	km	1 km = 1,000 m
meter	m	1 m = 100 cm
centimeter	cm	1 cm = 10 mm
millimeter	mm	1 mm = 0.1 cm
AREA	SYMBOL	
square kilometer	km^2	1 km^2 = 1,000,000 m^2
square meter	m^2	1 m^2 = 1,000,000 mm^2
square centimeter	cm^2	1 cm^2 = 0.0001 m^2
square millimeter	mm^2	1 mm^2 = 0.000001 m^2
VOLUME	SYMBOL	
cubic meter	m^3	1 m^3 = 1,000,000 cm^3
cubic centimeter	cm^3	1 cm^3 = 0.000001 m^3
liter	L	1 L = 1,000 mL
milliliter	mL	1 mL = 0.001 L
MASS	SYMBOL	
metric ton	t	1 t = 1,000 kg
kilogram	kg	1 kg = 1,000 g
gram	g	1 g = 1,000 mg
centigram	cg	1 cg = 10 mg
milligram	mg	1 mg = 0.001 g
TEMPERATURE	SYMBOL	
Kelvin	K	
degree Celsius	°C	

▲ Figure 1

COMMON METRIC PREFIXES			
micro-	0.000001 or 1/1,000,000	deka-	10
milli-	0.001 or 1/1,000	hecto-	100
centi-	0.01 or 1/100	kilo-	1,000
deci-	0.1 or 1/10	mega-	1,000,000

▲ Figure 2

METRIC-STANDARD EQUIVALENTS	
SI to English	**English to SI**
LENGTH	
1 kilometer = 0.621 mile (mi)	1 mi = 1.61 km
1 meter = 1.094 yards (yd)	1 yd = 0.914 m
1 meter = 3.28 feet (ft)	1 ft = 0.305 m
1 centimeter = 0.394 inch (in.)	1 in. = 2.54 cm
1 millimeter = 0.039 inch	1 in. = 25.4 mm
AREA	
1 square kilometer = 0.3861 square mile	1 mi^2 = 2.590 km^2
1 square meter = 1.1960 square yards	1 yd^2 = 0.8361 m^2
1 square meter = 10.763 square feet	1 ft^2 = 0.0929 m^2
1 square centimeter = 0.155 square inch	1 in.^{2} = 6.452 cm^2
VOLUME	
1 cubic meter = 1.3080 cubic yards	1 yd^3 = 0.7646 m^3
1 cubic meter = 35.315 cubic feet	1 ft^3 = 0.0283 m^3
1 cubic centimeter = 0.0610 cubic inch	1 in.^{3} = 16.39 cm^3
1 liter = 0.2642 gallon (gal)	1 gal = 3.79 L
1 liter = 1.06 quarts (qt)	1 qt = 0.946 L
1 liter = 2.11 pints (pt)	1 pt = 0.47 L
1 milliliter = 0.034 fluid ounce (fl oz)	1 fl oz = 29.57 mL
MASS	
1 metric ton = 0.984 ton	1 ton = 1.016 t
1 kilogram = 2.205 pounds (lb)	1 lb = 0.4536 kg
1 gram = 0.0353 ounce (oz)	1 oz = 28.35 g
TEMPERATURE	
Celsius = 5/9(°F – 32)	Fahrenheit = 9/5°C + 32
0°C = 32°F (Freezing point of water)	72°F = 22°C (Room temperature)
100°C = 212°F (Boiling point of water)	98.6°F = 37°C (Human body temperature)
Kelvin = (°F + 459.67)/1.8	Fahrenheit = (K × 1.8) – 459.67

▲ Figure 3

Appendix B Science Terms

Analyzing Science Terms

You can often unlock the meaning of an unfamiliar science term by analyzing its word parts. Prefixes and suffixes, for example, each carry a meaning that comes from a word root. This word root usually comes from the Latin or Greek language. The following list of prefixes and suffixes provides clues to the meaning of many science terms.

WORD PART	MEANING	EXAMPLE
astr-, aster-	star	astronomy
bar-, baro-	weight, pressure	barometer
batho-, bathy-	depth	batholith, bathysphere
circum-	around	circum-Pacific, circumpolar
-cline	lean, slope	anticline, syncline
eco-	environment	ecology, ecosystem
epi-	on	epicenter
ex-, exo-	out, outside of	exosphere, exfoliation, extrusion
geo-	earth	geode, geology, geomagnetic
-graph	write, writing	seismograph
hydro-	water	hydrosphere
hypo-	under	hypothesis
iso-	equal	isoscope, isostasy, isotope
-lith, -lithic	stone	Neolithic, regolith
magn-	great, large	magnitude
mar-	sea	marine
meso-	middle	mesosphere, Mesozoic
meta-	among, change	metamorphic, metamorphism
micro-	small	microquake
-morph, -morphic	form	metamorphic
neo-	new	Neolithic
paleo-	old	paleontology, Paleozoic
ped-, pedo-	ground, soil	pediment
peri-	around	perigee, perihelion
-ose	carbohydrate	glucose, cellulose
seism-, seismo-	shake, earthquake	seismic, seismograph
sol-	sun	solar, solstice
spectro-	look at, examine	spectroscope, spectrum
-sphere	ball, globe	hemisphere, lithosphere
strati-, strato-	spread, layer	stratification, stratovolcano
terra-	earth, land	terracing, terrane
thermo-	heat	thermosphere
top-, topo-	place	topographic
tropo-	turn, respond to	tropopause, troposphere

▲ Figure 4

Appendix C Astronomy Tables

PLANETARY DATA				
Planet	Diameter (km)	Time for One Spin on Axis	Time for One Orbit of the Sun	Average Distance From the Sun (km)
Mercury	4,880	58.65 days	87.97 days	57.9 million
Venus	12,103.6	224.7 days	224.70 days	108.21 million
Earth	12,756	23.93 hours	365.26 days	149.6 million
Mars	6,794	24.66 hours	686.98 days	227.9 million
Jupiter	142,984	9.93 hours	11.86 years	778.57 million
Saturn	120,536	10.66 hours	29.4 years	1.43 billion
Uranus	51,118	17.24 hours	84.01 years	2.87 billion
Neptune	49,528	16.11 hours	164.78 years	4.5 billion
Pluto	2,390	6.39 days	247.67 years	5.87 billion

▲ Figure 5

KEY ROBOT PROBES TO PLANETS, COMETS, AND ASTEROIDS				
Probe	Type	Target	Encounter	Achievements
Pioneer 10	Flyby	Jupiter	1973	First to cross Asteroid Belt; took close-up photos of Jupiter
Mariner 10	Flyby	Mercury	1974–1975	Only probe to Mercury
Venera 9	Orbiter/lander	Venus	1975	First views of surface
Viking 1 and 2	Orbiters/landers	Mars	1976	Photographed surface; searched for life
Pioneer 11	Flyby	Saturn	1979	First detailed views
Voyager 1 and 2	Flybys	Jupiter Saturn Uranus Neptune	1979 1980–1981 1986 1989	Details of all four planetary systems; Voyager 2 was first probe to Uranus and Neptune
Giotto	Flyby	Comet	1986	First close-up view of nucleus
Galileo	Flyby/orbiter	Gaspra Jupiter	1991 and 1995	First flyby of an asteroid; first orbit of Jupiter
Mars Global Surveyor	Orbiter	Mars	1997	Mapped surface and searched for water
Mars Odyssey	Orbiter	Mars	2001	Mapped surface and searched for water
Cassini	Flyby/orbiter	Saturn	2004	Detailed studies of the planet and its rings

▲ Figure 6

SOLAR ECLIPSES THROUGH THE YEAR 2030		
Date	**Duration of Totality (minutes)**	**Location**
Nov. 23, 2003	4.4	Central America
April 8, 2005	0.7	South Pacific Ocean
March 29, 2006	4.1	Africa, Asia Minor, Russia
August 1, 2008	2.4	Arctic Ocean, Siberia, China
July 22, 2009	6.6	India, China, South Pacific
July 11, 2010	5.3	South America
Nov. 13, 2012	4.0	Australia, South America
Nov. 3, 2013	1.7	North and South America, Africa
March 20, 2015	2.78	Europe, Africa
March 9, 2016	4.15	Asia, Australia
August 1, 2018	2.7	North America, Europe
July 22, 2019	4.5	Asia, Pacific Ocean
Dec. 14, 2020	2.2	Pacific and Atlantic oceans, South America
Dec. 4, 2021	0.38	Antarctica, Southern Africa
April 20, 2023	1.3	Asia, Australia
April 8, 2024	4.5	North and Central America
August 12, 2026	2.3	North America, Europe
August 2, 2027	6.4	Africa, Asia
July 22, 2028	5.1	Asia, Australia
Nov. 23, 2030	3.7	South America, Africa

◀ Figure 7

Appendix C Astronomy Tables (continued)

Regularly Occurring Meteor Showers

Occasionally, 60 or more meteors flash across the sky in a single hour or two. These light displays are called meteor showers. They occur when Earth crosses a comet's orbit and groups of meteoroids from the comet's tail collide with Earth's atmosphere. The dates in the table below are peak dates. For most showers, the meteors can be seen for a few weeks, but the peak occurs somewhere around the middle of the time period.

METEOR SHOWERS		
Shower	**Approximate Peak Dates**	**Associated Comet**
Quadrantids	January 4–6	—
Lyrids	April 20–23	Thacher
Eta Aquarids	May 3–5	Halley's comet
Delta Aquarids	July 30	—
Perseids	August 12	Swift-Tuttle
Draconids	October 7–10	Comet Giacobini-Zinner
Orionids	October 20	Halley's comet
Taurids	Nov. 3–13	Comet Ericke
Leonids	Nov. 18	Temple-Tuttle
Geminids	Dec. 4–16	—

◀ Figure 8

Appendix D Star Charts

Spring Sky

To use this chart, hold it up in front of you and turn it so that the direction you are facing is at the bottom of the chart. This chart works best at 34° north latitude and at the following times: 10:00 P.M. on March 1; 9:00 P.M. on March 15; 8:00 P.M. on March 30. However, it can be used at other times and latitudes within the United States.

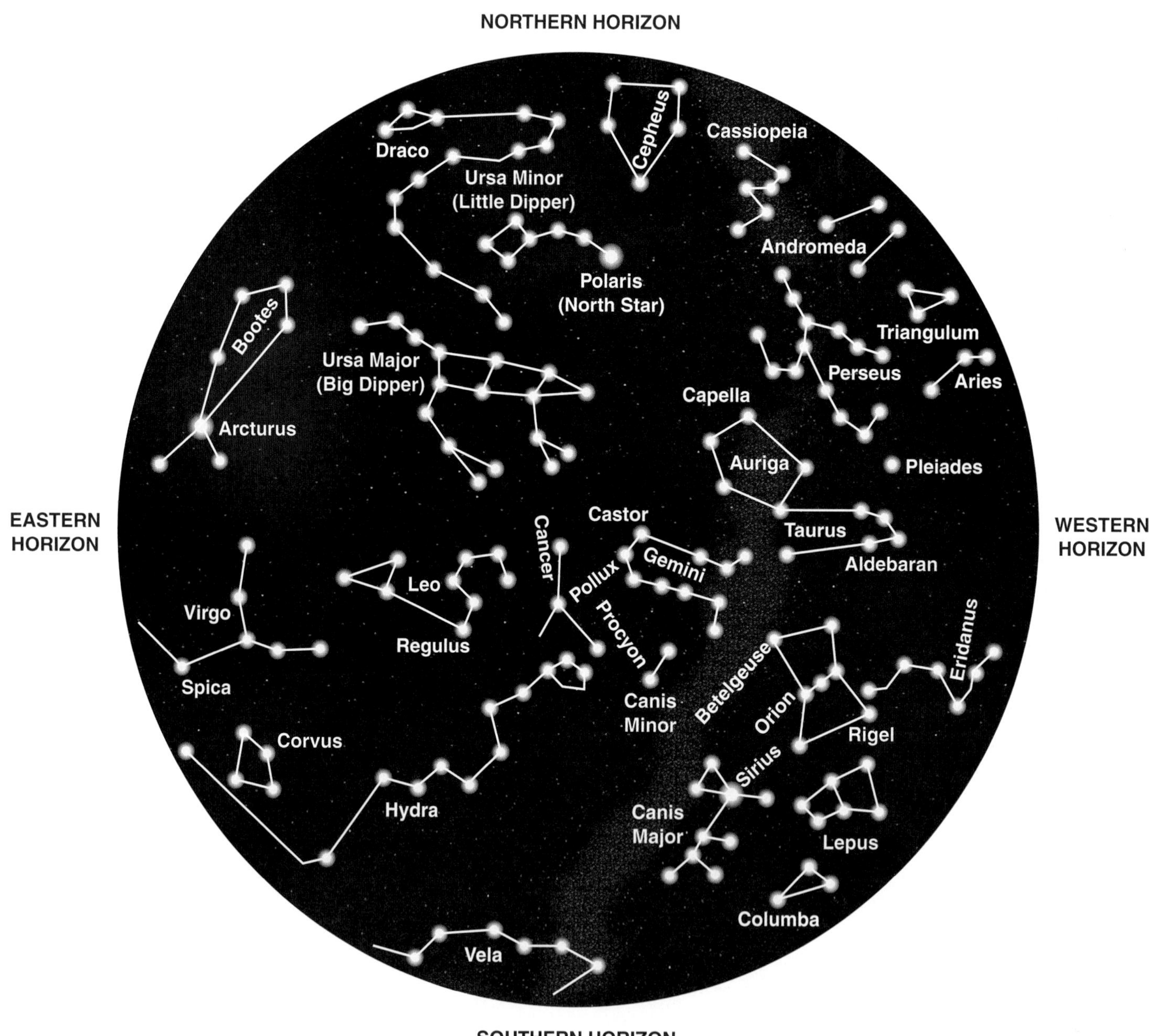

Summer Sky

To use this chart, hold it up in front of you and turn it so that the direction you are facing is at the bottom of the chart. This chart works best at 34° north latitude and at the following times: 10:00 P.M. on June 1; 9:00 P.M. on June 15; 8:00 P.M. on June 30. However, it can be used at other times and latitudes within the United States.

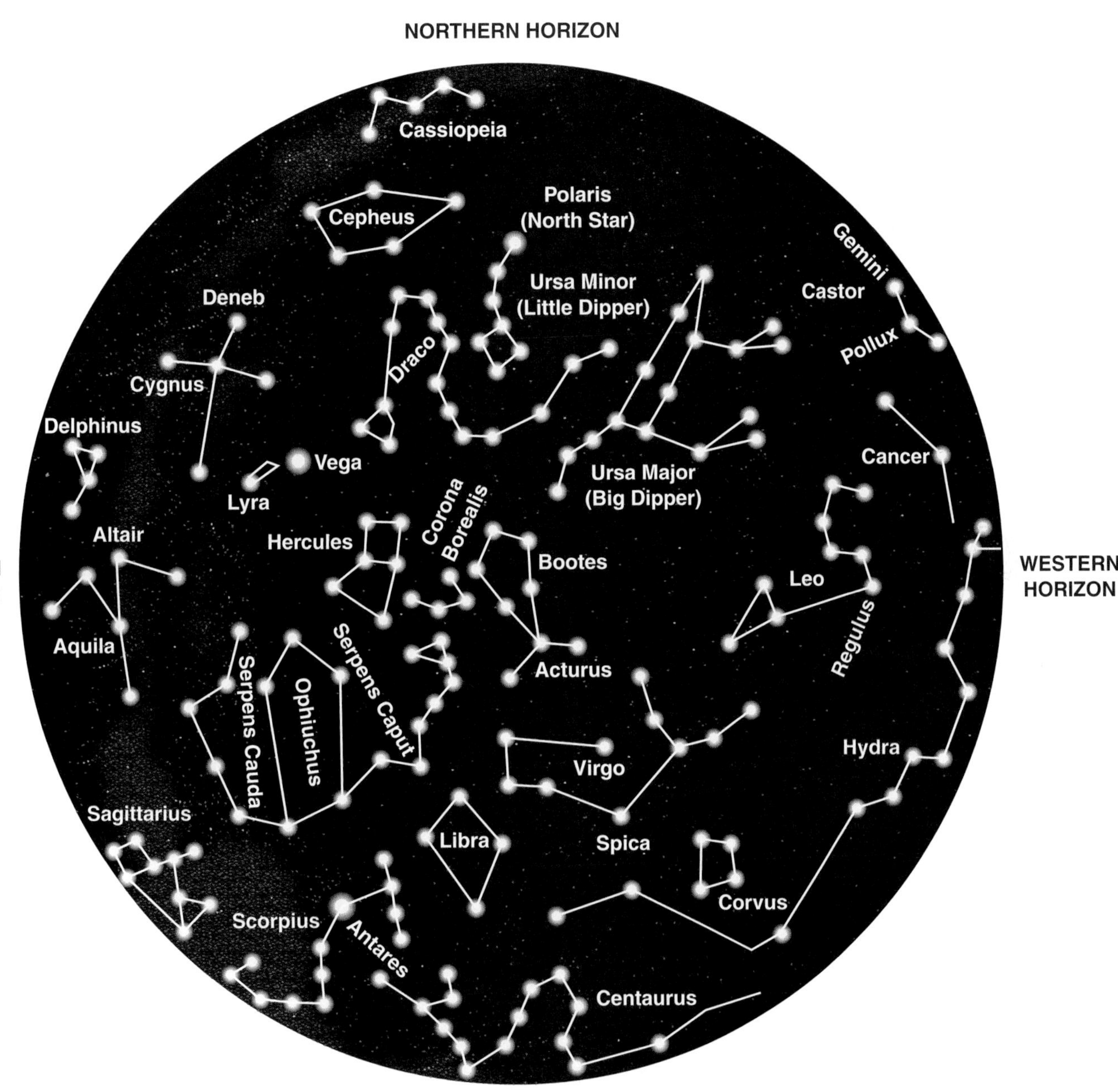

Autumn Sky

To use this chart, hold it up in front of you and turn it so that the direction you are facing is at the bottom of the chart. This chart works best at 34° north latitude and at the following times: 10:00 P.M. on September 1; 9:00 P.M. on September 15; 8:00 P.M. on September 30. However, it can be used at other times and latitudes within the United States.

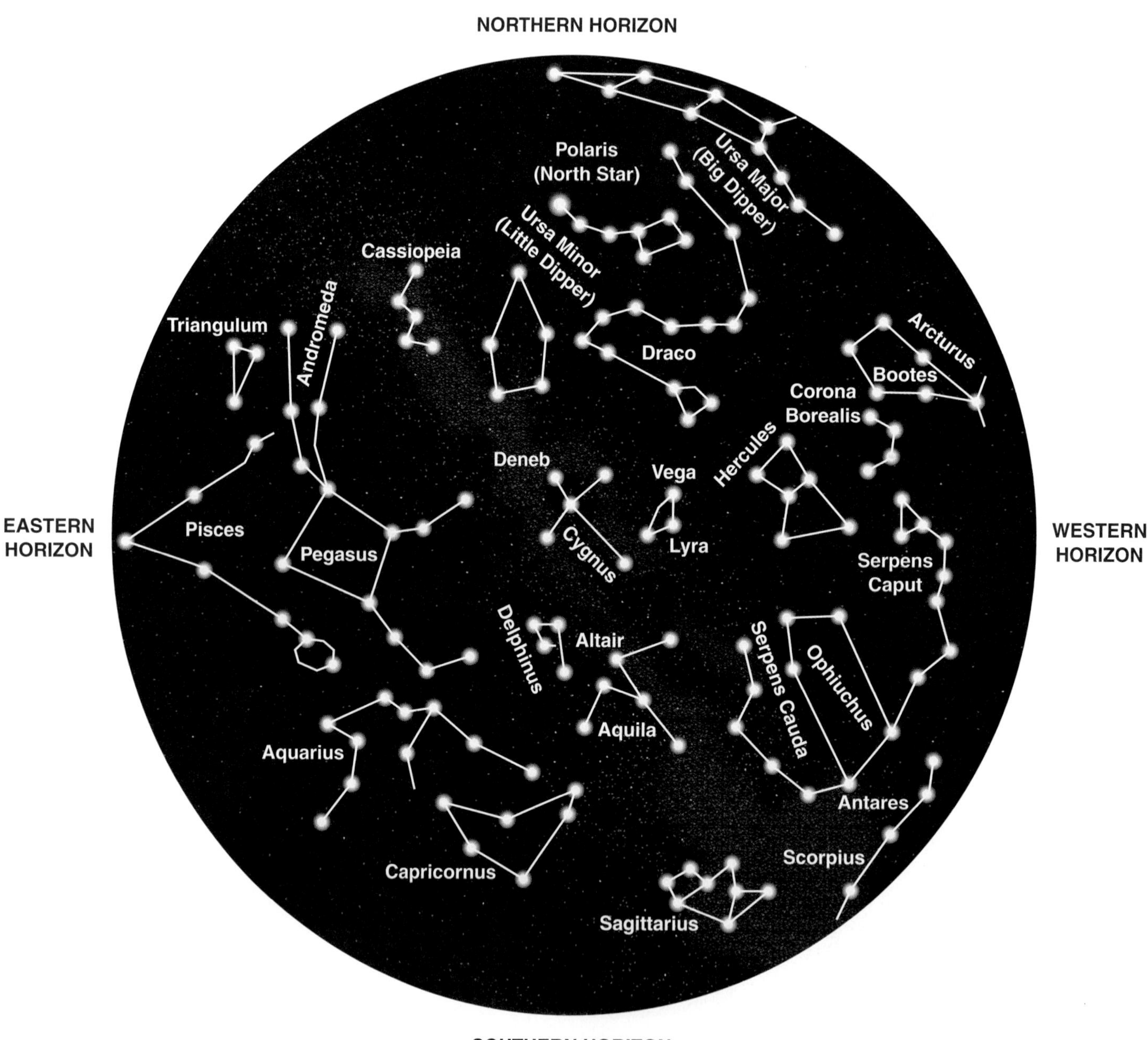

Winter Sky

To use this chart, hold it up in front of you and turn it so that the direction you are facing is at the bottom of the chart. This chart works best at 34° north latitude and at the following times: 10:00 P.M. on December 1; 9:00 P.M. on December 15; 8:00 P.M. on December 30. However, it can be used at other times and latitudes within the United States.

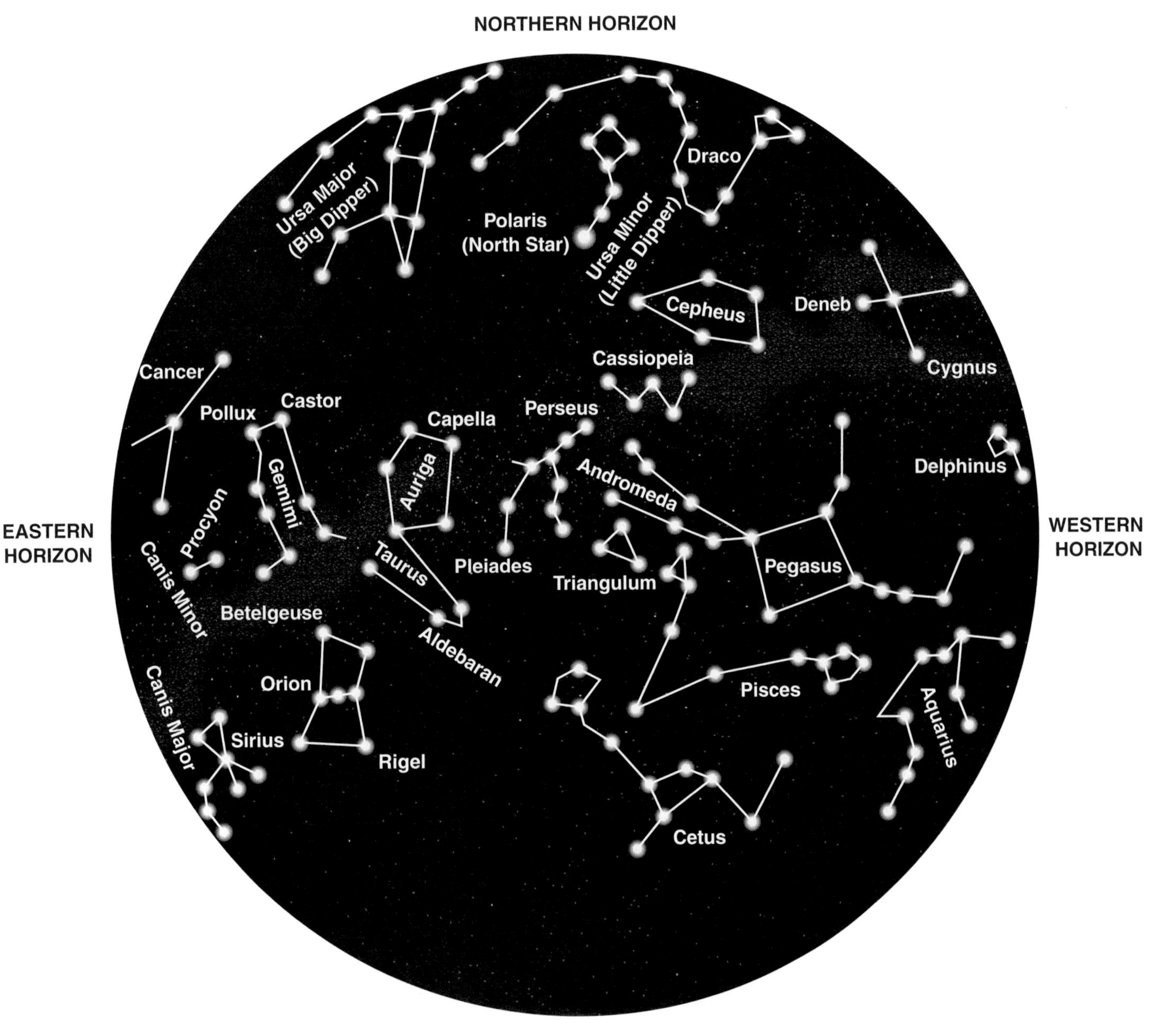

Appendix E Chemical Elements

LIST OF CHEMICAL ELEMENTS		
Element	Atomic Symbol	Atomic Number
Actinium	Ac	89
Aluminum	Al	13
Americium	Am	95
Antimony	Sb	51
Argon	Ar	18
Arsenic	As	33
Astatine	At	85
Barium	Ba	56
Berkelium	Bk	97
Beryllium	Be	4
Bismuth	Bi	83
Bohrium	Bh	107
Boron	B	5
Bromine	Br	35
Cadmium	Cd	48
Calcium	Ca	20
Californium	Cf	98
Carbon	C	6
Cerium	Ce	58
Cesium	Cs	55
Chlorine	Cl	17
Chromium	Cr	24
Cobalt	Co	27
Copper	Cu	29
Curium	Cm	96
Dubnium	Db	105
Dysprosium	Dy	66
Einsteinium	Es	99
Erbium	Er	68
Europium	Eu	63
Fermium	Fm	100
Fluorine	F	9
Francium	Fr	87
Gadolinium	Gd	64
Gallium	Ga	31
Germanium	Ge	32
Gold	Au	79

▲ Figure 9

LIST OF CHEMICAL ELEMENTS		
Element	Atomic Symbol	Atomic Number
Hafnium	Hf	72
Hassium	Hs	108
Helium	He	2
Holmium	Ho	67
Hydrogen	H	1
Indium	In	49
Iodine	I	53
Iridium	Ir	77
Iron	Fe	26
Krypton	Kr	36
Lanthanum	La	57
Lawrencium	Lr	103
Lead	Pb	82
Lithium	Li	3
Lutetium	Lu	71
Magnesium	Mg	12
Manganese	Mn	25
Meitnerium	Mt	109
Mendelevium	Md	101
Mercury	Hg	80
Molybdenum	Mo	42
Neodymium	Nd	60
Neon	Ne	10
Neptunium	Np	93
Nickel	Ni	28
Niobium	Nb	41
Nitrogen	N	7
Nobelium	No	102
Osmium	Os	76
Oxygen	O	8
Palladium	Pd	46
Phosphorus	P	15
Platinum	Pt	78
Plutonium	Pu	94
Polonium	Po	84
Potassium	K	19
Praseodymium	Pr	59
Promethium	Pm	61

LIST OF CHEMICAL ELEMENTS		
Element	Atomic Symbol	Atomic Number
Protactinium	Pa	91
Radium	Ra	88
Radon	Rn	86
Rhenium	Re	75
Rhodium	Rh	45
Rubidium	Rb	37
Ruthenium	Ru	44
Rutherfordium	Rf	104
Samarium	Sm	62
Scandium	Sc	21
Seaborgium	Sg	106
Selenium	Se	34
Silicon	Si	14
Silver	Ag	47
Sodium	Na	11
Strontium	Sr	38
Sulfur	S	16
Tantalum	Ta	73
Technetium	Tc	43
Tellurium	Te	52
Terbium	Tb	65
Thallium	Tl	81
Thorium	Th	90
Thulium	Tm	69
Tin	Sn	50
Titanium	Ti	22
Tungsten	W	74
Ununnilium	Uun	110
Unununium	Uuu	111
Ununbium	Uub	112
Ununquadium	Uuq	114
Uranium	U	92
Vanadium	V	23
Xenon	Xe	54
Ytterbium	Yb	70
Yttrium	Y	39
Zinc	Zn	30
Zirconium	Zr	40

Appendix F Mathematics Review

MEASURING ANGLES

Use a protractor to measure an angle. Place the center of the protractor's straight edge on the vertex. One ray must pass through 0°.

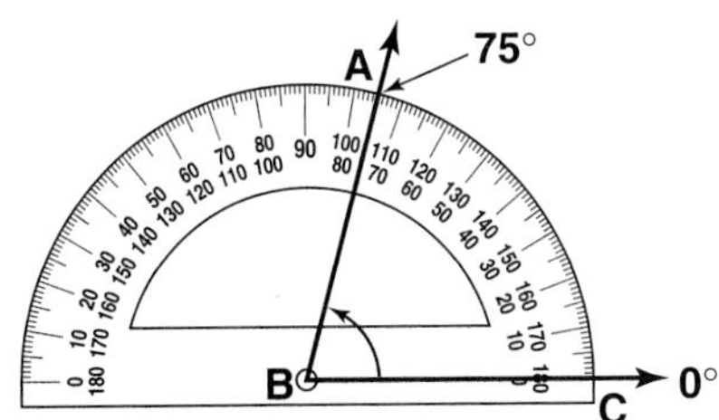

Angle ABC measures 75°.

SOLVING WORD PROBLEMS

To solve distance problems, you can use $d = r \times t$ or $d = rt$.

The Smiths drove 220 miles at an average speed of 55 miles per hour. How long did the trip take?

Plan

Substitute the values you know into the equation $d = r \times t$.

Then solve.

Do

$$220 = 55t$$

$$220 \div 55 = 55t \div 55$$

$$4 = t$$

Solution

The trip took 4 hours.

FORMULAS

Speed

Velocity is speed and direction.

1. Speed = distance ÷ time

   or

   $v = \frac{d}{t}$

   or

   $v = d \div t$

2. Change in velocity = final velocity − initial velocity
3. Acceleration = change in velocity ÷ time

Energy

Energy = mass × speed of light^2

or

$E = m \times c^2$

or

$E = mc^2$

Appendix G Map of the United States

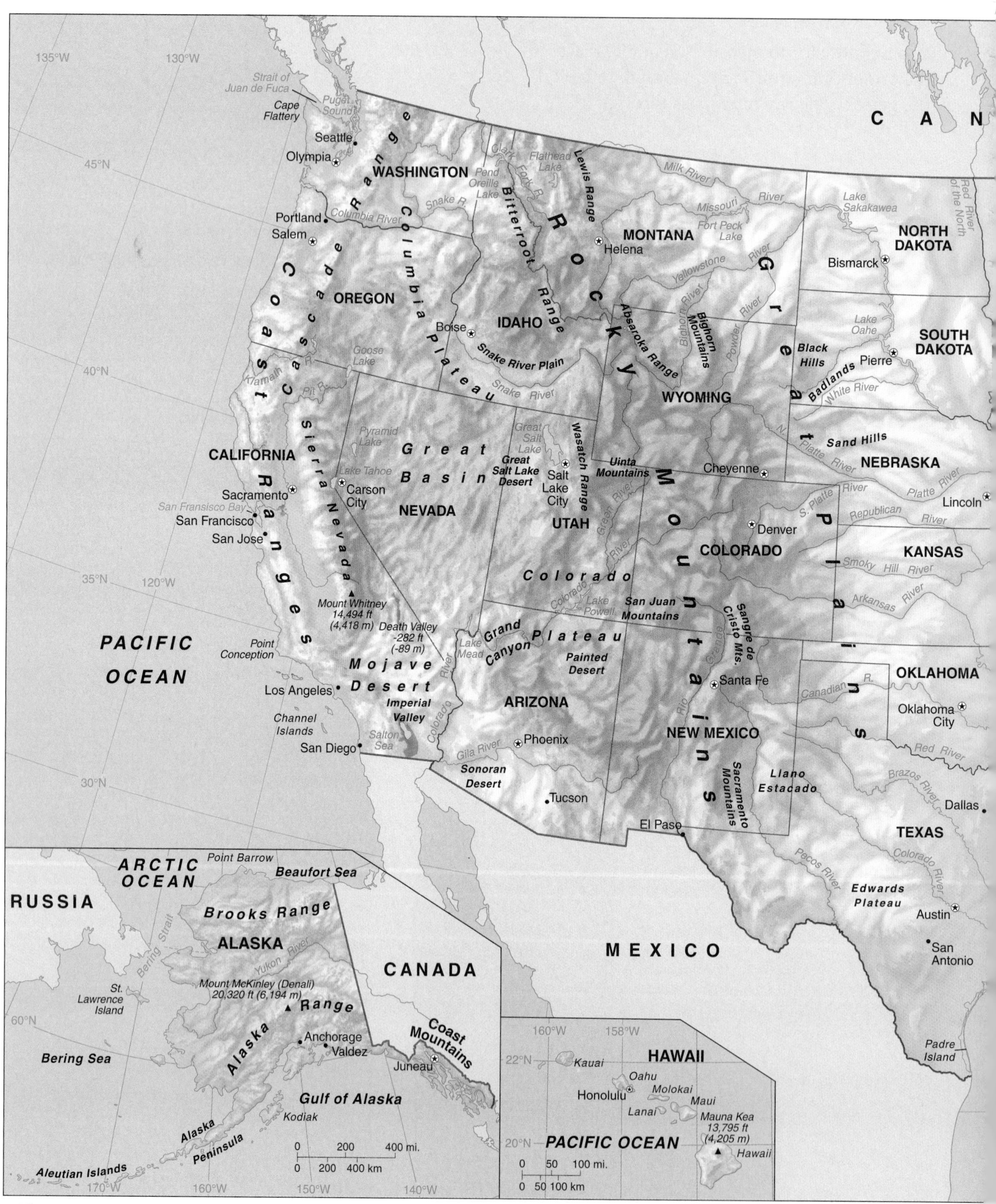

▲ Figure 10

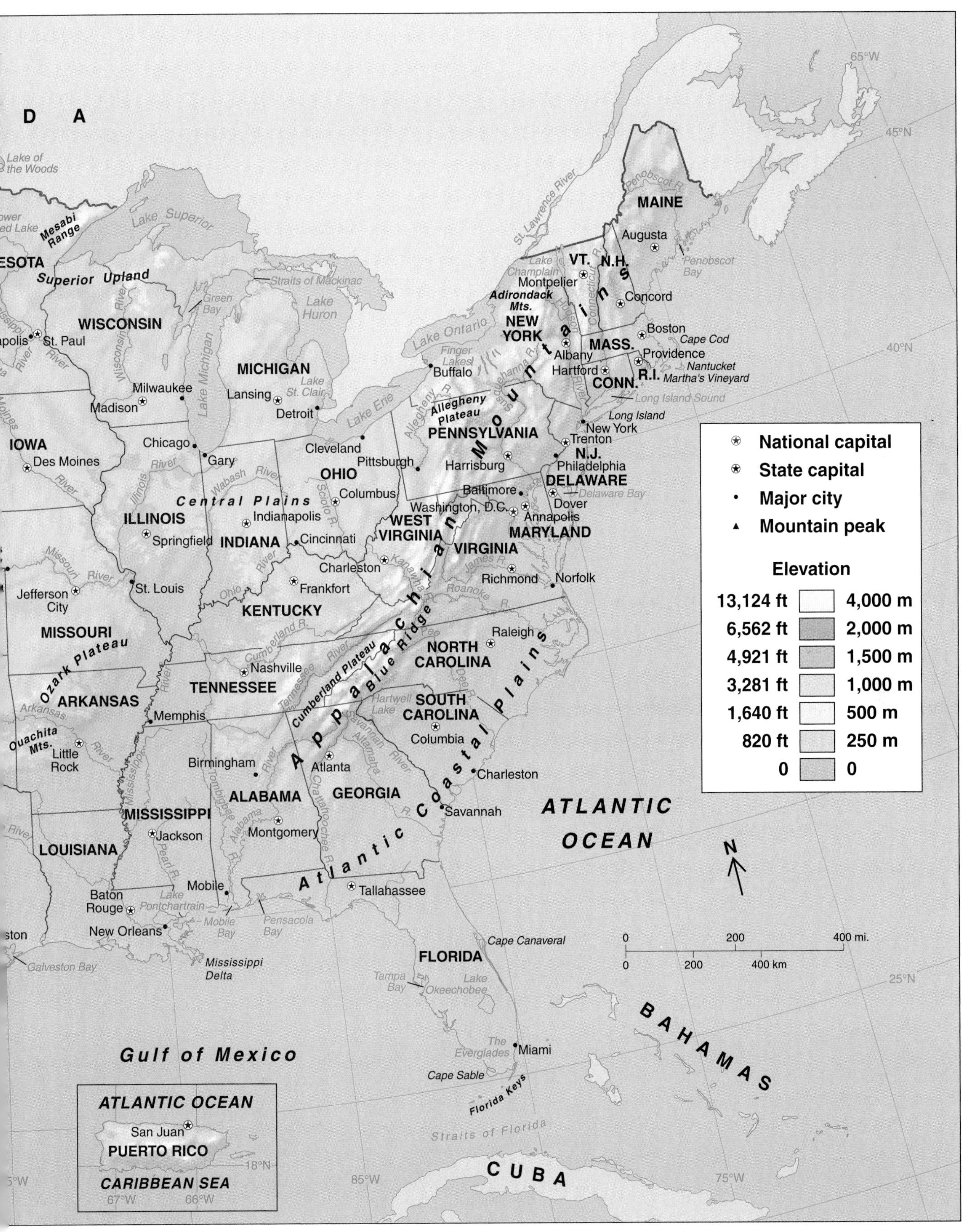

D A
MAINE
Augusta
VT.
N.H.
Montpelier
Concord
Adirondack Mts.
NEW YORK
Albany
MASS.
Boston
Cape Cod
Providence
Nantucket
Martha's Vineyard
Hartford
CONN.
R.I.
Long Island Sound
Long Island
New York
Trenton
N.J.
Philadelphia
DELAWARE
Dover
Delaware Bay
Baltimore
Washington, D.C.
Annapolis
MARYLAND
VIRGINIA
Richmond
Norfolk
PENNSYLVANIA
Harrisburg
Allegheny Plateau
Pittsburgh
Buffalo
Finger Lakes
Lake Ontario
Lake Erie
St. Lawrence River
Lake Champlain
Penobscot R.
Penobscot Bay
Connecticut R.
Hudson River
Susquehanna R.
Allegheny R.
Appalachian Mountains
WEST VIRGINIA
Charleston
Kanawha R.
James R.
Roanoke R.
OHIO
Cleveland
Columbus
Cincinnati
Scioto R.
MICHIGAN
Lansing
Detroit
Lake St. Clair
Lake Huron
Lake Michigan
Lake Superior
Straits of Mackinac
Green Bay
WISCONSIN
Milwaukee
Madison
Wisconsin River
St. Paul
Superior Upland
Mesabi Range
Lake of the Woods
IOWA
Des Moines
ILLINOIS
Chicago
Gary
Springfield
Illinois River
INDIANA
Indianapolis
Wabash River
Central Plains
KENTUCKY
Frankfort
Ohio River
Cumberland R.
MISSOURI
Jefferson City
St. Louis
Missouri River
Ozark Plateau
ARKANSAS
Little Rock
Arkansas River
Ouachita Mts.
TENNESSEE
Nashville
Memphis
Tennessee River
Cumberland Plateau
Blue Ridge
NORTH CAROLINA
Raleigh
Pee Dee R.
SOUTH CAROLINA
Columbia
Charleston
Hartwell Lake
Savannah River
Altamaha R.
GEORGIA
Atlanta
Savannah
ALABAMA
Birmingham
Montgomery
Mobile
Mobile Bay
Tombigbee R.
Alabama R.
Chattahoochee R.
MISSISSIPPI
Jackson
Mississippi River
Pearl R.
LOUISIANA
Baton Rouge
New Orleans
Lake Pontchartrain
Mississippi Delta
Galveston Bay
Atlantic Coastal Plains
Tallahassee
Pensacola Bay
FLORIDA
Cape Canaveral
Tampa Bay
Lake Okeechobee
The Everglades
Miami
Cape Sable
Florida Keys
Straits of Florida
CUBA
BAHAMAS
ATLANTIC OCEAN
Gulf of Mexico
ATLANTIC OCEAN
San Juan
PUERTO RICO
CARIBBEAN SEA
18°N
67°W
66°W
85°W
75°W
65°W
45°N
40°N
25°N
N
0 200 400 mi.
0 200 400 km
National capital
State capital
Major city
Mountain peak
Elevation
13,124 ft 4,000 m
6,562 ft 2,000 m
4,921 ft 1,500 m
3,281 ft 1,000 m
1,640 ft 500 m
820 ft 250 m
0 0

Glossary

Pronunciation and syllabication have been derived from *Webster's New World Dictionary*, Second College Edition, Revised School Printing (Prentice Hall, 1985). Syllables printed in capital letters are given primary stress. (Numbers in parentheses indicate the page number, or page numbers, on which the term is defined.)

PRONUNCIATION KEY					
Symbol	**Example**	**Respelling**	**Symbol**	**Example**	**Respelling**
a	transpiration	(tran-spuh-RAY-shuhn)	oh	biome	(BY-ohm)
ah	composite	(kuhm-PAHZ-iht)	oi	asteroid	(AS-tuhr-oid)
aw	atoll	(A-tawl)	oo	altitude	(AL-tuh-tood)
ay	abrasion	(uh-BRAY-zhuhn)	ow	compound	(KAHM-pownd)
ch	leaching	(LEECH-ing)	s	satellite	(SAT-uhl-yt)
eh	chemical	(KEHM-i-kuhl)	sh	specialization	(spehsh-uhl-ih-ZAY-shuhn)
ee	equinox	(EE-kwih-nahks)	th	thermocline	(THUR-muh-klyn)
f	hemisphere	(HEHM-ih-sfeer)	th	weathering	(WEHTH-uhr-ing)
g	galaxy	(GAL-uhk-see)	uh	volcanism	(VAHL-kuh-nihzm)
ih	anticline	(AN-tih-klyn)	y, eye	anticline, isobar	(AN-tih-klyn), (EYE-soh-bahr)
j	geologic	(jee-uh-LAHJ-ihk)	yoo	cumulus	(KYOOM-yuh-luhs)
k	current	(KUR-uhnt)	z	deposition	(dehp-uh-ZIHSH-uhn)
ks	axis	(AK-sihs)	zh	erosion	(e-ROH-zhuhn)

A

aphelion (uh-FEE-lee-uhn)**:** point in a planet's orbit at which it is farthest from the Sun (pp. 22, 70)

apogee (AP-uh-jee)**:** point at which the Moon is farthest from Earth (p. 26)

asteroid (AS-tuhr-oid)**:** large chunk of rock or metal that orbits the Sun (p. 84)

astronomical (as-truh-NAHM-ih-kuhl) **unit (AU):** unit of measurement based on the Sun's distance from Earth and equal to about 150 million km (p. 52)

astronomy (uh-STRAHN-uh-mee)**:** study of stars, planets, and other objects in space (p. 40)

axis (AK-sihs)**:** imaginary line through the center of a planet or other body around which that body spins (p. 16)

B

Big Bang: explosion that may have begun the universe many billions of years ago (p. 118)

binary stars: two stars that revolve around each other (p. 96)

black hole: massive star that has collapsed and whose gravity is so powerful that it pulls in everything, even light (p. 118)

C

chromosphere (KROH-muh-sfeer)**:** layer of the Sun's atmosphere above the photosphere (p. 106)

coma: gas cloud that surrounds the nucleus of a comet (p. 90)

comet: lump of ice, frozen gas, and dust that orbits the Sun (p. 90)

communication: sharing information (p. 8)

concave mirror: mirror that curves inward (p. 46)

constant: something that does not change (p. 11)

constellation (kahn-stuh-LAY-shuhn)**:** group of stars that form a pattern in the sky (p. 112)

controlled experiment: experiment in which all the conditions except one are kept constant (p. 11)

convex (kahn-VEHKS) **lens:** lens that is thicker in the middle than it is at the edges (p. 44)

core: center of the Sun (p. 106)

corona (kuh-ROH-nuh): outer layer of the Sun's atmosphere (pp. 34, 106)

crater (KRAYT-uhr): round hole on the Moon's surface (p. 74)

crescent (KREHS-uhnt) **phase:** phase when less than half the Moon is visible (p. 28)

data: information you collect when you observe something (p. 3)

ellipse (eh-LIHPS): flattened circle or oval (p. 70)

elliptical galaxy: galaxy shaped like a ball or slightly flattened ball (p. 114)

equinox (EE-kwih-nahks): day the Sun shines directly on the equator (p. 22)

fusion (FYOO-zhuhn): reaction in which atomic nuclei combine to form larger nuclei (p. 110)

galaxy (GAL-uhk-see): huge collection of stars, gas, and dust that travel together through space (pp. 42, 114)

gibbous (GIHB-uhs) **phase:** phase when more than half the Moon is visible (p. 28)

gram: basic unit of mass (p. 4)

gravity (GRAV-ih-tee): force of attraction that exists between all objects in the universe (p. 70)

hypothesis: suggested answer to a question or problem (p. 10)

International Date Line: boundary formed where the first and twenty-fourth time zones meet (p. 18)

irregular galaxy: galaxy with no definite shape (p. 114)

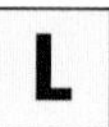

light year: unit of measurement equal to about 10 trillion km (p. 52)

liter: basic unit of liquid volume (p. 4)

lunar eclipse (ih-KLIHPS): passing of the Moon through Earth's shadow (p. 32)

magnitude (MAG-nuh-tood): way to measure a star's brightness (p. 100)

main sequence star: star that falls within a long, narrow, diagonal band across the H-R diagram (p. 102)

mare (MAH-ray) *pl.* **maria:** broad, flat plain on the Moon's surface (p. 74)

mass: amount of matter in something (p. 4)

meniscus: curve at the surface of a liquid in a thin tube (p. 4)

meteor (MEET-ee-uhr): rock or metal that enters Earth's atmosphere (p. 84)

meteorite (MEET-ee-uhr-yt): piece of rock or metal that falls on a planet or moon's surface (p. 84)

meteoroid (MEET-ee-uhr-oid): small piece of rock or metal that travels through space (p. 84)

meter: basic unit of length or distance (p. 4)

model: tool scientists use to represent an object or a process (p. 3)

neap tide: tide that is not as high or as low as a normal tide (p. 26)

nebula (NEHB-yuh-luh): cloud of gas and dust in space (pp. 68, 96)

nova: explosion where the outer layers of a star are blown off (p. 104)

nucleus (NOO-klee-uhs): head or solid part of a comet (p. 90); center, or core, of an atom (p. 110)

orbit: curved path of one object around another object in space (pp. 60, 68)

parallax (PAR-uh-laks): apparent change in the position of a distant object when seen from two different places (p. 52)

penumbra (pih-NUM-bruh): light part of a shadow (p. 32)

perigee (PER-uh-jee): point at which the Moon is closest to Earth (p. 26)

perihelion (per-uh-HEE-lee-uhn): point in a planet's orbit at which it is closest to the Sun (pp. 22, 70)

phases (FAYZ-uhz): changing shapes of the Moon (p. 28)

photosphere (FOHT-oh-sfeer): inner layer of the Sun's atmosphere (p. 106)

photosynthesis (foht-oh-SIHN-thuh-sihs): food-making process in green plants (p. 111)

prominence (PRAHM-uh-nuhns): stream of gas that shoots high above the Sun's surface (p. 108)

protostar: dense material in the center of a nebula that is about to become a star (p. 96)

quasar: continuous burst of brilliant light and enormous energy from a very massive black hole (p. 118)

radio telescope: telescope that can receive radio waves from sources in space (p. 48)

red giant: large, bright star that is fairly cool (p. 102)

reflecting (rih-FLEKT-ing) **telescope:** telescope that uses a concave mirror to collect light (p. 46)

refracting (rih-FRAKT-ing) **telescope:** telescope that uses convex lenses to produce an enlarged image (p. 44)

revolution (rehv-uh-LOO-shuhn): movement of a planet or other body orbiting another body (p. 16)

rift: valley caused by a crack in the crust of a planet (p. 82)

rotation (roh-TAY-shuhn): spinning of a planet or another body on its axis (p. 16)

satellite (SAT-uhl-eyet): natural or artificial object orbiting another body in space (pp. 60, 76)

simulation: computer model that usually shows a process (p. 3)

solar (SOH-luhr) **eclipse:** passing of the Moon between Earth and the Sun (p. 34)

solar flare: eruption of electrically charged particles from the surface of the Sun (p. 108)

solar noon: time of the day when the Sun is highest in the sky (p. 18)

solar system: Sun and all the bodies that orbit it (pp. 40, 68)

solstice (SAHL-stihs): day of the year the Sun reaches its highest or lowest point in the sky (p. 22)

spectrograph (SPEHK-truh-graf): device that measures the spectrum of an object (p. 98)

spectroscopy (spehk-TRUH-skohp-ee): study of light coming from objects in space (p. 98)

spectrum: pattern of different colors of light coming from an object (p. 98)

spiral galaxy: galaxy shaped like a flattened disk with spiral arms (p. 114)

spring tide: tide that is higher or lower than a normal tide (p. 26)

standard time: system whereby all places within a time zone have the same time (p. 18)

star: ball of gases that gives off light and heat (p. 96)

star cluster: large group of stars that travel together through space (p. 96)

sunspot: dark, cool area on the Sun's surface (p. 108)

supergiant: very large and very bright star (p. 102)

supernova: violent explosion where a star is blown apart (p. 104)

tail: long, ribbonlike trail of comet dust and gas (p. 90)

temperature: measurement of the amount of heat energy something contains (p. 4)

theory: set of hypotheses that have been supported by testing over and over again (p. 10)

thrust: forward force produced in a rocket engine (p. 54)

umbra (UM-bruh)**:** center or dark part of a shadow (p. 32)

unit: amount used to measure something (p. 4)

variable: anything that can affect the outcome of an experiment (p. 11)

volume: amount of space an object takes up (p. 4)

white dwarf: very small, hot star (p. 102)

Index

Photo Credits

Photography Credits: All photographs are by the Pearson Learning Group (PLG), John Serafin for PLG, and David Mager for PLG, except as noted below.

Cover: *bkgd.* Mount Stromolo and Siding Spring Observatories/Science Photo Library/Photo Researchers, Inc.; *inset* NASA/Peter Arnold, Inc.

Table of Contents: iv: b David Ducros/Science Photo Library/Photo Researchers, Inc.; v: t Nasa/Science Library/Photo Researchers, Inc.

Frontmatter: P001 bl Science VU/Visuals Unlimited, Inc.; P001 mr George Ranalli/Photo Researchers, Inc.; P001 tr Farrell Grehan/Photo Researchers, Inc.; P001 Comstock, Inc.; P002 bl Jane Grushow/Grant Heilman Photography, Inc.; P002 br Eric Kamp/Phototake; P002 tr AFP/Corbis; P003 Comstock, Inc.; P005 Pearson Learning; P005 r Comstock, Inc.; P007 r Comstock, Inc.; P009 br Bob Daemmrich/Stock, Boston, Inc.; P009 mr USDA/Natural Resources Conservation Service; P009 tr SuperStock, Inc.; P009 r Comstock, Inc.; P010 Frans Lanting/Minden Pictures; P011 r Comstock, Inc.; P013 r Comstock, Inc.;

Chapter 1: P15 Nancy Rotenberg/Animals Animals/Earth Scenes; P17 The Granger Collection; P22 Galen Rowell/Corbis; P23 Amos Zezmer/Omni-Photo Communications; P24 Neil Rabinowitz/Corbis; P25 l Sol Sexto/PhotoDisc, Inc.; P25 r Smari/Getty Images; P27 NASA/Science Photo Library/Photo Researchers, Inc.; P29 Nathan Beck/Omni-Photo Communications; P32 John Chumack/Galactic Images/Photo Researchers, Inc.; P34 George East/Visuals Unlimited, Inc.; P35 Roger Ressmeyer/Corbis; P36 Nancy Rotenberg/Animals Animals/Earth Scenes; P37 Nancy Rotenberg/Animals Animals/Earth Scenes; P38 John Sanford/Science Photo Library/Photo Researchers, Inc.; P38 Nancy Rotenberg/Animals Animals/Earth Scenes

Chapter 2: P39 NASA/Science Photo Library/Photo Researchers, Inc.; P40 Private Collection/Bridgeman Art Library; P41 b LOC/Science Source/Photo Researchers, Inc.; P41 t Roger Ressmeyer/Corbis; P42 b NASA; P42 inset NASA; P42 t NASA; P43 b D. Falconer/PhotoDisc, Inc.; P43 t Dr. Christian Brandstatter (d/b/a Austrian Archives)/Corbis; P44 l James A. Sugar/Corbis; P44 r Jessica Wecker/Photo Researchers, Inc.; P46 Bettmann/Corbis; P47 b Science/Visuals Unlimited, Inc.; P47 m USGS/EROS Data Center; P47 t Jerry Lodriguss/Photo Researchers, Inc.; P48 Dr. Steve Gull/Science Photo Library/Photo Researchers, Inc.; P49 b David Parker/Science Photo Library/Photo Researchers, Inc.; P49 t Dave Jacobs/Index Stock Imagery, Inc.; P50 bl AFP/Corbis; P50 br AFP/Corbis; P50 m Roger Ressmeyer/Corbis; P50 t Corbis; P50-51 Reuters NewMedia, Inc./Corbis; P51 bl NASA/Corbis; P51 br AFP/Corbis; P51 t AFP/Corbis; P54 Harvey Lloyd/Peter Arnold, Inc.; P58 Science VU/Visuals Unlimited, Inc.; P59 b Perkin-Elmer Corporation; P59 t NASA/Science Source/Photo Researchers, Inc.; P60 l NASA; P60 r ESA/CE/Eurocontrol/Science Photo Library/Photo Researchers, Inc.; P61 l David Ducros/Science Photo Library/Photo Researchers, Inc.; P61 r David A. Hardy/Science Photo Library/Photo Researchers, Inc.; P62 l NASA; P62 r NASA/Science Photo Library/Photo Researchers, Inc.; P63 Bettmann/Corbis; P64 NASA/Science Photo Library/Photo Researchers, Inc.; P65 NASA/Science Photo Library/Photo Researchers, Inc.; P66 NASA/Science Photo Library/Photo Researchers, Inc.

Chapter 3: P67 Phil Degginger/Color-Pic, Inc.; P67 inset Science VU/Visuals Unlimited, Inc.; P69 t Phil Degginger/Color-Pic, Inc.; P74 l NASA/Science Photo Library/Photo Researchers, Inc.; P74 r NASA/Science Photo Library/Photo Researchers, Inc.; P75 Science VU/NASA-JMP/Visuals Unlimited, Inc.; P76 NASA; P77 b Science Photo Library/Photo Researchers, Inc.; P77 t NASA/Science Photo Library/Photo Researchers, Inc.; P80 l NASA/Roger Ressmeyer/Corbis; P80 r NASA/Science Photo Library/Photo Researchers, Inc.; P81 Ken Lucas/Visuals Unlimited, Inc.; P82 NASA/Science Photo Library/Photo Researchers, Inc.; P82 inset Phil Degginger/Color-Pic, Inc.; P83 Gerald Cooyman/Animals Animals/Earth Scenes; P83 inset NASA/Science Photo Library/Photo Researchers, Inc.; P84 l MarkGlick/Science Photo Library/Photo Researchers, Inc.; P84 r David Parker/Science Photo Library/Photo Researchers, Inc.; P84 r inset Breck P. Kent/Animals Animals/Earth Scenes; P85 Chris Butler/Science Photo Library/Photo Researchers, Inc.; P86 l NASA/Peter Arnold, Inc.; P86 r Science VU/Visuals Unlimited, Inc.; P87 b PhotoDisc, Inc.; P87 t NASA Science Source/Photo Researchers, Inc.; P88 br NASA; P88 l Space Telescope Science Institute/NASA/Science Photo Library/Photo Researchers, Inc.; P88 tr Phil Degginger/NASA/JPL/Color-Pic, Inc.; P89 Roger Ressmeyer/Corbis; P90 Derke/O'Hara/Getty Images; P91 Phil Degginger/Color-Pic, Inc.; P92 Science VU/Visuals Unlimited, Inc.; P93 Science VU/Visuals Unlimited, Inc.; P94 Science VU/Visuals Unlimited, Inc.

Chapter 4: P95 Jeff Hester and Paul Scowen (Arizona State University)/NASA HQ Audio Visual Branch; P96 Larry Gilpin/Getty Images; P97 b Gary Ladd/Photo Researchers, Inc.; P97 t NASA/Omni-Photo Communications; P100 bl Paul Morrell/Getty Images; P100 bm John Sanford/Science Photo Library/Photo Researchers, Inc.; P100 br AFP/Corbis; P100 t col 1 Science VU/HO-RERDON-JMP/Visuals Unlimited; P100 t col 2 NASA/Science Photo Library/Photo Researchers, Inc.; P100 t col. 3 John Sanford/Science Photo Library/Photo Researchers, Inc.; P100 t col 4 Goddard Institute for Space Studies/NASA; P103 The Granger Collection; P106 Dr. Leon Golub/Science Photo Library/Photo Researchers, Inc.; P108 inset Mark Garlick/Science Photo Library/Photo Researchers, Inc.; P108 l Science VU/HO-Reardon-JMP/Visuals Unlimited, Inc.; P108 r NASA/Science Photo Library/Photo Researchers, Inc.; P109 t Science VU/Visuals Unlimited, Inc.; P110 b Roger Ressmeyer/Corbis; P110 t Historic VU/Visuals Unlimited, Inc.; P111 Kevin Schafer/Peter Arnold, Inc.; P114 l ESO-JMP/Visuals Unlimited, Inc.; P114 m Anglo-Australian Observatory/Dorling Kindersley Limited; P114 r Anglo-Australian Observatory/Dorling Kindersley Limited; P115 Anglo-Australian Observatory/Dorling Kindersley Limited; P117 Robert Williams and the Hubble Deep Field Team (STScl)/NASA; P119 Patrick Clark/PhotoDisc, Inc.; P120 b Cerro Tololo Inter-American Observatory; P120 m Royal Observatory, Edinburgh/Science Photo Library/Photo Researchers, Inc.; P120 t J. Baum & N. Henbest/Science Photo Library/Photo Researchers, Inc.; P121 Audio Visual Branch/NASA Headquarters; P122 NASA/Science Source/Photo Researchers, Inc.; P123 NASA/Science Source/Photo Researchers, Inc.; P124 NASA/Science Source/Photo Researchers, Inc.

Produce a Fashion Show from A to Z

Paula Taylor, M.S.
President, Paula Taylor Productions
The Art Institute of Tucson
Department of Fashion
Marketing and Fashion Design

PEARSON

Boston Columbus Indianapolis New York San Francisco Upper Saddle River
Amsterdam Cape Town Dubai London Madrid Milan Munich Paris Montréal Toronto
Delhi Mexico City São Paulo Sydney Hong Kong Seoul Singapore Taipei Tokyo

Editorial Director: Vernon Anthony
Acquisitions Editor: Sara Eilert
Editorial Assistant: Doug Greive
Director of Marketing: David Gesell
Senior Marketing Manager: Harper Coles
Senior Marketing Coordinator: Alicia Wozniak
Senior Marketing Assistant: Crystal Gonzalez
Associate Editor: Laura J. Weaver
Senior Art Director: Jayne Conte
Production Manager: Laura Messerly
Cover Designer: Karen Salzbach
Manager, Rights and Permissions: Mike Lackey
Cover Image: Newscom
Full-Service Project Management: Kiruthiga Anand
Composition: Integra Software Services, Pvt. Ltd.
Cover Printer: Courier/Kendallville
Text Printer: Courier/Kendallville
Text Font: 9/15 Helvetica Neue

Credits and acknowledgments for materials borrowed from other sources and reproduced, with permission, in this textbook appear on the appropriate page within the text. Unless otherwise stated, all artwork has been provided by the author.

Library of Congress Cataloging-in-Publication Data

Taylor, Paula (Paula Florence)
How to produce a fashion show, from A to Z / Paula Taylor.—1st ed.
p. cm.
Includes bibliographical references.
ISBN-13: 978-0-13-256036-8 (alk. paper)
ISBN-10: 0-13-256036-4 (alk. paper)
1. Fashion shows. 2. Fashion merchandising. I. Title.
TT502.T39 2013
746.9'2—dc23

2012008790

10 9 8 7 6 5 4 3 2 1

PEARSON

ISBN 10: 0-13-256036-4
ISBN 13: 978-0-13-256036-8

brief contents

contents

preface

Fashion show production is a high-energy, wonderful career choice as it is exciting, challenging, and ever changing. I have developed *How to Produce a Fashion Show from A to Z* to be a comprehensive step-by-step manual to guide students on current production methods. My own experiences with producing fashion shows and teaching in the classroom have been used throughout this book. This text takes a real-world approach to fashion show production and covers a broad scope of the business, adding the newest up-to-date tools, techniques, and individual adaptations by current professionals in the industry. This book explores the constant evolution of fashion shows and the important role they play in the business of fashion. *How to Produce a Fashion Show from A to Z* outlines what steps are needed to produce a high-quality, organized production, while providing an abundance of online resources, templates, and websites for the reader's use. Perforated worksheets and templates are provided at the back of the text and available online at www.myfashionkit.com. All worksheets and templates can be customized to fit any event. The text includes many in-class projects, and one ongoing fashion show project, which builds in intensity and depth as each chapter unfolds.

Many chapters include industry insider interviews with professionals currently working in the field, and case studies and problems crafted from real-world production challenges. *How to Produce a Fashion Show from A to Z* also highlights auxiliary career paths in fashion show production. The student or reader may be interested in any of a variety of these including public relations, modeling, or styling. Each chapter has information on these choices and how they can be accomplished.

The text will prepare the reader by underpinning every detail that is necessary to plan and execute a quality show, no matter what the size or budget. This book tackles the ever-changing fashion show industry in an interactive, project-based workbook style.

Supplements

How to Produce a Fashion Show from A to Z is supported by a complete package of student and instructor resources.

Student Resources

MyFashionKit website (www.myfashionkit.com). This online supplement offers media activities to aid student learning and comprehension. (Note: An access code is needed for this supplement. Students can purchase access directly with a credit card at www.myfashionkit.com or from your bookstore.) The supplement comprises the following:

- Chapter-specific Learning Objectives
- Chapter Summaries
- Flashcards
- Glossary
- PowerPoint Slides
- Web Link Resources
- Video Clips of Industry Insider Interviews
- Worksheets
- In-Class Activities
- Pearson e-text Upgrade Option

eBooks. *How to Produce a Fashion Show from A to Z* is available as a CourseSmart. CourseSmart eTextbook is an exciting new choice for students looking to save money. As an alternative to purchasing the printed textbook, students can purchase an electronic version of the same content. With a CourseSmart eTextbook, students can search the text, make notes online, print out reading assignments that incorporate lecture notes, and bookmark important passages for later review. Students can also access their CourseSmart book on an iPad by downloading the CourseSmart App. For more information, or to purchase access to the CourseSmart eTextbook, visit www.coursesmart.com.

Instructor Resources

The instructor will have access to Pearson Education's Instructor Resource Center (IRC), which will provide PPTS and an instructor's manual to accompany this content.

Download Instructor Resources from the Instructor Resource Center. To access supplementary materials online, instructors need to request an instructor access code. Go to www.pearsonhighered.com, click the Instructor Resource Center link, and then click Request IRC Access for an instructor access code. Within forty-eight hours of registering, you will receive a confirming e-mail including an instructor access code. Once you have received your code, go to the site and log on for full instructions on downloading the materials you wish to use.

Acknowledgments

I would like to thank my family for their patience, support, and love throughout the writing of this book and in particular my father, SarkiceNedder, who has been my right hand. He has read each chapter many times and offered countless key suggestions and edits along the way. I thank my mother, Florence, for making certain I was eating and in good spirits, and my sister Genevieve Nedder for being always a text away. Thanks to my husband Clifton Taylor for always making me laugh when I thought I couldn't do it.

I thank Bill and Elizabeth Heuisler for reading the text many times and offering valuable input and suggestions. I thank Sara Slavin, Susan Rondeau, and Melanie Corteal for their insights, input, and groundwork. I thank my husband Clifton Taylor and Allex Gregoire for the hours of filming the video footage. I am so grateful for the many industry insiders: Angel Sanchez, Andrew Weir, Barbara Kramer, Bruce Vassar, Crosby Noricks, Carolina Alvarez-Mathies, Matthew Trettel, Mazdack Rassi, Morton Myles, Jan Strimple, Sheree Hartwell, Thomas Muldoon, and Yeohlee Teng. Each gave me their time freely to share their insights, expertise, and perspective. I send a big thank-you to my dear friends John Calder, Omer Kreso, and Jose Beltran for supplying me with some amazing photographs. I am very appreciative of my students and all the ladies from the Tucson Ladies Council for inspiring me to create unique productions.

In addition, I would like to give a special thank-you to the reviewers of the manuscript for their input and valuable suggestions: Kate Campbell from the Art Institute of Tampa; Shawn Grain Carter from the Fashion Institute of Technology; Amber Chatelain from the Art Institute of Tennessee, Nashville; Crystal Green from the Art Institute of Charlotte; Nicole Harman from the United Tech Training Academy; and Wendy Markgraf from the Art Institute of Houston North. Finally, I would like to thank my editorial team from Pearson for their continued and professional assistance.

introduction

Thinking of becoming a fashion show producer or working on a production team?

The dream of many aspiring producers is to lead a fast-paced, glamorous lifestyle hobnobbing with designers, models, celebrities, and socialites. For the new producer or intern, this unrealistic idea of fashion show production will quickly disappear. The actual role of a producer or planner is much more mundane. Dealing with the task of organizing, meeting deadlines, putting out fires, creating a well-timed and visually aesthetic show, and fulfilling the needs of the client, while simultaneously making everything look seamless is the true reality. Fashion show production is demanding but rewarding work. Show production is one of the most important and sought-after careers in the fashion industry. When you have finished reading and studying this work, you will be well versed in the steps of fashion show production and in many of the secondary career paths under the umbrella of production. Whether you live in Nebraska or New York, whether your budget is $50 or $500,000, the fundamental steps of production are essentially the same. A positive attitude, a great deal of energy, and the information you have learned herein will provide you with the essential tools to start realizing your goal. Open the pages and begin dreaming of producing your show or landing a job on a production team!

Montana and Model

THE BEGINNING

LEARNING OBJECTIVES

After completing this chapter, you will be able to:

- Know what a fashion show is
- Discuss the key players in the history of the fashion show
- Explore the business of fashion shows
- Understand the views of industry insiders
- Understand the terminology of the trade

Every generation laughs at the old fashions, but follow religiously the new.

—THOREAU

1

The fashion show has emerged as a multi-million-dollar tool used by retailers, designers, and manufacturers to promote and sell their products within a highly fickle and constantly changing social and economic environment. Fashion show history is submerged within the variable fashion movements of the moment, profoundly influenced by economic struggles, social evolution, and shifting needs of the buying public. The shows, as we know them today, with all their glamour and excitement, have been part of the greater fashion picture for decades. They began with simple presentations of garments on mannequins and evolved into outrageous productions with live, high-profile models. Fashion shows have always reflected the times in which we live and among other things reflect a history of economic and social unfolding. In fact, at times, fashion shows were influential in social and economic change. Simultaneously, many designers and retailers were conducting fashion shows as a diversion from the struggles of the day and as a reflection of society at large. Fashion shows, as instruments of fashion movements, were and are on the leading edge of social, and sometimes economic, change. So what is a fashion show? Simply put, it is an event in which clothing is usually worn by live models and presented to an audience. The fashion show can be held on a raised runway and utilize various other structures and forms such as platforms and staging. The modern fashion show may utilize 3D technology, live streaming, and films. It often takes place outside of traditional venues. A show's purpose changes with motivation, including, among other things, the sale of clothing, branding of a designer or label, presentation of trends, promotion, and education.

The History of the Fashion Show

The runway show or fashion show is in many ways like the fashion industry itself, constantly in flux and ever changing. The fashion show has its roots in history and mirrors the transforming environment of the fashion industry. In order to have an understanding of what a fashion show is today and how the production aspect of it evolved, we must take a look at the history of and the inception of fashion shows. Hence, in this chapter we discuss the evolution of the fashion show and the creation of the catwalk. We will review many influential designers' and retailers' specific contributions and creations that helped shape the modern catwalk.

As early as 1851 **Charles Frederick Worth**, an Englishman, became known as the father of haute couture as he initiated the first known use of models and cleverly fostered a sense of ritual around shopping by ingeniously incorporating the ladies of society as his **brand ambassadors**. He was well known for making custom clothing for his elite clientele. Brand ambassadors are friends and clients who wear the designers' clothing and represent it in a positive light. Marie Vernet, who became Mrs. Charles Worth, wore his designs and visited clients as a means to show the garments. At the same time she brought additional ones to share. As business grew, Worth hired more women to wear his clothing and show it off to his high society customers.

Mr. Worth saw the power in having prominent socialites wear his clothing to public events. He was one of the first designers to create a cult of fashion and even coined a term for the women who wore his designs while visiting clients: **mannequins**. These mannequins were the first real-life models to work with designers and to wear and model clothing. Prior to this, miniature dolls called **fashion dolls** were used to show dressmakers' work to the ladies of the high court (Quick, 1997).

The fashion dolls were small figurines, exact replicas of the designers', or in those days the dressmakers', latest creations. The earliest record of the fashion doll was from the fourteenth century. Shipping those dolls, clothed in the latest fashion trends, from one royal court to another was a common practice among the European royalty and the only way women were able to view designs beyond that of seeing a sketch or illustration (Fraser, 1963).

The most notable of the dressmakers who used these fashion dolls was **Rose Bertin**, the French fashion dressmaker to Marie Antoinette. This form of presenting fashion designs and style hit its peak circa the early 1800s. After Charles Worth began using live models or mannequins, several prominent designers developed, expanded, and created unique ways to use women in fashion shows and productions. This was the beginning of the modern way of presenting clothing, and the initiation of the model as a designer's muse. It was Worth's groundbreaking realization that encouraged many designers and retailers to use models or real-life mannequins to display their collections and in practically no time they realized its importance in drawing people's attention to their collections.

French fashion designer **Paul Poiret**, a former student of Worth, took models to the races dressed in Turkish trousers as early as 1912. He was the first designer to travel with models to other countries to present his collection. He was well known for throwing elaborate parties and became one of the first celebrity designers. Traveling and participating in trade shows for the purpose of presenting and selling a collection is a common practice for current designers (Stegemeyer, 2004).

One of the first women of haute couture was the designer **Jeanne Paquin**. Paquin took models or mannequins out of the couture houses and into unique locations to promote her collection. Mme. Paquin took several mannequins in the same outfit to the opera and the races and created what we know today as the **finale** at the end of the show. Paquin had her models troop together one after the other at the end of her show. This became the forerunner of today's final parade of models in which each model walks down a runway, one after the other, signaling the end of the show (Everett and Swanson, 2001). Paquin was the first to see the importance of marketing a fashion presentation and feeding the press a unique story. She combined fashion and cultural events. She knew that her target market as well as the press was attending other popular high-profile performances such as races. Therefore, wherever possible she incorporated those cultural happenings with a fashion presentation.

Jean Patou was the first Frenchman to employ American business ideas and concepts. Mr. Patou's shows were major events in Paris, with the audience consisting of silk manufacturers, socialites, and customers. He was the first to hire the American mannequin/model. He had received feedback from clients suggesting that American women would not relate to the bodies of the French mannequins and, as a savvy businessman, Patou didn't wait for commerce to come to him; instead he traveled with his mannequins to America and Eastern Europe. He hosted grand gala openings, with champagne cocktail bars, hors d'oeuvres, and beautifully dressed models showing off his latest collection (Stegemeyer, 2004). Jean Patou essentially created the first designer **trunk shows and presentations**.

These designers and many others understood the importance of branding and marketing. They adopted the concept of using women as mannequins and set the precedent of **fashion models** as an integral and important part of the fashion show. This was most apparent in the 1980s and early 1990s with the birth of the "supermodel." The term "supermodel" was

A PROMENADE DES TOILETTES

Large Display of Imported Paris Costumes on Living Models.

About 200,000 persons yesterday, Friday, and Thursday witnessed the novel costume exhibition of Gimbel Brothers, in which the most attractive features of the Bois de Boulogne, Paris—the gorgeous Spring costumes—were reproduced.

The stage setting was unique. The porch of a Colonial residence fronted a handsome interior garden, outside of which was a larger garden, through which was a center path nearly 350 feet long, bordered by a flower-bedecked pergola.

Right and left were flowerbeds and seats for the thousands of guests who went to see the show morning and afternoon. Here and there were cages in which canaries voiced their thrilling songs. Electric lights glittered on all sides, resembling big diamonds amid verdure.

This reproduction of a corner of Fairyland was first enlivened by a reception and a parade of nearly a hundred bright-costumed people of all ages, from a five-year-old upward, who had gathered to attend a wedding in the Colonial mansion described. Then came the wedding march through the two gardens, along Bermuda lily lined pathways, through the wisteria and smilax twined pergola, furnishing an occasion for showing off the hats and gowns to the watching assemblage.

A more graceful scene was perhaps never produced in a dry good store. It was prettiness depicted in the most delicate manner possible, to the accompaniment of music from an orchestra hidden in a bower of flowers.

The several little girls (two of them twins) who acted as bridesmaids were of particular interest to the crowds of women and children who flocked to the show, which will be continued next week. In short, the "Promenade des Toilettes" in Greeley Square proved a new and brilliant chapter in the history of refined presentations of imported novelties.

Of course the so-called "Harem gown" was in evidence, and so was the latest Trouville bathing creation, and they were not the least admired of the many startling costumes.

FIGURE 1.1 *A news article featuring an in-store event "A Promenade des Toilettes."*
Courtesy of NY Times

coined by the press about a group of models who rose to celebrity status expanding the model's role, paycheck, and importance to branding.

Each of the above designers added, in his or her own way, to the evolution of the fashion show. Simultaneously, in the early 1900s, according to William Leach in his book *The Land of Desire*, many major American department stores, like Gimbels and Wanamaker's, were hosting extravagant productions, marketing exclusive Paris fashions shows to the masses. (Leach, 1994). These events can arguably be said to have been the first American fashion production shows and they ultimately created the form of the fashion show as we know it today. Living, breathing models parading through stores, theaters, parks, and other unconventional locations were precedent-setting events. These models and actors were taking part in the crafting of several big theatrical and outrageously huge productions. Over-the-top sales and marketing events, held at retailers in America and Europe, were the instigation of the classic runway show. What happened in between then and now is intriguing and can unveil much about not only the history of the fashion show itself but, perhaps even more importantly, about the times when fashion production was conceived.

Americans, throughout their fashion development, were constantly driven to find their place in the fashion world. This urge for self-sufficiency in the American design community was primarily apparent during the early 1900s. The inflow of Americans, and their move from rural life into urban city dwellings, drove department stores and designers to carve out their own fashion culture. This was the onset of the American fashion industry becoming independent from the chains and attendant high prices of **haute couture** in Paris. This was the salient factor in the birth of the American fashion industry. Americans craved their own style, reflective of haute couture but without the exclusive nature and contract dependence on Europe. These establishments created huge marketing campaigns and productions aimed at enticing customers, and thus defining some of the first fashion shows.

As early as 1910 stores like **Wanamaker's** and **Gimbels**, located in New York City and Philadelphia, held extrovertly themed productions based on Paris fashions, mysterious locations, and novels like *The Garden of Allah*, which mirrored the fashion trends of the day. The budgets were big. Wanamaker hired Broadway actors, built theatrical and provocative sets, and spent substantial dollars on décor and advertising. They paraded the actors and models around the store in themed costumes and clothing reflective of the trends in Europe. The goal of these major marketing productions was to give the **mass market** a taste of fashion and the glamour of Paris and other romantic locations without leaving New York City, or even better, without leaving the department store itself (Leach, 1994) (Figure 1.1).

Americans democratized fashion by taking fashion out of the control of couture and bringing it to the collective public, thus creating a fashion consciousness even among the masses. This was most significant during World War II when rations on materials such as nylon and silk and the closure of most of Paris's fashion houses forced Americans to create their own appropriate styles. (This mirrored the lifestyle of a hardworking nation at war.) This concept of opening the private world of fashion to the masses continues today to be an important part of sales and branding for most designers and is extremely relevant with major designers and retailers of the twenty-first century.

American fashion existed long before the 1940s and was centered in New York City. A group of designers and manufacturers rose to prominence during World War II, creating a particular style and crafting an authentic American look. This look highlighted **separates**. Women's fashion focused on items or pieces, such as blouses, skirts, pants, and suits. Soon these pieces became the norm. The female consumer moved away from one-piece dressing and defined American ready-to-wear and **sportswear**. Out of necessity and patriotic duty, women were not only volunteers but they worked in defense plants and manufacturing factories, replacing men. This naturally induced the acceptance and the popularity of the sportswear style (Milbank, 1989).

It was during this time that many American designers like **Claire McCardell, Bonnie Cashin, Vera Maxwell, Clare Potter,** and others brought creativity and ingenuity to their clothing. Additionally, as a result of working within the wartime rationing restrictions, they led the way in selling clothing at a substantially lesser price than couture pieces. Americans, following the trend of their department stores decades earlier, had now not only opened up the clothing industry to the masses but also created their own "American Style" and for a brief moment ruled the fashion world. During this period in New York City in 1943, one well-known press agent and publicist named Eleanor Lambert single-handedly launched American designers by hosting the first organized fashion week, named **Press Week** (Tiffany, 2011). The function of Press Week was to highlight American designers and again free America from its dependence on Paris as the fashion leader. Press Week took place while Paris fashion was essentially closed down due to World War II. Lambert had been hired by The Dress Institute in 1940 to help promote American fashion. The Dress Institute was a propaganda vehicle created by the labor unions and manufacturers to boost retail sales through strategic ad campaigns (Collins, 2004). New York City was then a chief apparel-manufacturing center, but its designers were basically unknown. Although Press Week started off slowly it grew into a hugely successful event. Today it is known as **Mercedes Benz Fashion Week**. It is currently held at Lincoln Center and produced by **IMG** (International Management Group), a global marketing agency and management company. IMG Fashion owns and operates many fashion events around the world. Although American Fashion Week still takes place twice a year, its function has varied little since Eleanor Lambert's reign. It is a time to bring American fashion designers together under one roof twice a year and to show their collections to the fashion press, buyers, and clients.

Although America had firmly set its feet in the fashion world with young bright, talented designers and manufacturers, and with Press Week on the way to becoming an American Fashion institution, Paris managed to regain its hold on the fashion world in 1947. It did so with Dior's new and revolutionary collections Number 8 and Corelle, known as the "**New Look**." The New Look was a design reaction against the wartime **silhouette**. Dior not only revolutionized the shape of women's clothing but also changed the way fashion was presented, marking another major step toward the modern catwalk presentation. After launching and using this manner of showing clothing, salon style presentations became commonplace in France. The staging in his salon or townhouse was themed and was delivered in a very theatrical manner for its time. The models themselves became part of the show, rather than simply being hangers upon which the clothing was draped. Dior asked his models to play a role and to become like the women who would wear his clothing. Dior had the models spinning, walking in a fast pace while making eye contact with the clients (Pochna, 1996). Dior's efforts were the seedlings for what is currently known as the **salon style show** or informal fashion show. (Refer to the interview with Morton Myles for more on salon style shows.)

FIGURE 1.2A *Models wearing an original 1947 Dior outfit (right)—known at the time as the New Look—and Dior's Newer Look.*
Courtesy of © Mirrorpix/Lebrecht Authors

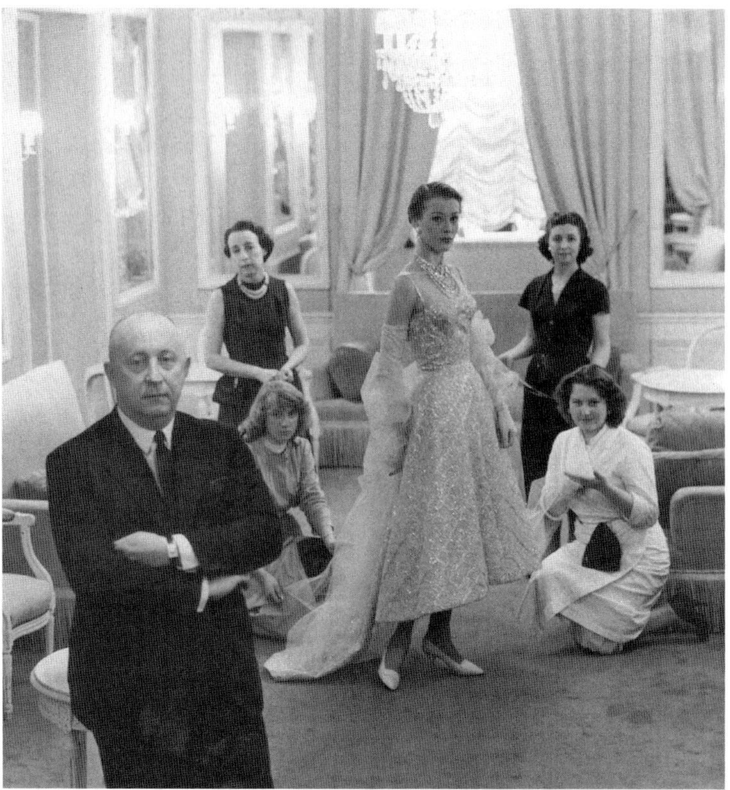

FIGURE 1.2B *Dior in studio.*
Courtesy of © Sueddeutsche Zeitung Photo/Lebrecht Music & Arts

Dior proffered a lifestyle. Ultimately, he was ahead of his time in branding a **lifestyle collection**. He was one of the most notable designers to successfully produce secondary and divisional collections such as hats, furs, and accessories. The most famous of his products was perfume, which was created in 1947. He was the first **couturier** to **license** his products. Licensing is the act by which an owner of a product or brand proclaims and retains the sole legal right to allow commercial use of that product or brand. There is no limit to what can be licensed. Examples of items that can be licensed are designs of watches, sunglasses, jewelry, and so on. Dior saw the potential of the clothing label itself eclipsing the designer, creating a longevity that still dominates the fashion world. It was Dior who brought Paris back into commanding the fashion world after it had essentially closed its doors because of World War II (Figure 1.2A and 1.2B).

America captured the fashion world in the 1940s. Paris rebounded in the late 1940s and 1950s with the return of Dior and his revolutionary collection. The 1960s, however, were consumed by Britain. They had the young market known as the "youth quake." They catered to the pop groups celebrated for their love of mod fashions. The active London streets and centers such as **Carnaby Street** and **Kings Road** supplied the disposable youth fashions and sold them to the musicians of the time. Carnaby Street, which housed popular stores, like "Biba," "His Clothes," and "Granny Takes a Trip," was the place to be and be seen. Passerbys, knowingly or not, were taking part in an ongoing organic fashion show of the trend-setting youth of London.

One of Britain's most influential designers, who changed the way runway shows looked and sounded, was **Mary Quant**. Mrs. Quant was acknowledged for designing and marketing her collection the "Ginger Group," which highlighted reasonably priced baby doll dresses and short skirts known as "the mini skirt," and defined the youth movement and market. She single-handedly changed runway shows forever. She catered to a new, younger clientele aptly named the **Youth Quake**. Mrs. Quant made fashion shows cool and hip. She added props and music, and made the milestone decision to take away commentary on the runway. She held a fast-paced, short runway show with over forty looks in just fourteen minutes (Quant, 1996). This set a new tempo, look, and sound for fashion shows. Quant and others focused on young people's need for change and saw the important role that youth would have as consumers (Figure 1.3).

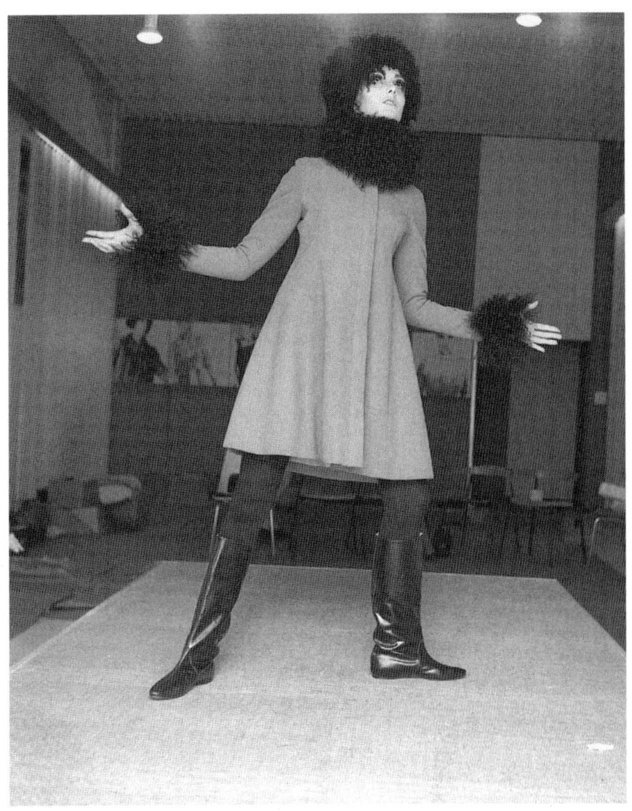

FIGURE 1.3 *Mary Quant Fashion Show rehearsal.*

Courtesy of © Lebrecht Music & Arts

Haute couture was becoming passé, overly priced, and unavailable to the general population. In England the Art School revolution was happening; in New York the underground art world was blossoming. By the late sixties another influential designer emerged who spoke to the artist, musicians, and creative people of the times. His name was **Ossie Clark**. Clark had a new approach to fashion shows and branding. He and his wife, printmaker **Celia Birtwell**, quickly became the new trend-setting designers of the area. Ossie was noted in London as the King of Kings Road (Figure 1.4).

The late 1960s was a time when models and celebrities started looking sexually ambiguous, reflecting musicians like Mick Jagger, from the rock and roll group the Rolling Stones, and New York artist Andy Warhol. Clark was the first contemporary designer to use celebrities and rock stars to promote and model his collection. The venue for the 1970 Quorum show was Chelsea Town Hall. In the show, musician Steve Miller played the music and **Lewis Leonard** of the renowned hair salon "The House of Leonard" styled the wild hairstyles. It was free and crazed with a myriad of innovations, including models dancing on the runway. As stated by Judith Watt, in her book titled *Ossie Clark 1965–1974*, "By now Quorum fashion shows had become major events at which a broad variety of London personalities met in a kind of chic melting-pot" (Watt, 2003). Ossie mixed tapes of music he liked and had his models dance and move with total creative freedom. These events were much more like a party than a fashion show.

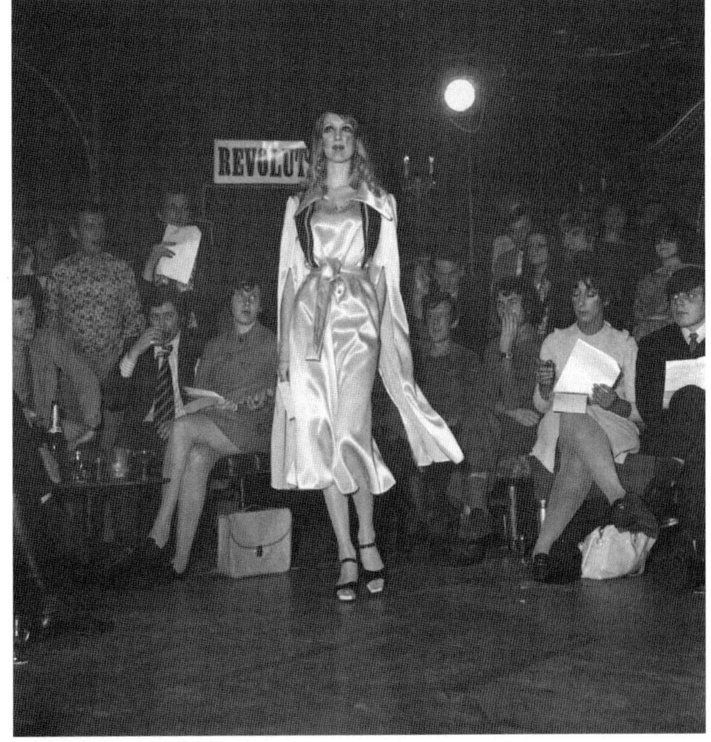

FIGURE 1.4 *Ossie Clark model on runway.*

Courtesy of © Lebrecht Music & Arts

In 1971 Ossie held a show at midnight at the Royal Court Theater, which didn't get started until 2:30 A.M. The A list attendees were just as much part of the show as the models. Ossie became part of the performance: With cigarette in hand he dressed each model behind a curtain that he ensured the audience could see through. All the models were famous friends, socialites, and clients—Linda and Paul McCartney, Twiggy, and Patti Boyd (the wife of George Harrison) were among them. Models were allowed to pace themselves, and the music was the newest and latest (Watt, 2003). The show itself took hours and was a surreal modern experience. Ossie Clark changed the idea of the runway show. He gave rise to and formulated the fashion show as a "must see" experience. The impact of his innovations was so profound that people desperately tried to get inside.

Clark was not the only designer of the 1970s to experiment with the fashion show. The Japanese designer Takada Kenzo and American designer Halston both majored ready-to-wear shows with innovation. **Kenzo** held his shows on a stage rather than a traditional runway. He was known for his avant-garde approach to design and for his use of experimentation on the runway. Halston held unique and creative shows in his newly opened showroom and did not use raised runways. He also had models walk barefoot. Clark, Kenzo, and Halston all broke with the haute couture tradition and focused on innovative self-expression.

The 1970s were a time of inventive expression on the runway, a redefining of the term "fashion show" into a union of art, music, and fashion. By the end of the 1970s, fashion shows would take another major leap forward.

The 1980s were an era that included the birth of American MTV, obsession with British royalty, and class extremes. It became a decade of worshipping status symbols and driving financial success. With designs such as the power suit for women and men's preoccupation with dressing in formal wear, clothing became the definition of the "new elite." Opulence and excess were the themes for many fashion shows across both continents. This was before the innovation of Internet, social media, and a groundbreaking time for the fashion show industry. The majority of fashion shows in the 1980s became big productions with excessive lighting, costumes, and ornate staging. The media began covering major shows and sharing the information, which once was exclusively for press, buyers, and elite clientele, with the general public.

It was during the 1980s that fashion shows became more inclusive events, rather than exclusive industry-only productions. This was the time when savvy designers, like **Bill Blass**, Pierre Cardin, and others, expanded the licensing of their names to companies handling or producing such things as perfumes, chocolates, cosmetics, wines, and cars. In 1980 CNN had just started on the air and launched a new fashion segment called *Style with Elsa Klensch*. This television show that was broadcast internationally was the first of its kind. It was a regularly scheduled program on style, fashion, and beauty. The show ran from 1980 to 2000. Elsa built a market that had not existed before, opened the world of fashion and fashion shows to the unassuming viewer, and created a very loyal following. Mrs. Klensch helped launch many young designers' careers, highlighted retailers, and gave the world a view into the fashion show milieu, previously reserved for the fashion elite. According to Jason Gay, in an interview with Elsa for the *Observer* in 2001, "Mrs. Klensch acknowledges that her business has changed—and not necessarily for the better. She brought a journalist's serious eye to fashion. Many of her successors are bubbly chatterboxes with great teeth but little expertise" (Gay, 2001). This was a time before bloggers, but also a precursor to the shift in who would be the gatekeepers of fashion information

For French designers **Thierry Mugler** and **Claude Montana**, the 1980s was their strongest and most profitable period. Both designers used big staged production shows as a tool for advertising and branding. Mugler had thousands of people attending his shows and for the first time provided a large number of tickets for the general public to purchase (Quick, 2004). This marked an important change in fashion shows: It was the first time the general public was allowed to attend a couture show in large numbers and thus began the trend for fashion shows becoming not only inclusive public events but also vehicles for entertainment. Montana and

Mugler both grabbed the attention of the press and media by holding over-the-top fashion shows. These shows that were reflective of the 1970s became much more about the "event" than the clothing itself. By the end of this opulent and decadent era in fashion a new fashion show norm would emerge, led by a group of models that quickly rose to fame in the late 1980s and early 1990s. These models spawned a new era and coined the term **supermodel**. (Figure 1.5).

FIGURE 1.5 *Mugler used nontraditional models.*
Courtesy of Mirrorpix/Newscom

Five powerful women were on the cover of *Vogue*'s first issue for 1990: Naomi Campbell, Linda Evangelista, Tatijana Patitz, Christy Turlington, and Cindy Crawford. These women and other highly paid supermodels graced the runways of many designers (Watson, 2008). They eclipsed celebrities for magazine covers and became, for many designers, equally important as the clothing they wore. These supermodels emerged as celebrities and advertising tools almost overnight.

Yet there was a downside to their presence; they were expensive. Some began acting as though they were more important than the clothing they modeled. This was aptly indicated by the famous quote from Linda Evangelista in an interview with Jonathan Van Meter "We don't get out of bed for less than $10,000 a day" (Van Meter, 1990). This started a backlash of negativity from the buying public, designers, and advertisers. Clever retailers and designers used these models as tools for advertising yet never lost control of their own brand and collection.

During the early 1990s, another distinctive period of change for the fashion show emerged as clothing once again mirrored the political, social, and economic environments. The 1990s runway shows were responding to the backlash of the decade and superfluous attitude of the 1980s. The zeitgeist or spirit of the 1990s was more subdued. Designers like Donna Karen, Calvin Klein, and the emerging new face Marc Jacobs scaled down the drama of the highly produced shows and focused instead on the clothing itself. Models walked with a normal pace. All emphasis was concentrated on the garments they were modeling. Hair was simple and makeup natural (Everett and Swanson, 2001). It was in this period that the Council of Fashion Designers of America created Seventh on Sixth as a nonprofit organization, with Fern Mallis as its executive director. This was an important change in the runway show for America. It built upon Lambert's Press Week and secured New York as one of the major players in fashion weeks around the world, paving the way for more American designers to highlight their collections on the runway. The organization has grown from its humble beginnings to become one of the largest, most influential fashion centers in the world. New York Fashion Week is home to the largest, well-known designers; however, emerging American designers also find their place at this fashion week. The event brings buyers, retailers, and fashion press from around the globe to view, comment, and place orders for the collections.

By the late 1990s a new crop of creative experimental designers emerged and, once again, the fashion show became the new performance art, which combined elements from different eras. For the last two decades the fashion show has become even more diversified, with designers seeking unique locations, utilizing different models, and looking to redefine the traditional runway show. Designers like Alexander McQueen were known for outlandish antics and theatrics on the runway and for avant-garde clothing (Watson, 2008). In 2004 the innovative and modern women's designer Yeohlee Teng held a distinctive fashion show titled "Fashion Underground" on a subway platform underneath Bryant Park. It celebrated the centennial of the New York Metro. Yeohlee used real women and celebrities like Farrah

Fawcett as models and hired street drummers to keep the beat. She had all the press from Bryant Park running from their tents, rushing to be present at her alternative underground location. Yeohlee's show is a perfect example of redefining the runway. The audience was able to see functional clothing in a real-world unconventional setting (Personnal Interview May 11, 2011).

Currently, designers are changing the nature of the fashion show yet again. For example, Alexander Wang focuses more on gathering an urban crowd to mirror his hip New York girl collection and recreates the Ossie Clark celebrity party feel of the 1970s. Tom Ford opts for a return to exclusivity with the launch of his much-anticipated 2011 women's collection. Mr. Ford had a limited guest list of 100 and very little press was allowed inside. His models were some of his favorite famous muses. He brought back commentary by announcing each of his models, including Lauren Hutton, Julianne Moore, and Beyoncé Knowles, as they came down the runway. Ford had no live streaming of the show and there was no rush for photographs to be posted online (Mower, 2010). Mr. Ford returned to a simpler, more refined fashion show template, which directly reflected the clothing and spirit of his collection. Numerous others nodded to the past and moved forward with their own resourceful additions or subtractions to the runway, combining different historical references, types of shows, and concepts to strengthen their own images (Figure 1.6).

FIGURE 1.6 *Model and designer Erin Wasson poses backstage with designer Alexander Wang.*
Courtesy of John Calder

We are presently in a period of change where the only rule is that there are no rules; for example, the tents at Bryant Park, the iconic American home for Mercedes Benz Fashion Week, no longer exist. Fern Mallis, the former executive director of the CFDA and current vice-president of IMG Fashion, has stepped down to start her own production company, and bloggers, rock stars, and everyone in between feel a part of the fashion week experience. Celebrities are creative directors for historic fashion brands and many are designing their own collections. Sarah Jessica Parker has come and gone as creative director for Halston Heritage and the child-actors-turned-fashion-moguls Mary Kate and Ashley Olsen have seen great success with their coveted Row collection. Since 2000, social media and Web have had the biggest influence in changing the way fashion shows are viewed, held, and experienced. Designers like Norma Kamali and Hussein Chalayan both created short films as a medium to showcase their 2012 collections.

These vehicles for promotion have both intentionally and unintentionally created an inclusive environment for the masses, enabling their participation in the fashion week experience. Stylists, producers, and creative directors have never been busier. Retailers are back to holding fashion events in their stores, and fashion is part of most people's daily life. Designers are streaming their shows live on YouTube, tweeting about the show as it happens. Bloggers and journalists are posting photos from shows immediately. Simply put, "There is no place to hide"—no secrecy. This openness and immediacy have not only changed the way fashion shows look, sound, and feel, but also began to alter the fashion business itself. The timeliness for production, the ability to gain press awareness, and the consumers' need for immediate goods, among other things, have caused many designers to keep limited items from the runway collection available for purchase. International retailers like Zara, the Spanish fashion chain, control the designs, production, and distribution of their product, owning their production in house to speed up delivery times and cut cost. In 2008 Zara stores sped up production even further so they could fill the need of the consumers' impatience for the new. They replenished inventory with new designs every week (Johnson and Rowhieder, 2008). This trend toward speeding up production continues to grow. Norma Kamali stocked product available for sale on her website immediately following her 3D presentation at Lincoln Center (http://www.normakamali3d.com).

The business of fashion shows continues to evolve and directly affect the look, feel, and function of the fashion show. Industry leaders are consistently searching for ways to directly connect the consumer to the world of fashion. One successful strategic attempt to connect the consumer with the retailer and fashion industry is the creation of Fashion's Night Out.

Fashion's Night Out

Anna Wintour, the editor-in-chief of *American Vogue,* and the Council of Fashion Designers of America (CFDA) launched **Fashion's Night Out (FNO)** as a way to connect with the consumer during fashion week. Special late-night retail events are held throughout the city and the world. FNO includes everyone who wants to experience fashion week and the 2010 Fashion's Night Out held the largest open-to-the-public fashion show in New York City's history. Tickets were sold at Lincoln Center with a portion of the proceeds benefiting the New York City AIDS fund (Strzemien, 2010). FNO has expanded to cities all over America hosting their own micro version of the event. They encouraged live streaming and public participation of the shows and fostered retail sales (Figures 1.7 and 1.8).

The growing nature of the runway show and fashion business has opened doors providing many more opportunities for young designers, retailers, manufacturers, and those of us bringing it all together, the **production teams**.

FIGURE 1.7 *Anna Wintour and other fashion press in the front row.*
Courtesy of John Calder

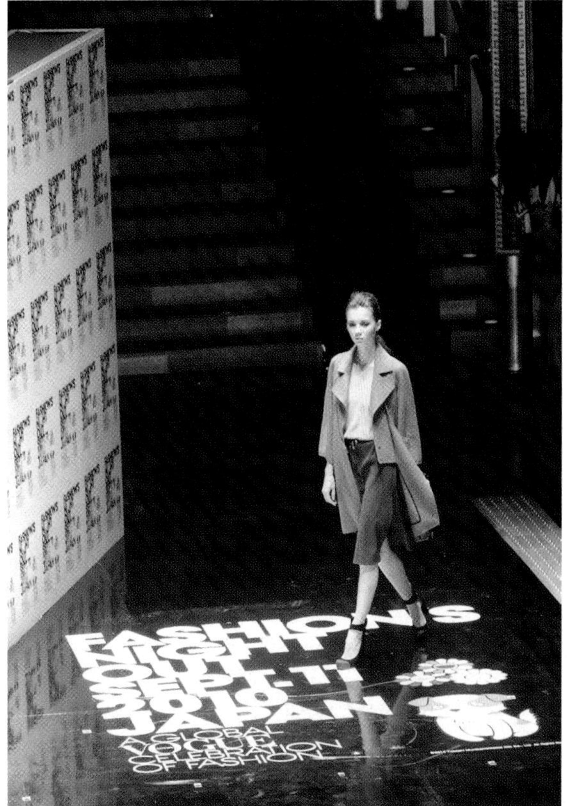

FIGURE 1.8 *Fashion's Night Out in Tokyo, Japan.*
Courtesy of EVERETT KENNEDY BROWN/EPA/Newscom

Timeline of Influential Designers and Events

This is a brief timeline of influential designers and events that helped shape the modern fashion show.

1847	- Charles Fredrick Worth—First person to use live women as models and coined the term "mannequin."
Late 1800s	- Jeanne Paquin—Took models/mannequins to unique locations like the opera and races; creator of the Finale.
Early 1900s	- Jean Patou—First to hire American models. Takes them on the road, creating one of the first trunk shows.
	- American department stores Wanamaker's and Gimbels bring the glamour of Paris fashion into the mass market with in-store large-scale theatrical fashion events, creating the modern production show.
1940–1945	- American designers launch their own unique style known as sportswear. Publicist Eleanor Lambert launches press week.
1947–1957	- Publicist Eleanor Lambert Dior's "New Look" revolutionizes fashion. Dior's innovative use of models changes the way fashions are presented, creating the salon style show. Paris dominates fashion once again.
1960s	- Mary Quant's successfully targets the youth market, named the "Youth Quake." Quant changes the runway show, adding music, staging, and props, and doing away with commentary.
1970s	- The birth of avant-garde performance as fashion shows with designers such as Takada Kenzo and Ossie Clark.
1980s	- The beginning of the era of the super model. CNN launches *Style with Elsa Klensch*. The era of the big production show with designers such as Claude Montana and Thierry Mugler.
Early 1990s	- A backlash to the opulence of the 1980s. Designers lean toward more simple fashion shows. CFDA creates 7th on 6th.
1998	- The first cybercast fashion show features the YSL Couture collection partnered with *Fashion Live*. The fashion show became the new performance art, which combined elements from different eras.
2000	- A return to big production and inclusion of technology with Victoria's Secret Fashion Shows and designers like Alexander McQueen.
2004	- Many designers look for alternative locations for runway shows. Designer Yeohlee Teng hosts "Fashion Underground."
2008	- MAC and Milk Initiative.
2010	- *Vogue* and CFDA launch Fashion's Night Out Tom Ford launches exclusive women's collection and uses celebrities as models, bringing back commentary to the runway.

Now that we understand the general history of the fashion show, we must examine what is the function of a fashion show and why designers, manufacturers, and retailers hold such events. Have the reasons changed in a hundred years? Are fashion shows still an important part of the business of fashion? Does understanding the past help in executing a strong, unique, and profitable collection?

The Business of Fashion Shows

The twenty-first century has been a time of change in the fashion world. Over the last decade, America and much of the Western world have been at war. Recession and economic hardship have hit most of the globe. No industry has been immune to the challenges of the era, including the fashion industry. Many historic fashion houses closed their doors, filed bankruptcy, created mergers, or **vertically integrated** in order to stay afloat. A business that is in control of production from raw material to retailing is referred to as being vertically integrated. In 2009 the fashion world was shocked to hear that luxury designer and French couturier Christian Lacroix had filed for bankruptcy. The enormous cost involved in producing several fashion shows a year has driven many designers to find alternative locations and new ways to show a collection. Many designers have turned to the Internet to reach a wider audience and have sought out unique locations that use technology and traditional presentations.

Advertisement, Branding, and Promotion

Why are fashion shows produced? They are produced because they are a vital and integral part of the business of fashion. Fashion shows continue to be one of, if not the best, ways for designers, manufacturers, and retailers to sell their product, showcase the latest in apparel trends, and promote their brands. The fashion show, regardless of its specific category, is one of the greatest vehicles for **advertising** and **branding** a collection. Advertising is the activity of attracting public attention to a product or business, by means of paid announcements in print, broadcast, or electronic media. Branding is a means of distinguishing one's company, products, or services from another's and of creating and maintaining a positive image. Fashion show is one of the oldest forms of **advertising and promotion** and can breathe new life into a dying brand, showcase a new designer to the masses, test the market, and cater to a new audience. The current trend in the industry is to showcase not just a garment but also a lifestyle. Dior was one of the first designers to do this and many others have followed in his footsteps. The catwalk is one of the best places for up-and-coming designers and seasoned houses to launch or reinvent their lifestyle image. The hope is that the consumer will relate to the image they are projecting and buy into the lifestyle pitch. This rebranding can work in more than one way. Some designers like Tommy Hilfiger missed the mark with their rebranding strategy and actually hurt the image of their collection. In 2000, Hilfiger deviated from his classic American image and strong logo placement in an attempt to drive sales and be on or ahead of trend. Hilfiger's customer was both the preppy set and the hip-hop urban community. Hilfiger made the decision to deviate from his formula "classics with a twist," losing many of his loyal customers. After much examination and collaborations including that of his exclusive relationship with Macys, Hilfiger is now more than back on track. He reported that 2009 was his best year in his twenty-five years of business. Tommy Hilfiger returned to his original brand and slowly regained his customer base (Ritson, 2006). Tom Ford has used exclusivity and celebrity muses to launch and brand his new collection. Branding and advertising are two of the most important vehicles a designer or retailer has. The fashion show can both build a brand and hurt a brand depending on the targeting of the proper audience, awareness, and its execution.

Fashion Shows and Education

Selling, branding, and promotion of products are not the only reasons to hold a fashion show or event. Students studying fashion design and marketing execute fashion shows as real life-learning tools and also as a merchandising exercise in preparation for marketing their own designs. By learning the process at every level, students gain a stronger understanding of the role of fashion show production in marketing and design. Many young designers can gain knowledge of their own collections by holding and participating in small community shows. If the student's work is strong and presented well, a student can be highlighted in larger local and even national fashion events and runway shows.

Fashion Shows and the Community

Community partnerships and charitable works are other very popular reasons to hold a fashion show. Many local retailers, designers, schools, and specialty boutiques will take part in community fashion events and shows as a way to build awareness, raise money for charities, and showcase their product. This type of fashion event is a great way for potential producers, models, stylists, and others interested in the fashion industry to get real-world experience without leaving their own city. Many local and regional shows have large budgets, raise thousands of dollars for needy causes, and hire professional producers. This type of show can range from a luncheon with tearoom modeling to a full-scale runway event.

Technology and Fashion Show Production

In our modern high-tech world, designers will quickly know the results of their latest collection simply by checking Facebook, Twitter, or any blogger who has seen the show. In 1996, Yves Saint Laurent (YSL) was the first to hold a live cybercast of his show partnering with Fashion Live Today. Use of technology as a vehicle to inform customers and press about a collection in real time has become the norm. Technology feeds consumers' insatiable need for information about current trends. The buyers and traditional reviewers (i.e., the gatekeepers) from fashion periodicals and magazines are still attending shows, yet they too have had to change the way in which they report and review. In a response to the public's need for immediate information, they have incorporated technology and ways to disseminate information quickly to their clients, readers, and the general population. Journalists also use mobile twitpics and live tweeting as the show is happening. In addition, some designers are employing technology as the driving vehicle for their fashion presentations. For example, designers like Norma Kamali, Hussein Chalayan, and Burberry all employed technology as a vehicle to highlight and present their 2012 collections.

Although Lincoln Center is the new home for New York Fashion Week, other unique locations—most notably Milk Studios, the premier photography studio that combines music, fashion, and art—have become paramount with young innovators of fashion. Mazdack Rassi, the creative director from Milk, stated in his industry insider interview for this text that he just recently read an article from *The New York Times* stating, "Lincoln Center may have the crème of the crop of designers and the tents, but Milk studios has the Internet." Milk has embraced technology, and transformed the way fashion presentations, photo shoots, and shows are experienced.

Location of Shows

The business of the fashion show also depends on the location of the show. Fashion events in Dallas have a very different need to fill than fashion shows during fashion weeks in New York, Paris, or Milan, which are generally for the press, bloggers, and wholesale buyers. Designers, students, and retailers are always looking for the right location to help bring the desired customer base, highlight work, generate energy about the collection, and promote sales.

Regional markets, like Dallas, according to Jan Strimple of Jan Strimple Productions are for the purpose of motivating the consumer to purchase the product. It is the producer's job to create a sense of drama and excitement to ultimately sell the designer's product. The Dallas ladies, who lunch, need to relate to the clothing they are seeing coming down the runway. At the same time it needs to be entertaining. Regional shows outside of major fashion markets are, most often, charity shows, student shows, and retail events executed solely for the consumer.

New York Fashion Week has seen a trend in designers seeking unique locations. Erin Wasson held her RVCA 2010 collection at the ABC carpet store, and many emerging young designers on a budget are flocking to Milk Studios to showcase their collections during fashion week.

MAC and Milk Initiative

The **MAC and Milk Initiative,** which began in spring 2008, had thirty emerging fashion designers display their collections in West Chelsea rather than in the Lincoln Center. The collaboration between MAC Cosmetics and Milk Studios continues with its initiative and proactive approach to highlighting young talent and utilizing technology. According to comments by Rassi, "MAC and Milk is now a major part of fashion week. It's still free of charge to all of the designers. A lot of people compare MAC and Milk to the tents, but we are completely different. We don't charge. We raise money through sponsorships. MAC and Milk has become a launch pad for young talent."

FIGURE 1.9 *A peek at MAC and Milk during fashion week.*
Courtesy of Joe Schildhorn/BFAnyc.com

Mazdack Rassi hopes the space will allow imaginative ways of showing clothes, as well as a place to be creative and push the envelope. Milk is tied to its roots, supporting young talent. **Milk Made** is an online extension of MAC and Milk and a community website featuring artists, photographers, editors, and bloggers who contribute to the site. This diverse group of talented individuals share experiences, and projects, providing the public a peek into the world of Milk. The website includes written editorial blog posts, exclusive photo commissions, cell phone content, and an interactive events calendar (Figure 1.9).

Industry Insider

American Designer Morton Myles

Morton Myles, the distinguished American designer who created the iconic robin's egg dress, which Jacqueline Kennedy wore on the cover of the 1961 *Look* magazine, talks about his time as a young designer working for Jacques Fath in Paris and his journey to 7th Avenue (Figure 1.10). He became one of a handful of American designers whose name eclipsed the manufacturer for whom he was designing. Mr. Myles addresses in this interview the functions of fashion shows, types of fashion shows, roles of models, and the business of fashion as he has experienced it during his esteemed career.

WHAT WERE THE FUNCTIONS OF FASHION SHOWS DURING YOUR TRAINING IN EUROPE?

There was really only one function in the past and it was to sell clothes. The function has since transgressed into other areas. Now the great big fashion shows are there to sell accessories, perfume, and all the products the designers and their backers make. The clothes seem to be the very last thing. My original concept of what was the function of the fashion show and what I saw when I was training in Paris was a means of showing and selling clothes. They were presented in salon rooms in townhouses in Paris. The best example was Christian Dior. The House of Dior, which went from one townhouse, spread down the street to Avenue Montagne to another. They kept adding more townhouses. The professional buyers were assigned seats, and you had a ribbon in your passport, which allowed you to see the collection that you already paid for through your commissionate (deposit). That proved that you were serious.

FIGURE 1.10 *Morton Myles and model in showroom.*
Courtesy of Morton Myles

WHAT WERE THE ROLES OF THE MODELS IN PARIS AT THAT TIME AND HOW DID THEY DIFFER FROM MODELS TODAY?

Paris was different from New York because in Paris the house employed house models like in New York. However, the house models were also the show models. In New York the house model was a lovely person that was paid less but had a perfect figure. She wasn't chic enough (had enough style) to show. In Paris the fitting models all showed, and if there were three or four fitting models they showed along with the models that were hired. But by the time show time came/collection came, there might have been only eight or ten models, not like the twenty-three or thirty-three models they would have used today. The French would have laughed at that. They thought that money should be spent for the clothes, the accessories, the perfumes, and everything else, and the models were paid next to nothing.

FOR WHOM DID YOU WORK IN PARIS AND HOW LONG WERE YOU THERE?

I worked for Jacques Fath for three years. The reason I keep talking about Dior is that I went in to an interview at Jacques Fath to practice, and to get the courage, and to know what to say when I went to Dior. But I got the job at Jacques Fath as a gopher, and then moved all around the fashion house. I worked in the embroidery house, the button house, and the fabric and trim departments. I wanted the ability to learn all the ways designers work and so I never got to Dior. But I met Christian Dior at a cocktail party in New York a few years later. Of course, he assured me that I had made a very wise choice. Of course I knew Jacques Fath loathed him and he loathed Jacques Fath. He invited me to come back and see him. By then I was secure in my job. This is just before he passed away. But I did go back and I did see him there (Paris) and that's when I had a tour of his workroom. I was there all together for three years. If you totaled all the years I stayed and bought fabrics and went to the collections it was a century.

(*Continued*)

Industry Insider (Continued)

American Designer Morton Myles

HOW DID YOU MAKE YOUR WAY TO NEW YORK CITY AND 7TH AVE?

I asked Monsieur Fath if I had a future in Paris. He said no. He said only a rare few make it because of strong family backing giving the example of Givenchy. He said I was much better off with all the skills I acquired to go to 7th Ave. As I was leaving he said he had an idea about America and said one day he may call on me. He did come back to America and was the first French designer to bring prêt-à-porter to the states in the early 1950s.

ONCE YOU WERE IN NEW YORK HOW WERE COLLECTIONS SHOWN?

In 1959 I was a second designer for Herbert Sondheim. It was my job to show the collection. I had never seen a collection shown in New York and had to ask the models what to do. The models introduced me to the best mannequin agencies (model agencies). These agencies were the backbone of 7th Ave. We used six or eight models and we showed the collection from a model room outside of the showroom for four days a week for four weeks. On Friday the fifth day of showing was always reserved for writing orders. We didn't have hair and makeup people. The models did it themselves. They were hired by the hour and made around fifty dollars an hour. The fit models were paid around thirty dollars an hour.

HOW DID SHOWING A COLLECTION CHANGE ONCE YOU HAD YOUR OWN BUSINESS?

Once I had my own company you had to add another dimension called the cost of doing it all. The cost of fashion shows skyrocketed. I did two kinds of shows, a showroom and Press show. The showroom show was to sell clothing. It was no longer every day for four weeks. It was done once. After the show buyers would return and house models would give them a private showing to make them feel special. We had people in seats out toward the elevator; it was so crowded. We started putting runways in because the people in the third or fourth row couldn't see anymore. No longer could anyone touch the fabrics, and the salon-style intimate show like in Paris was gone. Background music was added. We never had music in Paris; there was commentary and names given to the collection. It was "jardin" this and "jardin" that (garden this garden that). They spoke about the collection. In New York, they gave the collections numbers and names. Sometimes it took so long to write down the names and numbers you missed items.

As time went on, the shows became more dramatic. In 1981 for instance, Saks asked me to do a ball gown for a charity for the Philharmonic and I did a whole collection of ball dresses. This hadn't been done in ages and I made ten or twelve of them. I had music from the ballroom scenes of great waltzes and it tore down the house at the showroom and it tore down the house at the Press show. For the Press show I showed a few daytime dresses at the plaza hotel and then stopped everything. Everything went dark. It was a chance for all the models to get on stage. They were all wearing ball gowns and it was still pitch dark. Suddenly you heard this triumphant waltz music and all the lights went on at once. The models were told they could peel off any way they wanted.

WHERE DO YOU BELIEVE FASHION IS TODAY?

I'll never forget what Christian Dior told me at that cocktail party so many years ago. He said you had to get a lot out of a collection. The first collection was for the fat duchesses; you need to cover their arms and back. The second collection was for their daughters, who in twenty years will be the fat duchesses, but now are fashion forward French women. The third collection is for the Press. They make sure the first two groups buy the collection. I always tried to apply that. My goal was to make clothing that was accessible, with quality fabrics, sold to more than just the very wealthy.

The problem with fashion today is that there is no leadership, no expertise. The kids took over. Once the inspiration for clothing came from the streets, the music, the drugs, it cannot be fashion. Therefore, it is simply clothing. There is a big difference between fashion and clothing. No one needs fashion. It satisfies your inner self. There is a desire to look like you know what you're doing or be part of the fashion forward group, the group that makes things happen. But there are no groups that make things happen anymore.

IS THERE ONE ASPECT OF YOUR CAREER FOR WHICH YOU WOULD LIKE TO BE REMEMBERED?

I would like to be remembered for having honesty and integrity in delivering what I showed. I never wanted to do couture prices and never did. I kept prices at one point below 200 and in the later years 300 dollars, using the most expensive fabrics that I could. Most of the fabrics came from Milan and Paris—the same fabrics that were used in haute couture. The quality was there.

Excerpts from Morton Myles Interview, February 18, 2010.

Industry Insider

Fashion Designer Angel Sanchez

Venezuelan architect-turned-fashion designer Angel Sanchez discusses his evolution from showing his collection in Bryant Park to his own New York showroom (Figure 1.11). He shares his process for designing and manufacturing all of his collections and the importance of a look book as a sales tool and his new role in Project Runway Latin America.

WHERE DO YOU CURRENTLY SHOW YOUR COLLECTION?

I showed with a presentation in the tents at Bryant Park for years. This kind of presentation, when you share a venue with other designers, is the best way to save money. Then I decided to show in house and do a look book. The look book is the most important tool after the fashion show to send to buyers and to send to the stores. It is the only way people remember, because during the show it is so much information at once.

WHAT IS THE FUNCTION OF THE SHOWROOM?

I designed this space to be easy to work in while designing the collection and holding fashion week. During fashion week we, in the showroom, work for very private personal shoppers. We are not open to the public. It's by appointment. We have built a very small runway, so we have a fashion week in the showroom. We lay two rows of chairs and then my two fitting rooms in the back are used to change models. Normally after the presentation we have two or three days of market appointments and that's when the buyer comes with the paperwork to place the order. Then we present the whole collection with one or two models and they (the buyer) take notes. They like it so much that they say it reminds them of the European way to show—the old fashion way. That really works so well.

FOR WHAT ARE YOU MOST WELL KNOWN?

My bridal collection. It is very clean. It's romantic, but it's not too decorated. I design my bridal collection for many different celebrities and clients. I did the Eva Longoria and Sandra Bullock wedding dresses.

FIGURE 1.11 *Industry insider designer Angel Sanchez.*
Courtesy of Angel Sanchez

Excerpts from interview with Angel Sanchez, April 20, 2011.

I have a lower-price bridal line called Angel; it is simpler than my Angel Sanchez line. In addition I have ready-to-wear collections and evening Sanchez is my new ready-to-wear collection geared for a younger market. In the Angel Sanchez Evening collection the approach is young and graphic, but still there is separation with each of the collections.

TELL US ABOUT PROJECT RUNWAY LATIN AMERICA.

I am the Michael Kors version in Spanish. This is the second season. The show is fantastic! It's a little complicated. It's far away. I have to move there for almost two months to do the filming.

HOW DO YOU CONSIDER THE TALENT OF THE CONTESTANTS ON PROJECT RUNWAY LATIN AMERICA?

For the first year I was very surprised honestly, because you never know how you would find new, younger designers. The winner was from Colombia and we have contestants from all around South America. So it's not like here. Here it's all United States. In Latin America it's a competition between countries. It's about a designer, who is the winner in Columbia or Peru. So it's fun. It's intense when you are at the end; it's hard you have to eliminate one person every episode, but they've gained experience by being there.

WHO HANDLES PUBLIC RELATIONS FOR ANGEL SANCHEZ?

Carolina Alverez is in charge of press. It's nice to have an in-house PR director because they are involved with the whole philosophy of the collection, everything about our company.

WHAT IS YOUR PROCESS FOR DESIGNING A COLLECTION?

I go to my private space, my office, and I close the door, so I can hide myself and work on my fabric selection. I sacrifice having a window to the street to having a window to my sample room. We normally start working with the first ideas and then Armando, who's my assistant, and my team develop a sample. We are always checking proportion and details. We're always sketching. We also do special orders in the showroom. We don't manufacture here. We only do special orders and samples. We have two or three companies that make the production for the retail stores. Then we have people in house working with fabrics, quality control, and packaging before we send the merchandise to the stores. They have to check the store orders and put it all together. I really enjoy also having control over our quality control in house. I don't allow the factories to send it to the store. The garment comes here and we check everything. If everything is fine, we pack and send it.

Mazdack Rassi

Mazdack Rassi, the founder and creative director of Milk Studios, talks about Milk's beginnings, their relationship with MAC Cosmetics, and the important role that MAC and Milk play in fashion week and in fostering new talent.

HOW DID MILK STUDIOS BECOME SUCH AN IMPORTANT PART OF FASHION WEEK?

Our main business is photography, creating media, and content, but fashion shows were always with us because we learned from the best and were able to do it better than everyone else.

So for us it's kind of part of our DNA. Before Milk was even finished, it was under construction, in New York City, right between Chelsea and the West Village, a little sliver of land called "meat-packing." We bought this building where Milk is. Milk today occupies about one-third of the building. So we have about 80,000 square feet here, but we started very small. We just had the eighth floor and the rest was empty. I used to skateboard to work. There was this PR guy downstairs. His name was Keith Baptista. He is a big shot at KCD. Back then I didn't even know what KCD was. It is one of the largest public relations firms and they also produce tons of shows. He was downstairs and he was basically scouring the neighborhood to find alternative spaces, to Lincoln Center, for a client. That was in 1998. The client ended up being Calvin Klein. Calvin made Milk his home. We ended up doing it for eight years, which is sixteen shows in a row. Calvin really helped shape the DNA of Milk. Most people don't know that. He was sort of a mentor on aesthetic and where we come from and how we handle ourselves. The first few shows for Calvin we were just the space. Then we started to help produce it, building it—and that changed everything for us.

HOW HAVE MILK FASHION SHOWS CHANGED SINCE THE CALVIN KLEIN YEARS?

So after Calvin Klein we were like, we have to go back to our roots, to who we are. I didn't want 1,100 people in the show anymore. I wanted to be a part of the younger generation, which Milk was known for. So we looked around. Who's going to be next? Who's going to be the next kids who are going to make it? We found these two young, incredible guys; their line was Proenza Schouler. Jack and Lazaro are part of the Milk family. We said do you guys want to show at Milk? Just pay us what you can in the beginning. They came and we did about three years (six shows) with them. During that period, they won the CFDA award, and became the biggest designers in the world. They sort of outgrew us, so we went back to our roots. We found this young girl named Do-Ri. By the way, they're all Parson's kids. Milk was so successful we thought we had to give back to the young designers. We started building this community of young designers who do presentations around the show, so we would drive the traffic here to see Proenza. We would say, "Hey, there's like ten young kids upstairs. Do you want to go see them?" It started building this momentum.

HOW DID MAC AND MILK GET STARTED?

It was 2008, and the economy tanked. We found ourselves in a position in which none of the young kids were calling us. They were all broke, and their companies were literally folding. We always had a program with MAC Cosmetics, which is an Estee Lauder brand. It was called "MAC and Milk." It brought young makeup artists doing symposiums with the great makeup artists at Milk. I was speaking with the MAC cosmetics people. I said, "You know, the program is great, but we have to do something about all these kids. You guys could give me half the money perhaps that you spend at the tents. We could then take all these kids and go out of the way to help them. It cost money to put on a show." She said, "You know what? Actually I was calling you because I had an idea, to do the same thing." It all came together. It was sixty days before September fashion week, four seasons ago. MAC was on board! KCD produced the show. We had Proenza back within forty-eight hours and we had a roster which was free of charge to every designer. We had Proenza back downstairs as our anchor, and we had thirty-seven young designers that got to show for free. We had presentations upstairs, runway shows downstairs, and Proenza in the gallery on the first floor. It was called MAC and Milk. In one week we had to produce thirty-seven shows, presentations, parties, and concerts, because we can't do anything without throwing a party these days. It was all about the youth. It was about these kids and giving them the opportunity to show their clothes. It became this unbelievable thing.

DO YOU HAVE SOME ADVICE FOR YOUNG PEOPLE IN THE INDUSTRY?

The one person who I think taught me how to work within the industry and how to create fashion shows was Julie Mannion who is one of the owners of KCD. I come from the school of Julie Mannion. I think that today a lot of the young people in our industry don't have the mentors we used to have, the people that we got to work with like Calvin, and Julie. Everyone is growing up very quickly without paying their dues and really working in the industry under greats.

Today all the young people in our industry tend to jump from company to company very quickly. Ten or fifteen years ago people stayed at a company under a mentor and they were there for a long time. They learned their ways. The most successful people in the industry have been people who just stuck around long enough, and paid their dues. For young people to intern, or to go into a company, which is really great to do, you have to treat it as an internship or a mentoring program, and not try to get to the top as fast as possible.

Excerpts from an interview with Mazdack Rassi, May 2011.

Chapter Review

In summary, the fashion show has a long global history with many influential designers and retailers paving the way for its content evolution. American department stores helped pave the way for fashion events, as we know them today, and they did so as early as 1912 by holding extravagantly themed events in their stores. Shows were quickly recognized in the trade as a unique marketing tool. Fashion shows can be vehicles to strengthen brands, drive sales, introduce new trends, and educate students and communities on critical issues. The current fashion show industry, led by industry leaders like Milk Studios, has incorporated technology as a way to include the masses into this once-exclusive environment. Historically and currently, they are mirrors of economic, social, and political change. Since the early twentieth century, shows have proven to be much more than entertainment. They are crucial to driving sales for and branding a collection or retailer. An understanding of the past and the reasons for the development and evolution of fashions shows enables and helps us in the execution and marketing of a strong and profitable collection. Now that we understand the history of the fashion show and its current place in the business of fashion, it is time to examine in detail the categories of shows and the role of the producer.

Questions for Review and Discussion

1. How has the fashion show changed in the last 100 years?
2. What factors made America the center for fashion during World War II?
3. Visit www.fashion-era.com to view the wartime rationing restrictions of clothing, cloth, and footwear. Discuss the challenges of these restrictions for both families and retailers.
4. Give two examples of how fashion shows reflect social, economic, or political history.
5. Explain how fashion shows can help brand a retailer or designer.
6. What is Fashion's Night Out? How has it made the industry more inclusive rather than exclusive?
7. How did America democratize fashion?
8. What designer's response to the wartime silhouette brought Paris back into its fashion dominance?
9. Who was the first designer to use rock stars and celebrities to model in his shows?
10. Who made the groundbreaking decision to take commentary off the runway?
11. When did media begin covering fashion shows and sharing it with the general public?
12. Explain how an understanding of the past helps in creating and marketing a strong, unique, and profitable fashion collection.
13. What makes the MAC and Milk project unique in the industry? How has it changed the runway show?
14. Who was the first designer to hold a live cybercast of his show?
15. How are designers using technology to highlight their collections?
16. Why was *Style with Elsa Klensch* a groundbreaking television show?
17. What designers opted out of a traditional runway show and are using technology as a medium to showcase their collections?

Out and About Activities

1. Go online to the CFDA website (www.cfda.com) and research Eleanor Lambert's history as the founder of Press Week and the founder of CFDA. Write a one-page summary of her influential role in creating New York Fashion Week.
2. Go online and research alternative locations for fashion shows during fashion weeks around the globe.
3. Attend a local fashion show and summarize what eras, if any, by which they were inspired.
4. Examine the fashion shows of one of the designers listed on the timeline. Discuss the characteristics that made his or her shows unique. How did these designers reflect the times in which they were holding their fashion shows?
5. Go online to www.milkstudios.com and summarize how they use technology to promote all the divisions of their business?

6. Go online and research one vintage fashion show from 1940 to 1990 and compare and contrast to a current fashion show.
7. Go to YouTube and watch several segments of *Style with Elsa Klensch* from 1980 to 2000. Answer the following questions:
   a) How did the runway show change over the years?
   b) How did models walk and pace on the runway change from 1980 to 2000?
   c) What major trends are highlighted from 1980 to 2000?
      1. Have you noticed a return of any trend highlighted?
8. Go online and research current designers who are using technology as a way to showcase their collections.

Terminology of the Trade

Advertising 14
Advertising and promotion 14
Bill Blass 10
Bonnie Cashin 7
Brand ambassadors 4
Branding 14
Carnaby Street 8
Celia Birtwell 9
Charles Frederick Worth 4
Claire McCardell 7
Clare Potter 7
Claude Montana 10
Couturier 8
fashion dolls 4
fashion models 5
Fashion's Night Out (FNO) 13
Finale 5
Gimbels 6
haute couture 6
IMG 7
Jean Patou 5
Jeanne Paquin 5
Kenzo 10
Kings Road 8
Lewis Leonard 9
license 8
Lifestyle collection 8
mannequins 4
MAC and Milk Initiative 16
Mary Quant 8
mass market 6
Mercedes Benz Fashion Week 7
Milk Made 16
New Look 7
Ossie Clark 9
Paul Poiret 5
Press Week 7
production teams 13
Rose Bertin 5
salon style show 7
separates 7
silhouette 7
sportswear 7
supermodel 11
Thierry Mugler 11
trunk shows and presentations 5
Vera Maxwell 7
vertically integrated 14
Wanamaker's 6
Youth Quake 9

Web Resources

www.fashion-era.com
www.fashionsnightout.com
www.style.com
www.nymag.com
www.cfda.com
www.normakamali3d.com
www.truthplusblog.com/2011/01/20/fashion-historian-john-tiffany-on-eleanor-lambert-and-the-coty-awards/

Bibliography

Apselund, K. (2009). *Fashioning Society: A Hundred Years of Haute Couture by Six Designers.* New York: Fairchild Books.

Clifford, S. (2010). Watching the catwalk, and clicking "add to cart." *The New York Times.* Retrieved December 6, 2010, from http://www.nytimes.com/2010/09/12/business/12shows.html?_r=1&pagewanted=print

Clothing and Fashion Encyclopedia. (2009). *Fashion Shows.* Retrieved November 2, 2010, from http://angelancartier.net/fashion-shows

Collins, A. (2004). The lady the list the legacy. *Vanity Fair*. Retrieved June 2, 2011, from http://www.vanityfair.com/style/features/2004/04/eleanor-lambert200404

Everett, J. C., and Swanson, K. K. (2004). *Guide to Producing a Fashion Show* (2nd ed., pp. 12–14). New York: Fairchild Publications.

Fraser, A. (1963). *Dolls: Pleasures and Treasures.* New York: Putnam.

Gay, J. (2001). Madison Avenue shopkeepers weep for CNN style diva Elsa Klensch. Retrieved June 1, 2011, from http://www.observer.com/2001/06/madison-avenue-shopkeepers-weep-for-cn

Johnson, K., & Rowhwedder, C. (2008). Pace-setting Zara Seeks more speed to fight rising cheap-chic rivals. *The Wall Street Jouranl Online.* Retrieved July 4, 2008, from http://onlinewsj-com/public/aricle_print/sb120345929019578183.html

Leach, W. (1993). *Land of Desire* (pp. 101–111). New York: Vintage Books.

Menkes, S. (2009). Lacroix files for bankruptcy. *The New York Times.* Retrieved November 20, 2010, from http://www.nytimes.com/2009/05/29/business/global/29lacroix.html

Milbank, C. R. (1989). *New York Fashion: The Evolution of American Style* (pp. 8–16). New York: Harry N. Abrams, Incorporated.

Mower, S. (2010). Mr. Ford returns. *Vogue.* Retrieved November 16, 2010, from http://www.vogue.com/magazine/article/tom-ford-returns/

Pochna, M. (1996). *Dior.* New York: Universe Publishing.

Popik, B. (2005). Fashion week (7th on 6th). *The Big Apple.* Retrieved December 4, 2010, from http://www.barrypopik.com/index.php.new_york_city/entry/fashion_week_

Quant, M. (1995). *Quant by Quant*. London: Cassell.

Quick, H. (1997). *Catwalking: A History of the Fashion Model* (pp. 23, 145). Edison, NJ: Wellfleet Press.

Ritson, M. (2006). *Mark Ritson on branding Hilfiger has learned the hard way*. Retrieved April 8, 2010, from http://www.marketingmagazine.co.uk/news/559423/Mark-Ritson-branding-Hilfiger-learned-hard/?DCMP=ILC-SEARCHom.

Stegemeyer, A. (2004). *Who's Who in Fashion* (4th ed., pp. 184–198). New York: Fairchild Publications.

Strzemien, A. (2010). Fashion's night out to produce largest show in NYC history. *Huffington Post.* Retrieved November 20, 2010, from http://www.huffingtonpost.com/2010/04/22/fashions-night-out-to-pro_n_547501.html

Thomas, D. (Spring 2000). Ossified. *New York Times Magazine,* p. 92.

Tiffany, J. (2011). On Eleanor Lambert and the Coty Awards. Retrieved January 28, 2011, from http://truthplusblog.com/2011/01/20/fashion-historian-john-tiffany-on-elanor-lambert-and–the-coty-awards/

Van Meter, J. (October 1990). Pretty women. *Vogue*.

Watson, L. (2008). Chapter title. In *Vogue Fashion* (pp. 326, 330, 384). Buffalo, NY: A Five Fly Books Ltd.

Watt, J. (2003). The king of the king's road. In *Ossie Clark 1965/74* (pp. 95–96). London: V&A Publications.

NCHEZ

THE SHOWS, THE PRODUCER, AND THE TEAM

LEARNING OBJECTIVES

After completing this chapter, you will be able to:

- Know the types of fashion shows
- Understand the role of the fashion show producer
- Create a production team
- Discuss the available jobs on a production team
- Understand the views of industry insiders
- Know the terminology of the trade

The important thing in this industry is passion ... and I don't care if you're a model, a stylist, a student or a producer. You have to have passion, not a desire to be famous—a passion for the industry.

—JAN STRIMPLE

2

General Overview

Chapter 1 explored the history of the fashion show and the major influences in shaping its evolution. Those include the culture and economies of varied time spans presented, as well as those of the most influential designers, and retail and fashion movements worldwide. The chapter discussed the fashion show growing beyond a tool for entertaining clients and generating sales to become a multilayered vehicle for long-term branding.

Simply listing different types of current fashion shows, and categories of these shows, although important, would miss the true point of this book, and its approach to fashion show production. The "fashion show," like the fashion industry itself, is in constant flux. The catwalk is currently being redefined, relocated, and reshaped each season. Each type of show is molded to fit the needs of the individual, business, or group sponsoring the event. The book shows how fashion shows have always been and continue to be a response to what is happening in the world around us. These shows can shock, entertain, and magically seduce the audience. Producers need to have a clear understanding of the different types of shows currently in vogue in the industry. The importance of becoming familiar with the general categories of fashion shows is simply for use as a reference or guide when it is determined what type of show is to be created. Keep in mind that new categories are being invented daily. The examples presented are not exclusive of each other. The lines of separation among the various categories of shows have become blurry. As technology improves, more designers are incorporating high-tech elements to craft "new" types of shows.

Social media, the Internet, video technology, and live streaming of shows all help designers and manufacturers reach a wider audience and unlock the once-secretive world of fashion shows to the general public. In March 2010, during London Fashion Week, Burberry launched the first 3D (three-dimensional) virtual show in some of the world's most fashion forward cities, including New York, Los Angeles, Dubai, Paris, and Tokyo. Guests at each location had a virtual front-row seat, with 3D glasses allowing people to see the texture of fabrics. If people missed the 3D version they could always visit the website live. burberry.com to see the show in 2D. Directly following the show, they offered a selection of twenty outerwear garments and bags for sale. For spring 2011 Burberry continued to live stream their shows and sell even more items directly off the runway collection. The clothing was made available for immediate online purchase after the Prorsum show during London Fashion Week. Instead of customers waiting the traditional four to six months for the items to be in stores, people who purchase during the time of the fashion show receive their orders six to eight weeks later (Scott, 2010).

It is imperative that producers be aware of the technological advances in production and use them when applicable. It is necessary because 3D is just the beginning. Ralph Lauren launched a 4D light show in November 2010 for over 1,000 people at Ralph Lauren on Madison Avenue. According to Karimzadeh in his *Womens Wear Daily* article. "The technology involved architecturally mapping the store and digitally recreating 3-D replicas. Lauren, who just built the imposing mansion to house his women's and home categories, was prepared to see it disappear in a David Copperfield-like stunt" (Karimzadeh, 2010).

The future evolution of technology as it will be used in the fashion industry is simply not predictable. However, what is certain and foreseeable is that technology will reach new and unimaginable breakthroughs that will be applicable and adaptable to the fashion industry. Yet with all its promise of a brave new, technologically infused fashion world, where so many designers will use technology and social media simultaneously, others like Tom Ford, for example, have opted for a return of a more exclusive and perhaps throwback template. Ford shunned mass press and created a mysterious buzz around his elite fashion show for his 2011 women's collection. He used an alternative location to Lincoln Center. He had friends and celebrities model the clothing and he opted to include commentary. He exploited all aspects of the traditional **salon style show.**

Types of Fashion Shows

This book classifies fashion shows into three general categories as adapted from Judith C Everett and Kristen K Swanson in their text *Guide to Producing a Fashion Show:* **the production show, the formal runway show,** and **the informal show**. (Everett and Swanson, 2007). The majority of these are defined by the categories of the product they have to present such as: **ready-to-wear, bridge,** and **designer**; **contemporary,** high fashion, or haute couture clothing. The shows are also defined by their elements. These elements may include lighting, sound, staging, and video technology. The audience, the press, the trade, and the consumer further define such shows.

Three General Categories of Fashion Shows

Production Show

The production show is a full-size theatrical event with music, choreography, and professional lighting. Frequently, a production show makes use of performances, dancers, singers, and ornate light shows concurrent with an unlimited variety of multimedia components. The 1980s were the production shows' major period. Clothing was bold, and models were curvy and sexy. The economy was strong. Designers like Thierry Mugler and Claude Montana produced extravagant shows, which grabbed the attention of the media and helped catapult the success of many individual careers (Quick, 1997). In the early 2000s, with designers like Alexander McQueen for Givenchy, Dolce & Gabbana, and the lingerie giant Victoria's Secret, the production show saw a strong resurgence. Many regional and local charitable organizations use production shows as a vehicle for fundraising.

History Connect

The big American department stores like Gimbels and Wanamaker's started what evolved into production shows as early as 1912.

Formal Runway Show

The formal runway show presents a traditional and straightforward parade of models coming down the runway. The models may walk alone, in pairs, or in a group. Most of these events include music, lighting, and some variety of staging. This form of show is most commonly seen during fashion weeks across the globe and is best suited for ready-to-wear collections. It was in the 1990s, with the strong minimalist movement in clothing, that this class of show

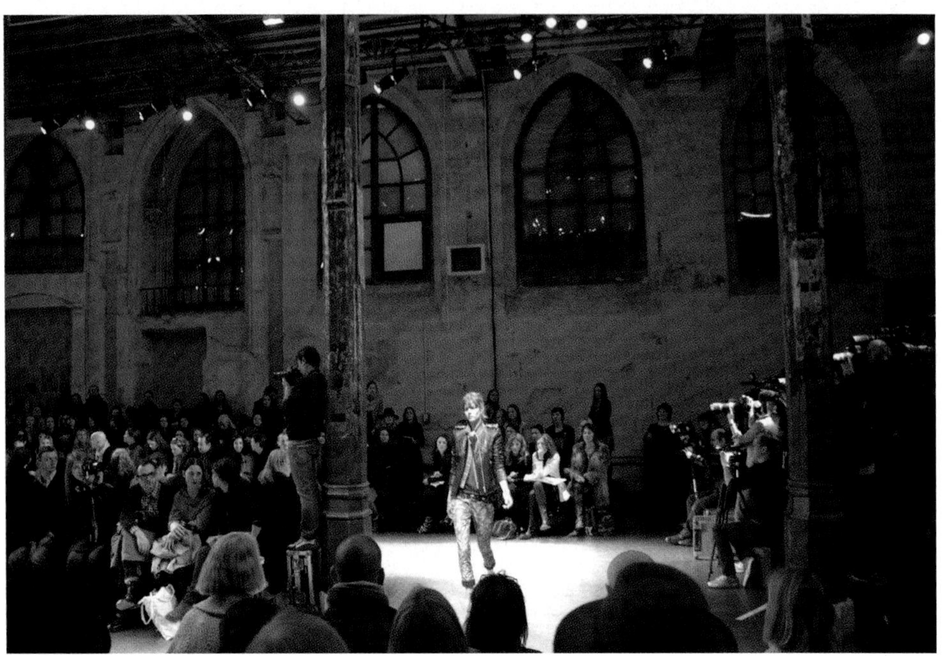

FIGURE 2.1 *Model walks the Parisian runway.*
Courtesy of John Calder

History Connect

Mary Quant helped shape this type of show in the 1960s.

became the industry norm. This particular type of show is completed in about fifteen to thirty minutes. It requires advance planning and involves staging, lighting, and special locations. The target audience for formal shows varies and may be retailers, consumers, or the press. Clothing is the highlight of the show and can be either formal or informal. The current trend at most fashion weeks is to stream these shows live for the public to view online (Figure 2.1).

Informal Shows

An informal show is a more simplified presentation of garments and accessories on a model. This variety of show rarely has any theatrical elements such as additional lighting or props. It can be held at retail locations, restaurants, showrooms, schools, hotels, and other alternative spaces.

SALON SHOW/TEA ROOM MODELING

The salon show/tea room modeling is an informal fashion show without the runway. Models, wearing the design of the moment, walk around tables while people are enjoying lunch or dinner. This show is often used for charity luncheons or as a sales tool in retailers' establishments. Boutiques frequently partner with restaurants to execute this type of show. The benefit is mutual, but the salon show at restaurants has

History Connect

The salon show has its roots with Dior and other French couture designers. Buyers visited their "maison" and their models would parade around them in the designer's latest collection.

fallen out of favor in recent years. One of the perceived reasons for its unpopularity is related to the fact that long lunches are not currently as popular as they were in the 1980s and 1990s. Charitable organizations still use this type of show for fundraising luncheon events.

TRUNK SHOW

The trunk show is one of the most effective of the informal shows. The trunk show is used as a direct sales tool for retailers and designers. Its purpose is to highlight specific pieces of a collection, or unique items not normally featured in the retail establishment. Designers or representatives from the company often make public appearances during a trunk show. Better department stores, like Neiman Marcus, Saks Fifth Avenue, Bergdorf Goodman, and Barneys New York, hold trunk shows several times a year to indulge VIP customers and drive sales. The trunk show usually involves some manner of informal show with professional models donning the garments. These events are small and exclusive, and frequently include champagne, hors d'oeuvres, and gift bags for the customers. The key to the success of the trunk show is the creation of an intimate shopping experience and availability of "new" merchandise for the customer. The trunk show also functions as a way for new designers to build their brand with minimal investment.

Bill Blass was one of the first American designers to brand the trunk show and use it to his advantage. He continually used the trunk show as both a marketing and sales tool throughout his career. Blass applied the trunk show model of selling and presenting clothing into his seventies. In 1993 he took his couture trunk show into twenty-four American cities ("Bill Blass Ltd.," 2010).

History Connect

Patou traveled with models to different locations, hosting cocktail parties and showing his collection.

POP UP SHOP

Pop up shops are an extension of the trunk show. They utilize a temporary retail space or can be held in an existing retail store. They may be open for as little as one day or as long as six months. Like trunk shows, pop ups can highlight a specific brand, retailer, or a number of products all at once. Pop ups have grown in popularity as vehicles for potential designers, retailers, and brands to test market product and location without incurring the cost of a long-term lease. The majority of pop up shops take over empty retail space and hold fashion and sales events during their limited residence in the location.

SHOWROOM

This category of informal show is exclusively used for wholesale trade or industry professional. The retail customer does not have access to this kind of informal show. At a showroom, buyers for retail businesses order merchandise by visiting a showroom during market week and periodically throughout the season. The showroom fashion experience is different and dependent upon the level or category of product. Among other things, it depends upon pricing and breadth of the potential market. For buyers purchasing designer clothing and accessories, the representatives usually provide one or two models to highlight the garments. This type of model is called a showroom model. Showroom models are discussed in greater detail in Chapter 6. The showroom model, or house model as traditionally known, models clothing that the buyer and the designer's representative have pulled for review. Most often the buyer is served lunch while taking notes and photos of the garments on the models. Each showroom has its own version of a show.

FIGURE 2.2 *Angel Sanchez shows his bridal wear in a salon style setting.*
Courtesy of Angel Sanchez

Many showrooms host actual fashion shows for selected VIP retailers. In 2008, the Los Angeles Nicole Miller showroom held an exclusive runway show for their regional West Coast buyers that mirrored the New York City Fashion Week show. They had the same clothing line up as the New York City show; each buyer had a gift bag; and the president of the company was there to promote the collection and answer any questions (Figure 2.2).

PRESS SHOW

Although the press attend shows during fashion weeks and market weeks throughout the globe, press shows have evolved into press events. Depending on the category of merchandise, the manufacturers and designers will hold exclusive events specifically for the press. All have websites available, which contain press releases, photos, and articles about the company for editors, bloggers, and journalists to use. The primary function of a press show is to encourage press coverage of the designer's latest collections. Creating a special event for the members of the press gives a sense of exclusivity to the fashion media. It creates insider opportunities for fashion writers, bloggers, and editors. The experience is then expressed in its own particular press venue, sharing opinions, judgments, and multimedia with the public at large. All of this is the core reason d'être for this type of event.

FASHION PRESENTATION

Designers or manufacturers hire models to present their collection to press and buyers. They are static presentations. Presentations are held in rented spaces at places like Milk Studios, or in the designers' or representatives' showrooms. Models are hired to wear the clothing, and stand and pose on an elevated platform for hours while the press and important buyers see the garments on human forms. During this time, the designer answers questions about the collection. Press presentations can be long and exhausting experiences for models. Many designers have created events out of fashion presentations that fall somewhere between full-scale shows, fashion exhibitions, and traditional presentations. For example, Hussein Chalayan opted out of a traditional runway show for his spring 2010 collection. He presented his collection to buyers and press individually. Instead of a major show he created two films around his designs and showed them at two separate art galleries in London (Jones, 2006). Fashion presentations can have many manifestations; traditionally they were simply a presentation of the collection for the press and specific buyers (Figure 2.3).

TRADE SHOWS

Trade shows are an industry-only exhibition for manufacturers and designers to showcase their new collections. Trade shows are not open to the public and can only be attended by company representatives, retail buyers, and members of the press.

Regional and National Trade Shows Los Angeles, New York, Dallas, and Miami are just a few of the cities in the United States that host market week trade shows within their **fashion marts**, or near their fashion district. A fashion mart is located in a specific city. The mart is the building or buildings where clothing is produced, manufactured, and sold on a wholesale level. Most major marts, such as the California Mart located in downtown Los Angeles or the Dallas Market Center in downtown Dallas, Texas, are open year round. However, the majority of the buying happens during market weeks. The major market weeks for ready-to-wear

FIGURE 2.3 *Presentation example.*
Courtesy of Alexander Porter/BFAnyc.com

and designer clothing correlate with fashion weeks around the globe. They happen twice a year during spring and fall. Nevertheless, to address the growing industry needs, the majority of fashion marts have created additional shows at least four times a year, targeting many different categories of apparel such as contemporary, bridge, junior, children's, and ready-to-wear markets. In every major market center new progressive marts have emerged as the "new" centers catering to younger contemporary, innovative collections. The Cooper building in Los Angeles and the FIG in Dallas are examples. These marts started as a place to highlight the growing contemporary and fashion forward market and have grown into major marts in their own right.

International Trade Shows An international trade show is a show for the trade or industry professionals located in countries around the globe. The most popular are located in fashion centers such as Paris, Milan, Tokyo, and London. One of the world's most iconic international trade show is the Prêt a Porter, which focuses on French and international designers. It is held in Paris, France. The new movement in international shows is to create partnerships with other fashion capitals and trade shows. These collaborations provide an opportunity for the international fashion industry to connect with the buyers throughout the world. Prêt a Porter continues to hold an innovative **international show,** "Train," in New York City and Los Angeles during market weeks. In 2005 with the support of the Federation of Women's Ready-to- Wear, they launched "Living Room" in Tokyo. "Living Room" is a cutting-edge international show that aims to get designers in front of the Japanese market. Recently a new South-West collaboration has emerged with WWDMAGIC and Prêt a Porter. The show, called "Heart of Prêt," takes place at WWDMAGIC in Las Vegas, Nevada. It highlights 20–30 apparel brands selected directly from the Prêt a Porter show in Paris. It is clear that shows are evolving into international collaborations. Producers of these shows are searching for new ways to meet the growing buyer's market, and looking for ways to stand out in the industry. D&A and others are providing more than just exhibit space, by offering an environment of creative partnership and one-stop shopping (Figure 2.4).

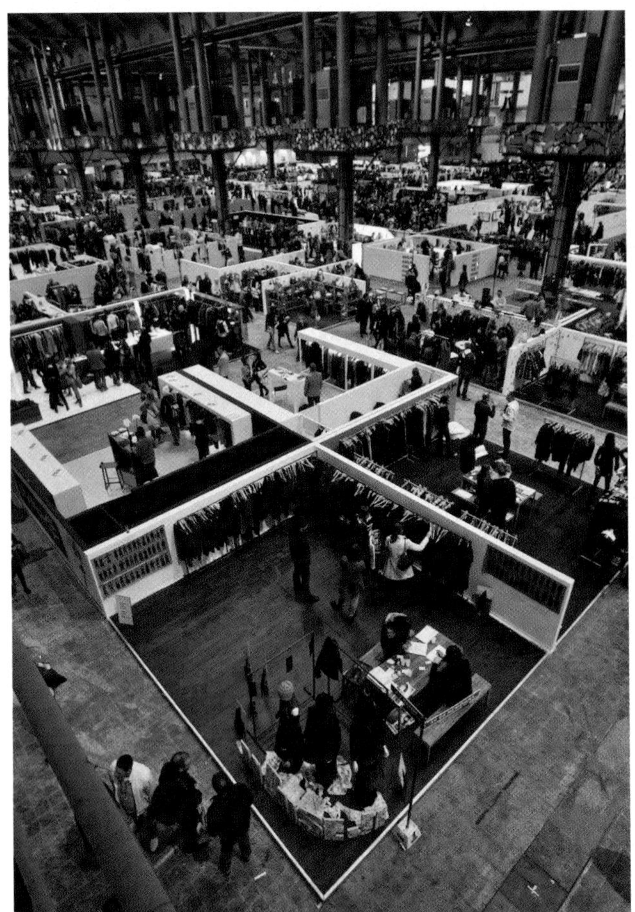

FIGURE 2.4 *International trade show.*
Courtesy of Alberto Estevez/EPA/Newscom

Temporary Shows In addition to the regular showrooms, major temporary shows hold events in the mart during market weeks. The landlords rent space to these well-known shows. Contemporary fashion forward shows like "Designers and Agents" travel to New York, Los Angeles, and Paris. Designers and agents have blossomed into a unique and innovative show highlighting well known apparel brands as well as emerging designers. According to Barbara Kramer, one of the founders of D&A, in an interview for this text, this is a new model for the trade show platform, which constantly caters to both the vendors' needs and the exhibitors' comforts. In these shows the attendees are provided with healthy meals and comfortable custom exhibit booths. In 2007 they launched the Green Room, in which they provided dedicated and gifted space to temporary shows (Personal Communication, May 8, 2011). D&A and other trade shows accommodate retailers who purchase clothing encompassing every market level. Ready-to-wear, designer, bridge contemporary, sportswear, juniors and missy, swim, and ecofriendly clothing collections are some of the categories of product one might expect to see at a trade show. Different regional locations may focus on specific items. Miami is known for swimwear; Los Angeles has gained a reputation for contemporary clothing lines as well as designer and bridge merchandise. The MAGIC show in Las Vegas, which was once a men's show only, has grown into both men's and women's designer, contemporary, and bridge collections. It also houses Project—a contemporary show that also provides a one-stop shopping experience for a variety of buyers. The majority of all trade shows host collective fashion shows periodically throughout the day, highlighting specific vendors. Major fashion hubs like New York have a fashion district and have designer showrooms all over the city. During fashion weeks and market weeks, additional shows are held throughout the city. The Jacob Javits Center is home to ENK's Coterie, a well-known industry favorite with row after row of recognizable brand names and new emerging designers. Simultaneously, many other smaller shows are happening all over the city (Figure 2.5).

FIGURE 2.5 *Dollhouse trade show booth at MAGIC.*
Courtesy of Reuters

Role of the Producer/ Coordinator

The producer/coordinator is the person hired to bring together all the components of the fashion show, making the magic happen! The producer's job is to coordinate and direct every detail of the show. The client determines how extensive the producer's role will be. The need for qualified producers continues to escalate in our contemporary fashion environment. There is no absolute educational qualification required to prepare one to be a producer. Experience in the fashion world is fundamental, combined with a variety of attributes and skills. A clear understanding of the trends in the fashion world, on the runway, and in print will help in realizing one's production goal. Working or interning at an established production company is a good way to see the inner workings of the business. In addition, an understanding of the client's needs, the target audience, and the type of clothing to be highlighted is paramount to success. The personality of a producer must be one that maintains composure under great stress, is detail oriented, and at the same time is able to multitask. A clear grasp of the past will provide insight and inspiration for implementing a unique and memorable show.

A producer is challenged with bringing the designer's, retailer's, or client's vision to life. The role can be varied depending on the budget and goals of the show. In general the responsibilities include, but are not limited to casting the models; styling the looks; calling the show; creating the theme; overseeing the stage and set design; and working with and directing music, lighting, and the sound crew. Finally, one of the most important roles is putting together a strong production team. (A detailed list of potential services provided by a production company is outlined in Chapter 3.)

One of the largest fashion production companies and PR firms in the world is KCD Worldwide. KCD shapes the brands and produces the shows for many of the big name designers such as Diane Von Furstenberg, Chanel, and Gucci. Looking at their large menu of services and capabilities, it becomes clear that they have captured a significant part of the industry and rely on a major global staff. KCD is the company that many of the well-known brands turn to for production and PR. The majority of smaller regional producers, however, still provide a variety of services and execute professional shows. The services are provided with a smaller budget and fewer paid staff. It is clear that no one person can execute a fashion show. Any prepared producer, whether he or she works at a large firm like KCD Worldwide, has one's own company, or is simply a student or volunteer understands that success depends on a strong team.

Production Team

There are many people who help execute a runway show and fashion event. Below are some general titles or positions and job duties of people who may be hired or volunteer to be part of a production team. However, these are by no means the only jobs available. A brief job description for each is given. In later chapters more detailed information will be provided on these positions (Figure 2.6).

Fashion Show Director: The person in charge of producing the show, delegating responsibilities, and maintaining strong communication with all members of the team. (This position can be synonymous with fashion show producer.)

Stage Manager: The person in charge of all talent performing and timing issues dictated by the producer or director. He or she schedules and keeps track of timing issues and tech rehearsals. This position is needed for bigger production shows that incorporate theatrical elements and talent beyond just the models. Generally, a stage manager is required only for large productions runway shows.

Stylist: The person or persons in charge of selecting the clothing and accessories each model will wear while walking down the runway.

Backroom Coordinator: The person in charge of the backroom. This person is responsible for creating the backroom layout, schedules, dressers, and dressing tracks. The backroom coordinator coordinates with hair and makeup and deals with any other backroom issues.

Merchandise Coordinator: The person who is responsible for pulling and keeping an inventory record of all clothing used in the show. He or she will work closely with the stylist and producer to make sure the show's image and theme are accomplished.

Fashion Show Producer/ coordinator	The person in charge of producing the show, delegating responsibilities, and maintaining strong communication with all members of the team.	Persuader—Works as a leader to produce
Stage Manager	The person in charge of all talent performing and timing issues dictated by the Producer or Director. He/She schedules and keeps track of timing issues and tech rehearsals. This position is needed for bigger production shows that incorporate theatrical elements and talent beyond just the models. Generally, a Stage Manager is utilized only for large runway shows.	Organizer—Works with details and precision
Stylist	The person or persons in charge of selecting the clothing and accessories each model will wear while walking down the runway.	Creator—Works creatively and independently
Backroom Coordinator	The person in charge of the backroom. This person is responsible for creating the backroom layout, schedules, dressers, and dressing tracks. The Backroom Coordinator coordinates with hair and makeup and deals with any other backroom issues.	Organizer—Works with details and precision
Merchandise Coordinator	The person who is responsible for pulling and keeping an inventory record of all clothing used in the show. He/She will work closely with the stylist and producer to make sure the show's image and theme are accomplished.	Helper—Works cooperatively, helping and supporting
Model Coordinator	The Model Coordinator assists in the hiring of models, creating the line up of models before they hit the runway, and coordinating all issues with models and modeling agencies.	Helper—Works cooperatively, helping and supporting
PR Coordinator	This person is in charge of all public relations regarding the show. This person writes and distributes the press release and all other written material regarding the event.	Persuader—Works as a leader to sell
Program Editor	This person is in charge of the written program. This person works closely with the PR Coordinator to guarantee consistency in printed material.	Thinker—Works with information and ideas
Dressers	This person is in charge of dressing models and fitting models. He/she sets up the model rack, following styling procedures.	Doer—Works hands on
Assistants	This person works closely with the producer on the needs of the production team. This usually is a paid position.	Helper—Works cooperatively, helping and supporting
Interns	An Intern is usually a student who works in order to obtain course credit from his or her college or high school. This person may also work for the purpose of getting real world experience. Interns can be utilized in capacities where their skill sets are best maximized. Often Interns will be dressers for shows.	Doer—Works hands on; or Helper—Works cooperatively, helping and supporting
Volunteers	These individuals work in unpaid positions and are placed wherever they are needed.	Doers and Helpers

FIGURE 2.6 *Production Job Description Sheet.*

PR Coordinator: This person is in charge of all public relations regarding the show. He or she writes and distributes the press release and all other written material regarding the event.

Program Editor: This person is in charge of the written program. He or she works closely with the PR coordinator to guarantee consistency in printed material.

Dresser: This person is in charge of dressing models and fitting models, setting up model racks, and following styling procedures. (A detailed dressers job description is located in Chapter 6.)

Assistant: This person works closely with the producer on the needs of the production team. This usually is a paid position.

Intern: An intern is usually a student who works to obtain course credit from his or her college or high school. This person may also work for the purpose of getting real-world experience. Interns can be utilized in capacities where their skill sets are best maximized. Often interns will be dressers for shows.

Volunteer: This individual works in unpaid positions and is placed wherever he/she is needed.

Each producer has a diverse approach to building a team and executing the show. The best way to understand the role of the producer and process of building a production team is to

Industry Insider

Fashion Show Producer Jan Strimple

FIGURE 2.7 *Jan Strimple.*
Courtesy of Anthony Chang Photography

Former runway model and founder of Jan Strimple Productions, Jan Strimple is one of the most successful producers in Dallas, Texas (Figure 2.7). Jan has walked runways and produced shows all over the country. Mrs. Strimple is known for her over-the-top theatrical productions. Jan continues to work with a variety of emerging designers, retailers, and seasoned professionals like Carolina Herrera, Rodarte, YEOHLEE, and Philip Lim. Jan shares with us her insights on the role of the producer and her concrete ideas about forming her team. Jan addresses how she transitioned from model to producer and the importance of branding shows for the Dallas consumer.

WHAT IS THE ROLE OF THE PRODUCER?

Good production is about empowering people, being organized, being able to anticipate problems, careful planning, and setting up a structure where you give ownership of part of the show to someone else. It is your job to make sure they fully understand what they are doing!

I spend a lot of time and energy going beyond what I was hired for. You have to decide what your own standards are in this industry and you have to decide what your brand represents. I do not celebrate mediocrity. I just like it over the top. You do your work. You do your research. You figure it out and you wow them.

WHERE DO YOU PRODUCE FASHION SHOWS?

I actually produce all over. I have never gone after this. I have never pursued it; I have never said I want to be a producer. But that's all I do now. I still walk a few runways every once in a while and I still do a few personal appearances.

HOW DID YOU TRANSITION FROM MODEL TO FASHION SHOW PRODUCER?

During the 1980s when Dallas began its legendary Dallas Collection AIDS/HIV fundraising efforts, known as Design Industries Foundation Fighting Aids (DIFFA), I always gave my time to model in the shows. One year, my dear friend Jimmie Henslee was producing it and he asked if I would give him some assistance the week before the show to help him complete the production design. We delivered a fun show.

The following year Jimmie and I were invited to produce the show together. He was not available, but I was, so I took it over. Two women who attended the show were slated to chair the upcoming Kidney Texas fashion luncheon and wanted to do something different—add some "juice" to what had become a predictable formula of fashion luncheon shows. When they saw my DIFFA show, they approached me about producing their luncheon show. I accepted and delivered a show that was much more than a parade of fashion and Dallas received it with rave reviews. It's a great message I share with my interns: Let your work speak for you. Too many people today spin their wheels trying to convince others how fabulous they are. Hype can be an effective "excitement" tool but without substance, the results are generally frail at best. I teach them to learn it then earn it.

HOW DO YOU KEEP THE SHOW NEW AND EXCITING? HOW DO YOU GET INSPIRED?

The diversity of the projects that I work on keeps it new. You have to ask yourself, who is this merchant and what is their image? How do they see themselves? Then we have to duplicate that. It is really all in the styling.

HOW MUCH CREATIVE FREEDOM ARE YOU GIVEN AS THE PRODUCER?

I have a phrase; it's called, "It's a show in a box." If a designer creates a collection show, and it's presented once, it's done! The design work is done. The music stops. The collection's styled out. If this is the type of model they want then it's not my vision, it's their vision. I'm redelivering it. I am adjusting it to Dallas. If it happens in Dallas, if the designer comes here and I'm presenting their collection, I will look at their music. I will listen to the music. I will look at the way they cast it. We'll take and make up direction from there. I will duplicate it if I feel that it's appropriate for our audience here. But I am not afraid as a producer to voice the audience's point of view as well. And, their point of view is lost a lot. For a long time it

(*Continued*)

Industry Insider (Continued)

Fashion Show Producer Jan Strimple

was lost. For a long time it was about the stores, the designers, and the press. What happened? Why do I have mile-long marked-down racks? Talk to me. I can tell you. I'm in the dressing room with these ladies who can't find anything. Because you're buying and pandering to what the press tells you is correct, and to what a person in sales with the designer tells you to buy. What happened to listening to your customer? YEOHLEE is a great example. I walked for her in the eighties and she has come to Dallas and I produced a couple of her shows. I did 100 percent of the casting, because there was a trust. I understood who she was and what she was about. I did the show for a store which is the only store in Dallas where you can buy YEOHLEE; she didn't micromanage me at all. I feel that I've always been in this market the voice of the women in the audience.

If you have a small store you understand who walks through the door. When the power shifted, things changed. When the powers that be are that large, they don't know who walks through their doors. I feel that I've always been the voice of the women in the audience.

WHO DO YOU HAVE IN YOUR TEAM?

For a small show, a forty-five-piece show, my stylist and my assistant can mange backstage just fine. I have a headset person. It is the backstage manager and he or she manages the people flow, but they don't touch wardrobe. "Stylists do the final look."

The show I just did called "Outrageous" I had three people on headsets. I had one person over in the costume character area because I had drag performers. I had a stage manager in the character area, and a stage manager in the hair and makeup area.

DO YOU USE ANY PROFESSIONAL DRESSERS?

Dallas has the Kim Dawson agency, which is an in-house agency and production office for the Dallas area. They have professional dressers. They have rates and you can hire them by the hour. There is so much photography that goes on in Dallas. You can hire them to prep photo shoots all day long. I might bring in four professionals for a show. Also, because I'm a huge supporter of students, I will use interns. It could be eight, ten, or twelve depending on the show. The interns dress one on one. The professional dressers dress one on two. The show Outrageous had 140 looks in it. They are pop up scenes so there were sixteen or twenty girls. I had eight or nine minutes between scenes. That's a lifetime!

HAS TECHNOLOGY HELPED BRING AWARENESS TO FASHION SHOWS AND PRODUCTION?

Television made it more accessible in the eighties. I didn't know of any social woman in Dallas who wasn't sitting and watching *CNN* Saturday morning seeing what was happening in fashion with Elsa Klensch. Elsa was the high priestess of fashion to them. It wasn't necessarily the editor of *Vogue* in those days because they didn't know those people. Somebody like Elsa comes into their living room with coffee, they know her. So what Elsa Klensch said was more powerful than any magazine editor they'd ever read. Now that Anna Wintour, the editor of *Vogue*, has become who she has become, it's different. It's about press and the Internet. It started with television in the eighties and moved on through the nineties through a mix of television and the Internet and continues with social media.

DO YOU HAVE PERMANENT STAFF MEMBERS?

My husband said the other day, "What you do is very strange. You have this huge production company. You do all these shows and you have no employees." I said, "That's right because one day when I wake up and say that's been fun, I don't have to fire anybody."

WHAT IS THE FUTURE OF THE RUNWAY SHOW?

I think it is being redefined. The runway show used to always be on a raised runway and everyone sat and watched it. Then the press show concept changed things. We responded to new venues by going to floor level and raised the audience a little. I think we are in a mode where anything goes.

Jan produces over seventy shows a year. She has no permanent staff members and builds her team around each show. Jan is known for going the extra mile and creating unique and outrageous productions. The cornerstone to her success is fashioning shows that speak to the Dallas audience. Her career-making extensive intern program is well known and based on securing two dedicated interns each season. The interns receive college credit for their work. Those two interns are in charge of managing all the other interns. These students end up hand picking their replacements. Jan believes that since these students are on the front lines communicating with the others, they are best suited to choose the replacement. Everyone wants to intern for her. It is hard work. By the end of the show Strimple and her managing interns sit and evaluate the "winners" and "losers" of the event. The winners are asked to come back, while the losers may consider alternative career options.

Courtesy of Jan Strimple

Industry Insider

Wedding Fashion Show Producers Bruce Vassar and Matt Trettel

FIGURE 2.8 *The Wedding Guys.*
Courtesy of Matt Trettle and Bruce Vassar

Bruce Vassar and his partner Matt Trettel are The Wedding Guys (Figure 2.8). The Wedding Guys produce couture bridal fashion shows and events for private clients, the press, retailers, and the consumer. They are considered the premier wedding event producers in the country. They were the only wedding producers from America asked to cover the Royal wedding and have won several awards from Bridal Show Producers International. They revolutionized and redefined the traditional bridal show. Below Bruce and Matt explain their approach to production, how they staff the production team, and how The Wedding Guys have modernized the traditional bridal show.

HOW DID YOU GET STARTED IN THE WEDDING TRADE SHOWS/EVENTS BUSINESS?

Bruce and I have been working together for almost ten years now. In 2002 we were working for another company and there was a need coming from big national participants like Pottery Barn and Williams-Sonoma and high-end designers who really wanted to get in front of brides on a national and international level but had no platform that would protect their brand. They couldn't find any shows around the country they wanted to be associated with. So we created the unveiled wedding events that take place in Dallas, Atlanta, and Minneapolis. We also do a New York Show Press and buyers show called Wedding Trend Spots.

WHAT IS THE ROLE OF THE PRODUCER?

We like to be in control of all the details. We are in charge of the entire event, the sales process, the execution, and the final wrap up of the show. We do the selection of the gowns, and styling of the looks and décor. We also create a "look book" for each show. Traditionally, the producers in the bridal show industry focus on sales, creating a trade show feel. They do not have a fashion background. It is not uncommon to see a producer do the same thing each show. We started The Wedding Guys out of a need that existed to modernize the bridal show. Our job is to give the bride an elevated and exclusive experience, while creating an immersive event. We take out the trade show feel. We continually try to evolve and keep the bride in perspective. Ultimately, it is the bride and her family that are important. We see ourselves as trend spotters and bridal forecasters.

WHO DO YOU HAVE IN YOUR TEAM? AND WHAT IS IT LIKE SETTING UP?

We have permanent staff, Bruce and myself, and a national sales director, who handles the majority of our sales and operations. We also have an operations manager and dedicated show staff that travel with us. The dedicated show staff deals mostly with logistics and set up. From that point on we bring in temporary help from each city in which the event is held. For instance, we will fly into Dallas on Thursday and our advanced team has arranged loading of our semi that takes our equipment to the show. The truck will arrive and meet us on Friday morning. At that point, our show staff assist in the setup. We will carpet the fashion show area and bring in backdrop pieces. From that point on, we bring in our temporary staff in each market and they will do things like setup the seating for the fashion show. Bruce and I will put together a look book for each show and direct staff to additional setup needs. We bring in hair and makeup from a New York company that has branches in each of our markets. Dressers are brought in from the regional markets or from staff of boutiques or companies we work with. We fly the same models from our New York Press Fashion Show out for all of the unveiled shows. We have one dresser per model. Bruce helps with dressing and final looks while I call from

(*Continued*)

Industry Insider (Continued)

Wedding Fashion Show Producers Bruce Vassar and Matt Trettel

the front and Matt calls the show from the back of the house. We train all dressers before the fashion show. We have a seamstress on site. Friday night we bring the models over and on Saturday morning we start the alterations. The alterations must not be permanent, as all garments need to be returned to the retailers and designers after the show.

HOW HAVE YOU MODERNIZED THE BRIDAL FASHION SHOW?

We spend so much time taking what we do to the next level. Our inspiration for Unveiled and all of our events we produce comes from outside of the bridal industry. We look at culinary, art, the red carpet, and fast-track these trends into our industry. We have created elements within the show to put them in a design atmosphere. We took an opportunity to create trend forward events. We wanted it to feel like a department store-style format and created the ceremony setting at the show. We took out the trade show feel of the experience and have created a wedding reception experience as part of the event itself. We have no commentary; we create an entire show program with all the descriptions of the gowns and designers so they can follow along. It's actually a souvenir program. The brides follow along while the show is happening and take notes. We use a plasma TV that names the designer or salon on the runway. There is a very short introduction to each segment so the bride knows where they are in the run of the show. It was necessary to elevate the fashion show component because brides are very familiar with what fashion shows should look like, because of reality TV and access to high-end fashion shows. We are constantly striving to out do ourselves.

WHAT IS THE FUTURE OF BRIDAL FASHION SHOW PRODUCTION?

I think it is evolving. However, it's not uncommon in our industry to see a producer that's produced shows for twenty-plus years. Their fashion shows are not really different from twenty years ago. I think if you were to do a survey across the bridal show producer landscape, you would find that most of the bridal show producers nationally are salespeople. They don't have a fashion background. They are not producers the way Bruce and I are event producers. They are much more involved in sales and exhibit space.

WHAT'S NEXT FOR THE WEDDING GUYS?

You just never know. For us something new comes along every day great shows for great clients; elevating weddings to be something more than just a party; to include secrets, surprises, a TV show, and maybe a line of clothing.

Bruce Vassar and Matt Trettel.

look at the approaches of professionals in the field. Therefore, we provided summaries from extensive interviews with two regional producers. These interviews examine each producer's definition of production and their method of building the right team for their shows. These interviews will give the reader a "real world understanding" of professional production methods and a comparative step-by-step approach of modern-day fashion production. The reader is given a series of examples of the production process. These examples illustrate the practical, concrete steps that are used in the industry today.

Every producer approaches creating a team differently. Many regional producers work for nonprofits with small budgets. The majority of their teams are composed of interns, students, and volunteers. They often hire a backroom manager and have assistants that work for them. Industry Insider Jan Strimple of Jan Strimple Productions and Bruce Vassar and Matt Trettel of The Wedding Guys were asked what they consider to be the role of the producer and how each utilizes staff and builds a production team. They have been chosen because they represent a diverse approach to regional and national productions. They are all currently active and successful in the industry.

Industry Insider

Thomas Muldoon

Thomas Muldoon has worked as a director of sales for many major designer labels such as YEOHLEE, Nicole Farhi, and Helen Morley. Thomas gives insight into the process of how a showroom works, sharing the important roles fashion shows, trades shows, and social media play in the success of selling and promoting a collection.

WHAT DOES THE JOB OF A DIRECTOR OF SALES FOR A CLOTHING BRAND ENTAIL?

As director of sales you are responsible for maximizing all wholesale distribution across multiple channels, that is, traditional brick-and-mortar retailers, online sales, and off-price. The job entails a strong mathematical background and the ability to decipher those numbers to build a sales strategy to ensure future success. Working with merchandisers, marketing, and public relations is crucial to having the right product at the right time for the right consumer. It is the job of the director of sales to link these efforts to the proper sales channels and translate them into sales.

WHY DO WHOLESALERS PARTICIPATE IN TRADE SHOWS?

Wholesalers participate in trade shows for two reasons: immediate sales and exposure. Trade shows are an excellent way to see a great volume of wholesale accounts in a short period of time. The other aspect of trade shows is connecting with new or potential retailers and the fashion community in a format that is fast and easy. Since seasonal markets are very short, trade shows are essential to giving a synopsis of what your brand is doing. In my experience, trade shows are great for new accounts or smaller accounts that are just starting with a new collection. Once an account is established and has reached a certain volume, it is ideal to present your collection in a showroom where they can be more deeply immersed in the brand. For a successful trade show you must decide whom in advance you will be able to connect with and present to at the trade show. This is done by being in constant contact with your accounts and your potential accounts and making appointments to see them at the show. Most of the preparation for making appointments is done eight to ten weeks in advance.

The setup and breakdown of trade shows vary greatly by venue and the extent of the booth you have chosen to use. Most trade shows offer the option to bring your own booth or to use their booth and fixture package for a flat fee. Most companies use firms that specialize in designing, building, installing, and storing large custom booths. These firms will typically handle the complicated logistics on the ground or recommend a company to do so. The physical setup and breakdown is done by the labor that is provided by the venue if unionized or outsourced to a production company. Sales teams will typically arrive the day before to unpack samples, and steam and merchandise the garments in the booth with the aid of a visual merchandising team.

IS FASHION SHOW AN IMPORTANT PART OF SALES FOR A BRAND AND PROMOTION OF CLOTHING?

Shows are important to the sales and marketing of apparel as they engage people very differently than a rack of clothes in store or a picture of a dress in an ad. Fashion shows ultimately make a statement about the brand to a captive and actively engaged audience. I cannot think of a better way to create desire and exhibit control over how your brand is presented to consumers than this format. Most brands use production companies for fashion shows that will ensure that the event goes smoothly and looks professional. There are many groups of people that have to interact for a fashion show to get produced. Stylists, models, hair and makeup, sound and music, lighting, photographers, and location scouts are just a few of the many people it takes to put on a fashion show. Having a great producer or production company is key to a great show as he or she can manage many of the relationships and get the work done efficiently.

HOW DOES THE SHOWROOM APPOINTMENT PROCESS WORK? IS THERE ANY PRESENTATION OF MODELS FOR THE BUYERS AT THIS TIME?

The general way that showroom appointments work is that a buyer will view the collection and then take notes and pictures on what they will buy. Most buyers take this information home with them to then work their selections into their budgets. Every brand is different in how they want their collections presented to buyers in a showroom. Many times this depends on the size of the collection and the amount of deliveries you are showing at one time. I find it most helpful to first show a few looks on models that are most representative of the major trends and innovations of the season. This is usually a great starting point to start building their assortment for the season. Some accounts buy collections by category and some buy collections by full head-to-toe looks. I think it is important that you always offer options that are great representations of the brand and that will resonate at retail with the end buyers.

HOW DO YOU INCLUDE SOCIAL MEDIA AND TECHNOLOGY IN MARKETING AND SELLING A COLLECTION?

Social media and technology in wholesale apparel is much like a great editorial in a magazine fifteen years ago. It allows brands to get feedback as soon as they put a look on the runway. Today buyers and merchants use the information that comes from Internet chatter on trends as they are happening. This information allows wholesalers and retailers to react and satisfy demand more rapidly.

Courtesy of Thomas Muldoon

Comparisons

Jan Strimple and Bruce Vassar and Matt Trettel have many similarities in their approach to fashion show production, yet there are inherent differences. The greatest similarity is that both are regional producers. They are not huge companies, but have generated national work and built solid reputations as the best in their field. The first difference lies in the category of show produced. Jan produces general fashion shows and events ranging from the designer to the contemporary market. Bruce and Matt are wedding show and events specialists. Second, staffing approaches are very different. Jan has no permanent staff and relies on temporary staff and her extensive internship program. The Wedding Guys have permanent staff in addition to hiring local help as needed. The third significant difference is the manner in which each manages the production of the event. Jan believes the producer must be organized, and willing to empower others. Once she has placed someone in a position in her team she relies on their decisions and oversees all aspects of the show through her team. The emphasis is to rely on her creative freedom to continually keep the varied audiences engaged. The Wedding Guys are bridal fashion forecasters and it is through a series of regional events and shows that they introduce new trends to the bridal market. Bruce and Matt control every aspect of their events, and have detailed hands-on involvement. For example, Jan Strimple hires a stylist that executes her vision. The Wedding Guys style all of their looks on their own. Matt is backstage calling the show from a headset, while Bruce oversees dressing and styling. Jan prefers to call from a headset out in the audience or at the technical table, trusting her staff can manage the lineup. Scrutiny of the comparative approaches of these two different producer types is valuable.

The decision to use one or the other method is influenced firstly by the producer's personality and preferences. Secondly, the nature of the production will dictate certain decision-making processes that will lead to one or the other approach. Each has its valuable characteristics and each has some drawbacks. The successful producer must be adaptive to functioning within all the approaches.

Chapter Review

The fashion show regardless of the categories presented in this text is expanding and evolving even as this is written. Many now include some use of technology and live streaming. The producer's decision about what type of show to hold is dependent upon the budget, trends, target market, and client's needs. This chapter has defined three general categories of fashion shows for use as a reference or starting point: the production show, the formal runway show, and the informal show. It has highlighted the importance of regional, national, and international trade shows as collaborative and innovative shows for buyers. The role of the fashion show producer is conditioned on the goal of the client. In general, the producer is the person in charge of every detail of the fashion show. Hiring an appropriate team for each show and cultivating the right people to execute the client's demands are just some of the producer's responsibilities. Each member of the team, regardless of title or position, can be a paid employee or a volunteer. To help the reader gain a stronger understanding, three professional producers from different locations in the United States were asked to explain their approach to fashion show production. The reader has been presented with examples of the different production and management approaches for review and analysis.

Questions for Review and Discussion

1. Discuss the key members of a production team and the job duties for each member, using the Production Team Job Responsibility Worksheet. Please fill in the general job description of production team members.
2. Compare and contrast our industry insiders' approach to building a team. What are the pros and cons to each approach?
3. What are the U.S. cities that hold temporary fashion trade shows? What is the function of these shows? How are they changing?
4. Compare and contrast the functions and benefits of the types of informal shows.
5. Define the role of the producer.
6. What factors must a producer consider in building a production team?

Out and About Activities

1. Go online and research, using YouTube, all the Victoria's Secret Fashion Shows. Start from the first 1996 show. Write a one-page summary about the evolution of the show and the level of production.
2. Volunteer to help with a local charity fashion show. Summarize your duties. Explore the duties of the other members in the production team.
   (a) Define the type of management style used by the producer in the charity fashion show above.
   (b) If you are unable to volunteer at a fashion show, contact a local coordinator or producer and interview him or her about his or her production team and style.
3. Go online to KCD Worldwide.com and research all the services they provide, the clients they represent, and how they describe what it is they do?
4. Visit the websites listed below and compare and contrast the professional industry trade shows.

   http://www.magiconline.com/
   http://designersandagents.com/
   http://www.pretparis.com/en
   http://www.enkshows.com/coterie/

   Answer the questions below.
   (a) What category of merchandise do they represent?
   (b) What type of buyer will attend this type of show?
   (c) Where is the show located? Is there more than one location?
   (d) Who can attend the trade show?
   (e) Which shows have created international partnerships?
5. Go online and research the current apparel trade shows. What are the trends in the trade show industry.

   www.apparelnews.net/calendar/2011-Trade-Show-Calendar/
6. Go online and research current international fashion weeks and shows.

   http://lakmeindiafashionweek.indiatimes.com/
   www.fashionfringe.co.uk
   http://www.pfdc.org/
   http://www.londonfashionweek.co.uk/
   http://www.belgradefashionweek.com/english/

   Answer the questions below.
   (a) What category of designer participates in the show?
   (b) What is the objective or goal of the show?
   (c) What is the application process?
   (d) Who attends this type of show?

In Class Activity

Joining a Production Team

After reviewing the Production Job Description Sheet, ask the students to explore the possible positions they would consider applying for in a production team. Have a class discussion on skills needed to obtain a position in a production team.

After reviewing the list of positions available on many fashion show production teams, the students should select the three roles/titles that appeal to them the most. In written summary form students should describe the skills and talents they currently posses. How do these skills and talents translate to the jobs they've chosen on the Production Team Responsibility Worksheet? Lead a discussion and exercise outlining the additional skills the student will need to foster to perform these roles proficiently. Address the importance of these skills and how they can be developed.

Ongoing Fashion Show Project

Introducing the Project; Defining Your Role

1. After students have completed the Joining a Production Team in class project, use the Production Team Job Responsibility Worksheet available at the end of the text and break into production teams. Each student chooses a job on the production team.

Terminology of the Trade

assistants 34
backroom coordinator 33
bridge 27
contemporary 27
designer 27
dressers 34
fashion marts 30
fashion presentation 30
fashion show director 33
formal runway show 27
informal show 27
international show 31
interns 34
national show 30
PR coordinator 34
press show 30
producer 32
production show 27
program editor 34
ready-to-wear 27
regional show 30
salon style show 27
stage manager 33
trade show 30
trunk show 29
volunteers 34

Web Resources

www.prcouture.com
www.tradeshow.globalsources.com/TRADESHOW/TRADESHOW.HTM
www.apparelsearch.com
www.apparelnews.net/about/publications/tradeshow/
www.designersandagents.com/english/no_flash.html
www.cosmoworlds.com/fashion_luxury_goods_trade_fairs.htm
www.premiumexhibitions.com/

Bibliography

Advanstar Communications, Inc. (May 5, 2011). *The Business of Fashion*. Retrieved from http://www.magiconline.com/press-release/pret-porter-paris-partners-wwdmagic-launch-%E2%80%98heart-pret

Burberry to sell even more straight off the runway for spring 2011. (August 27, 2011). *Fashionologie* (n.p.). Retrieved November 11, 2011, from http://www.fashionologie.com/Burberry-Sell-Even-More-Straight-Off-Runway-Spring-2011-10597630

Everett, J. C. and Swanson, K. K. (2004). *Guide to Producing a Fashion Show* (2nd ed., pp. 24–26). New York: Fairchild Publications.

Funding Universe. (2010). *Bill Blass Ltd. Company History.* Retrieved November 28, 2010, from http://www.fundinguniverse.com/company-histories

Jones, N. (September 15, 2010). Chalayon's Film Fest. *Women's Wear Daily*. Retrieved November 15, 2010, from http://www.wwd.com/fashion-news/fashion-scoops/chalayans-film-fest-3272774

Karimzadeh, M. (2010). Ralph Lauren stuns crowd with 4-D shows. *Women's Wear Daily.* Retrieved November 20, 2010, from http://www.wwd.com/menswear-news/ralph-layren-stuns-crowd-with-4-d-shows-338081

Pret A Porter Paris. (2011). More than a salon, a brand, and a label, the hub of fashions [Press release]. Retrieved August 9, 2011, from http://www.pretparis.com/en/le-salon/presentation

Quick, H. (1997). *Catwalking: A History of the Fashion Model* (p. 145). Edison, NJ: Wellfleet Press.

Scott, K. (2010). Burberry to broadcast fashion show in 3D Wired, CO. UK. Retrieved March 1, 2011, from http://www.wired.co.uk/news/archive/2010/02/8/burberry-to-broadcast-fashion-show-in-3d

Stone, E. (2008). *In Fashion Fun Fame Fortune* (4th ed.). New York: Fairchild Publications.

The Train New York. (2010–2011). The train and the box fall/winter 2010–2011 the wardrobe international [Press release]. Retrieved November 20, 2010, from http://www.thetrainnewyork.com/en/press

London Callin

FROM PITCH TO PROPOSAL AND BACK

LEARNING OBJECTIVES

After completing this chapter, you will be able to:

- Explore the qualifications needed to be a producer
- Know how to land a production job
- Draft a fashion show proposal
- Gain knowledge on storyboarding a vision
- Know how to present and pitch the theme
- Understand the terminology of the trade

You can't just make clothes. You have to be an architect, a filmmaker; you have to be a little bit of everything.

—MAZDACK RASSI, founder and creative director of Milk Studios

3

By now, the reader should have garnered an understanding of the history of the formation, development, and evolution of the fashion show and the relationship of it to the cultural and economic times of the moment. Clear understandings of the salient factors; individuals; and economic, technological, and cultural influences have been presented demonstrating and tracing the shaping of the fashion show to its present status. In addition, Chapter 1 presented the various categories of fashion shows and an explanation of each type of show, enabling the student to understand the reason for using one over the other. Chapter 2 outlined how to participate in or build a production team. Now, it is necessary to take a step back. The producer must first land the job before planning the show. For the aspiring producer it is vital to have or acquire some basic skills before interviewing or drafting a proposal. The pitch to the client is one of the best ways to outline the business approach and plan. Whether pitching a new client, a teacher from school, or a charity, the steps taken and skills needed are generally the same. The producer needs to articulate his or her talent and skills in both verbal and written form. Being qualified and enthusiastic and having the ability to deliver what has been proposed are basic requirements to the process. It is important to prepare for the interview. Create a clear and organized proposal. Storyboard the likely theme, vision, or mood. As you will learn throughout this book, the producer interacts with various industry professionals and others (Figure 3.1).

FIGURE 3.1 *Jan Strimple calling the show.*
Courtesy of Anthony Chang photography

Personal Qualifications and Skills Needed for a Production Career

In the current environment of reality TV and people's obsession with fame, most careers in the fashion business appear to be about ego, narcissism, and self-determination by whatever means necessary. The reality is that hard work, internships, education, and enthusiasm can get the potential producer much further than ego-driven selfish behavior. Below are examples of the qualifications needed to pursue a career as a producer or coordinator.

Education

Although there are no specific degrees in fashion show production, a college education is an advantage for anyone interested in fashion show production. The skills acquired by earning a college degree are directly transferable into the production business. Courses such as marketing, fashion merchandising, business management, introduction to the fashion industry, and communication are considered essential.

Fashion Industry Knowledge

A passion for the industry; a grasp of the current trends and movements; and an understanding of the contemporary fashion innovators, trends, and countertrends are imperative to successful production. Many of these topics are taught in college courses. Internships are another means to stay informed. Reading trade press such as *Women's Wear Daily* ("WWD") and the *Apparel News* will help build the knowledge and language of a fashion show producer. Visiting and signing onto forecasting sites like www.stylesight.com and www.WGSN.com will inform you of the latest trends in the industry. It is also necessary to keep up with current fashion blogs, and participate in fashion events.

Strong Writing Skills

Producers are expected to write proposals, create press releases, and show summaries. Each of these endeavors requires a superior ability to clearly articulate thoughts on paper. Take a writing course in college. Start a personal fashion blog and write on topics in which you are interested.

Analytical Skills

Every production has a budget, staffing issues, and a series of critical decisions that must be made. Analysis of each and every aspect of the production is the obligation of the producer. Analytical skills are perfected in a variety of ways. College education and work experience are two examples of how skills are perfected.

Drive and Enthusiasm

A producer works long hours in hectic, unpredictable environments dealing with needy clients and overworked, underpaid staff. Being enthusiastically driven is a must-have personality trait. If the leader is driven, positive, and passionate about the work, the energy and drive will trickle down to the whole team.

Appearance

A fashion forward approach to his or her own professional dress is an important characteristic of a producer. The producer should be a fashion leader or innovator.

Succeeding at the Interview

The first step in landing a job is getting an interview. Those properly prepared for the interview will have a better chance of getting the job. Producers are constantly interacting with people. A producer's communication skill and ability to articulate concepts and thoughts must be strong. Being able to present yourself in an interview in a compelling manner is an asset. Some basic steps when preparing for executing interviews either as the producer or as a member of the production team are given:

Step 1: Schedule the Interview: Once asked by a potential client, schedule the specific time and date.

Step 2: Research the Client or Organization: How can a producer understand the needs of the client without the necessary information about the client? Technology makes this endeavor easy. Spend some time reading and researching about the clients, brand, image, and goals. Know the proper pronunciation of their business's name, the key players, and what their message is.

Step 3: Show Up on Time: In life showing up is half the battle, but showing up late is a sure way to make the worst first impression.

Step 4: Dress Appropriately: Remember this is the fashion business, so have some style and flare. Keep it appropriate.

Step 5: Leave Them with a Takeaway: A takeaway is a small token, an item left with the interviewer. Some examples of takeaways are handkerchiefs, mints with a logo, stationery, or even a personal business card. In short, leave something, anything that will enable the potential client or employer to remember you.

Step 6: Present Examples of Work: These examples can come from portfolios, media kits, and a business website. Remember that some student or volunteer work you have accomplished is fine to share. (See Chapter 5 for further discussion of portfolios and media kits.)

Step 7: Listen and Take Notes: This is the time when the client is telling you what is needed. Listen carefully and take detailed notes. Attempt to address all of the client's requirements in the proposal.

Step 8: Ask Questions: In order to understand the client's needs ask probing questions, for example: What are the goals of the event? Who is the target market? What is the production budget? Be confident.

Step 9: Update Your Resume: Keep your resume current using the most contemporary templates, multimedia, and layering of content. Make sure to direct clients to your company, organization, or school's website, blog, and Facebook page.

Step 10: Be Realistic: Don't accept just any job offer. Understand your limits. New producers often fail because they take on more than they can handle.

Step 11: Bring a Few Ideas, but Don't Give Too Much Away: The goal is to demonstrate your ability to adapt to the client in a unique way. Entice the client with little indications of new ideas for the event. Keep in mind to save the meat of the concepts until a contract is signed.

After the successful interview, it is time to work on the proposal. Having listened and taken notes as to the requirements of the potential client, simply list how the proposal will meet their needs. It's important to understand the potential services required and to determine if you or your company is capable of providing the necessary services.

List of Production Services

This list is an example of producers' services. Many companies offer these services as a package or "a la carte" and are priced accordingly. Basic definitions are provided below. However, more detailed explanations are given in Chapters 7 and 8.

Technical—Lighting, Audio/Visual Scenic

Lighting design: Hiring and working with lighting technician to meet all illumination needs for the show.

Audio visual design (AV): Working with and hiring the AV technician to meet all audio (sound) and visual needs for the show, which include but are not limited to items such as logo placement and image and video projection. The AV provides all sound and visual components of the show as well as the equipment involved in presenting such works.

Scenic design: Involves providing the stage design, set design, and/or production design.

Video projection: In charge of hiring the video projector technician and renting the equipment. A video projector takes a video signal and projects the equivalent image on a projection screen using a lens system. Most video projection can be effectuated through computer systems.

Video documentation/filming: The responsibility of hiring a videographer to film the event.

Event photography: Involves hiring a photographer to take pictures during the event.

Music selection: Involves working with a DJ, or band, in selecting the music for the show.

Headset technician: The person in charge of securing headsets for hands-free communication. Usually sound or AV technicians can supply headsets.

Clothing and Merchandising

Coordination of designer collections

Selecting clothing from retail establishment

Backstage

(See Chapter 2 for definitions.)

Styling

Backstage managing

Coordination

Directing

Calling show

Dressing

Alterations

Fittings

Hair and makeup

Assistants/runners

Supervising

Pressing/steaming

Stage management

Models, Talent, and Agencies

(See Chapter 8 for definitions.)

Casting models

Model choreography

Casting entertainment

Securing talent

Securing celebrities

Other Services Defined

PR coordination: The responsibility of creating and/or directing all public relations information that is disseminated to the press. Often this person develops information such as media kits, press releases, and invitations. This person can also be in charge of creating and updating all social media.

The program creator: The person in charge of developing the entire list of planned events for the production, the program. This person works closely with the PR coordinator and graphic designer to ensure all printed information is accurate.

Security and transportation personnel: Hired individuals in charge of security, safety, and human movement during the show. This is true for both the front of the house (the public space) and the back of the house (the private workroom).

Public speaker: Usually the person that a producer secures as a high-profile popular individual to moderate or make a verbal presentation for the event. These speakers can be local celebrities such as college athletes or newscasters, and nationally recognized celebrities such as reality TV stars, models, and actors.

Commentary writer: The individual who under the instruction of the producer writes the word presentations provided to and for the master of ceremonies, talent, and all other speakers.

Décor coordinator: The party (individual or company) that provides the themed material for the decoration of the event location. A producer can hire a third-party events company or supply the décor from his or her own production house if available. (Décor is discussed in greater detail in Chapter 7.)

Every producer has a different and somewhat distinctive way of presenting the written proposal. Paula Taylor LLC Productions addresses each issue that the client needs within the proposal and clearly defines the role and responsibilities of Paula Taylor LLC Productions. See the proposal format example below.

THE PROPOSAL

Traditional proposals have many components. They include, but are not limited to, the following:

1. **Executive summary:** Although the executive summary appears at the start of the document, it is preferable to wait until all other sections are finished before you write it. It contains a short summary of key points that are included in the proposal.
2. **Statement of purpose:** This section clearly delineates the purpose of the event/show. It must include the main functions of the event such as fundraising, promotion, selling, education, and so on.
3. **Project plan and list of services:** A list of all production services you intend to provide.
4. **Resources:** A resource can be people, information, and objects. This includes staff members, interns, and volunteers. Information technology, relationships, concepts, education, and expertise are some examples of information resources. Maintaining a style warehouse full of accessories, staging, and costumes is a classic example of object resources.
5. **Budget:** In traditional proposal development, budgets are created by first obtaining the service cost. In the fashion industry, more often than not, the client dictates the total

funds available. Therefore, all services provided must be customized to fit the limit of funds available.

6. **Conclusion:** A conclusion reviews in summary form the following:
   a. Purpose and goal of the event.
   b. Benefits the client will receive.

FIGURE 3.2 *Male model on runway.*
Courtesy of Omer Kreso

A FORMAT EXAMPLE OF A FASHION SHOW PROPOSAL

Proposals for fashion show productions can vary. For example, they may include client's funds available, individual desires, and scope of the required production services. Below is an example of the format of a basic small-budget production proposal, using the business name of Paula Taylor LLC Productions (Figure 3.2).

Paula Taylor LLC Productions

PROPOSAL FOR (Insert client's name)

Executive Summary

Paula Taylor Productions (your business name here) has leveraged her extensive industry knowledge, community relationships, and experience to produce, direct, and create fashion shows and events. Paula Taylor has a network of support to ensure the success of the event. The event will be conducted on. (include date of event here) Paula Taylor Production will manage and direct for a flat fee of (insert proposed fee) all the aspects of the fashion show stated below. In particular, Paula Taylor Productions will handle the back of the house services as provided in the menu of services below.

Statement of Purpose

The function of this event is to assist (insert client name) in their fundraising by providing a professionally produced and executed fashion show.

Menu of Services and Resources

- **Production staff:** Paula Taylor LLC ("PTLLC") will contract all the necessary production staff to ensure a seamless show.
- **Coordination of designers/clothing and retail selection:** PTLLC will schedule pick up and shipping of clothing with all retail stores and designers. It will choose, inventory and style all looks and photograph them.
- **Back of house direction and management:** PTLLC will provide experienced dressers, run the back of the house, and coordinate with contracted hair and makeup provided by the client It will also provide racks for each model, information, and storyboards for all model looks.
- **Casting models:** PTLLC will select and hire professional models through an agency or casting agent that has had runway experience and provide headshots for review by the client if requested.
- **Choreography/timing:** PTLLC will work directly with the models to create a memorable and entertaining, well-timed event. Paula Taylor and staff will organize the timing of the production to align with the music and choreography.
- **Rehearsal and preparation:** PTLLC will work with models and lighting, music, and information technology personnel to ensure that all aspects of the show are in sync. PTLLC will conduct a final run-through and rehearsal.
- **Lighting:** PTLLC will work with the venue, client, and lighting technician to create lighting, which matches the vision and or theme of the event. (The actual lights are not included in the quoted fee but can be provided for an additional charge.)
- **Scripting:** PTLLC will work with the client to create a seamless, well thought-out script for the fashion show.
- **Runway and stage design:** PTLLC will work with the client, venue provider, and décor company on the size and design of the runway and stage (The runway itself is not included in the quoted fee.)
- **Theme:** PTLLC works closely with the client to ensure its vision is met while bringing our own expertise and knowledge to create an unforgettable runway experience.

(Continued)

(*Continued*)

- **Day of event management and direction:** PTLLC will direct all day event needs, including final approval of each model's look before calling the show.
- **Sound and audio:** PTLLC will work with venue provider and the DJ to have all appropriate sound and audio required.
- **Striking the show:** PTLLC will break down the backroom and return it to its original condition.
- **Merchandise return:** PTLLC will return all merchandise in original condition to appropriate parties.
- **Event summary:** PTLLC will provide a written report within two weeks of the event, which will measure the successes and the challenges of the event.

SUMMARY

Paula Taylor Productions looks forward to executing a successful, unique, and professional fashion show using proprietary in-house resources where appropriate and brings to the production her extensive experience, staff, and expertise.

Date of event is scheduled for	
Total investment:	$
Payment requirements:	
Deposit upon signing:	$
Preevent payment:	$ (due on or before ____________________)
Balance due:	$ (due no later than ____________________)

This quote is valid until:

Accepted and approved by:

______________________________ Date: ______________________________

For (Client Name)

Creating the Show Concept

If the client does not require "a show in a box" as Jan Strimple put it, be creative and come up with your own concept for the show. The best and most organized approach to formulating a theme is brainstorming and storyboarding. After spending extensive time researching ideas, reading magazines and books, browsing the Internet, watching movies, and taking in all that is around as inspiration, decide on a theme. The theme can be a feeling, a word, or something literal such as the Hollywood glamour of the 1930s. All of the producer's decisions are based on the client's needs, the target audience, and the product. Once the theme is determined, dream big. This is not the time to worry about budget. Create a wish list for the show, including props, music, lighting, and staging. If it's a big production show, incorporate and include dancers, actors, and singers on the wish list. Brainstorm with your team, your friends, and people you trust about potential ideas. The best way to keep all these ideas organized is on a storyboard. It can be online, in PowerPoint form, or on poster board.

Storyboards

A fashion show storyboard or mood board is a visual summary and outline of the concept of the fashion show (Figures 3.3 and 3.4). It is used in many creative industries. It

FIGURE 3.3 *Example of vision board.*
Courtesy of John Calder

FIGURE 3.4 *Model wearing Osman Yousefzada.*
Courtesy of John Calder

is developed in the early stages of production and is a tool used to help organize inspiration and solidify the theme. The physical board or Web application for the same purpose can include magazine tears, fabric swatches, old photos, buttons, and ribbons. Any visual reference can be included to reinforce the theme. The main function of a fashion show storyboard is to communicate the concept to the team and the clients. Making a storyboard is fun and easy. Once all the materials are gathered, simply cut and paste them onto thick poster boards or use a Web application. Include copy and inspiring text. If the producer chooses to only create a physical storyboard, then he or she should take a digital photo of it and send it to team members including the backroom manager, hair and makeup artist, and the stylist. Many producers also have a separate storyboard for hair and makeup (Figures 3.5 and 3.6).

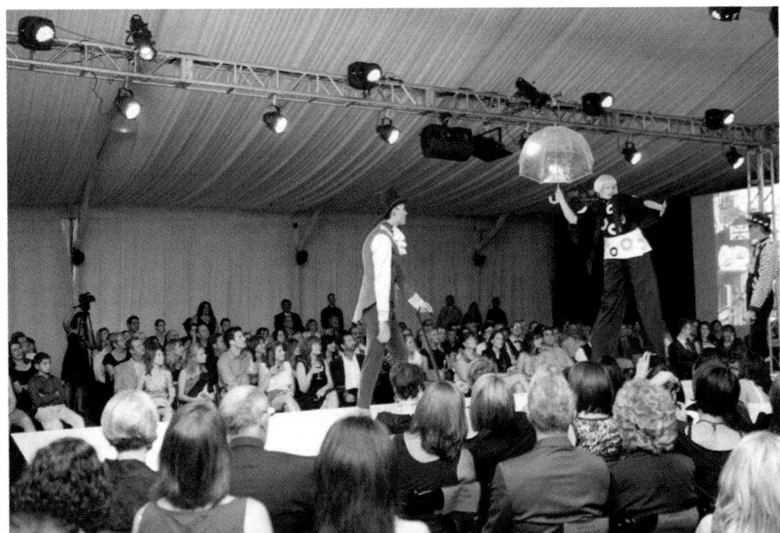

FIGURE 3.6 *Carnaby Street Characters opening the London Calling Show.*
Courtesy of Omer Kreso

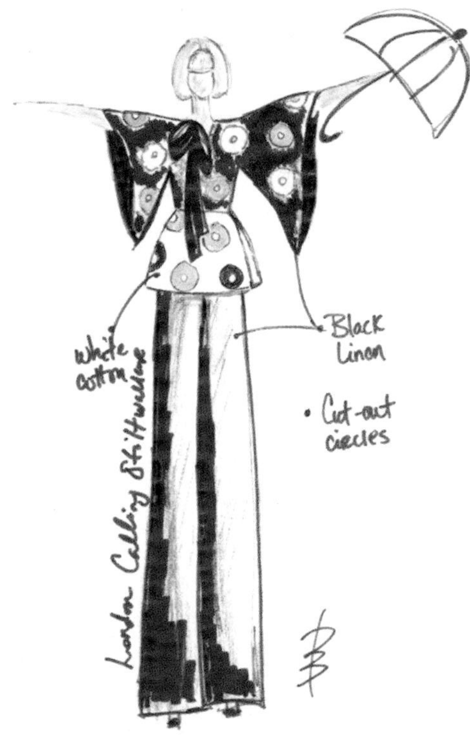

FIGURE 3.5 *Sketch for costume.*
Courtesy of Dustin Bever

Pitching the Theme or Concept

Although it is encouraged to discuss preliminary ideas regarding the theme or vision in the interview and proposal, it is not until the contract is signed that the final theme/vision is actualized. Pitching the theme is selling the idea! It is the producer's role to make it sound new, exciting, and uniquely created for the client's purposes. In most cases the client will have the producer come to his or her office for the presentation. If technology is part of the presentation, such as use of a laptop, PowerPoint, or video presentation in addition to the storyboard, arrive early to check all your technology. Have a backup plan if something isn't working. The presentation should be no longer than twenty minutes. During the pitch it is the responsibility of the producer to take the client on a visual journey. Incorporating a short PowerPoint that may include a video presentation that reinforces the storyboard can enhance the visual sojourn. It can include music, clips from movies, YouTube, or other fashion shows. Pitch the theme! The clients determine the degree to which the production company has control over the theme. Often PR firms and casting agents have developed the concept and it is the production company's job to execute their vision. They will be delivered such items as layouts and mood boards.

The Preview

This is the moment the show becomes real. It is the time for the producer to give a glimpse of the big idea. The more the five senses are involved (i.e., sight, sound, smell, taste, and feel), the easier it will be for the listener to be engaged and comprehend the theme.

In the attempt to set the mood, turn the lights off. Play some music, something that speaks to the theme. For example, if it is a British 1960s MOD theme, play The Beatles, The Who, The Kinks, and so on. If it's a conceptual theme, use a feeling or word like "ethereal" or "dreamy." Play some soft appropriate music. It is now time to tell the story.

Storyboard/Mood Board Step by Step

Do not give everything away; rather, generate excitement by using your board and PowerPoint to explain the general ideas of the show. For a local nonprofit charity *London Calling* show, Paula Taylor LLC created a surreal version of Carnaby Street in the1960s as the theme. The show opened with three absurd characters: a stilt walker, a juggler, and the MC known as the Dandy. The Dandy was a character created using inspiration from Beau Brummell, the first known British Dandy and Malcolm McDowell's sinister character from the movie *A Clockwork Orange*. The storyboard included sketches of the potential costumes and magazine tears for styling, hair, and makeup. Street music from London was the backdrop, with police sirens, shoppers' feet, and "newsies" calling out the exciting events of the day. The pitch to the client included setting this scene visually and walking step by step through the opening number. Storyboarding is the beginning of the show development and a key aspect to organizing thoughts. See Figure 3.7 to know how to create a theme for a fashion show.

The theme/vision worksheet has been provided at the end of the text to guide you in this process.

Clients will provide direction regarding the theme or vision of the Fashion Show. It is the Producer's responsibility to meet and exceed their client's expectations. Follow the guidelines below to help you develop a theme/vision. Begin by answering the following two questions:

1. What is the **function** of the show? (Remember that a show can have multiple functions)
   - To drive sales?
   - To highlight or introduce a brand?
   - To entertain the audience?
   - To raise funds for charity?
   - To educate the public on the new fashion trends and looks of the season?
2. Who is the potential **target audience**? Remember the show can have a variety of audience members such as:
   - Buyers
   - Retailers
   - Students
   - Community Members
   - Board Members
   - Press

Once you have addressed and answered these questions you are ready to select a general theme for your Fashion Show. Begin with a 10-15 minute brain storming session. Everyone in your group will contribute to the brainstorming session. Creativity is encouraged; the goal is to create a theme or vision that will help direct the look and feel of the show. Select a group member to serve as secretary and record ideas with a marker on poster board for all to see. Next, examine your list of ideas, grouping similar ideas together and come to a common consensus on the best idea presented. A vote will most likely be needed.

The elements that will bring your theme to life are both visual and auditory. Visual elements include: color, texture, space, and lighting. Auditory elements include: music, rhythm, pacing, and sound effects. Together, visual and auditory elements create emotion, mood, and atmosphere.

Once you've answered the questions above and brainstormed as a team, it's time to determine what your general theme and vision for the show/event will be. As your show/ event progresses, your theme and vision will evolve to include elements such as décor, lighting, color, merchandise, music, models, pacing, and sound effects. These elements will bring your theme to life incorporating many of your senses.

A worksheet has been provided at the back of the text to guide you in this process.

FIGURE 3.7 *Creating a theme for your fashion show.*

Chapter Review

In summary, the production industry is ever growing. A qualified, educated, and experienced producer has a better chance than most in securing work. Chapter 3 outlines the qualifications and skills a potential producer needs to acquire to enter the career path in production. In addition, several tangible interviewing tips are specified in this chapter summarizing how to conduct a successful interview. The chapter investigates the importance of writing and pitching a proposal. In addition, it provides a detailed list of production services. It defines storyboarding and its function as a real-world tool for the organizational foundation of the show.

Questions for Review and Discussion

1. What are the skills required to be a producer and why are they vital to a career in production?
2. List the key elements that are included in a proposal.
3. Discuss and explain successful methods used in pitching a proposal.
4. Explain the importance of storyboarding.

Out and About Activities

1. Using the Web resources provided, research fashion show production/fashion show coordinating websites. Review the services they provide. Choose two and compare and contrast their available services.
2. Go online and research the latest online applications for storyboarding.

In Class Activity

1. Break the class into groups and role-play interview scenarios. Have one student play the role of the producer and the others play that of a client. Incorporate many of the tips on succeeding at the interview.
2. Have teams of students come up with themes for a fictional fashion show. Storyboard the themes. Pitch the storyboard themes. (Use the theme form at the end of the text.)

Ongoing Fashion Show Project

Getting Started

Start your own fashion show by following the steps given:

(a) Create a theme. (Utilize Theme/Vision Worksheet at the end of the text.)
(b) Brainstorm with class members on the purpose or message of the show to help create the theme.
(c) Storyboard the theme.
(d) Create a working title or name the show.

Terminology of the Trade

pitch 54
production services 48
proposal 50
storyboard 52
target audience 55
theme 54

Web Resources

www.atinytribe.com/apps/moodboard
www.polyvore.com/
www.moodboard.com/
www.groundcrew.net
www.shannondavidson.com/
www.theweddingguys.com/about.html
www.facebook.com/JanStrimpleProductions
www.facebook.com/paulataylorllcproductions
www.paulataylorllc.com
www.proposaltemplatedepot.com

Bibliography

Osborn, A. F. (1963). *Applied Imagination Principles and Procedures of Creative Problem Solving* (3rd ed.). New York: Charles Scribners Sons.

Roland, J. (1985). *Questorming Outline of the Method*.

The Purdue Online Writing Lab (OWL). (2012). Retrieved February 11, 2012, from http://www.owl.english.purdue.edu

PLANNING THE SHOW

LEARNING OBJECTIVES

After completing this chapter, you will be able to:

- Gain an understanding of the timelines, budgets, and planning calendars
- Define who is putting on the show
- Identify and address your target market
- Understand the terminology of the trade

The truth is, when there are so many problems in the world... why would anyone be interested in fashion? The ability to make a woman look lovelier, more beautiful, and a word that's no longer used, more glamorous...is something akin to magic.

—MORTON MYLES

FIGURE 4.1 *Angel Sanchez's showroom/office.*
Courtesy of Angel Sanchez

The previous chapter discussed the methods and interview techniques that are helpful when you are in consideration for the job. The chapter also described the creation of the theme and the use of storyboards, once the contract to produce the show has been obtained. After the creation of a successful storyboard and a strong team, the producer's next job is to plan the show. Planning the show requires rigorous organization, commitment to a timeline, and planning calendar and budget. In this chapter, we will explore in detail the steps it takes to create and organize timelines, budgets, and planning calendars. The chapter also addresses how to identify and secure the target market for the event (Figure 4.1).

Timeline

A **timeline** is a tool used to help organize dates and deadlines for all-important facets of the show. The timeline keeps everyone on track and ensures that significant deadlines are met. Creating the timeline may take several hours. Once a timeline is completed, syncing the information with your computer's or phone's calendar will assist in reminding you of specific dates and deadlines. It is generally recommended to start a timeline three to twelve months prior to the event. The actual start date is determined based on the nature of the show, for example, whether it is a professional, charity, student, or combination show; the budget for the show; and the target audience. Each type of show has special challenges; some have small budgets and short deadlines while others have massive budgets, major staff, and a great number of key milestones before show day. Before a timeline is started, it is important to consider a few fundamental questions that will help determine what type of timeline you need to create and who will manage the details. *The Complete Idiot's Guide to Meeting and Event Planning* suggests that you ask yourself some questions about the event before you start the timeline.

> For whom is the timeline? The producer? The staff? The clients?
>
> Who is in charge of the timeline?
>
> How long is the timeline?
>
> Will task completion dates be required?
>
> Is the timeline only for certain key events or a comprehensive compilation?
>
> Will some of the tasks be on going—like monthly meetings? (Craven, R. E., and Golabowski, L. J., 2006).

How detailed the timeline is can be determined by the producer's needs. Many producers fill in only major events and deadlines while others create an exhaustive list. A timeline is best begun only after the show's location and date have been set. Once the date and location are secured, all other aspects of the event can be addressed. Timelines can be broken into two categories: **key events** and **comprehensive information**. In both cases the following list provides some items that may be included:

- Assign job duties to the team
- Book hair and makeup

- Book fittings
- Book models; negotiate contracts
- Conduct site visits
- Create a site contacts list
- Create model boards
- Create lineup
- Create day of show plan/timeline
- Meet with hair and makeup and present storyboard
- Meet with technical team
    - Audiovisual
    - Disc jockey/music
    - Lighting
    - Sound
    - Videography
- Order food and beverage for models
- Hire a photographer
- Prepare the budget
- Select inventory
- Review product and theme connection
- Schedule rehearsal
- Style looks
- Schedule staff meetings
- Schedule new staff/intern orientation
- Return merchandise
- Prepare written show evaluation

Once you have made a general list of items to be added into the timeline, Craven and Golabowski suggest it is a good idea to put each task into a main category. Categorizing tasks will help the producer ensure his or her team clearly understands their task. Once categories and key events are determined, make sure you clarify who will be in charge of the specific tasks. Here are a variety of applicable categories:

- Audiovisual
- Back of the house
- Front of the house
- Hair and makeup
- Models
- Site

For example, task and deadlines that would fall under the model category are:

- Contracts
- Casting
- Evaluations
- Fitting
- Hair and makeup
- Line up
- Model board
- Rehearsal(s)

It is important to remember that significant events like rehearsals, castings, and fittings should have permanent dates and times certain for completion. In addition, a timeline should list the staff member in charge of the task, meeting, or event. Once the major tasks and categories are listed in detail, the producer will gain a better understanding of the amount of preparation time needed to meet the task. As stated before, timelines, like every other aspect of production, are dependent upon the needs of the show, the amount of staff, and the time frame within which you are working. Let's create a timeline!

The best way to start is simply writing down all the important dates that are set in stone and filling in the blanks. If you are unsure of a date or how long a task may take, make an educated guess. An example of a fashion show key events timeline is given in Figure 4.2. Remember to include all postshow task and meetings in your timeline, such as:

- Billing
- Dry-cleaning
- Evaluations
- Returning inventory
- Shipping
- Wrap-up meetings

Events	Notes
Initial Staff Meeting	
Start:	
End:	
Creation of Storyboard	
Start:	
End:	
Hair and Makeup Meeting	
Start:	
End:	
Model Call	
Start:	
End:	
Merchandise Pull	
Start:	
End:	
Styling Looks	
Start:	
End:	
Creation of Lineup	
Start:	
End:	
Tech Meeting	
Start:	
End:	
Backroom Layout	
Start:	
End:	
Model Boards	
Start:	
End:	

FIGURE 4.2 *Key events timeline example.*

Events	Notes
Rehearsal	
Start:	
End:	
Top of Show	
Start:	
End:	
Breakdown	
Start:	
End:	
Return Merchandise	
Start:	
End:	
Wrap-up Meeting	
Start:	
End:	

FIGURE 4.2 *(Continued)*

The Budget

Once you have created a timeline and outlined the goals of the show, the next order of business is to draft the budget. The budget is an essential planning tool. No fashion show producer can live without one. Budgets are time-consuming and efforts should be made to make them painstakingly detailed. The salient issue for new producers and seasoned professionals is to remember that everything has a price—even donated items and volunteers. It is important to predict cost and make educated guesses where needed. Start by making a list of all expenses you think you want or need to create your dream show. Then highlight the essential items.

What Is a Budget?

A budget is a financial presentation that defines all expenses and income as an operational goal, and derives from that a statement of profit or loss known as an Income Statement. Budgets are presented as proposed income, expenses, and profit as compared against actual performance—in short, what you plan on spending and what you actually spend. The budget is an essential planning tool, which defines precise expenses and expenditures.

What Is Included in a Budget?

Everything! Often important items, such as cost of meetings; expenses for stamps, cell phone calls, and rehearsals; and personal expenses related to the show are left out of a budget. How detailed a budget should be and what should be included will depend on what the producer's job entails. The producer's role may simply include back of the house, show, and runway issues. In some cases, the producer secures and pays for the location and front of the house issues, or décor. Below is a list of categories commonly used in fashion show budgets?

- Audiovisual
- Custom or in-house costumes
- Dressers
- Entertainment
- Food and beverage
- Hair and makeup
- Headsets and monitor
- Insurance
- Invitations
- Lighting
- Models
- Promotional materials
- Phone and fax
- Photography
- Runway
- Seamstress
- Staging
- Staffing
- Shipping
- Transportation
- Videography

Each show is different and unique unto itself. The list above should be viewed simply as an example of some items and expenses that could be included in a budget.

Once you have created a general list of items needed to be included in the budget and their estimated cost, it is time to establish which expenditures will require competitive bids. For example, hair, makeup, and models all may require more than one bid to find the best price and suitable company with which to work. Many first-time producers or coordinators obtain several bids. Once they have done so, they have a much better ability to estimate actual and future cost. Many charity shows have items like hair and makeup donated by a salon for free. This type of donation is considered an "**in-kind donation**." This type of donation includes products, services, and time, instead of a monetary gift. All in-kind donations need to be reflected in the budget.

Fixed and Variable Costs

It is also crucial to include both **fixed** and **variable** costs in the budget. Fixed costs are any charges (expenses) that must be paid without variation. In traditional business budgets, there are many fixed costs whereas in fashion show production there are fewer fixed and more variable costs. Examples of fixed costs are insurance, location rental, and taxes (e.g., sales tax).

A variable cost is any charges that are not constant and are subject to variation. In the case of fashion shows, almost all categories of expenses are variable.

Understanding your financial goals plays an important role in the creation of a budget. All expenses should be listed and accounted for before considering revenue. **Revenue** is the gross amount of money a business receives before deductions for cost of goods and services. Remember, keeping a budget realistic will help in all facets of producing the show. List every single expense and revenue in the budget. In today's modern world, there are numerous examples of budget templates to use and manipulate in creating your own. We have fashioned a simple budget form with some potential categories included. In addition, a blank template has been provided in the back of the text that you can use and change to help manage your show.

An example of a fashion show budget is given in Figure 4.3.

	Budgeted	Actual
INCOME:		
Donations	$15000	$10000
Ticket Sales	$45000	$45000
Sponsorships	$25000	$30000
Other	n/a	n/a
Income Total	$85000	$85000
EXPENSES:		
Front of House		
Location rental	$2500	$1500
Insurance	n/a	n/a
Food & beverage (catering)	$3600	$3000
Entertainment	$500	$500
Audiovisual	$1500	$1500
Lighting	$2800	$3000
Sound	$250	$250
Security	n/a	n/a
Videographer	$400	In Kind
Photography	$250	In Kind
Décor	$2500	$1800
Staging and runway	$1000	In Kind
Guest Speaker(s)	n/a	n/a
Master of ceremony	n/a	n/a
Phone & fax	n/a	n/a
Printing	$500	In Kind
Front of House Expenses Total	$15800	$11550
Back of House		
Staffing		
Producer	$5350	$5350
Production assistant(s)	$600	$600
Stage manager	n/a	n/a
Backroom manager	$350	$350
Stylist(s)	$100	100
Dresser(s)	$600	In Kind
Seamstress	$100	$100
Intern(s)	n/a	n/a
Other	n/a	n/a
Hair & makeup	$600	In Kind
Models	$3450	$2850
Costumes and custom designs	$350	$350
Shipping	$300	$300
Miscellaneous	n/a	n/a
Back of House Expenses Total	$11800	$10000
General Other		
Promotional materials	n/a	n/a
Advertisement	$5000	In Kind
IT support		
Other Expenses Total	$5000	$0
Total Expenses	$32600	$21550
Profit (LOSS) before Taxes	$52400	$63450

FIGURE 4.3 *Fashion show budget example.*

Planning Calendars

A planning calendar is a daily, weekly, or monthly schedule containing important dates and deadlines taken from the timeline and put into **calendar/time** format. The planning calendar is yet another tool used by producers and staff to have a quick glance at daily, weekly, or monthly schedules. A copy of the planning calendar should be on the producer's computer, phone, and binder.

It is essential to understand that just as the fashion industry is constantly moving and changing, some items in one or all of the organizational and financial charts may change. We have discussed the timelines, budgets, and planning calendars and now proceed on to learn about how to create fashion show binders and flash drives for management and staff.

Fashion Show Binder

Almost every producer I have interviewed, worked with, and seen in action uses some form of binder to hold all of his or her critical materials. It is a quick and easy way to stay organized and have access to all the vital show information. Purchase several three ring binders and divide important information within them. Title dividers and keep the planning calendar readily available for easy reference to day-to-day meetings and deadlines. By show date, this folder and flash drive will be full of all the imperative information a producer and management staff need about their show at hand's reach. Each team member's folder will have a variety of items. While the producer's binder will hold all information regarding the show, the stylist or backroom management binders will be limited only to the information that the individual may need for his or her specific job duties. Below is a list of some items one may find in a producer's folder:

A contact list
Day of show timeline
Evaluations
Final model lineup
Floor plan/layout
Model list/notes
Merchandise selection
Model release forms
Makeup direction
Public relations
Production job title sheets
Receipts
Stylist notes
Set list

In Chapter 2 we defined the categories of shows such as production, traditional, runway, and trunk, among others. It is extremely important, especially in planning the use of media kits, budgets, and press releases, to understand which category of show is to be produced. One must have a clear grasp of the function of the event. Consider, for example, whether the show is to support charity; the expected participants, for example, whether the participants are students; and the potential audience, if the audience comprises the community at large or only members of the charity. The function can be varied; for example, it could entail the support of students, charities, designers, or retailers. Frequently, fashion shows are a combination of all these components. On the one hand, students might be executing a runway show to benefit a local nonprofit. On the other hand, larger charitable organizations may hold a production show hiring professional producers for an event, thus raising funds for the needy. Most designers hold shows simply to promote, brand, and sell their collection. Retailers may align themselves with charities, providing the clothing for the show. Many regional shows partner with retailers, like Neiman Marcus, Dillard's, Stanley Korshak, and Saks Fifth Avenue. It is a great way for retailers to showcase their products and at the same time donate to a worthy cause. In addition, in order to increase traffic and sales, many retailers hold fashion events and shows inside their establishments. Regardless of which group is undertaking the show, budgets, timelines, and planning calendars should all be used. The depth and breadth of these items will vary depending on the size of a production, allocated budget, and planning time needed. Budgets and timelines change with the nature, function, and category of the show or event.

Category and Function of the Show

Student Shows

A student show is a fashion event coordinated by the students under the supervision of faculty of a specific educational institution such as a college, university, or high school. Generally, the budgets are small. Volunteers and students are often used as models, DJs, and videographers. Students, faculty, and staff plan and execute all aspects of the show. Budget restrictions will dictate what, if anything, is spent on such things as additional lighting, décor, and entertainment. The purpose of the show can vary. Normally, student shows promote education and positive public relations about and for the school. Such shows also highlight student work, and raise money for programs and charities, while providing entertainment.

Charity Shows

The main functions of a charity show are fundraising, education, and branding. Raising money for a needy cause through a fashion show and educating the audience on the charity's mission are the most significant reasons for conducting a charity show. Branding the charity, its board members, and events is another important aim of holding charity shows. The audience is generally the consumer, not the press. Many charity fashion shows have large budgets and hire fashion producers to execute a professional show. The professional producer works directly with the charity's committee members. These shows often secure lighting and sound technicians and include a multimedia presentation. Smaller nonprofits hold more humble events having the board members or committee members coordinate the show. Depending on the goals and budget, they may hire models directly from a modeling agency or recruit committee members, board members, and prominent community members as volunteer models (Figure 4.4).

Professional Fashion Shows

The function of a professional fashion show is to highlight, brand, advertise, and sell a collection of a particular designer. Sometimes it is to sell various collections from a specific retailer. These shows are generally for the trade, buyers, press, and VIP customers.

FIGURE 4.4 *Angel Sanchez with clients.*
Courtesy of Angel Sanchez

The VIP clients for major brands are usually celebrities, socialites, musicians, and athletes. They are the people you see sitting in the front row. Industry or professional shows hire local big-name production companies and fashion show coordinators to work with the designers and retailers in executing their vision. A professional runway show can have a budget in the hundreds of thousands of dollars (Figure 4.5).

FIGURE 4.5 *Models on the runway.*
From Dreamstime

Shows in a Retail Setting

The purpose of a show in a retail setting is to drive sales and highlight the product. The shows are for the consumer, especially VIP customers. Outside producers are rarely hired to execute these events. Staff and designer representatives coordinate the events. They can be everything from a full runway show to a simple, salon style presentation.

Once you have determined both the category and function of the fashion show, it's time to secure the target market and potential audience.

Target Market/Audience

A target market is a specific group of consumers or potential customers to whom a company aims to sell its product. Every fashion show has a different target market or audience that will attend the event. In most cases, the company or organization that hires the producer knows who their target audience is and has already started securing them as participants. The producer's role is to balance creativity, theatrics, and styling to make the show exciting and fresh without losing the audience. The audience can come from many different sources depending on who is holding the fashion show. A retailer, for instance, may target current customers, while seeking new ones from mailing lists and through direct advertising campaigns. Designers generally target bloggers, press, and retailers. Charity or school shows draw from mailings, social networking, public service announcements (PSAs), word of mouth, free press, and membership lists. It is crucial to define the potential audience prior to the event. Understanding the audience's needs is critical to designing and planning a successful fashion show. Asking some basic questions regarding the **demographics, geographics, psychographics**, and **behavioral patterns** will help in determining one's target market. In short, it is necessary to look at the age, income, interests, and lifestyles of the potential audience member.

Geographics

Look at the area or climate within which the consumer resides. For example, it may not speak to the target market in Florida or Arizona to have a great deal of heavy clothing or fur displayed down the runway—no matter how much they are in trend.

Demographics

Demographics explores the age, race, educational background, and household income of the consumer and expected or targeted attendee to the fashion show. If the average age of the attendee is 65 or over, styling, décor, and other choices should be fashionably age appropriate, as an overemphasis on certain design and other types of trendy urban fashion may only disconnect with the mature audience. Sometimes even the nature of the music must be carefully reviewed so as to ensure the listeners remain engaged. Be aware of current or local events that may influence or are presently affecting the particular attending demographic. Incorporate current events where and when appropriate.

Psychographics

Look at the potential attendees' lifestyle. For example, do they have a great deal of free time and discretionary income? **Discretionary income** is the amount of money left over after taxes and day-to-day expenses are met. Have there been any noteworthy recent events, local, regional, national, or global, that may affect their mood and willingness to go along with the fantasy event you intend to create and present? In light of such potential events, consider how you might customize your show to hold your audience.

Behavioral Patterns

Is the audience's attendance at the show about status, charity, responsibility, entertainment, or a combination of all of these? Understand the complex motivations of the expected target audience. Pick out the top two motivations and be sure your show, in both direct and subtle ways, reinforces such motivation. Behavior patterns and motivation are regularly the most ignored and mishandled aspects of a runway show and can lead to a mediocre response, not just from the audience but also from the employer who hired the producer of the show (Stone, 2007).

The most effective way to find answers to these questions is to conduct a survey or give a questionnaire to be completed by the organization, designer, retailer, or charity that has hired you to produce the show. A **questionnaire** is a set of printed or written questions that provides for a multiple-choice answer or for a written response. They should already know the answers to these basic questions about their target market. If they do not know them or if the answers they provide to you are inconsistent, you should suggest and encourage the organization to take a real survey of their expected market and to provide those answers to you. Surveys and questionnaires determine significant factors and motivations of a specific group and are somewhat complex to interpret. Careful attention should be given to the stated motivation for support of the organization. The producer should summarize the relative information and attempt to incorporate, where appropriate within the show, the issues discovered. The following are examples of questions one might include in a questionnaire or survey about target market/audiences:

QUESTIONS TO CONSIDER WHEN APPLIED TO THE ATTENDEES

What is the average age of the attendee of the show?
What is the average income of the attendee?
In what part of town does the attendee reside?
Why is he or she participating?
How did the attendee hear about the show?
Is this the attendee's first time to the event?
How many events a year does the attendee support?
How many for charity? How many for other purposes?
What is the single most important issue for the attendee concerning this event?
What is the least important issue for the attendee concerning this event?

QUESTIONS ABOUT THE FASHION SHOW TO BE DIRECTED TO THE EMPLOYER/SCHOOL /CHARITY

Is this a charity event? If so who is the beneficiary?
Are board members required to attend?
What restrictions, if any, are there for the event?
What is the goal of the fashion show?
Why have they chosen a fashion show to meet their stated goals?
What type of attendance are they expecting?
What are the steps they are taking to ensure attendance?
How many events a year do they have for this purpose?
What is the single most important reason for them to attend this event:
raise money, see the latest fashions, or socialize with friends?

Chapter Review

This chapter has laid out the various important organizational and financial tools to aid in the planning of a well thought-out and detailed show—leaving very little to chance. Budgets, timelines, and planning calendars are all essential and basic tools of the trade. They should be kept close by and secured both on a flash drive and in a three-ring show binder.

The producer's binder is an easy, must-have resource to help store, find, and organize the show information. Understanding what category of show you are to arrange and who the target market is through an exploratory process of handing out surveys and questionnaires is paramount information and will help determine how extensive the budgets and planning calendars will be. Ultimately, no garments can be styled, no models hired, and no music determined until the budget, the planning calendar, timeline, and target market have been fleshed out.

Case Problem

You have been hired to produce a luncheon fashion show for the Symphony Association. They have given you a production budget of 5,000 dollars. The show will be thirty-five minutes long, highlighting three local boutiques with a total of sixty-five looks to be presented on the runway. All clothing will be donated for use in the show by the boutiques. With a show consisting of sixty-five looks, you will need at least fifteen models, which will cost an average of $150 per professional model. Keep in mind, this is a charity event; many agents or models will discount their price. In addition, you may consider using students or volunteer models to reduce cost. You are only responsible for the back of the house or backroom responsibilities, such as hiring models, dressers, and backroom staff. Budget everything that has to do with the runway show itself. One week before the show date the major sponsor dropped out and your budget has since been cut 1,800 dollars. Using the Event Budget Example Form, create two budgets:

1. The first with the 5,000 dollar budget.
2. The second with the modified budget.
3. Highlight where you have cut, discounted, or substituted "in-kind donations" to meet the new reduced budget limitations. Tip: Review Chapter 6 and 7 for all items to be addressed in the back of the house.

Questions to Consider

1. What kind of items could be donated?
2. Where in the budget did you have to cut to meet the new budget?
3. What solutions are there other than producing a smaller show to cut the budget if a sponsor is lost?
4. How could this situation have been prevented?

Questions for Review and Discussion

1. What is the difference between a timeline and a planning calendar?
2. Why do fashion show producers use timelines?
3. What is the difference between a fixed and a variable cost?
4. What is the first planning tool that should be created?
5. Why and when is a questionnaire or survey utilized?
6. What are the basic differences among the charity, student, retail, and professional runway shows?
7. What determines the breadth and depth of planning calendars, budgets, and timelines?
8. What is a target market?
9. What information is kept on the flash drive/USB?

Out and About Activities

Break the students into groups. Each group should create a questionnaire aimed at learning more about the target market. Have each group give the same questionnaire to students their age, friends, or parents the same age. Tip: Remember to address the geographics, demographic, psychographics, and behavior patterns of the target market.

Ongoing Fashion Show Project

Planning Your Show

Using templates and worksheets at the end of the text:

1. Begin creating folders for the production binder.
2. Create a planning calendar, timeline, and budget for the show.

Terminology of the Trade

behavioral patterns 69
budget 63
charity shows 67
comprehensive information 60
demographics 69
discretionary income 69
fixed costs 64
geographics 69
in-kind donation 64
key events 60
planning calendars 66
professional show 67
psychographics 69
questionnaire 70
revenue 64
student show 67
timeline 60
target audience 68
variable costs 64

Web Resources

Storyboard/Mood boards
www.stylesight.com
www.beeclip.com
www.polyvore.com/
www.moodboard.com/

Regional, National, and International Production Companies
www.groundcrew.net
www.shannondavidson.com/
www.theweddingguys.com
www.facebook.com/JanStrimpleProductions
www.paulataylorllc.com
www.KCDworldwide.com
www.IMGworld.com

Bibliography

Allen, J. (2000). *Event Planning* (N. pg.). Ontario: Wiley.

Craven, R. E., & Golabowski, L. J. (2006). *The Complete Idiot's Guide to Meeting & Event Planning* (2nd ed., pp. 85–91). New York: Penguin Group.

Rabolt, N. J., & Miler, J. K. (2009). *Retail and Merchandise Management* (2nd ed.) New York: Fairchild Books.

Stone, E. (2007). *In Fashion: Fun! Fame! Fortune!* (pp. 30–33). New York: Fairchild Publications.

Nikon
SPEEDLIGHT SB-80DX
Nikon

GETTING THE WORD OUT

LEARNING OBJECTIVES

After completing this chapter, you will be able to:

- Write a press release
- Describe the "new" public relations/marketing
- Use social media
- Create a press kit
- Create invites, e-vites, and save the dates
- Understand the views of industry insider Crosby Noricks
- Understand the terminology of the trade

Every successful company today has to be a media company first. It doesn't matter what you sell, you have a new way of telling your story with digital media and a new voice.

—MAZDACK RASSI, creative director and founder of Milk Studios

FIGURE 5.1 *Angel Sanchez talks to press prior to the show.*
Courtesy of Angel Sanchez

It wasn't so long ago that the only way to promote an event was with very basic traditional public relations ("PR"), marketing, and direct advertising. *Promotion included such activities as writing a* press release *advertising in a local newspaper or magazine, and sending "save the date" invites. The promoter would hold his or her breath and hope people would RSVP to the phone number on the invite. Currently, most local newspapers and other print media have taken a backseat to websites, blogs, and social networking sites, like Facebook and Twitter. Snail mail or the postal service is used as a last resort or as a tool only to reinforce the varied social media and other modern ways of advertising.*

In Chapter 2 we discussed the business of fashion and how technology has helped catapult the fashion industry and fashion shows into mainstream consciousness. These same technologies that facilitate showcasing and selling product can also be utilized to promote runway shows and fashion events. This chapter discusses both the traditional methods of PR and the new and forthcoming innovative strategies. We will look at the use of technology, social networking, modern media kits, and the latest breed of fashion press gatekeepers, the bloggers. Each of these public relations vehicles has shaped our modern PR environment. Interviews with such industry insiders as blogger Crosby Noricks, from the blog PR Couture, give the reader insight and advice on the new PR, and how to get the word out about an event.

In Chapter 4 there was extensive discussion on planning the actual event. No event, however, can maximize its potential for success without a comprehensive PR and marketing effort. Grab your fashion show binder already equipped with the timeline, the budget, and the planning calendar. Title the next section PR and marketing (Figure 5.1).

Public Relations and Marketing

The goal of public relations and marketing is beyond that of direct advertising. In advertising you pay to have your copy, brand, and message placed in a magazine, newspaper, website, radio, or television. The most effective PR is about getting the word out without having to pay for it. The goal is free coverage in a magazine or having an article placed in the paper covering the event. Although this is free publicity, it doesn't mean it is easily accomplished or fast to obtain. Free PR when mentioned in a blog or highlighted on a social networking site reaches a wider audience and has the potential to be picked up by national and international online media. In the fashion show production industry it's about creating a BUZZ, a must-see event, and branding that event in ways that ensure repeat audiences. The producer's job is to create an unforgettable experience that will capture bloggers' and press attention and will ensure that they write about it. The producer must get people to talk about the event such that those who didn't attend will be the first to buy tickets for the next year. Although most designers, companies, and charities hire a PR firm or have in-house staff working on PR, it is important for those of us on the production side to have a basic understanding of all the "new" and traditional ways to promote and market runway

FIGURE 5.2 *Photographers and press in the pit at a fashion show.*
Courtesy of John Calder

shows and fashion events. The actual flow, look, and timing of the event all fall under the producer's umbrella of responsibilities. The successful show is a calling card for the next event. Understanding the importance of PR, marketing, and advertising and how you get it, keep it, and utilize it for future projects is an indispensable knowledge set. Public relations is defined as, "Using the news or business press to carry positive stories about your company or your products; cultivating a good relationship with local press representatives" ("Public Relations Definition," n.d.). In short, it means making sure your brand, image, and event are strengthened and heard about by others (Figure 5.2).

The Publicist

In the past the main responsibility of the public relations professional or **publicist** was to highlight and make public a client, or a client's products presented through a variety of means such as a runway show. The most common way information was provided to the media was with press releases and media kits. Today's publicists and **PR firms** still write press releases, create media kits, and manage image issues, but simultaneously handle several other responsibilities for their clients. Depending on the size of the firm or if the publicist is a freelance consultant, there may be more than one PR professional tackling the needs of the clients. Examples of publicist responsibilities are listed below:

Public relations and marketing—Overseeing and creating all PR and marketing for clients including, but not limited to, social media, advertising, media kits, ads, and all written press.

Online publicity—Websites, blogs, and other online media are targeted to cover, review, and write about the client's events.

Community relations—Partnering with targeted, qualified community members, nonprofits, and organizations to create built-in qualified target markets, while branding the client's image and building community bonds.

Social media—Managing Facebook, Twitter, and other social media to drive business and promote branding.

Event planning—Planning, managing, hiring staff, and executing clients' events.

Website, graphics, advertising—Building, creating, and managing websites, blogs, all branded graphics, and ads for clients.

Celebrity endorsement—Connecting with qualified celebrities, socialites, and community members; obtaining endorsements, appearances, and master of ceremony opportunities.

Brand and image consulting—Helping clients create and maintain image and a constant public presence and awareness of the client's product.

Press kit creation—Creating and compiling all materials for online and hard copy press kits.

Copywriting—Writing the advertisement and publicity copy.

Editorial placement—Securing the placement of stories about the event or business in online newspapers, blogs, and websites.

Product placement—Embedding product or brand in nonstandard advertising situations in media such as television and films.

Image Control

The right PR team and/or freelance consultant are image control consultants or spin doctors, spinning all press into highlighting the company in the best "light." The team helps the client stand apart from others who are competing and appealing to the media and the public for their attention. Thus the team is able to shepherd a business, event, or person to the next level. The publicist's goal is to get the client's product, event, or business in front of all types of media and potential clients. The skill sets needed to succeed in PR as a professional are specific and critical to the nature of this fast-paced, often-stressful, career. The news is flooded with PR firms and client breakups. It is a difficult and precarious business. Even the most seasoned of PR firms or professional can be at a loss when a brand, image, or person is permanently damaged by inappropriate behavior, numerous bad reviews, or unethical business practices. In 2011, designer John Galliano was removed as creative director from the House of Dior for making inappropriate and anti-Semitic remarks while drunk, which was caught on tape. Although he publicly apologized and went to a rehabilitation facility to address his problematic drinking, his image is permanently damaged. He has lost his job and now clearly his bad behavior and PR nightmare has eclipsed his undeniable talent (Socha, 2011). Most producers, designers, or charities have a PR coordinator, who is the person who communicates the company's needs to the publicist or a staff member, volunteer, or student in charge of the PR needs for the event. If you are considering going into the fashion PR business or taking it on as a designer, staff member, volunteer, student, or small business owner, the skills below are crucial for your success.

Communication skills—Both written and verbal skills are essential. It is the publicist or PR coordinator for the event who writes and creates the press release, media kits, and public statements. The ability to articulate thoughts and information about the event, product, or client in a clear, concise, and engaging manner is elementary.

Time management and multitasking—These are other significant skills that a PR person should have. Juggling several responsibilities at once is commonplace for those in the image-making business. Having strong organizational and time management skills will help to keep the PR team focused and clear when they are in the midst of solving critical issues and creating a contingency plan, especially when something goes wrong.

Use of social networking and new technology—A clear understanding of how to use social networking sites, online media kits, and websites as vehicles to drive positive PR and branding is a key element to successful marketing.

Good sense of humor—Although this is central to any career, it is most essential for people working in a very stressful job such as PR. The fashion industry is chaotic, demanding, and constantly in flux. Being able to face each challenge with laughter will ease the tensions on the road to solving problems. Every fashion show coordinator and producer will need to have these skills or get someone on their team, committee, or business that has them.

The Press Release

The press release continues to be an integral part of getting the word out about events. It is, simply put, a concise article on a newsworthy event. The press release remains one of the mainstay elements to a media kit and one of the most highly used vehicles to obtain press. The press release is sent to predetermined, specific media and press, with the hope of publication. The press release is a powerful and cost-effective tool for branding, building creditability for your event, and generating sales. Best of all, it is free! Writing a clear, appealing press release is a skill few people have obtained. Many make a press release too short, leaving out important "newsworthy" information. Others put too much useless information, making it hard for the reader to find essential news within the release. The press release can stand alone or be part of the media kit. Most press releases are faxed or e-mailed to the targeted press. There are no guarantees for publication. However, there is an industry standard formula and format. Sticking to it will help improve your chances of getting media attention. Prior to writing a press release the producer, charity, designer, or retailer must clearly understand the objective of their event. Make sure you understand what it is you hope to accomplish, the reason for the press release. Once the objective is defined, the crafting of the press release can begin. The release should always address the 5 Ws and they should be addressed within the first two paragraphs of the release. The 5 Ws are *who, what, where, when,* and *why*.

Who is conducting the event?
What is the event?
Where is the location of the event?
When is the event?
Why are you having the event?

The 5 Ws must all be answered in the press release. How they are answered could have an impact in the press by either getting the public's attention or being ignored. Although publication is never guaranteed, there are some general guidelines and formatting rules for writing a successful press release that may give a leg up toward publication. Here are some general formatting rules:

Keep it short—No more than two pages, that is, 400–500 words. Too much text and too many words may distract the reader.

Write a positioning statement—A few sentences that summarize what makes this event different from the competition, other events, or a previous similar event. This is what makes your event special and unique.

Include the company or event name and logo—The reader needs to know the source of the information. It builds creditability and promotes the brand. This information should be obvious within the first few paragraphs. In addition, include the contact information of the qualified and appropriate person. This person must be the one who can speak expertly about the event and provide more information, such as a media kit and additional multimedia, if so requested.

Date and time the press can release the information or "For Immediate Release" on top of the page is also correct—Make sure that bloggers and editors know when the event will happen and at what date the information can be highlighted (released) within their publications. Knowing lead-time for publications is a key factor to getting your information printed.

The words "Press Release"—The news release is identified as such when the words "Press Release" are at the top of the page.

Include a bold headline and strong first paragraph—The first paragraph should clearly state your news. The rest of the release should give the details of the event in a concise, logical, and professionally written manner.

Proofread—Write the press release in a word document. Once you have written it, proofread. Make sure the date, time, and location of the event are correct. Proofreading should involve two people. One should be reading the text and the other following.

Include multimedia, anchor text, and features—Multimedia like photos, video files, audio files, and PDF documents have been proven to keep bloggers and online editors reading your release longer. The online media may use the images and links on the blog, making their job a little easier and creating great press for you. Include anchor text. An **anchor text** is the link title or clickable text in a hyperlink. This provides an easy ranking for search engines and a great way for media to access more information regarding the occasion.

Include Title Sponsorship Information—A title sponsor is the person or company that underwrites the largest portion of the cost of the event in return for getting their name or brand out in the public.

Brag! It is ok—Don't be shy about providing information about the company, designer, school, retailer, or charity. If it is a charity fashion show that continues to raise a large amount of money for a very needy cause, make sure you include this information.

Have some surprises—Do not give away all the secrets about the event in the press release. In addition, engage the reader into wanting to learn more by visiting the links you have provided.

End with three hash symbols (###) centered at the bottom of the release—This signifies the end of the press release.

Use active verbs—Use active or action verbs such as "parading," "exploding," and "bursting." This will set the tone of the release as one that is full of high energy.

TELL THE TRUTH

Make sure your information is newsworthy and that the writer deals with facts. Never make promises that the event may not live up to. Stay focused on the content. The media must be only given the information they need. It is crucial to share only the information that is essential.

Don't bury the lead—Always put the main point of the release first. Avoid overelaborate fancy language and jargon.

Provide contact information—Make certain the contact person is well versed on the event and prepared to speak to the press ("How to Write," n.d.).

What is the bottom line? It does not matter how much press you receive but whether it translates into real results. For fashion shows this means tickets sold, sponsorship dollars raised, and postevent coverage.

Below is an example of a charity fashion show's press release—As you read through the press release, make sure you observe whether it includes the 5 Ws and all the necessary information and formatting information provided in this chapter. Is anything missing that might make this press release stronger?

Press Release Example

For Immediate Release http://www.tucsonladiescouncil.org/the-fashion-show

August 25, 2010

For more information contact:

Ciara Meyer

Assistant Director

(520) 555-5558

HYPERLINK "Ciara@tunidito.org" Ciara@tunidito.org

Tucson, Arizona—August 25, 2010—The Tucson Ladies Council is proud to present the sixth annual FASHION SHOW benefiting Tu Nidito Children and Family Services Saturday, September 25, 2010 at the Westin La Paloma Resort. The theme of THE FASHION SHOW is London Calling.

Tickets are available for $150 and guarantee an evening full of exhilarating events beginning at 6:00 P.M. including a silent and live auction, a spectacular runway fashion show, and fabulous cuisine. THE FASHION SHOW is a high-profile community event, highlighting top fashions from Tucson's trendiest boutiques and showcasing today's hottest designers.

Another highlight of THE FASHION SHOW is the children's runway walk, which features Tu Nidito children who are battling a serious illness or experiencing grief from the loss of a loved one wearing fun costumes of their choice. The children's runway walk gives Tu Nidito kids the opportunity to have some fun amidst the challenges they face every day.

For tickets please log onto Tu Nidito's website www.tunidito.org/tlcfashionshow or call (520) 322-9155.

The sole mission of Tu Nidito Children and Family Services is to provide individual, family, and group support through emotional, educational and social services to children and their families as they deal with serious illness and death.

Each year Tu Nidito supports more than 800 Tucson children impacted by serious illness and death.

(Press release courtesy of Tu Nidito Children and Family Services, Tucson, Arizona)

Distributing to the Press

Once the release is written, it is time to distribute it to the qualified press. Creating a **contact/media list** of local and national press is important and should be an active ongoing process. File online as well as in the PR section of your production folder. Keeping an updated list will save you and your staff hours of time. Remember! Papers fold. Editors change. Assistants get promoted. New divisions are constantly being added such as online editions and blogs. Sending the release to the correct editors, bloggers, and other media is requisite. Once the press release has been sent, it is your responsibility to distribute and follow up with the correct person. The majorities of press releases are sent via e-mail or fax. Larger companies, advertising firms, or publicists often hire a wire service to distribute and follow up on the press release. Many small businesses distribute their own press release using their proprietary press contact list. Having a contact that knows you personally at the publication is a powerful way to ensure your release is read. The best way to make contact with editors, bloggers, and other media is by having a strong presence in the community and to be seen as the expert in your business.

How to Get Press

Developing story lines for the press is a superb way to assert oneself as the expert. Suggest story lines when following up or imply such in the lead of your press release. Volunteer! Become a board member or take part in events and fundraising for a charity in which you believe. Sometimes, the best way to advertise and brand yourself and your event is by giving back, and building a network of support in your city. Contact industry trade publications or blogs and volunteer to write articles or columns. Speak at schools and other organizations on the subject. Consider hosting workshops and seminars, thus demonstrating your specific skills. Some producers work with aspiring models, teaching them how to walk. Paula Taylor LLC holds dressing workshops for young college merchandising and retail students desiring to work backstage in a professional fashion show. If you undertake just a few of these suggestions, when it is time for you to contact the press, your name will be recognizable as the expert in the field and you will receive a willing reception from the press. Still, some people seem to get all the press while others, no matter what they do, never get noticed. The key to getting and keeping publicity is to create a plan that includes all aspects of the media. The new public relations encompass several different mediums and sharing discernibly branded information among them.

The New "PR"

Building PR, contacts, and advertising networks has become much easier with the ever-growing and shifting face of technology. It has opened a great number of marketing and advertising opportunities. **Social media** or **the social web** is one of the simplest free and measurable PR tools for modern public relations. Today's PR and marketing encompass layering and connecting newsworthy content while simultaneously sharing the story or information. The Web provides a platform for sharing information. It is an excellent place to give the viewer an opportunity to actively learn more about the event by video streaming, viewing photographs, and visiting links to important sites. This affords anyone an opportunity to read articles about previous events, charities, and the audience who attended them. Keep in mind that people participate in fashion events for a multitude of reasons.

In Chapter 4 you learned how to identify your target market. Once the **target market** is unmistakably defined, all marketing should be geared toward capturing this intended group of people. Many business professionals and fashion designers are using social media as a way to market their product or event but still are failing to approach it with a strategic plan. According to Paul Chaney in his article "4 steps to effective marketing strategy," content is king and the greatest vehicle to create content is a blog. Mr. Chaney considers the blog to be the center of operations from which other digital vehicles distribute the information. Effectively, all social media that are used should be linked back to your blog (Chaney, 2010). Blogs are online journals that are inherently interactive and universal. Anyone who uses the Web can access your blog as compared with social media, which can only access your information once you join. Highlighting a blog on the main website or in a subfolder will help attract search engine attention. The key to a successful blog is frequent updates of information while making certain all information on the blog defines and reinforces the primary function of the blog. Many successful fashion designers are now also creating blog content and determining where it should be positioned, either on its own or part of the proprietary website. It is necessary to determine on which social media to post the content. Examples of some social media are Facebook, Twitter, YouTube, LinkedIn, and Tumblr. Transmitting the information from one source to another can be time-consuming. Most people use the **RSS feed** button on their blog so consistent readers can be delivered information without having to visit the site. A RSS feed, sometimes referred to as really simple syndication, is a format for delivering regular changing Web content. A RSS feed lets the reader acquire content from a blog or other websites daily. **Dlvr.it** is a resource for bloggers, which does away with having to manually post updates to separate social media sites. All the laying of content and sharing of information is of no use if the readers do not feel a connection to your blog. Personalizing some information is an easy and effective way to build loyalty and create personal connection. Consider responding promptly to Facebook posts, comments, or messages from fans; re-Tweeting when appropriate is also beneficial. Younger bloggers do more than list information, and that is why they have such a following. Educate the viewer in clever ways through fashion trends surveys, style trivia, games, and helpful tips that capture the attention of the reader. Consider that social media is just another tool used to foster brand awareness and loyalty while sharing information. Writing a well-edited, unique, and informative blog solidifies you, your event, or your company as the experts.

Bloggers

In the last decade, these new and younger breed of fashion gatekeepers have emerged as power players in the fashion industry. Bloggers, like fourteen-year-old Tavi Gevinson from her blog, Style Rookie, are not only getting front-row invitations to coveted fashion shows but are also carving out lucrative business deals with the traditional media. Tavi, for example, just negotiated a partnership with industry expert, founder, and creator of *Jane* magazine, Jane Pratt. As a result, the young Internet star, who reportedly attracted

FIGURE 5.3 *Blogger Tavi Gevinson,* left.
Courtesy of John Calder

as many as 50,000 visitors to her blog in one month, will be part of a website and magazine geared toward teenagers which Jane is launching (Turner, 2011). With all this attention on her, it is fitting that Tavi recently changed the name of her blog from Style Rookie to Style Pro. Blogging by definition is a proprietary website that contains an online personal journal, which includes reflections, comments, and often hyperlinks provided by the writer. Fashion bloggers have asserted themselves as the experts, and new trend forecasters. The public and some of the trade have welcomed them with open arms. Blogging, however subjective, has eclipsed the traditional print media and journalists because of, it is argued, the speed and multimedia way by which news is disseminated compared to magazines and newspapers. Blogs provide immediate responses to runway shows and fashion events, including simultaneous video feeds, photo posting, and content sharing via Twitter and other social media outlets (Figure 5.3).

The inherent inclusivity of blogs welcomes all types of readership and opens a target market for many brands in a nonthreatening approach. It is part of the new fashion environment available to all. Blogging does have a downside. Many of the bloggers have no real fashion experience or expertise on the subject, and often do not play by the same rules and industry standards as traditionally educated and experienced fashion writers, editors, and journalists. In response to the great success and readership that blogs and bloggers have obtained, many traditional fashion media outlets, such as *Women's Wear Daily*, *In Style*, *Vogue,* and the *New York Times*, and professional fashion journalist and editors have created their own blogs. They have done so in order to compete in their industry's marketplace and reassert themselves as the gatekeepers of information.

Media Kits/Press Kits

All production companies, big or small, should create a press kit or media kit. The media kit is an informative, self-contained packet holding everything needed to enable the press to write a story about you and/or the event, and as a result learn more about the company or the event. Modern press kits are created online, facilitating the reader to actively find information about the event and driving business to your company. Media kits can also be well-branded packaged information in a pocket folder. Whether the kit is online or at arm's reach, it is imperative to include the following items:

Letter of introduction—A short detailed letter introducing you and outlining what is included in the press kit.

Short biographies of company officers, or production team—A brief biography giving important background, education, and past experience about the company's officers, designers, or production team.

All current press coverage—Include all current press releases, and any positive press coverage through links if the kit is online. Provide professionally photocopied version for the traditional kit.

Company website info, FB page or blog, and tweeting—Include links to all the social media and Web presence the company currently has. Include a printed version of the blog or excerpts from the site for the hard copy.

Multimedia of company's work—Include colored photographs, video clips, YouTube links, and anything that educates the viewer about the company, organization, or school. Include current and past samples of save the dates and invitations.

Info letter—An additional letter that includes more detailed information about the event or company may be included on the website or blog.

Business card/logo—Your business logo and card should be included, keeping your branding consistent and upfront. If you are using both an online and a hard copy version, make sure you invest in a good quality folder and high-end paper products. Be creative and brand the media kit (Lautenslager, 2011).

Invitations, e-vites, and save the dates—In the world of high fashion, if you are one of the lucky few to get an invite to a fashion show during fashion week, the invitation is always simple, clear, and informative (Figures 5.4 and 5.5). In addition,

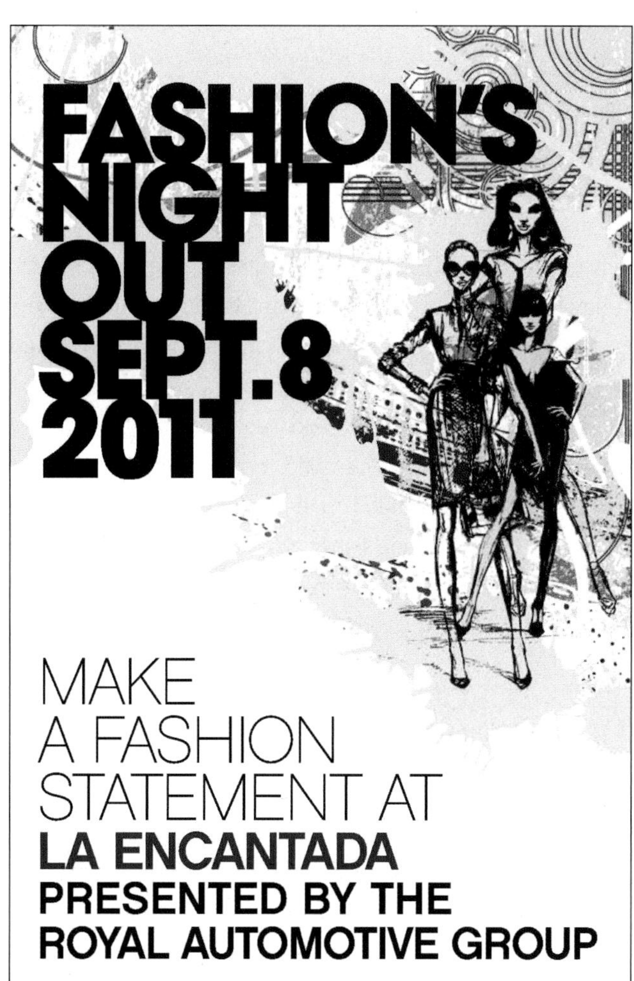

MAKE A
FASHION
STATEMENT AT
LA ENCANTADA

September 8, from 6 - 9pm,

Come be a part of Fashions Night Out Global Extravaganza

- Exciting in-store events; Participating stores: Ann Taylor, BCBG, Bluemercury, Coldwater Creek, Everything But Water, Fringe Hair Studio, Ilori, J. Crew, J.Jill, Lucky Brand Jeans, Pandora, St. John, White House Black Market, Solstice, United Colors of Benetton
- Special VIP Appearance by Designer Morton Myles
- Exclusive discounts and promotional items
- Select Restaurants including North & Ra Sushi, are participating as well with special offerings and menu items for that evening only!
- Shop Local Courtyard, featuring Pour Moi, W Boutique, My Closet, Siobhan, Tres, Avenue & Zoe Boutique
- Musical entertainment by The Occupants, Over The Wall and DJ PCparty

For a full line up of events, in-store promotions and everything you need to know about Fashion's Night Out – visit LaEncantadaShoppingCenter.com

Produced by:
La Encantada & Paula Taylor Productions

LA ENCANTADA

2905 E. Skyline Drive Suite 279 Tucson, AZ 85718
(520) 615-2561 | LaEncantadaShoppingCenter.com

FIGURE 5.4 *The front and back of a fashion's night out invitation.*
Courtesy of Melanie Sutton

FIGURE 5.5 *An e-vite example.*

Courtesy of Visual Communication

most designers send out an e-vite version as well. The save the date card is generally used for fashion shows and events. It is similar to the invitation, but with less information. It is a teaser to introduce the event, while encouraging potential attendees to clear their calendars and save the date. An invitation should include the following information:

Name of the event
Name of the business
Name of the show or event
Name of the designer
Day, date, and time
Location
Cost and ticket information
Sponsors
RSVP
Website URL

Additional information that can be included on the invitation is the following:

Celebrity appearances
Raffle items
Fashion show highlights

Many small designers, charities, and businesses have done away with printing and mailing invitations, as the process can be costly. They simply send e-vite invitations. However, we have stated earlier in this chapter the importance of layering content to help brand an image or event. Mailing invitations on high-quality card stock and following them up with an e-vite version that has been posted on the website or blog, and highlighted on social media sites is an excellent example of how one shares content and keeps the event fresh on the public's mind. Using all the venues gets the word out about the event in multiple ways. Understanding the target market and planning a budget that can bear the cost will also guide in decision making concerning whether to include both hard copy and online invitations. If the target market is older, a mailed invitation should be included to at least a limited qualified mailing list. This expense must be included in the budget.

HOW DOES ONE GENERATE AN AUDIENCE FOR AN EVENT?

Designers, during fashion weeks around the globe, send a majority of the invitations to the press, editors, bloggers, and fashion journalists in the hope of getting press for the show. In addition, potential buyers from retail stores and department stores are invited to encourage them and inspire them to write orders at the showroom thereafter. Finally, fashion innovators and leaders are included in this list. Many times the fashion innovators are celebrities, musicians, athletes, and socialites. They wear the clothing that helps to brand the collection while also catching the eye of the fashion gatekeepers, thus adding another potential reason for media coverage. For local designers, retailers, charities, and schools, creating a **targeted list** of potential attendees is a crucial endeavor necessary to ensure the success of the event. All the great clothing, fabulous food, and outlandish décor will mean nothing if no one attends the event. As mentioned in previous chapters, mailing lists, membership lists, and customer lists are all ways to attract qualified audience members. In addition, having a strong social media network is another easy way to acquire qualified potential attendees. Advertising in local magazines distributed to your potential market and purchasing mailing lists of addresses in affluent or qualified neighborhoods are yet other avenues to reach a specific target market. Let's ask our industry insider how to approach PR and use social media and bloggers in this contemporary world (Figure 5.6).

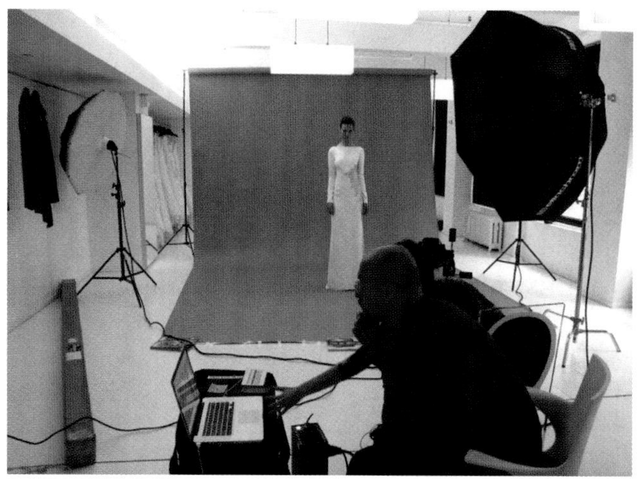

FIGURE 5.6 *Angel Sanchez and photographer preparing for a photo shoot.*
Courtesy of Angel Sanchez

Industry Insider

Crosby Noricks

FIGURE 5.7 *Industry insider Crosby Noricks, founder of PR Couture.*
Courtesy of Crosby Noricks

Industry insider Crosby Noricks (Figure 5.7), the creator of the blog PR Couture, shares her unique approach to fashion PR, describes the importance of public relations in the fashion industry, and gives us her opinions on social media and the role of bloggers in the fashion press.

WHY DID YOU START PR COUTURE?

I became interested in fashion public relations while pursuing a graduate degree in communication because it appeared to be a profession that combined many of the things I loved, fashion, of course, but also a chance to be both strategic and creative, with a large amount of writing and storytelling. However, the academic journals I read and the textbooks assigned either ignored fashion PR altogether or lumped it and dismissed it as a category of entertainment PR. PR Couture began as an attempt to bring visibility to the profession, while also providing a space for those either curious about it (like me) or working in it, to read content relevant to the industry.

WHY IS PR/MARKETING SUCH A CRUCIAL TOOL FOR FASHION PROFESSIONALS?

Well, simply put, you can create the most gorgeous garments on the planet, but if no one knows that they exist, you won't get very far! Also, PR and marketing help designers to think critically about their brand and target customers. This process is integral to creating a fashion business, and sustainable growth and success.

HOW HAS NEW TECHNOLOGY PLAYED A CHANGING ROLE IN PR AND MARKETING FOR FASHION SHOWS AND THE BUSINESS OF FASHION?

Primarily, it has to do with access and immediacy. Shows like *Project Runway* and *Kell on Earth* brought the fashion industry to the masses, while social media tools, reality television, live streaming, self-publishing tools, and mobile phone applications have changed the ways and the rate at which the consumer experiences fashion shows. Fashion bloggers sit front row at fashion shows, shows are streamed live online, and photos are made available immediately through our mobile phones, with professional shots circulated online soon afterward. Oscar de la Renta and DKNY both leverage women on their PR teams to provide behind-the-scenes quips and photos and engage in conversation on Twitter, and have amassed quite formidable followings as a result!

(*Continued*)

Industry Insider (Continued)

Crosby Noricks

WHAT ARE SOME NEW SUCCESSFUL PR/MARKETING TECHNIQUES TO HELP PROMOTE FASHION SHOWS?

When working with independent or lesser-known designers, it's important to start outreach early and to augment that outreach beyond just the invitation. Provide look books or previews of the looks and designer Q&As, and be sure to identify which aspects of the show (clothes, hair, production, etc.) might be of interest to the person you are inviting.

I think it's also important not to forget the experience your guests have once they show up, and once they have left. For media guests specifically, there is nothing more frustrating than not being on the right list, not being escorted to one's seat, and so on. Have a point person assigned to media and make sure interview opportunities are facilitated, backstage access is granted, and photos are welcomed and wine is never far away!

For follow up, a gracious thank you, professional images of the show attached for use, and a quick line about welcoming feedback are also great.

HOW HAS SOCIAL NETWORKING CHANGED THE FACE OF PR?

Fashion public relations have primarily dealt with fashion media, but social media has, in many cases, removed the "media as gatekeeper," and now, anyone and everyone has one's own sphere of influence. In a certain way, it's great to be able to engage directly with the customer, but it also means that everyone has a megaphone to broadcast messages about your client, positive or negative. Smart publicists (and business owners) look at negative coverage or a poor customer service experience as opportunities, but sometimes a tweet communicated in jest, a misguided attempt at humor, or a poorly executed campaign requires a bit of old-fashioned crisis communication.

WHAT ARE SOME GENERAL MISTAKES PEOPLE MAKE PROMOTING FASHION EVENTS?

Digital media has made it easy to attach an event flyer in an e-mail and call it a day, but this is a bad idea for several reasons. Media receive hundreds of event invitations each week, and should never have to click on your hi-resolution JPEG and wait even thirty seconds for it to load. Plus, many of us are working off of our mobile phones, and need to copy and paste an address or event information directly from our phones.

Other mistakes include sending an e-vite, sending out event reminders daily, not inviting anyone until three days before the show, forgetting to include the city the event is taking place (helpful if you are inviting a girl from San Diego to your event in Berlin!), not sending a confirmation e-mail acknowledging the RSVP, and of course, having a mess of a line when your attendees arrive.

WHAT ARE SOME TIPS FOR EASY, INEXPENSIVE, AND USEFUL WAYS TO PROMOTE FASHION EVENTS? IF YOU COULD, ADDRESS SOME GENERAL GUIDELINES/ TIPS FOR FINDING THE RIGHT PR FIRM OR PROFESSIONAL?

Here's a tip! Write a personalized message with all the pertinent information and provide a link to the flyer for more information. Create a link for an optional instant Google or Outlook Calendar invite that includes the cell phone number of their contact for the evening. Send a follow-up to only those who have confirmed forty-eight hours before the event and see if they need anything, with a reminder of who their point person is and a note that you are excited they are attending.

Prep your team, use photographs and bio information if you need to, so that anyone running your event knows your VIPs and your media.

When it comes to hiring support for your event, recognize that fashion show production and fashion PR are two very different things. Hire someone for your front of house who will handle invites; RSVP's; manages list; and, as the name implies, "stays front of house" to welcome guests and, of course, watch for show crashers and so on.

WHAT IS THE ROLE OF A BLOGGER AS THE "NEW" GATEKEEPER OF FASHION INFORMATION?

Fashion bloggers provide a unique perspective on fashion and are able to say and do what they want, without a large parent media company dictating content length or point of view. As such, fashion bloggers provide a welcome alternative to print media and an element of real girl, real-world fashion information. This is changing, however, as major print media publications are creating their own fashion blogger networks and top-tier bloggers are working directly with major media and brands to produce and curate content.

ARE THEY (BLOGGERS) HELD TO THE SAME STANDARD AS OUR TRADITIONAL GATEKEEPERS, EDITORS, JOURNALISTS, AND FASHION EXPERTS?

I don't think it is appropriate to say that a fashion blogger must consider herself a journalist, nor is it appropriate to say that because she is a fashion blogger she must not have any journalistic integrity. Each blogger has his or her own goals, point of view, and experience. Some are, in fact, former fashion editors; some are current models; and some have no experience in fashion whatsoever. If a fashion blogger wants to make a career out of her blog, her personal brand, or her particular passion or area of expertise, then yes, she should conduct herself with integrity and be held to the same code of all industry professionals.

One part of the problem is that many fashion bloggers without industry experience don't understand the rules of the game, and therefore don't actually know what they should or should not do, or how to negotiate with major industry powerhouses. We also need to be careful not to lump all fashion bloggers together. Instead, we (the industry) should work to preserve and allow for each blogger's right to pursue his or her own endeavors, and be mindful of the value of multiple perspectives as opposed to turning fashion blogging into a homogeneous sector of fashion media.

Excerpts from an personal Interview with Crosby Noricks, June 12, 2010.

Chapter Review

The success of a runway show or fashion event depends in part on getting the word out to the proper media outlets. Publicists and PR firms are hired to address all press-related matters. Traditional PR has been focused on press releases, advertising, and branding. The modern-day PR firm and publicist, however, tackle many job responsibilities for their clients, including, but not limited to, branding, marketing, copy writing, advertising, event planning, and managing social media and websites. A press release follows specific formatting rules and includes hyperlinks, multimedia, and anchor text. The new PR includes all traditional press while incorporating social media, like Facebook, MySpace, Twitter, and blogs. Both sides are today's essential PR tools. With this change, the role of being gatekeepers of the fashion press has extended from a qualified few to also include anyone with an opinion and strong following online. In response to the bloggers' dominance of the industry, traditional fashion press like *Women's Wear Daily* and *Vogue* have included blogs and online presence to secure their standing as the experts in the field. The modern approach to PR trends is moving toward layering and sharing information from traditional advertisements to blogs and social media. The more information is shared among all the potential outlets, the greater the ability to track and predict success. In the fashion events arena, success translates to audience attendance, money raised, branding, press coverage, and sales of product. The media kit is an essential PR tool. It is a folder that holds the salient information about the company or event readily available for online media publication and in printed form. Media kits house examples of previous press, biographies, press releases, blogs or newsletter samples, and multimedia such as photos or videos. It also includes previous work samples such as invitations, save the dates, and e-vites. All press information needs to be consistent and accurate, and needs to be proofread. The press information should include visuals, multimedia, and hyperlinks to ensure that the reader spends time learning more about the company or event. For the producers and coordinators of fashion shows and events, PR, marketing, and advertising are indispensable components of the industry.

Questions for Review and Discussion

1. Why are multimedia and anchor text such important parts of a press release?
2. What are the job responsibilities of the publicist and the PR firm? How have they changed with the onset of social media?
3. List the items that are included in a media kit.
4. How is having a media kit online as well as in a folder beneficial to PR?
5. Discuss the role that bloggers play in the fashion industry today. Why do some bloggers pose a challenge to traditional media?

In Class Activity

Create a "fashion event" ongoing blog and FB fan page. Make sure to include information on school shows, local and national fashion shows, and events.

Ongoing Fashion Show Project

Promoting Your Show

1. Create a press release. (Use the press release worksheet at the end of this text.)
2. Create a media kit.
3. Design invitations, save the date, and e-vite.
4. Create a Facebook fan page or blog, or use other social media outlets to begin promoting your event.

Terminology of the Trade

advertising 78
anchor text 80
blog 85
contact list 82
Dlvr.it 83
e-vite 85
gatekeepers 89
invitations 85
media kit 84
press release 79
PR firms 77
publicists 77
RSS feed 83
social media 82
the social web 82
targeted list 87
target market 83

Web Resources

Marketing and PR
www.Prweb.com
www.publicityhound.net
www.entrepreneur.com
www.prcouture.com

Social Media and Blogs
www.blogspot.com
www.tumblr.com
www.formspring.com
www.twitter.com
www.trendalertdaily.com
www.weblinknow.com

Bibliography

Chaney, P. (2010, September 14). Social Media: 4 Steps to an effective marketing strategy. *Practical Ecommerce*. Retrieved April 10, 2011, from http://www.practicalecommerce.com/articles/2244-Social-Media-4-Steps-to-an-Effective-Marketing-Strategy

How to Write a Successful News Release. (n.d.). Retrieved April 10, 2011 from http://service.prweb.com/learning/article/how-to-write-a-successful-news-release

Lautenslager, A. (2011, November 18). The ingredients of a press kit. *Entrepreneur*. Retrieved April 10, 2011, from http://www.entrepreneur.com/marketing/publicrelations/prbasics/article57260.html

Public Relations. (n.d.). Retrieved October 10, 2011 from http://www.entrepreneur.com/encyclopedia/term/82434.html

Socha, M. (2011, March 1) John Galliano: Downfall of a Couturier. *WWD*. Retrieved April 10, 2011, from *WWD Style issue* March 02, 2011, from http://www.wwd.com/fashion-news/dior-ousts-galliano-in-wake-of-anti-semitic-allegations-3528611

Turner, Z. (2011, March 23). Jane Pratt Plots Her Comeback. *WWD.* Retrieved April 10, 2011, from WWD Style issue March 23, 2011, from http://www.wwd.com/media-news/jane-s-big-comeback-helped-by-tavi-3562469

MODELS AND MERCHANDISE

LEARNING OBJECTIVES

After completing this chapter, you will be able to:

- Know the types of models
- Understand the functions of modeling agencies and casting agents
- Discuss the Power agencies
- Gain an understand of merchandise styling and pulling
- Review industry insiders' views
- Understand the terminology of the trade

Yes, there is technique with modeling, but it's more about being comfortable and confident. The more you look like you don't care, the better.

—SHANE GAMBILL, male model with ADAM agency, NY

The show and event have been promoted. The budget is set. Timeline and planning calendar are a go. It is now time to cast models, *find and select the merchandise, and style the looks. Chapter 5, "Getting the Word Out," reviewed the planning stages of promotion. It detailed the tools that producers, designers, retailers, and students need to acquire to promote their fashion shows and events. It is in that arena that the branding of the collection and event begins. This chapter takes the concepts, vision, and themes fleshed out in earlier chapters and translates them into reality. The reader is given a clear understanding of the various kinds of models and physical requirements for each type of model such as runway,* commercial, *fashion, and showroom. The chapter explains the roles of modeling agents and casting agents. It outlines and makes clear the process of inventory and merchandise selection, styling, and creating final looks for the event or fashion show.*

The **merchandise pull** *or selection and the modeling needs to hold professional large-scale fashion events and shows are very different when compared with that required for regional, emerging designer, retailer, and student shows. The smaller community, student, and retail shows may engage local production companies and professional models from agencies in their area. Productions with tighter budgets often use the free and volunteer services of members of the community, modeling schools, or students to showcase and/or model garments. Unlike fashion week shows where each designer provides the merchandise for the show, specialty boutiques and larger retailers in the community more often than not provide the merchandise for local shows. The differences are many; for example, locations can vary from big hotels to small restaurants. Even local museums, parks, and schools are often used. Models used can also vary from volunteer to professional. The garments worn may be from different resources as well. As previously mentioned, they most likely do not come from designers or large retailers but rather from local specialty boutiques. The show may or may not be professionally produced. Budgets most likely will be small. Bloggers and press will be local, not national or international. The audience may be attending a fashion show for the first time. Regardless of all the above-mentioned differences, the steps taken to secure or to produce the show; cast the models; and select, pull, and style the merchandise are all very similar. Remember, despite the differences, the coordinator of either type of show should think outside the box, work within the client's needs, challenge his or her idea of beauty, and push the audience beyond its comfort zone.*

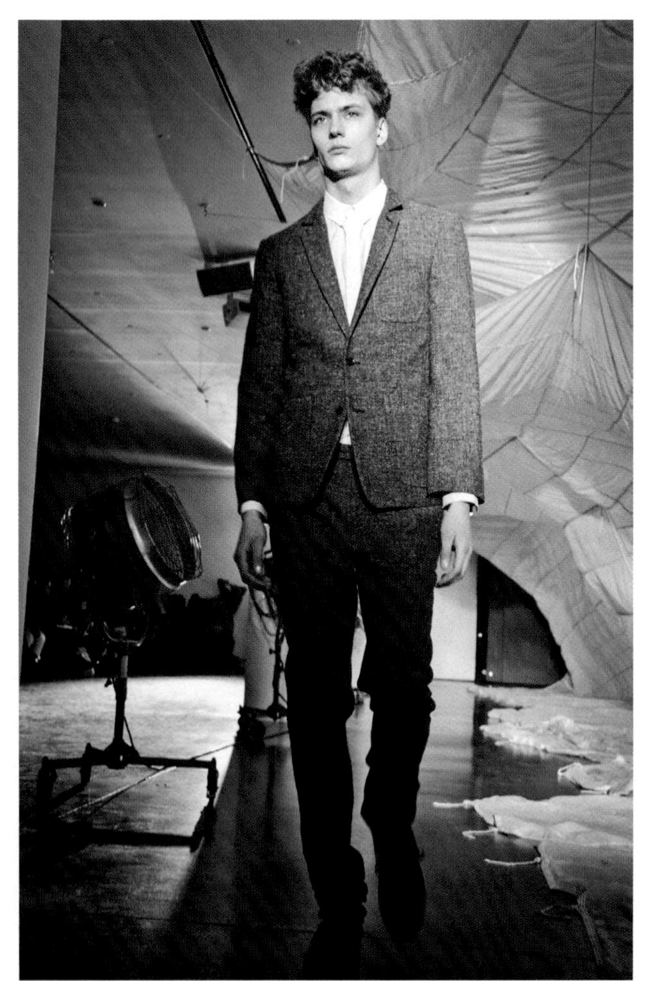

FIGURE 6.1 *Male model on the runway.*
From Carly Otness/BFAnyc.com

Models

The model coordinator or producer must have completed the budget and ascertained the goals of the show before models can be secured (Figure 6.1). He or she must have an understanding of the basic needs of the event and the target audience. Referencing the storyboards/vision boards will help in the model selection process. Larger production companies work closely with casting agents to find just the right high-profile model. Fashion week shows traditionally last no longer than fifteen minutes, with one or two models walking the runway at the same time. This timing is strategic and meant to provide audiences made up of buyers, editors, and bloggers the chance to focus on the details of the garments. Casting the correct and appropriate model is an indispensable necessity. Models are more than a hanger for the clothing. They are a tool that helps to communicate the image and brand of the particular designer and/or retailer. The models must possess the right body type, confidence, and look to showcase the highlighted garments. While they are walking, posing, and even acting, models are connecting with the audience. This ultimately aids in selling the lifestyle and image desired by the customer. Models for fashion weeks throughout the globe are idealized versions of the designer's clients or artist creations styled with theatrics and branding in mind. There are many designers who are and have been using lesser-known models and changing the pacing and patterns of shows. Meadham Kirchhoff's autumn/winter London Fashion Week 2011 show featured unfamiliar faces as models. The designers changed the pacing of the show so dramatically that it caused a shock wave throughout the fashion press community. The models were sent out on the runway in a tight parade one after another. This challenged the viewer's ability to see, analyze, and photograph easily (Singer, 2011). These forward-thinking designers and others are always changing the roles of models and the rules of the runway. They force fashion media to break out of its traditional ideas concerning runway shows and model choices. Model and merchandise preferences vary depending on the audience and goal of the event. Understanding the variety and differences among model types will help with the selection process for diverse events. There are several differing types of modeling categories. Each modeling category has a specific and unique set of requirements. The general modeling categories are as follows:

- Fashion models/editorial/runway
- Advertising
- Commercial/print
- Fitness
- Plus size
- Fit model
- Showroom
- Celebrity
- Child
- Teen
- Other
- Volunteer/amateur

Fashion Models

It wasn't until the twentieth century, with the advancement of photography, women's shifting roles in society, and the change of clothing needs of women, that fashion models appeared in magazines (Quick, 1997). It was in the 1980s that the concept of supermodel was created. This era created celebrities out of many models. The most notable were five iconic women: Cindy Crawford, Linda Evangelista, Naomi Campbell, Christy Turlington, and Tajana Patitz. They appeared on the cover of *Vogue* in 1990. The supermodels, or "supes" as they were known in the industry, changed the modeling world forever. They made a career out of fashion modeling, and became more than just pretty faces, with perfect bodies. The supermodels established modeling as a real business. They were able to gain financial security for themselves while catapulting the images and brands. Throughout the decades, the ideal model body and look has shifted from "heroin chic" in the early 1990s with models like Kate Moss to curvy in the late 1990s with bombshells like Gisele Bundchen from Brazil. Gisele, like Kate Moss before her, took the modeling world by storm. Her arrival according to "Vogue Magazine" (1999) declared the return of the sexy curvy model and the official end of the heroin chic model.

Editorial Fashion Models

Whatever the current trend for models may be, today's **editorial fashion models** are hired through modeling and casting agencies. They are found in the pages of magazines such as *Vogue*, *Elle*, *Glamour*, and *W* and the online versions of the magazines. High fashion models

FIGURE 6.2 *Supermodel Jessica Stam.*
Courtesy of John Calder

are the women and men seen when opening a fashion magazine; they can also be hired for big branded fashion campaigns and advertisements. Editorial work does not pay the same high dollars as commercial high fashion campaigns pay. However, it does provide exposure for up-and-coming models and keeps familiar faces in the public eye. This type of modeling by necessity is a partnership among photographer, stylist, hair, and makeup. Editorial modeling involves selling a story. A shoot can take all day, giving the editors plenty of solid material from which to choose to create a fluid story for the viewer. Editorial work is essentially for the model's self-promotion.

Runway Model

Professional runway models are hired through modeling and casting agents (Figure 6.2). They work fashion weeks around the globe as well as regional shows. They can be seen in both advertisement and editorial work. High fashion runway models must meet specific requirements. Easily recognizable, they are the tall, thin "glamazons" who glide down the catwalk during fashion weeks in Paris, New York, London, and Milan. They are young, between the ages of 15–26. Usually they are signed with major agencies like IMG or Ford. The lucky ones can become famous household names in the footsteps of Gisele, Tyra, Tyson, and Chanel Iman. Runway work requires a great deal of travel. It is heavily focused during fashion weeks. Depending on the popularity of the model, pay can be hundreds of dollars or even into the thousands. Rehearsal and fittings are considered additional casting and require payment (Figure 6.3).

FIGURE 6.3 *Finale example.*
Courtesy of John Calder

Guidelines for Professional Fashion Models

The height and weight requirements are strict and very narrow. The general height requirement for runway work is 5′9″–6′0″ for women and 5′9″–6′2″ for men. For fashions spreads and ad campaigns the minimum height requirement for women is 5′8″. The pendulum is always swinging back and forth when it comes to the requirements. The current weight trend for runway models leans toward the low end. Female weight requirements are 90–120 lb. The weight of runway models is constantly being addressed in the industry and among consumers. In 2007 the Council of Fashion Designers of America (CFDA) created a health initiative to bring to light and raise awareness of the eating disorder problem in the fashion industry (Von Furstenberg & Herzog, n.d.).

Guidelines were also put in place to help change the extreme trend of casting only super thin New York runway models. A few designers, such as Lakes and Stars, have used more realistic-looking models and included plus-size models on their runways. The majority of the industry still demands fashion editorial and runway models to be unrealistically thin. Most high-fashion runway and print models are dangerously thin. Many of these runway models are actually "photoshopped" for print media because they are not representative of the magazine's reader. Robin Derrick, creative director of British *Vogue*, stated in *The London Times,* "I spent the first ten years of my career making girls look thinner and the last ten making them look larger." This clearly shows the change from a decade ago when models were artificially made to look thinner (Pavia and Rochell, 2009).

A high-fashion modeling career is short-lived. The normal period is only five to ten years, with the exception of big names or supermodels that leverage their celebrity status into a variety of postmodeling careers. Tyra Banks now hosts her own reality TV show and daytime talk show. Molly Sims has made a career as an actor, while Heidi Klum is the host and executive producer of *Project Runway*. For the majority, however, a runway and editorial career is relatively brief, fast paced, lonely, and stressful. Many models turn to alcohol and drugs to deal with the everyday pressures of the modeling business. Emerging American models that are serious about the business must relocate to a major fashion capital city such as New York. New models are often sent overseas by their agency to get practice in front of a camera and on the runway. The pay varies and is dependent on experience, demand, and talent.

Once a model has gained popularity on the runway and in the pages of magazines, websites, and blogs, the real money is earned. It is earned by being hired for advertising campaigns and becoming the face of a brand.

Advertising Model

These types of models are most often high-fashion editorial or runway models. They are hired to promote clothing brands, fragrances, and other merchandise through print, online, point-of-purchase displays, and other media like billboards. The current trend is collaboration. Models are not just brand ambassadors; they are collaborators with companies. Supermodel Gisele Bundchen has collaborated with the shoe and accessories brand Nine West, creating an exclusive vintage jewelry collection for the company. In 2011 Gisele also secured a traditional advertising champagne contract with Rampage worldwide. Traditional advertising models are hired as the face of a fragrances or clothing line. Georgia May Jagger, the daughter of Mick Jagger, was the face of Chanel's 2011 resort line. Model Karen Elson replaced "uber" celebrity Angelina Jolie as the face of St. John for the 2010 collection. Actress Kate Winslett has since replaced her. An advertising campaign contract can last one year or more. The company determines the length of the contract under agreement with the model. Exclusive contracts with high-profile models can bring in millions of dollars for one campaign.

Commercial

Some commercial models are high-fashion models. However, commercial models can also vary in age, size, and height. Commercial modeling involves selling a product. The model must fit the client's needs. These models may be representing a retail establishment, a product, an online catalogue, and/or may be featured in a television commercial, all with the direct purpose of selling. Depending on the needs of the client and their target demographic, the commercial model represents the brand. They are not required to be as thin as editorial or runway models. Many high-fashion and editorial models can transition into commercial work. Commercial models who have a strong, attractive image and appropriate appearance can have a lengthy career. It is essential that the model fit the company's image. For companies such as Brooks Brothers, J. Crew, and Ann Taylor, for example, the target audience is an "All American" relatable appearance, not a surreal runway body. In short, the All American "boy" or "girl" next-door image is what these companies require. Commercial models chosen must fit the brand's image. Measurements for commercial work demands are less strict. Height is still 5′8″ but the age and weight can vary depending on the target audience and the client's needs.

Fitness Model

Fitness models represent the fitness industry and market. They are athletic and muscular, the opposite of editorial models. They work for the fitness industry, promoting fitness and related products. Additionally, they may have print and trade show work.

Plus-Size Models

Plus-size models are gaining popularity in the fashion world. More designers are highlighting them on the runway. Fashion weeks around the globe are testing the waters with their own plus-size shows. For example, London Fashion Week 2010 held its own plus-size show with the online retailer oneplus.com. Plus-size Celebrities like Gabourey Sidibe from the movie *Precious* and TV actor Nikki Blonsky came out to support it. Magazines and designers who traditionally have ignored this market are now addressing its ever-growing needs. American designer Teri Jon is now manufacturing up to size 18 in her collection. Franca Sozzani, the editor of *Italian Vogue,* has recently launched Curvy, a separate section on her site Vogueitalia.com dedicated to the plus-size customer.

PLUS-SIZE MODEL REQUIREMENTS

Plus-size models are required to meet the same height requirements as runway and print models. They must have model features and a proportionate body. They are generally a size 10–18 and are starting to be recognized as an important part of the fashion world, both in print and on the runway. Plus-size models are not overweight women. They are larger, well-proportioned women. The plus-size model, according to Sheree Hartwell (personal communication, September 19, 2011) from Ford Robert Black agency in Scottsdale, Arizona, must have the right look, beautiful features, and fit the requirements. These may vary depending on where they live. Typically, for Ford in Scottsdale, Arizona, the plus-size model is 5'8 and a size 14. Often they are in local fashion events and shows where they are representative of the retailers and consumers in the area. As the high-fashion world continues to largely ignore these women, the debate among consumers and retailers around the globe on what is considered "beautiful" continues. As the purchasing power of the plus-size women and men continues to grow, so will their presence on the catwalk, in magazines, and on websites around the globe.

Fit Models

Fit models are live mannequins who try on clothing for designers and manufactures prior to production. Unlike fashion models, the ideal fit model is a size 6–8 with measurements 34, 26, 38 for women. Children, teens, plus-size individuals, and men are also hired as fit models. Fit models provide immediate feedback for manufacturers and designers. They are active participants in the construction process. They can address comfort, fit, and style issues on the spot, enabling the designer and manufacturer to work out the kinks before production. The pay is good, and the work is consistent. Fit models are mainly found in fashion capitals such as New York, Milan, London, and France and large manufacturing centers like Los Angeles. Being a fit model is not a glamorous job. It is a good, well-paid, potentially long-term career, if the model's measurements stay consistent (Admins, 2010).

Showroom Models

Showroom models work at the designer-representative showrooms or in house for a specific manufacturer. They are hired during market weeks and during important private buying appointments. These models wear the sample garments for the buyer informally in the sales area. Showroom models enable the potential buyer to have a glimpse of how the garment looks, feels, and is cut on the human body. Showroom models can be editorial and fashion models, as they must fit into sample-size clothing. This type of modeling happens during fashion weeks, trade shows, and at private appointments throughout the year. The casting for a showroom model is handled through an agency. These are professional models that most likely are doing other modeling work throughout the year.

Celebrity

Tom Ford held a groundbreaking return to the fashion world with his spring 2011 show. A great many of Ford's models were what he referred to as his muses and friends, but to the viewing and buying public they were all very famous celebrities. For example, singer Beyonce Knowles, actress Julianne Moore, and iconic 1970s model Lauren Hutton all walked down his low-key yet luxurious runway. Tom Ford, like others throughout history, has found the value in using celebrities and socialites as models. In Chapter 1 we discussed Ossie Clark and other designers who utilized musicians and celebrities as their models, cultivating the must-see press darling experience in which all wanted to partake. High-profile people attract the attention of consumers, and the press, providing a newsworthy reason to write about the show. **Celebrity models** are not required to have any specific measurements. Designers choose them for many reasons. The best motive is that celebrities may provide inspiration to the designer. He or she can be their muse. More importantly, they usually fit the image of the brand. The designer's clients or potential customers will relate to the celebrity and want to emulate them by purchasing the clothing, perfume, makeup, or shoes from the manufacturer. Oftentimes a major celebrity will become the spokesperson for a company or its secondary line such as perfume and accessories. Their image helps solidify the brand with the consumer through print ads, online advertisements, and public appearances. If they are not in the runway shows, they attend as the brand ambassadors. The celebrity's presence alone can create yet another reason for the attention of the press. In 2011 actress Natalie Portman became the face for Dior perfume, while actress Keira Knightley follows in a long line of famous women by representing Chanel. Celebrities as models both on runway and in print are considered an important marketing tool. Choosing the correct celebrity is the challenge, as he or she will be forever connected with the brand.

Teen Models

Teen models, that is, girls and boys between the ages of twelve and fifteen, represent a variety of demographic segments of the population. The market they represent is called the **junior market**. The junior market continues to grow as teens and their clothing choices are expanding both at brick-and-mortar stores and in online divisions of teen apparel. More manufacturers are entering the juniors' market and the need for relatable young models is ever growing. Designers like Tommy Hilfiger, who launched a teen collection in 2011, and many others are entering the juniors' market. There are many agencies that cater only to child and teen models.

Child

Child models represent the merchandise for baby, toddlers, children, and preteens (Figure 6.4). Designer brands like Versace and Phillip Lim have children's collections and are part of an evolving trend toward high-end designer children's and toddler's clothing. The Young Versace brand is aimed at children from infancy to age twelve. Children can be challenging on a runway. If young children are used on a runway, it is advised to have a familiar adult walk them down the runway. They should have a rehearsal/practice on the runway so they are not shocked when show time begins. It is advised to have a separate changing area for children only (Zargani, 2011).

FIGURE 6.4 *Example of child model on runway.*

Courtesy of Omer Kreso

Other

There are several subindustry modeling categories such as artist models, body parts models, promotional models, and swimsuit models.

ARTIST MODEL

An artist model or figurative model poses for professional and student artists while they study, draw, or paint the human figure. The majority of artist modeling is done in the nude and requires the model to hold a pose for a long time. The artist models earn around $15.00 to $30.00 dollars an hour.

BODY PART MODEL

This category of modeling specializes in a specific body part. Body part modeling can be a lucrative industry and includes: hands, face, legs, feet, eyes, bottoms, hair, and the torso. There are many agencies that specialize in casting body part models.

PROMOTIONAL MODEL

This is a model hired to work promotional events such as trade shows, conventions, sporting events, and concerts. He or she promotes items and brands like automobiles, beauty products, alcoholic beverages, and sports drinks. The physical requirements for promotional models vary and depend on the company's needs.

SWIMSUIT MODELS

Swimsuit modeling has become highly competitive since the popularity of the Sports Illustrated swimsuit issue. Swimsuit models must have great proportioned bodies and are often high-fashion editorial models. In the past no noticeable tattoos or body piercings were acceptable but, as fashion trends change, so do these hard-and-fast rules regarding swimsuit and all categories of models. In addition to print and commercial work, swimsuit models work on runways, participate in tradeshows such as boat shows and car shows, and are hired for catalogues and websites.

Volunteer/Amateur

This is a model that is not signed to a professional agency and does not require a fee for his or her services. A volunteer model can be an aspiring model, a student from a modeling school, a community member, a high-profile local celebrity, or a friend who fits the image of the show. The model coordinator must keep in mind that he or she is not dealing with professional models and be patient with volunteers. It is vital that a **model application/information** form be filled out for all volunteer models (Figure 6.5). This is a form listing all measurements, notes about the model, and vital contact information. In addition, creating a **model contract** is another tool that coordinators should use when dealing with volunteers. (Professional agencies will provide a contract.) The contract sets forth the details, responsibilities, and expectations of the model. The simple act of signing the contract should instill a sense of responsibility and yield professional behavior from the volunteer. Amateur models often require training and extra rehearsal time. The extra rehearsal and training time should be noted in the budget and timelines. There are pros and cons to using volunteer and amateur models. Many may not be willing to wear the garments selected, or be able to walk or model the clothing in the manner in which the producer or designer had planned. The extra time for rehearsal can burden the timeline and affect the budget. However, volunteer models and amateurs can also bring audience members, create energy, encourage community support, and help reduce cost.

AI SENSE OF STYLE SHOW

Name: Ashley Martin

Phone: 555-555-5555

Address: 1234 N Apple Drive

E-mail: am@email.com

Date of Birth: 09/21/93

Measurements:	Women:	Men:
Height: 5′11	Bust: 34	Chest: ____
Weight: 115	Dress: 6	Shoe Size: ____
Waist: 25	Shoe Size: 10	Inseam: ____
Pant Size: 6	Inseam: 32	Sleeve Length: ____
Hair Color: Brown	Hips: 35	

Eye Color: Blue

Models Experience: *I've done one local fashion show and a couple photo shoots for some aspiring photographers.*

Coordinators Notes: I liked her look because of her lack of experience her walk needs some work, I think with a little work we should cast her.

You will need to attend a dress rehearsal on Saturday, March 23

Model Applicant's initial here: ____

Signed Release form: ____

FIGURE 6.5 *Model application example.*

Courtesy of Paula Taylor

The Modeling Agency

Modeling agencies are companies that represent a variety of models and act as their representative. Models are placed in divisions based on their body type, look, and particular strengths. A model might meet the requirements for runway, commercial print, or plus size, for example. Agents book the models for jobs and take a fee, which is generally 20 percent of all the models' bookings. They send models out on casting calls and, if booked, will receive the contracted percentage as payment.

There are hundreds of modeling agencies around the globe, and many of them are scams and disreputable. They take young, impressible girls' and boys' money. They promise fulfillment of dreams of superstardom to people who clearly do not meet the physical requirements of modeling. Reputable modeling agencies do not ask for money upfront. They stick to very strict guidelines for height requirements and weight. New models looking for representation can contact their local professional agencies and simply set up an appointment. In addition, they can contact the major modeling agencies via the Internet. Send in a photo and honestly address the questions of height and weight. Most agencies will ask for the photo to be taken outside in natural light with very little to no makeup.

The Portfolio

If hired, the new model must update and create a **portfolio**. A model portfolio is a collection of the model's best, professionally produced photographs. However, depending on where the model is in his or her career, the portfolio can contain professional photographs, which the model had previously taken to show versatility and range of looks. In the case of working professionals, the book or portfolio is already full of photographs produced from real-world work,

tear sheets, published photographs from past assignments, all torn out of magazines. Today's portfolios are available digitally as well as in a hard book.

Model Card

It is still the industry standard for a model to bring in his or her portfolio during a casting. In addition, the model will need to bring a **composite** or **model card** (Figure 6.6). This is an informative card listing all the imperative information about the model, including the model's name and measurements, and agency information, including its contact info. It also contains a headshot and additional photographs. All composites are also available at the modeling agency's website. They are excellent PR tools. Websites have helped expand the opportunities for several agencies and models. Many agencies include videos as well as composite cards. Some of the most powerful and popular current agencies are: IMG, Women Model Management, Ford, DNA, Supreme Management, Marilyn Model Mgmt, Elite New York, 1 model management, and New York Model Management.

FIGURE 6.6 *Example of model card.*
Courtesy of Ford /Robert Black Agency

Although both Ford and Elite are legends and are the only universal brands in the model world, IMG is the most successful agency dominating the trade. It currently defines model management and branding. With supermodel clients like Gisele and Kate Moss, IMG continues to dominate the business. Each agency has its own strengths and weaknesses. An aspiring model should do his or her research before signing with just anyone, even if they are the biggest and the best. Sometimes a smaller agency will give the models the needed attention and guidance.

Many of the top agencies cater to both men and women, such as Ford, DNA, Elite, and New York model management.

Male Modeling Agencies

As the male modeling industry grows, the demand for agencies solely focused on the male model has also increased. A few of the current best American male agencies are VNY Model Management, Wilhelmina, Major Model Management, and Red Model Management.

Modeling Schools

Modeling schools are formal training facilities for modeling that can be found in almost every major city. However, attending a modeling school is neither a requirement nor a necessity to become a model. For a fee they can provide instruction on makeup application, walking, nutrition, voice projection, and self-confidence. Many of these schools have access to modeling contests across the globe and either have an affiliation with a professional agency or have their own agency. These are unlike professional agencies that have strict guidelines and do not charge an upfront fee. Modeling schools are open to a wider variety of people and are facilities that charge for the specific classes the student may take. Many modeling schools focus on commercial potential and local work, emphasizing that height and weight restrictions may be less strict in these markets.

Casting Directors

Once a model is hired, the agent can begin sending his or her client out on casting calls (Figure 6.7). Casting calls are the model's interview. The casting agent holds the call for a designer or brand for which models are sought. The casting can have several people attending including the designer, the stylist, and, of course, the casting agent or director. Casting agents generally contact an agent with specifics for a project. The agent will put together the appropriate talent. During the casting, the models are asked to walk and answer a few questions. The models should wear clothing that shows their body such as jeans and tank tops or a basic dark-colored fitted dress. Women should always be in heels. The casting director needs to see if the model can actually walk in heels. Casting directors do more than simply hire models for photo shoots and runway shows. Casting director Andrew Weir from ACW worldwide holds an open casting each season in New York City, where over 500 boys and girls from all the major agencies and all over the world come to walk for Mr. Weir.

As the global social, economic, and political environment changes, the trends in the modeling world will also change. Sometimes these trends may mirror, react against, or ignore the world climate. History has proven that in the fashion world things are constantly changing. As designers' collections evolve each season, the need for specific types of models grows. It is fair to say the current "it" models will soon be replaced with new and different models more representative of the fashion trends of the moment. The best examples of these changes are seen in the pages of high-fashion magazines, on blogs, and, of course, strutting down the catwalk. The catwalk or runway is the most obvious and expressive vehicle to showcase current designer trends and artistic visions.

Once the casting of the models has taken place, and you have completed your model selection, it is important to sign a contract with the agency as well as obtain from the agent or model a signed **model release**. A release is necessary to allow producers and designers to use the model's photographs for publication and promotional purposes (Figure 6.8).

FIGURE 6.7 *Example of a fashion presentation at Milk studios.*

From Alexander Porter/BFAnyc.com

1122 Fashion Drive, CA

I, Jane Fashionista, hereby give Fashion All Stars, its successors, and assigns the absolute and irrevocable right and permission with respect to the photographs taken of me or in which I may be included with others during the rehearsals and production of (name of event) on (date[s] of event):

(1) To copyright the photographs,

(2) To use, reuse, publish, and republish the photographs individually or in conjunction with other photographs,

(3) To use my name in connection therewith.

I understand that any and all photographs taken become the property of Fashion All Stars.

I hereby release and discharge Fashion All Stars, its successors, and assigns from any and all claims and demands arising out of or in connection with the use of photographs, including but not limited to any and all claims for libel or invasion of privacy.

Name (of individual being photographed): Jane Fashionista

Signature: Jane Fashionista Date: Sunday May 3

Address: 1234 Fashion Lane

City: Los Angeles State: CA Zip: 98902

Telephone: (555) 444-3333 Date of Birth: 10/10/1992

E-mail: fashionista@email.com

FIGURE 6.8 *Model release example.*

The Merchandise

Pulling and styling merchandise is one of the most important aspects of the show. Most designers will dictate the merchandise that is to be put in the show.

If the stylist and merchandise coordinator are working with retailers, the merchandise should be previewed several weeks prior to the event. The actual merchandise selection may not happen until a week or even a few days before the show. This is dependent on how much inventory the store has and what is available.

Merchandise Selection Record Sheet

This is a description of and a listing of the type and quantity of items used in the show. It is the stylist's and producer's job to coordinate, pull, and style the garments for the show. The stylist working with one particular designer will work closely with the design team, executing the image the designer has set forth. They will make editing, lineup, and provide styling suggestions. However, the final say is that of the designer. Producers working in markets promoting shows that highlight several retailers or designers often have more freedom. They must visit each boutique, retailer, or designer showroom and pull the accurate merchandise. The producer, stylist, or merchandise coordinator is responsible for the merchandise and must inventory all items used. The process for an inventory of garments is simple. Keep a record and photo of each garment; write a brief description of the garment. Make certain to have a version of the merchandise selection record online. It is recommended to create a physical sheet online to enable easy, clean changes styling the garments. In shows and

FIGURE 6.9 *Model boards backstage.*

Courtesy of John Calder

events that highlight several retailers and brands, the producer and stylist, with direction from the client, will pull and style the merchandise.

When the merchandise has been selected it is time to create the **model/style boards** (Figures 6.9 and 6.10).

Model styling boards function as direction for the stylist and dresser. Every designer has his or her own way of creating the boards. Generally it is a poster board with the model's name, photo, the order of appearance on the runway, and number of looks or changes each will have. Details about the outfit and a photo are provided so that dressers can follow the information and have a clear comprehension of how the garment should look going down the runway. The stylist should also have a **stylebook**.

STYLEBOOK

This is a book with information on each garment and styling notes. Some examples of items that may be addressed in a stylebook are as follows: it specifies the shoes the model will wear; it explains how clothes should be presented, for example, how a scarf should be tied, and so on. The stylebook is ideally kept as a working document online until show date and after final fittings, so all information can be kept current. Prior to creating the model boards, the **model lineup** must be completed.

A model lineup is a list delineating the order in which the models come down the runway. This is a vital tool for calling the show. Until show day the lineup is tentative and can change if a model is a no show, sick, or unavailable. When booking models, always have a backup list that have similar features, hair color, and measurements. The person in charge of timing the show uses the model lineup as a guide when sending the models out to the runway one after another or in whatever manner the producer has constructed the event. The lineup or order of appearance will also alert the dressers on how much time they actually have to dress the models. It is a good idea to have a large print of the model lineup posted by the entrance to the runway. This enables both models and backstage management to be aware of the order (Figure 6.11).

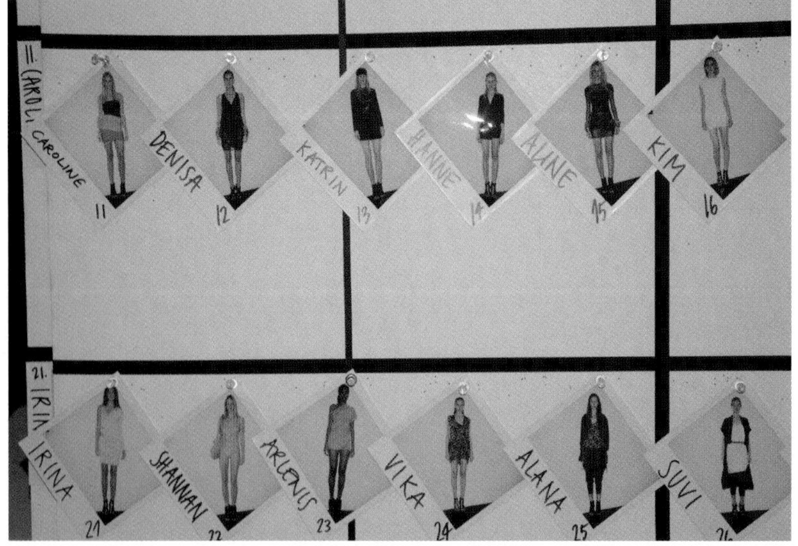

FIGURE 6.10 *Model style/lineup polaroids.*

Courtesy of John Calder

Merchandise Return

After the show, the coordinator or stylist must return all merchandise highlighted in perfect condition to the designers or retailers that provided the garments. If problems or damages occur, the production team should notify the designer or retailer immediately and have the garment repaired or dry-cleaned. If the garment is damaged beyond repair, it may be the responsibility of the producer to reimburse the owners for the destroyed or badly damaged item. Keeping merchandise clean and safe is an important task, as damages and dry-cleaning bills could destroy reputations and cut away at the profit.

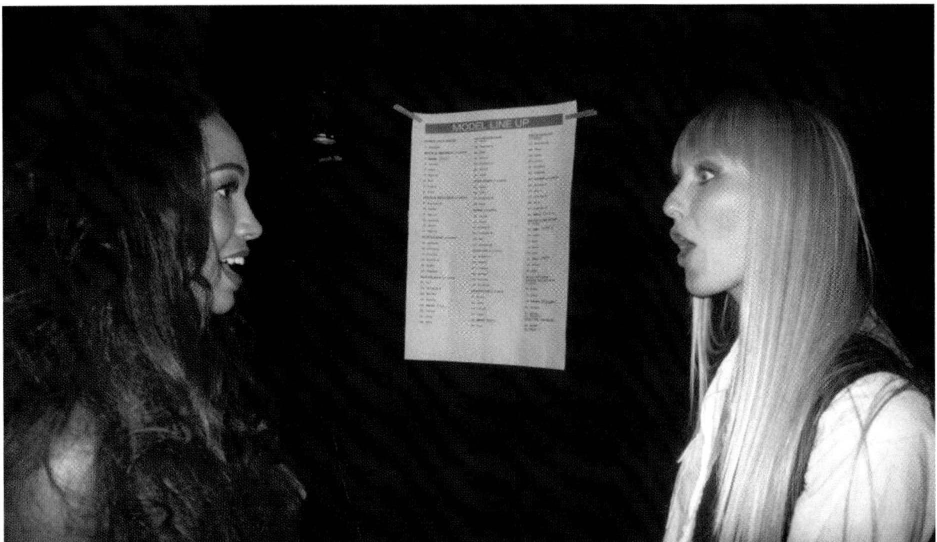

FIGURE 6.11 *Models and lineup by Eric Kroll.*
Courtesy of Eric Kroll

A detailed job description of styling and how to pull and select merchandise is provided below:

Styling and Merchandise Pull Job Description and Instruction Sheet

What Is the Function of a Stylist?

The stylist works closely with the producer and merchandise coordinator. He or she assists in pulling and styling garments for the show. The stylist works with the models to create their final looks.

What Is a Merchandise Pull?

A week or two prior to the show the merchandise coordinator, stylist, or producer will pull (select clothing for the show. This can happen at a designer's showroom or studio, a retail store, or specialty boutique.

Supplies Needed

The following items for the merchandise pull are needed:

- Pens, pencil, a clipboard, a notebook, a camera to take styling notes, and mult.iple merchandise selection record sheets.

Take copious notes, regarding the styling of the garment. Write quickly and be very attentive to the direction from the producer or the merchandise coordinator.

- Pay specific attention to the model's names, which look he or she will be wearing, and what sizes will be pulled. It will be helpful to make a list of the models with their names, pictures, and sizes prior to the slection process to reference during the pull.

The Pull

The merchandise coordinator, stylist, and, depending on the team, the producer will look around the store or showroom and decide what kind of merchandise will be chosen. The challenge when pulling merchandise from several stores is finding garments that work within the vision of the show as well as being appropriate for representing the store/brand that you are pulling. Be mindful of the vision of the show, client's goals and the target audience.

The person in charge will then begin to pull complete looks for certain models, which may range from two to five looks per model. This is where detailed styling notes are a must. You will refer to these notes when making the styling boards and stylebook.

Each of the looks will be pulled from the store racks and shelves and hung on to a rolling rack. Each garment will be selected in the appropriate size for the respective model that is wearing the look. Some stores may hold the garments for you until the day of the show, but often the garments will have to be put back on the shelves so they can potentially be sold. This depends entirely on the decision of management or corporate rules in dealing with fashion shows. If they need to be placed back on the store floor make certain you have selected more looks than needed.

(Continued)

(*Continued*)

Photos of individual garments and full outfits should be taken for use in the styling book and model boards.

Tips for Changing into Looks, When a Model is Present

Makeup bags must be worn over the model's face when changing a model into his or her look. This is necessary so that makeup does not rub off on to the garments.

Spray tanner must be completely dry before a model can change into a look; ask your model to rub a piece of white cloth over various parts of his or her body where the tan has been applied. If any of the tanners can be seen on the cloth, do not allow your model to change into the look.

Help the model change into the garmets.

When changing your model into his or her look, be sure to keep the dressing area neat and organized. Keep each look together and in the order it was pulled. Hang all garments on their respective clothing hangers and/or in the original store packaging.

Merchandise Selection Record

Merchandise Selection records (MSR) must be filled out: These should contain the model's name, size, and description of the looks and garments being borrowed. All of the garment style numbers are to be recorded on this sheet.

You will use the MSR for your own records. A copy of the MSR should be made and given to the selected store as well. Copies of the model's photos should be shown to the store manager for approval (if required) and additional copies should be made for them if requested.

Styling Book

The style book is a book or PowerPoint that has all the models looks photographed and inventoried

Supplies needed: Color printer, camera with photos, paper, notebook, and styling notes, laptop.

A styling book will aid in familiarizing yourself with the looks as well as for a reference tool when making the model boards.

The pictures that you previously took at the merchandise pull should be arranged by look and model name. Make sure to include the store or designer name from which the look was pulled. The notes you took from the merchandise pull for each look should be included on this same sheet.

Compile all the styled looks into a notebook and have an online version available. Once your styling book is completed you will need to make additional copies for the executive team and other backstage management.

Keep a copy on a jump drive.

Model Boards

Supplies

Large poster board (one for each model), a black sharpie, the photos of the looks and models, spray mount, twine, and a whole punch.

Each of the models' photos and looks will be compiled on one large white poster boards. They should be arranged with the first look at the top of the board with the store name, or designer, below. Then place the second look with store name and so on. On the other side of the board, a large photo of the model should be pasted and his or her name should be written in large letters.

All of the photos should be spray mounted. All written information included (store name, model name).

A small hole should be made with your hole punch at the top of the board. You will tie twine through this hole into a loop in order for it to be hung on the rolling racks during the fashion show.

Fashion Show

During the fashion show, the stylist will work with dressers to make sure the interpretation of the stylebook and model boards are executed to perfection.

The stylist will then consult with the producer or executive production assistant for approval of the total look and styling.

The stylist will make sure these total looks are sent into the lineup correctly throughout the show.

Post Show

After the show, the stylist will assist in returning the garments and accessories to their respective stores or designers.

In the post show evaluation with your executive team or producer, you will discuss and evaluate the looks of the show, strengths and weaknesses of the looks, as well as what you can do better for the next fashion show.

Industry Insider

Andrew Weir

Andrew is one of the world's leading casting directors and consultants and the founder and director of ACW Worldwide. Andrew speaks to us about his ever-evolving and multifaceted approach to casting and branding. He explains how he became a casting director and the function of fashion presentations while giving us a peek into the creative process he and his team use when branding a client.

WHAT IS THE ROLE OF A CASTING DIRECTOR? WHAT SERVICES DOES ACW WORLDWIDE OFFER CLIENTS?

Someone involved with a brand, whether it's a designer, a stylist, or the head of public relations, will hire us to help find and negotiate which model, actor or celebrity would best represent their brand. We consider who is going to generate dollars for the client. We also want to inspire the consumer, and give them something to aspire to without it being out of reach. We also strive to make sure our choices translate to social media and generate buzz around the brand.

We collaborate with our clients and their creative team to identify what the brand wants to convey. We analyze market trends as well as the brand's demographic, its aspirational values, and its advertising and casting history. We combine all of that research, and through the process of many discussions with the client, we develop a message and cast those we feel will help move the brand forward.

There's a misconception that casting directors pick "pretty" faces and connect them with a client. This business is actually very research driven. To do this job well and to keep clients, you have to do your research. There is no one-size-fits-all approach because each brand's DNA is different.

We recently brought on a new client. She makes amazing custom jackets, pants, and handbags out of leather and denim. We will facilitate the entire branding process, including logo creation, website, and e-commerce development, and identify from where to source the materials. Part of this process is identifying the kind of person and face that should represent the brand from the beginning. Who is that girl? Where does she hang out? What does she like? What's her aesthetic and personal sense of style? That girl becomes the archetype for the brand and then we try to find someone who can portray that.

We also do projects with television and original programs. ACW proactively reaches out to clients to create co-ops. We constantly work with the talent and the brands we represent to create something organic, exciting, and new.

Then, in addition to advertising, there is the business of casting runway models for shows for fashion week, which is an extremely hectic time.

HOW DID YOU GET STARTED IN THE INDUSTRY?

I was a producer at KCD, the world's premiere fashion production company, for two years. I had the opportunity to travel the world working on projects for designers such as Alexander McQueen and Louis Vuitton. At the end of it I said to myself, "I'm not a producer." It wasn't for me. I wanted to do something fun, and it seemed like the person who was having the most fun was the casting director. I went to the vice-president who took a chance on me and sent me to Milan to cast Calvin Klein's men's show with Joe McKenna and Mr. Klein. That was my first big casting job. Not too long after that I became Calvin Klein's director of talent, and in 2001 I started the casting company, ACW Worldwide.

HOW DOES ACW WORLDWIDE USE SOCIAL MEDIA AND TECHNOLOGY IN ITS BUSINESS MODEL?

Weir Diary (http://www.weirdiary.com) is the company's blog. We use it to promote some of the work we do as well as many of the models we work with. It's also a great way to increase the visibility of new faces that we believe in. Recently a girl from IMG came through the door. She had "it"—an amazing face mixed with that special something. After her visit with us, I immediately uploaded the photos I had taken of her to the blog and Facebook. The response was amazing. That girl was going to be a star. Within minutes I was able to show the entire world this girl's face and get feedback from my colleagues in the industry. Then she went on to walk for Rebecca Taylor, Preen, Badgley Mischka, and Helmut Lang this past season.

Social media also makes it easier to maintain relationships and keep in touch with agents, models, and other clients. Casting is based on relationships. Social media allows us to connect much more easily with people and have meaningful interactions, despite having such busy lives. Social media also helps us to keep our finger on the pulse of fashion. When time comes for us to do research for our clients on market trends, and find the models with the most buzz, we use information from social media to help us.

Additionally, even though it's rare, the Internet provides scouting opportunities. Sean O'Pry, now one of the biggest male models in the world, was discovered by Nole Marin via Myspace. Social

(*Continued*)

media has given casting directors the ability to discover new faces, whether it's from an editorial you see on a blog or someone's Facebook profile.

HOW HAS THE FASHION SHOW CHANGED AND WHAT HAS ACW DONE TO ADDRESS THOSE CHANGES?

It hasn't really changed much. The same groups of people are putting shows together all over the world. The budgets have changed, so we don't get to be as extravagant. Several years ago we did a show for Hugo Boss Black in Berlin. There was a set of steps that descended from the ceiling, and the models were coming out of the ceiling down this grand circular staircase. Carmen Kass was floating in the air. It was performance art. There's a lot less theatricality now. Shows have gone back to being very simplistic and minimalist.

WHAT IS THE FUNCTION OF A FASHION PRESENTATION?

In comparison to runway shows, a fashion presentation is more static. The models are like live mannequins. They stand in a garment, often for hours at a time, and buyers and editors are able to view the collection more intimately. You can see what type of material the garments are made of and spend time with the clothing. It's a great way for new designers to showcase their clothing to key people who aren't yet familiar with the brand, and it's less expensive than a runway show. A runway show, by contrast, is more dynamic. The energy of a runway show creates an exciting atmosphere and allows the designer to tell more of a story. It's also a status symbol because runway shows require more money, more coordination, and more workforce.

There are many challenges that are inherent in casting presentations. In many cases you are competing with runway shows for bigger designers where there is more press coverage. Presentations also tend to pay less than runway shows even though they require a larger time commitment from the model, so you have to be persuasive, a good negotiator, and savvy enough to leverage the relationships you have established with agents and models to get them to commit to doing a presentation. It can be exciting, but it's also challenging.

Presentations usually use fresh faces. You will almost never see a top model doing a presentation. Models don't like to do presentations; they like to do runways. It's awkward and uncomfortable for them to stand there for hours. They're necessary and we need them. Not everyone can do a runway show, and we don't want to show the clothing on mannequins. We want to show how the clothing functions on people, how it drapes, how it fits, and how it moves, so we do presentations.

WHAT ADVICE WOULD YOU GIVE A STUDENT WANTING TO ENTER THE CASTING INDUSTRY?

1. Go intern. See what you like before you commit. Freelance. Get out there and network. It's tough out there right now. Intern twelve hours during the day and then go get a job across the street and work all night. People respect the sacrifices that interns make, especially if they're smart and if they consistently go above and beyond the call of duty. Word spreads like wildfire if you're smart.
2. Be patient. Kids these days expect to work for six months and then get promoted to be vice-president with a six-figure salary. They want to walk through the door and straight into a meeting with Calvin Klein and Mario Testino. Building a career in this industry takes time, but hard work certainly pays off.
3. Above all else, have integrity. Your reputation precedes you and you only get one. A lapse of integrity can permanently destroy people's perception of you. It may get you ahead in the short run, but it always, *always* comes back to you. Being dishonest can very easily ruin your career and your credibility.

Excerpts from interview with Andrew Weir, May 8, 2011.

Industry Insider

Sheree Hartwell

Sheree is the owner and director of Ford/Robert Black Agency (Figure 6.12). She started modeling with Robert Black at the age of twelve. Her dream was to someday own her own modeling agency and fourteen years later Sheree took over ownership and became the director and owner of Ford /Robert Black Agency in Scottsdale, Arizona. She is actively involved in all aspects of the business including maintaining client relationships and scouting new talent. Sheree often sends models overseas and to national markets outside of Arizona. She shares with us some details about running an agency and what requirements it takes to be a Ford model.

WHAT DOES A MODELING AGENT DO?

Scout, sign, and negotiate contracts for models.
Proof film and compile portfolios.
Procure new clients.
Place talent in markets outside of the market they are working in.

FIGURE 6.12 *Industry insider Sheree Hartwell.*
Courtesy of Sheree Hartwell

WHAT ARE THE REQUIREMENTS TO BE A FORD MODEL?

Women-5′8″–5′11″ sizes 0–6.
Men-5′11″–6′2″.
Great skin, smile, hair, bone structure, and personality!

ARE THE REQUIREMENTS DIFFERENT FOR RUNWAY THAN COMMERCIAL OR EDITORIAL?

Yes, commercial models don't have to have the height. They can be really any size or shape. Editorial models tend to be much edgier in look, thinner, and have different features. Runway models are most successful at 5′10″ size 2–4.

HOW MANY DIVISIONS OR CATEGORIES OF MODELS DO YOU HAVE?

Men, women, teens, kids, actors, voice-over, and runway.

WHAT IS THE AVERAGE AGE OF A PROFESSIONAL MODEL?

Working catalogue models tend to be in their 20s and if they are truly successful, they can work into their 30s. Male models are fortunate to work much longer than female models, some well into their 50s! Campaign and editorial models are generally sixteen to twenty-four years old.

HOW DO MODELS LEARN HOW TO WALK OR POSE?

Most professional models work with runway coaches to help perfect their walk and be ready for the runway. Most models learn how to pose by practice shooting with photographers, studying images in magazines, and watching others.

DO YOU WORK WITH CASTING PEOPLE? IF SO HOW DOES THE PROCESS WORK?

Yes, we work with many casting directors here locally and nationally. Most of the time they will contact us with specifics for a project and then we will submit talent that is appropriate. The casting director's client decides whom they would like to see in person and then schedule a casting time to meet.

OFTEN MODELS ARE AWAY IN EUROPE OR ASIA WORKING; HOW DOES THIS PROCESS WORK?

Traveling is essential for models. They constantly need to be moving around to markets that are current at the time. There are different seasons in every market, so for a model to stay busy and continue to develop his or her talent base, it is imperative they travel. Asian markets are great for newer models that are looking to build their books. It essentially acts as a model "boot camp."

Models can go on anywhere from six to twelve castings a day and book one to four different jobs per day. The market is conducive for young talent, as all models are chaperoned to/from all castings and bookings.

(*Continued*)

Industry Insider (Continued)

Sheree Hartwell

Tear sheets are the main reason models travel. The majority of the cover models on the American magazines are actresses, celebrities, and so on—not models. It is very difficult for an American model to land on the cover of a major fashion magazine, unless he or she is a supermodel. The other markets overseas are not this way. There are so many versions of *Vogue,* for example, that a model could land on the cover much easier.

DO YOU SEE PLUS-SIZE MODELS GETTING MORE WORK? WHAT ARE THE HEIGHT AND WEIGHT REQUIREMENTS OF A PLUS-SIZE MODEL?

The plus-size market is dependent on the actual market. There are many catalogues and lingerie clients that cater to the PLUS market, so that is a great way for PLUS models to make money. Height requirement varies but typically is 5′8″ and a size 14. Some PLUS models work at much smaller sizes depending on where they live and if they are able to "pad-up."

IT APPEARS THAT THE TRENDS FOR MODELS IN NEW YORK AND EUROPE IN BOTH THE RUNWAY AND EDITORIAL ARE SUPER SKINNY. DO YOU SEE THIS CHANGING OR STAYING STATUS QUO?

Unfortunately, I don't see this trend ending any time soon. The designers really depict what sizes the models should be. They design clothes with specific measurements and find models that fit those clothes. Couture clothing hangs much better on taller, thinner models.

Excerpts from interview with Sheree Hartwell, September 19, 2011.

Chapter Review

Models and merchandise are two indispensable components of a fashion show. Models are more than hangers for the garments; they are direct advertisements and help with brand development of a designer's collection. Since the majority of fashion shows and events are streaming live, the modern-day model must translate visually offline and online. The general categories of models are as follows:

- Editorial fashion/runway/print
- Advertising
- Commercial/print
- Fitness
- Plus size
- Fit model
- Showroom
- Celebrity
- Child/teen
- Other
- Volunteer

Each type of model has height and weight requirements and plays a different role in the fashion business. Models are represented by modeling agencies and are cast for jobs by casting directors. The model coordinator or producer works with the agencies and casting directors to guarantee that the appropriate talent is secured. Once the casting of the model is confirmed, it is essential to create a contact list, model lineup, and begin selecting merchandise.

Merchandise selection is critical to the success of a show. It is the job of the stylist and merchandise coordinator to edit and style the appropriate looks for the runway. Stylist and merchandise coordinators work directly with designers, retailers, and small boutiques, pulling (selecting) garments and styling the final looks. When pulling from retail stores, it is imperative to record all items on a merchandise selection record sheet. Once the merchandise is selected and models are cast, creating a model lineup will delineate the order in which the models will be directed down the runway. An individual model board must also be created to highlight style notes, present the number of changes a specific model will have, and provide direction for the dressers. Models and runway trends are always changing. All merchandise should be returned in perfect condition immediately after the show.

Case Problem

Nicole is a new, eighteen-year-old, recently signed, professional regional model. She has been contracted through her agency for a charity event. Nicole's job is to model an evening gown and hand out auction items to the winning guest. The event starts at six in the evening and will be covered by the local news. The model coordinator has negotiated a great deal with the agent since Nicole is new to professional modeling. The agent, as contracted with the client, has told Nicole to arrive by 4 I .Y. for hair and makeup to be completed before the event begins. The model coordinator has worked with the agency before and feels confident that although Nicole is new, she will do a fine job.

Nicole arrives on time and is taken to the back of the hotel to have her hair and makeup completed. Nicole does an excellent job modeling and presenting the auction items. After the auction, the model coordinator and Nicole's dresser cannot find her anywhere. Finally, after an in-depth search of the entire building, the dresser spots her in front of the hotel. Nicole is drinking a glass of champagne, smoking a cigarette, and still wearing the designer evening gown she was modeling that evening. To make matters worse, she is not alone. She is talking to the local news crew about the event as if she were some sort of representative for the evening.

Questions to Consider

1. What should the model coordinator's immediate reaction be? What further steps should be taken to troubleshoot the problem?
2. How could this situation have been avoided from the start?
3. Review the templates given at the end of the text and create a model expectation form, which outlines the requirements and financial repercussions if expectations are not met.
4. Do you believe the producer should dock Nicole's pay?
5. Should the producer contact the agent?

Questions for Review and Discussion

1. Please list the different categories of models and explain each category and its role in the fashion industry.
2. What is the role that celebrity models play in promoting fashion brands? What are the pros and cons in having a celebrity represent your brand?
3. What are the pros and cons of hiring a volunteer and an amateur model?
4. What should a producer consider when casting young children? How can he or she avoid problems?
5. What is the difference between a model agent and a casting director?
6. What are some of the services Casting Director Andrew Weir provides through ACW Worldwide?
7. Why is a model lineup critical to the success of a show?
8. Explain a fashion presentation.
9. Discuss the pros and cons of the current weight requirements for runway models.
10. Discuss why so few designers address the plus-size market.

Out and About Activities

1. Interview a local or regional model agent from a professional agency.
2. Interview an admissions person at a local modeling school.
3. Compare and contrast the goals of each business.

(If you do not have a professional agency and school, research via the Internet and schedule a phone interview.)

4. Go online and research who is the current face of Dior perfume, what celebrities are currently Cover Girls, and who is promoting for MAC cosmetics.
5. Visit several different professional modeling agencies' websites from the list provided and answer the questions following it.

http://www.dnamodels.com/
http://www.fordmodels.com/
http://www.suprememanagement.com/Models/List
http://www.imgmodels.com/

(a) In general are the agencies representing the same category of model? Explain.
(b) What makes one agency different from another?
(c) Evaluate how easy it is to maneuver around the website.
(d) Develop a list of similar trends in models.
(e) Which agency has the most recognizable models?

Ongoing Fashion Show Project

Selecting and Styling Models and Merchandise

Create two dividers: one titled models, the other merchandise. Refer to the templates given at the end of the text. The model coordinator and members of the team should be using online templates as a guide:

Hold a model casting.
Create a custom contact sheet.
Create a custom Model Release Form.
Create a custom Model Application Form.
Create a model lineup for the fashion show.

The stylist and members of the team should:

Pull and inventory merchandise on Merchandise Selection Record Sheet.
Create style boards.
Begin the style notebook.

Terminology of the Trade

advertising model 97
casting directors 104
celebrity 100
child 100
commercial 98
composite 103
editorial fashion models 95
fashion models/runway 95
fit models 99
fitness model 98
junior market 100
merchandise pull 94
models 94
modeling agencies 102
model application/information 101
model card 103
model contract 101
model lineup 106
model release 104
model/style boards 106
modeling schools 103
plus-size models 98
portfolio 102
showroom models 99
stylebook 106
tear sheets 103
teen models 100
volunteer 101

Web Resources

www.models.com
www.milkstudios.com
www.acwworldwide.com
www.weirdiary.com
www.modelinia.com

Bibliography

Admins (2010, April 13). *Behind the Scenes with a Fit Model*. Retrieved May 13, 2010, from http://www.39thandbroadway.com/scenes-fitmodel/

Moil, D. (2011, May 23). *Macy's speeds up innovation agenda*. Retrieved July 23, 2011, from http://www.wwd.com/retail-news/lundgren-talks-innovation-at-macys-annual-3620683

Quick, H. (1997) *Catwalking: A History of the Fashion Model* (pp.19–20). Edison, NJ: Wellfleet Press.

Singer, M. (2011, February 22). *Meadham Kirchhoff Review*. Retrieved April 10, 2011, from http://www.style.com/fashionshows/reviews/F2o11RTW-MKIRCH

Vogue Magazine. (1999, July). *The Return Of The Sexy Model*.

Zargani, L. (2011, May 11). *Versace to Launch Kids Line*. Retrieved May 28, 2011, from http://www.wwd.com/markets-news/versace-to-launch-kids-line-3610214

Pavia, W. & Rochell, H. (2009, June 13). *Size–Zero Models are no longer in Vogue, Editor Tells Top Fashion Houses* (p. 16). The Times London UK. Retrieved April 29, 2011, from http://search.proquest.com/arts/docprintview/320132557/fulltext?accountid=36308

Retrieved from http://www.associationofmodelagents.org/become-a-model/getting-started-as-a-model.html

Retrieved from http://www.modelinia.com/blog/ready-set-cast-acw-worldwide-begins-casting-for-new-york-fashion-week/17777

Retrieved from http://www.cdc.gov/nchs/fastats/bodymeas.htm

Retrieved from http://www.newmodels.com/school.html

Retrieved from http://www.vogue.com/vogue-daily/print/vd-new-york-spring-2010-the-mac-initiative-at-milk-studios/

Retrieved from http://www.barbizonmodeling.com/faq.htm

Retrieved from http://www.cfda.com

Von Furstenberg, D. & Herzog, D. (n.d.). *Healthier Standards*. Retrieved June 18, 2011, from http://www.cfda.com/healthier-standards-%e2%80%93-an-op-ed-by-cfda-president-diane-von-furstenberg-and-director-of-the-harris-center-dr-david-herzog

THE FRONT OF THE HOUSE AND THE BACK OF THE HOUSE

LEARNING OBJECTIVES

After completing this chapter, you will be able to:

- Know how to work with décor, floor plans, and layouts
- Understand staging, lighting, and runway options
- Discuss the variety of entertainment options
- Gain knowledge about backroom basics
- Understand the role of the dresser
- Review the given case study
- Understand the terminology of the trade

We spend so much of our time taking what we do to the next level. We look at culinary, art, the red carpet, and fast track these trends into our industry.

—BRUCE VASSAR and MATTHEW TRETTEL, wedding fashion show producers

7

Organizing the **front of the house** *and the* **back of the house** *for fashion events is no easy task. Simply put, the front of the house is everything the audience can see, take part in, and experience. The back of the house is also known as the workroom or backroom. It is the place where the magic happens, the secrets unfold, and the chaos ensues. It is hidden from the public's view and is the room where models, hair and makeup stylists, dressers, seamstress, and other staff create the show. Both parts of the house are important to setting the scene, branding the event, and executing the vision of the show. A prepared producer visits the location prior to the event and creates a plan based on the client's needs and the reality of the space. Many producers are charged with the task of working with décor and events companies to help translate the vision or theme into the location. In this chapter the reader will gain detailed knowledge about how to turn a backroom into a high-functioning fashion show machine. The chapter discusses the key backstage roles, such as that of the dresser, the seamstress, and the hair and makeup people. In addition, the chapter gives examples of layouts for both the back of the house and the front of the house. Different runway and staging options are explained; also, discussion on effective audience seating and details on how to work with décor companies and lighting technicians are provided. The chapter uses the runway show as an example for front of the house and back of the house issues and concerns. However, many of the steps provided and issues addressed can be used for many different categories of shows or events. For example, all of these steps can be modified for a show or event in a retail establishment.*

The Front of the House

The front of the house is the public area of an event where the audience views the event and experiences all the performance, and within which the guests interact—the space that helps brand the vision or theme of the event (Figure 7.1). It can be as dissimilar as the tents at Bryant Park, a wedding tradeshow in a convention center in Dallas, or a school auditorium

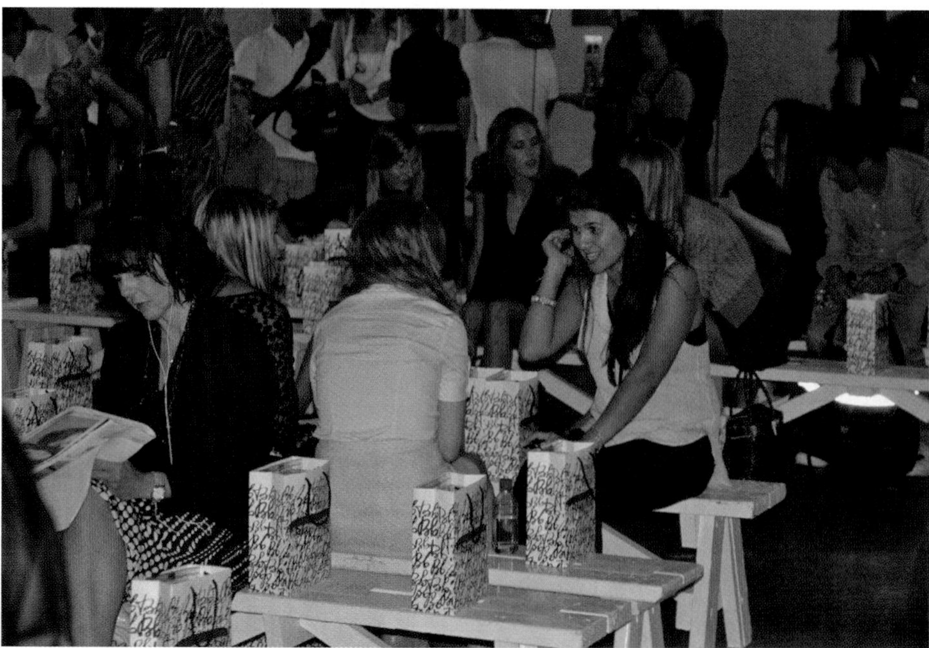

FIGURE 7.1 *Guests seated prior to the start of the show.*
Courtesy of John Calder

in Scottsdale. Each of these venues has different front of the house needs. Often production companies work with or contract décor/events companies to execute the theme or feeling of the event. Many producers and coordinators are hired to run both the back of the house and the front of the house. Others, like the Wedding Guys, own their own event supplies and décor. This enables them to create events in which they produce both the front of the house and the back of the house. In their industry insider interview in Chapter 2, according to B. Vassar and M. Trettel (personal communication, November 13, 2011), they created a trend-setting bridal trade show named "Unveiled" where they produced the front and back of the house. Their team physically sets up the location trucks and the décor, staging, and props. They arrive on site with their own staff and hire local help to execute the show. Whether the producer is solely running the back of the house or hired to take on the total event, gaining a detailed understanding on how to implement the front of the house is a critical skill. Below is a list of some general front of the house needs:

Before a planner or producer can execute the staging, runway décor, and seating, he or she should create a floor plan and a basic layout. Keep in mind that a producer may at any time contract or outsource all of these services. In such an instance the producer's responsibility is to ensure that he or she has hired the proper companies that will fulfill the vision as created by the producer or client.

Layouts/Floor Plan

A **floor plan** is a simple line drawing as if seen from above—used to organize the layout of the front of the house and/or the back of the house. A **layout** is a schematic or plan, which plots the manner in which the elements of the room are arranged. Basic floor plans and layouts can be completed with the aid of websites such as www.floorplanner.com and www.smallblueprinter.com. For more elaborate planning, hiring a professional designer may be necessary. Students might consider partnering with interior design programs and architecture departments to collaborate on detailed floor plans and layouts for fashion events. Once a simple layout is fashioned, the actual physical placement of décor can begin.

Staging and Runways

As you have learned in previous chapters, trends for the actual size and shape of runways and staging are regularly changing. Some designers hold over-the-top elaborate production shows using props, unique staging, and backdrops. Others opt for simple, stripped-down shows with traditional raised runways. Chapter 2 explored technology and the many tends in current fashion shows, giving examples of designers finding unique locations and alternative runways. Many have done away with the raised runway and turned to distinctive locations as a highlight or complement to their collections. Model and designer Erin Wasson held her RVCA Fall 2010 show around the carpets at the ABC carpet store in New York with no elaborate staging (Phelps, 2010). Hugo Boss in Berlin held an elaborate production within which the models made a unique entrance coming down a large spiral staircase before they arrived on a mirrored catwalk. When determining what type of staging and runway are right for your show, one must consider timing and location of the dressing area and the backroom. Specifically consider its physical proximity to the runway. The ideal runway should be close to the backroom and dressing area to accommodate for quick model changes. However, depending on the location, this might be impossible.

The proper staging, runway, and other front of the house requirements can be key PR and branding tools. This can further support a detailed theme or vision and ultimately translates into direct sales.

STAGING

Staging refers to building a stage and runway and creating a background. It can also include setting the lighting cage. The **stage** is a raised platform on which the show will take place or on which theatrical performances are presented. The **runway** is a physical extension of the stage. It can also be a freestanding elevated element. Small and charitable shows may be located in hotel ballrooms. The hotel may donate and execute the raw runway and basic staging. The décor or production team then dresses it within the vision of the show.

RUNWAYS

The physical runway is constructed after the dimensions, look, and shape are created and placed on the layout and added to the floor plan. Runways vary in height, size, and shape based on the layout and the convenience to audience visibility. They can be constructed out of plywood, plexiglass, metal, and other materials. The physical runway or platform is no longer limited to big fashion shows. Designer Angel Sanchez built small narrow runways in his showroom to highlight garments for clients and the press (personal communication, April 20, 2011). Retailers use temporary platforms to highlight garments on both live models and mannequins. Larger catwalks, as runways are often called, are most commonly rented from décor or events companies. They come in sections and have legs that lock in place. The customary size for the runway or stage is four feet by six or eight feet wide. The width of the runway determines the number of models that can come into view next to each other. The height of a runway can vary in increments from 24 inches to 36 inches and so on. The length of the runway should accommodate the location and the pacing of the models on stage. Longer runways are normally attached to the stage where the models can pose for a mark at the beginning of their walk and again at the end. Smaller runways may not have the space for a stage. Traditionally, the majority of shows have one long "T" runway, but like all things that are fashion related even the runway shapes and sizes come in and out of vogue. Common runway stage shapes include circular or box-shaped runways. This shape directs the model's walk in a circle or square without having to stop and change direction. An "I" shaped stage is an adaptation of the "T" but with staging at both ends of the runway allowing for dramatic posing and pacing of several models at once. This type of runway and stage design is conducive for showcasing an entire collection for a big finale. The X or the cross places two platforms at 90° angles. Additional shapes are the Y and the U, each with its own purpose and function. If you have a big enough budget, creative production crew, and the ability to rent or build unique raised platforms, almost any shape you can dream up can be executed. The surface or top of the runway is another important concern for the producer or planner (Figure 7.2).

The surface is covered with fabric or vinyl. The fabric is tucked and taped to the top. Many fashion designers use **muslin**, which is thin cotton, white, dyed, or printed. The muslin is placed on top of the runway. This fabric is what gives the runway its white, crisp look and feel. It is the industry standard covering for runways during fashion weeks. Muslin must be placed on the runway by experienced staff. It needs to be pulled taut and taped down. If placed incorrectly a serious accident could occur. Prior to showtime the muslin is covered

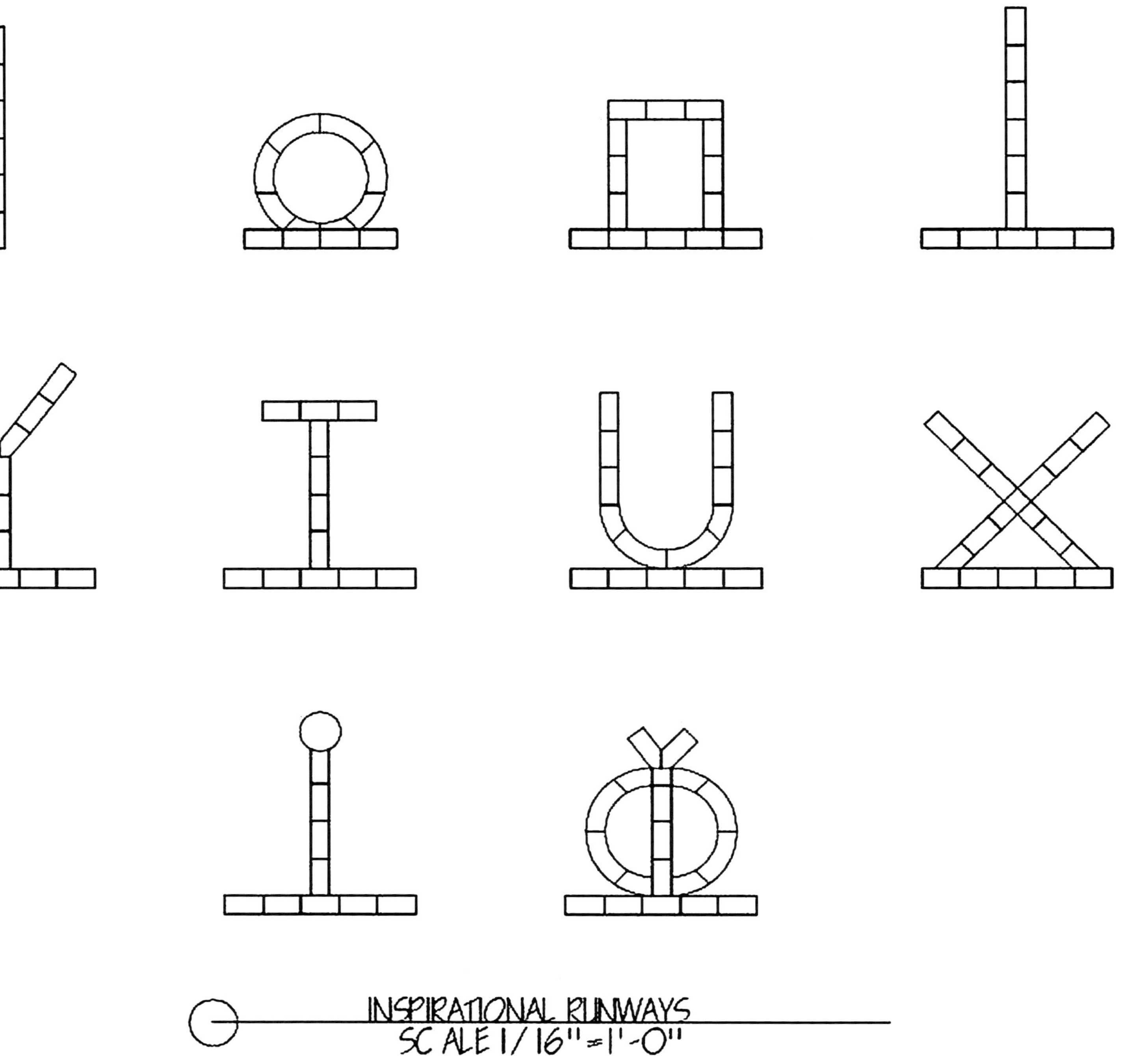

FIGURE 7.2 *Runway examples.*
Courtesy of Melanie Cortel

FIGURE 7.3 *Example of a runway at MILK Studios.*
Courtesy of Joe Schildhorn/BFAnyc.com

with paper or plastic to keep the integrity of the runway clean. There are many other coverings available on the market such as vinyl, fabric, and carpet. A unique and eye-catching runway adds to the vision and brand of the show (Figure 7.3).

Backdrops/Backgrounds

Custom flat backdrops can be built to allow multiple entrances and exits for models. The real function of a backdrop and background is to highlight the products shown. They are perfect for displaying logos, theme elements, designer, and sponsor names. How elaborate backdrop and background scenery is depends on the designer's theme and the budget for the show. Scenery, staging, and designer's backdrops can be built and painted. The more detailed the background scenery and staging, the greater the expense. Although over-the-top productions have become commonplace, it is crucial that the set and stage do not overshadow the product. For example, in Chanel's fall 2010 show, Karl Lagerfeld created an arctic scene with enormous chunks of iceberg transported from Scotland. He constructed a frozen landscape with imported real ice from Scandinavia within which the models dressed in fake fur-lined tweed walked around (Brody, 2010). Many young designers have opted out of big productions and have kept their shows simple, which are representative of the mid-1990s shows. The focus is on the product rather than big production.

FIGURE 7.4 *Model with guitar as a prop.*
Courtesy of Jackie Alpers

Props

The use of props is dependent upon the vision of the show and the available budget (Figure 7.4). Just like elaborate staging, props come in and out of trend. Props can be created for a specific show, rented, or borrowed for use on the runway. Props can be mobile or stationary or even live as in the case of designer Christophe Lemaire. He used a live eagle, bow, and quiver as props in his Hermes fall 2011 RTW show (Mower, 2011). Stylists may use props for drawing attention to a garment and to emphasize a theme. Prada in her Men's Spring 2012 RTW show had a runway made of Astroturf with blue cubes as the seats. She designed branded golf clubs as props emphasizing the kitschy golf theme and supporting the sporty collection. Motionless props are placed on the runway or stage to enhance the theme. For example, for the London Calling show Paula Taylor Productions used a vintage Vespa scooter as a prop on stage to strengthen the theme of the 1960s Mod era in London England. No matter what types of props are used, live, immobile, or mobile, they should always be considered highlights to the show. They should never overshadow the collection and distract the attention of the audience, buyers, and press.

Seating

THEATER SEATING

Most of us have seen photos of seating for fashion shows conducted around the globe. Such an arrangement has a runway in the middle and **theater seating** on either side. Theater seating entails placing chairs side by side and next to the runway and stage.

Theater seating is tight and crowded but usually provides a clear view of the show, since all audience members face the runway. This type of seating is optimally used for runway shows that do not include any variety of meal service or other entertainment that would require the guests getting up from their seats.

See Figure 7.5 for an example of a designer's seating layout.

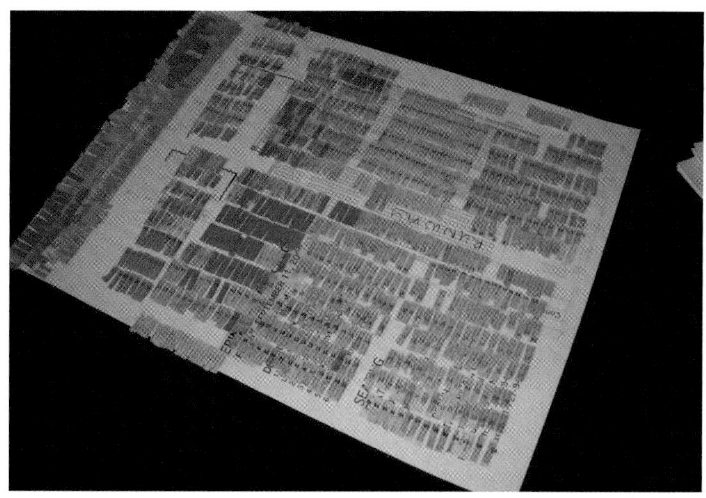

FIGURE 7.5 *Example of a seating chart.*
Courtesy of John Calder

SWAG BAGS

The audience may be assigned seats or seating may be open; **swag bags** or promotional gifts and materials may be placed on each seat prior to the attendee's arrival (Figure 7.6).

STADIUM SEATING

Stadium seating is raised seating with one row raised above the other. This is usually found in sport stadiums or school gymnasiums. Many high-school shows take place in the school's gymnasium where making use of stadium seating is practical. Community shows can rent high school space for little to nothing, and will have a built-in seating arrangement that bears no additional cost to the budget. Designer Rachel Antonoff held a unique fashion presentation for her fall/winter 2012 collection called "The Dance." She booked the band "The Like" to keep guests entertained while models danced and drank punch in LaGuardia High School's gymnasium. The audience could sit at round tables and on chairs apropos of a high school dance (Foreman, Bonet-Black, and Baraga, 2011).

TABLE SEATING

Table seating is the arrangement of tables within the location, generally placed around the runway. Tables are used for tearoom modeling and runway shows alike. Table seating may seat up to twelve people each at round tables. A meal service is generally part of the events, and the reason why table seating is necessary. Dependent upon where in the room the table is located, some visibility problems may arise. Often this type of seating is used as a fundraising tool for charity events, thus selling the tables at a certain price with the proceeds benefiting a charity.

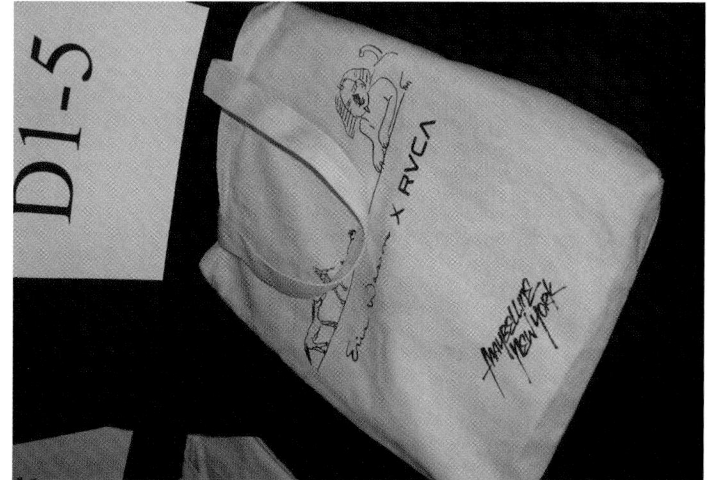

FIGURE 7.6 *Swag bag example.*
Courtesy of John Calder

COMBINATION SEATING

Subject to the goals of the event, location, and budget, some people combine both theater and table seating. Perhaps a meal is served in a separate area while the runway and theater seats are in yet another area altogether. High tops and cocktail tables can be used to supplement

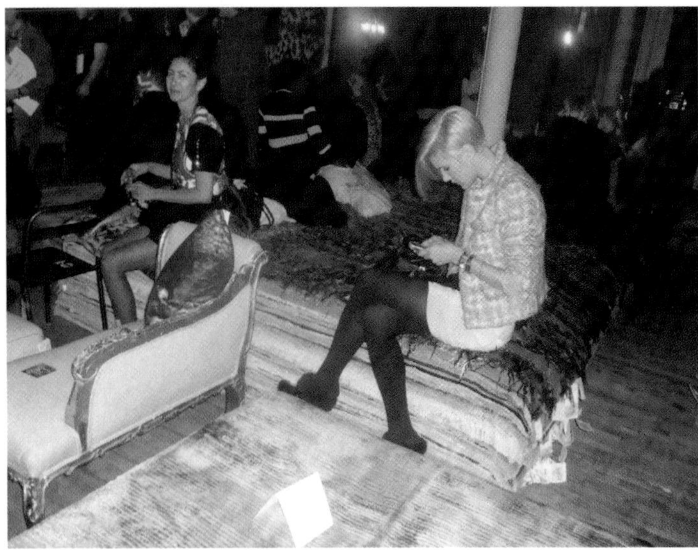

FIGURE 7.7 *Alternative show locations.*
Courtesy of John Calder

theater seating and provide additional seats. Lounge areas can be created to provide, with the help of décor companies, another venue for additional seating.

ALTERNATIVE

Throughout this textbook we have talked about many new approaches to fashion show production. We have discussed unique locations, unusual runways, and outrageous and varied staging and props. Seating is yet another way to engage the audience and support one's theme. As mentioned earlier, Prada created blue cubes as seats to enhance the golf theme of their men's collection. Model-turned-designer Erin Wasson used piles of carpets as the alternative to chairs or benches (Figure 7.7).

PRESS SEATING, SPONSOR, AND VIP SEATING

Press seating is reserved for specific members of the fashion press, such as editors, journalists, and fashion bloggers. VIP seating is seating for what is commonly known as "very important people." This may include celebrities, dignitaries, important donors, or other parties that in one way or another are significant to the event (Figure 7.8).

Lighting

Once the staging, runway, and seating are designed, the lighting plan needs to be created. Lighting helps set the scene for the stage, the show, and the entire location. **Lighting** refers to using specialized equipment to provide artificial illumination. Lighting for fashions shows and events is an excellent way to create atmosphere, highlight garments, and showcase specific areas during the event. Professional lighting technicians and designers are artists in their own right, using various lighting techniques to set a scene and create the mood. Larger lighting companies have an array of services and equipment available for every budget. Some basic examples of lighting equipment used in fashion shows and events are listed below:

FIGURE 7.8 *Diane von Furstenberg and Simon Doonan in the front row.*
Courtesy of John Calder

Moving lights are a computer-controlled stage lighting system under the direction of the lighting technician. It is capable of canvassing the entire runway and room.

The **truss** is a supporting structure or framework for lighting. The truss is generally set up around the catwalk and enables the lighting tech to attach movable lights to the structure. It is an excellent tool for the lighting technician and provides a platform to use every variety of light.

Spotlight is a focused beam of light that illuminates a single area. This type of lighting is used to draw attention to a specific area, model, or performance.

LED (light emitting diode) produces an alternative to incandescent light bulbs. LEDs are often used to light the runway and may be attached to the runway platform itself. They last a long time and do not get hot, making them an ideal product for runway and fashion events. They are safe and effective.

Depending upon how elaborate the lighting plan is, most lighting designers set up lights the day before the show using motorized lifts to build the truss and hang the fixtures. The lighting technician controls the light from a control panel located at a **tech table**. The tech table is one central area where sound, lighting, and audiovisual run the show. **Audiovisual** is anything concerning both hearing and seeing. For example, if the sponsor's or designer's names need to be video projected onto the backdrop or screens, the audiovisual person is in charge of this. He or she must work closely with the lighting tech and producer to create the scene securing any video or sound presentation.

Producers can spend tens of thousands of dollars on lighting. The lighting needs, like all aspects of the show, are dependent upon the requirements of the client, the budget, and the space; also, lighting trends on the runway vary. In the eighties during the larger production shows, extravagant lighting was commonplace. Designers like Thierry Mugler and Claude Montana used big theatrics and outrageous lighting. The early 1990s experienced a return to a more refined simple show. Designers like Marc Jacobs and others opted for bright, clear, crisp runways with little to no colored lights. As the millennium progressed and technology improved, we saw a return to the big production shows of the past. The most notable, Alexander McQueen's fall 2006 show titled "The Invasion of the Hologram," featured a state-of-the-art video projection of Kate Moss.

Currently, the Thierry Mugler collection designed by Nicola Formichetti is making a serious nod back to Mugler's grand theatrics of the 1980s by implementing unique and unusual lighting techniques. He uses large moving spotlights and creates and contrasts rich, dark, distinct colors. This supports his mysterious and sinister collection. A prepared producer works within the lighting budget to secure the best and most cost-effective lights for the show.

Tech Table

The lighting control panel is most often placed in the front of the house beside the audiovisual, sound, and DJ. The majority of tech tables are located at the front of the house so the people running the boards can work in real time and troubleshoot as the show and event is taking place. Producers are generally on a headset, calling the show for the models, technical team, and backroom staff. All coordinators and producers have their own approach to calling the show. For example, Jan Strimple calls from the front of the house. According to Jan, she sits at the tech table out front and allows key members of her staff to physically send and pace the models from her cue (Personal communication, October 24, 2010). Most producers use some version of a wireless headset to communicate with all parties that need direction. A **headset** essentially provides the same function as a telephone, with hands-free operation. It allows open communication and mobility. If technical trouble arises and headsets fail, the producers should make certain all cell phones are charged and have included a hands-free earpiece as a backup means of communication. The more elaborate the show, the more crucial clear communication becomes. All technical staff must be given detailed directions and a script prior to the day of show.

The Music/Entertainment

A disc jockey, also known as a **DJ**, is traditionally, for fashion shows, the person who selects and plays recorded music for the audience. Originally, the word "disk" referred to phonograph records. Today the term includes all forms of music, no matter the medium. DJs have become

FIGURE 7.9 *DJ booth.*
Courtesy of Omer Kreso

entertainers in their own right. The DJ for a fashion show will either make a recorded music set list or play music live synced according to the pace of the show. Depending on the medium the DJ wishes to use, the DJ plays music through a mixer and public address system (PA). Today many DJs perform by using a laptop computer with music software. Examples of music software are Serato or Ableton Live. The music can also be live or it can be recorded to use as a premixed music session. The music is sent through the laptop to the mixer. The mixer control into which the sound system is connected is where the overall volume is controlled. This equipment allows the DJ to have full control over the music throughout the show. See Figure 7.9 for an example of a DJ booth.

DJs use samples and beats from already recorded music. Although DJs are most commonly used for runway shows, rotating trends in major fashion shows throughout Europe and the United States shift back and forth from having live bands to well-known celebrity DJs spinning to mixed music in real time on the runway or stage. The year 2008 saw a big trend in using musicians and DJs to complement fashions shows. For example, the band Sonic Youth played live on the stage for the Marc Jacobs fall 2008 show. Currently, designers are hiring musicians of all varieties from big-name acts to smaller indie bands to perform live at their fashion shows. Los Angeles indie-rock band The Like performed songs at Rachel Antonoff. C'N'C Costume National featured Swedish pop group You Say France and I Whistle live. On the other hand, for fall fashion week 2012 DJ Thom Bullock has mixed the music for designer Daryl Kerrigan. Josh Madden has done the same for EMU ("Fashion Week's Musical," 2011). Music and entertainment trends continue to change and are always determined by the client or designer. Producers and music coordinators work with the designers and clients to hire musicians. They also work with DJs to create the set list for the show.

Sound System

In addition to hiring disc jockeys and live bands and preparing the music, the coordinator must hire a sound technician or arrange for a sound system and **public address system** at the show. The sound system is the equipment necessary for amplifying audio and playing music for an audience. The PA is an electronic amplification system, which includes equipment like a mixer, amplifier, and loudspeakers, used to strengthen a certain sound. PAs are needed for the MC, the DJ playing prerecorded music, and live mixing. The PA system distributes the sound throughout the venue. Many locations have sound systems available for use or rent. If a system is not provided, it can be rented from a local company. The sound system and PA are checked during technical rehearsal prior to the run-through with the models and talent.

Décor

Décor is the decoration consisting of the layout and furnishings of an interior or exterior space. Many of the items previously discussed can fall under the umbrella of décor.

For fashion events décor can range from props on the runway to seating on the floor. For big themed events, custom décor can be built or rented specifically to strengthen the theme. The major décor elements like additional seating, cocktail bars, and tables are placed after the runway, staging, and the backstage have been constructed. Décor includes everything from deco tables like the ones used in 1930s to Moroccan tents. Décor companies work with the lighting technicians and production team. Generally, they begin the loading of items the night before or very early on the day of the show. Some examples of décor that can be rented or custom built include sofas, bars, unique lighting, chairs, linens, drapes, tents, and tables. How elaborate and detailed the décor is for an event depends on the budget and the client's needs.

The Backroom

All fashion show backrooms are hectic, crowded, and chaotic. It is the function of the producer to make sense out of the chaos and create an organized workroom. Changes to the model boards, lineup, and styling happen until the last minute, as designers are scrambling to complete collections. Retailers may sell a garment slated for the show or decide on highlighting additional pieces, leaving the producer and backroom team to implement changes to be executed moments before the models hit the runway. The production team's process of organizing the backroom is in three basic stages: the setup, the show, and the **breakdown**.

Setup

Before the models, hair and makeup people, seamstress, or other auxiliary staffs arrive, a core group of individuals begin the setting up process. They are known as the **setup crew**. The producer or coordinator should provide the setup crew with a copy of the backroom layout and a supplies list.

BACKROOM LAYOUT

The setup crew will work from the layout created by the production team. The layout is a plan or arrangement of the area. The layout is often completed as a schematic on a computer similar to a floor plan. A layout is a helpful tool for visualizing the backroom area and planning the dressing area.

This early crew works off the layout or floor plan and places all racks, tables, chairs, and supplies in their proper preplanned position. If the show is in a hotel, the hotel staff or décor company may handle setting up the tables and chairs that have been contracted by the client under the advisement of the backroom management team. Most production companies bring their own rolling racks, steamers, sewing machines, and other necessary backroom supplies. The setup crew is in charge of setting up the clothing racks. They must work off the layout and create the working space for hair and makeup as well as the management office. This happens, of course, only if there is no additional room already available for these areas. Trash bins, fans, and all other setup items, as required, are put in place at this time (Figure 7.10). A general list of backroom necessities and supplies is provided in Figure 7.11.

Hairstylist tables in close proximity to outlets
Hairstylist seating
Optional mirrors
Make-up artist tables
Make-up artist seating
Backroom entry/exit
Runway models waiting area to line up before walk
Fashion show shot caller
Runway walk entry
Small refreshment stand
Seamstress/Sewing repairs and garment adjustments
Fashion garment rack labelled with models' names and pictures
Accessory and shoe tables partitioned in middle, equipped with shelving underneath
Backroom entry/exit
Optional refreshment stand
Runway exit FLE into garment area for garment change
PFE and drape
Little 1 runway configuration
Note: Configuration of this backroom can be modified to accommodate the needs of the size of the fashion show, and the size of the backroom that is provided for each fashion show, as they vary in size and location. All backroom items are modular and therefore can be moved in and out of the space, and around it inside as necessary. Any runway configuration can be utilized as well.
Floor plan call out of furnishings etc
scale $\frac{1}{4}$″–1′.0″
Fashion show backroom layout option designed for Paula Taylor LLC

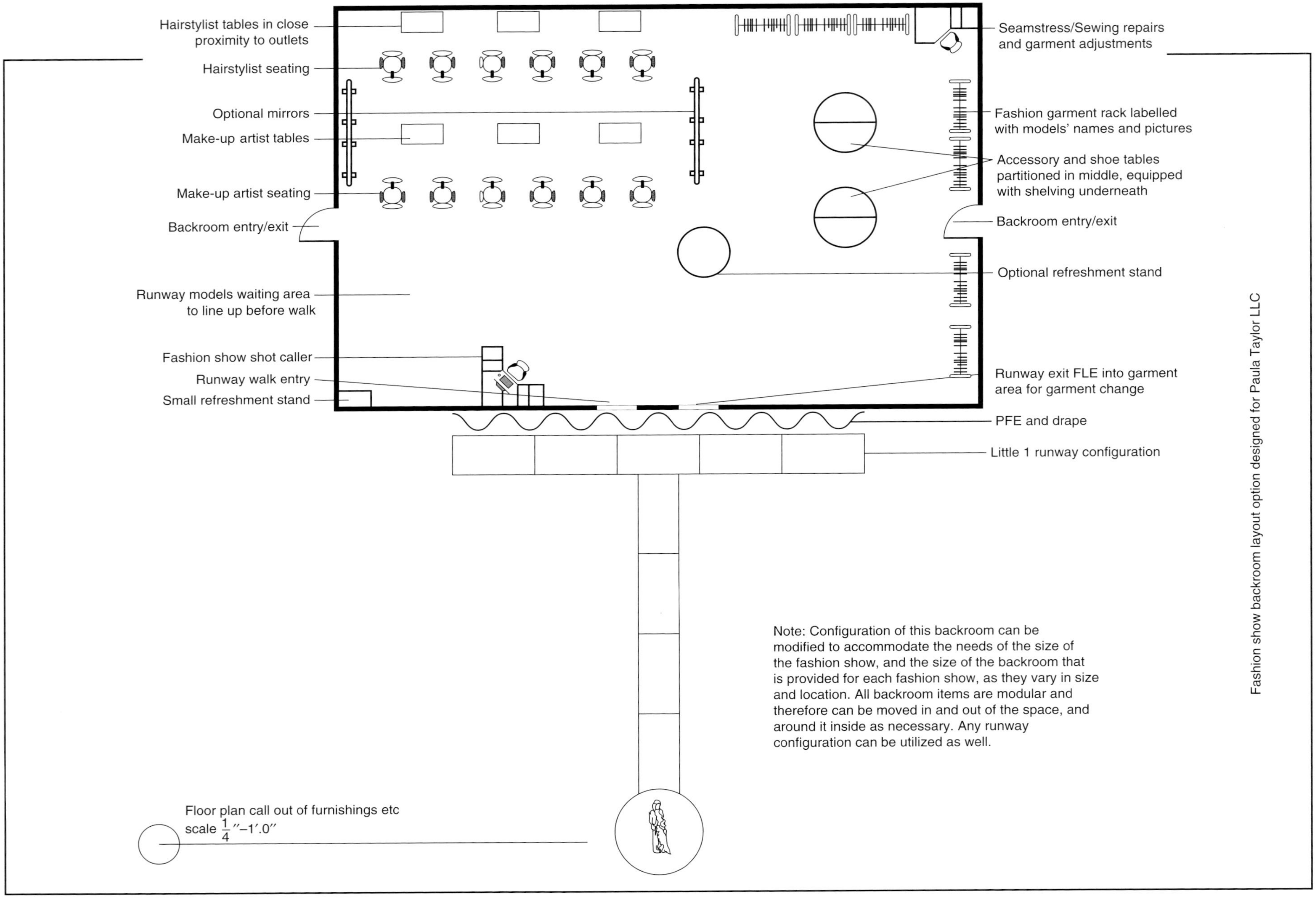

FIGURE 7.10 *Example of a backroom layout.*

Courtesy of Melanie Cortel

Supplies for Backroom Example	Complete
Tables	☐
Chairs	☐
Steamers/iron/ironing board/sewing machine	☐
Mirrors	☐
Hangers	☐
Garment bags	☐
Makeup and dress shields	☐
Trash bins	☐
Computer	☐
Printer	☐
Paper	☐
Monitor for calling the show	☐
Mirrors	☐
Dresser's aprons	☐
Accessories	☐
Inventory	☐
Additional lighting	☐
Headsets	☐
Food and beverage	☐
First aid kit	☐
Dresser tracks	☐

FIGURE 7.11 *Supplies for backroom example.*
Courtesy of Paula Taylor

PRODUCTION TEAM ARRIVAL

After the hotel staff, décor company, or production crew complete the basic setup, the members of the backroom staff arrive. Staff members, interns, and volunteers are all given backroom tasks to be completed throughout the day.

CLOTHING ARRIVAL

The clothing and accessories, having once been delivered onsite by a carrier company or the production team, must be separated and hung on specific model racks thus creating individualized **dresser tracks** (Figure 7.12).

DRESSER TRACKS

Dresser tracks are the actual racks delineated for each model. The rack holds all the clothing or looks the model is wearing in the show and has his or her model board and name attached to it. Depending on the size of the show there may be more than one model assigned per track. Each dresser is assigned a model or models and stays at the track to dress his or her models.

FIGURE 7.12 *Backroom at Angel Sanchez.*
Courtesy of Angel Sanchez

ACCESSORIES TABLE

The accessories table is the area where accessories are placed until the dresser tracks and looks are hung up on the specified rack (Figure 7.13). Often producers will bring extra accessories to have on hand for final fittings and styling of looks. At least one staff person is in charge of the accessories table. Accessories that have previously been placed with an outfit are stored in clear ziplock bags and hung next to clothing for which they have been styled. Expensive and exclusive jewelry may be safely kept on a nearby table with a representative from the designer or retailer in charge of the items and their proper storage and return.

MANAGEMENT AREA

Most producers and backroom managers create an office area to hold periodic staff meetings and work away from the total chaos of the backroom. The actual size of this area depends on the specific location and available space. It should be set up near outlets and good lighting, creating a work desk for the computer and printer as well as providing a safe place to keep the production folder, styling book, and other essential forms and materials.

FOOD AND BEVERAGE

Medium to large shows will have a minimum of twenty-three models, ten dressers, two seamstresses, hair and makeup people, and the production staff. Keeping these people hydrated and fed is crucial to creating a positive backroom environment. The day begins early and ends late. Keeping attitudes and energies high is a must. It is important not to supply heavy, greasy food that will slow people down. Focus on lean protein, power bars, fruit, and cheese. Absolutely no eating is allowed once the models are dressed and in their first looks.

FIGURE 7.13 *Accessories table.*
From David X Prutting/BFAnyc.com

DRESSERS

Dressers have one of the most important jobs in the fashion show business. They are responsible for getting models dressed quickly and correctly. The number of dressers for each show varies in direct correlation with the show's budget, garments highlighted, and the number of models cast. Most producers hire a few professional dressers and use fashion students and volunteers for the rest.

A detailed Job Description and Dresser Instruction Sheet is provided below:

Dresser Job Description and Instruction Sheet

THE FUNCTIONS OF THE DRESSER

Organized chaos! The dresser's job is one of the fastest paced and critical jobs in fashion show production. Dressers essentially help their assigned models to dress for the show. With most changes taking less than a minute, dressers and models need to create an organized fast-paced dressing system. The dressers must understand the lineup and who is in charge of getting the models to the lineup. They are responsible for executing the look in the manner the stylist, designer, and producers have created and for hanging all clothing as well as keeping their area organized. They must check off inventory sheets at the end of the show and sign off that all the garments are on the rack.

BEFORE THE SHOW IT IS SUGGESTED THAT DRESSERS

Wear comfortable shoes, as dressers will be on their feet for most of the day.

Make sure arrangements are made for transportation to the show before the day of the show.

Be on time and be ready to work.

UPON ARRIVAL

Check in at the designated entrance of the fashion event to confirm arrival with one of the assistants and sign in.

A lanyard with full name and duty (i.e., dresser) will be given, which the dresser will wear at all times when in the backroom area. If the lanyard is not worn, entrance to the backroom will be denied.

A black apron will be provided containing the following items:

- Small scissors, work lights, safety pins, threaded needles, a writing pen, sharpie, hem tape, lint roller, and makeup mask.

Wear this apron at all times in preparation of and during dressing duties.

One of the production assistants will provide a Dressing Track Assignment Sheet, which will assign tracks.

A tour of the backroom will be given to dressers by one of the production assistants. Become familiar with the dressing area(s).

Prior to the backroom tour, dressers will be escorted to the dresser track, which will be their work station.

PRESHOW TRACK DUTIES

A dresser track will have anywhere from two to five complete looks and a **model board** containing a photo of the model, photos of the looks, and styling notes attached for reference.

Remove the garment bags from the clothing (if necessary). Note which garment bags go with which garments. Store the bags in a place near the assigned track. If you notice any imperfections on a garment before the show, notify one of the production assistants immediately.

All the outfits should be placed in order on the clothing rack consistent with the order referred to on the model board.

If multiple clothing pieces are put on a single clothing hanger, remove the additional pieces and place each one on its own separate clothing hanger.

For all the garments on the rack/track unbutton all buttons, unzip all zippers, and untie all ties. This will make it easier to dress models quickly. Carefully remove all tags from all garments and accessories. Store them accordingly with the bags/boxes within which the garment came.

Fill in or adjust an already completed **inventory sheet**; write down every garment on the rack/track with descriptions— sign off on this after the show.

MODEL FITTING

When the model arrives, one of the production assistants will introduce the model to the assigned dresser.

Depending on the predetermined order the model will go to hair and makeup for a fitting.

If the model is sent to hair and makeup, then the dresser will do the following after he or she is finished and has returned:

- Fit the model one look at a time and style the look, referring to the model styling board. The stylist or producer must approve each one of the looks. Take the model for approval. Thereafter, make changes to the look in accordance with instructions.
- If a garment doesn't fit correctly, take the model to alterations (one of the professional dressers) and they will fit the garment. Occasionally, depending on the proximity of available garments, the producer or stylist will replace a piece of clothing or accessories.

Once assigned looks have been approved, undress the model and return the garment to its designated position on the clothing rack.

Send the model to hair and makeup promptly afterwards if this has not already been accomplished.

Twenty minutes before the show starts, dress the model in his or her first look styled and ready to go.

- Be careful of makeup staining clothing. Use makeup masks when dressing models with already applied makeup.

(Continued)

(Continued)

One of the assistants will line the model up when needed. Stay at the rack at all times during the show.

DURING THE SHOW

Dress models as quickly as possible in the looks and in the order predetermined.

Keep clothing off the floor at all times.

AFTER THE SHOW

Check your garments for damages, stains, tears, and so on. If there is a problem with a garment, take it to one of the backroom staff. Put all garments back into their respective garment bags and boxes and onto their racks. Deal with the accessories in the same manner.

An inventory sheet that the dresser must sign will be provided. This assures that all the garments are present and in their original condition.

Return the lanyard and apron if borrowed from the production team.

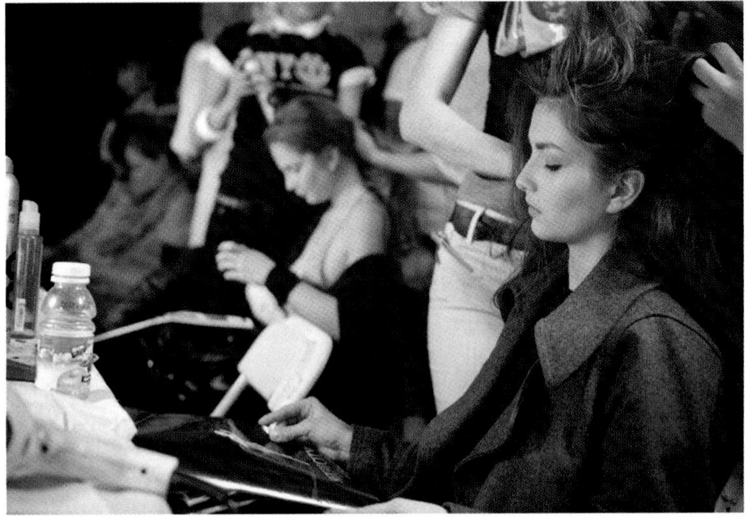

FIGURE 7.14 *Hair backstage at Angel Sanchez.*
Courtesy of Angel Sanchez

HAIR AND MAKEUP ARRIVE

A production staff member takes the hair and makeup team to their allocated area. Examples of the hair and makeup direction are provided by the producer, designer, or stylist and placed in a space as a visible reference for the makeup artist and hair stylist. The hair and makeup people should be scheduled weeks to months prior to the event (Figure 7.14). The producer or stylist should have previously given them directions about hair and makeup. Most stylists send examples via a vision board or by e-mailing photos. A practice session a week prior to show date with volunteer hair and makeup models is recommended.

MODELS ARRIVE

A model coordinator or staff member should check in the models as they arrive, and make certain that a model release has been signed. The model is then assigned to one of the following people: hair stylist, makeup person, dresser, or seamstress. If it is to the seamstress, it will be for the final fitting.

FITTINGS

Fittings are important elements of successful fashion shows. As stated in an earlier chapter, one of the main reasons to hold a fashion show or event is to sell product and strengthen a brand's image. Clothing highlighted on the runway must fit the model to perfection. A **fitting** is the act of trying on clothes for the purpose of enabling adjustment (tailoring) to the clothing to ensure a proper fit. It is completed by the designers, assistant designers, seamstress, and/or qualified dressers. Measurements are taken and the proper adjustments are made to the clothing or pattern to guarantee a proper fit. The locations of fittings can vary; most take place at the designer's studios prior to the show and continue to happen until the day of the show. The day-of-show fittings are considered **final fittings**. Regional shows and charity and student events with smaller budgets and borrowed merchandise generally only hold fittings the day of the event. It is important to have a qualified designer, seamstress, or dresser on site to assure the garments fit the model properly. Although models' measurements are supplied on their model card, it is important to update these measurements as bodies change. It is imperative to get proper measurement and perform a fitting to guarantee the clothing selected will work on the specific model. If clothing is borrowed from retail stores, actual alterations on the item are not allowed. In such cases the dresser or seamstress must apply some quick tricks of the trade to make the clothing appear as if it fits the model without damaging the integrity of the clothing (Figure 7.15).

FIGURE 7.15 *Bridal show fittings.*
Courtesy of Matt Trettel and Bruce Vassar

The Show

The backroom becomes highly chaotic and this naturally leads to great stress placed on all the backroom participants. The models are changing into looks and quickly taking their place in the final lineup (Figure 7.16). The backroom staff needs to be prepared for quick changes, makeup touchups, and fast returns to the lineup. This is the time when all the previous organization and preparation is taken to task. Can the team stay calm and organized, keep people moving in an orderly manner, and deliver a smooth successful show? The show begins with getting the models into look number one and sending them to the line. This happens twenty minutes prior to top of show (the start of the event). The dressers must have all the models dressed in their first garment and lined up according to the final lineup sheet and ready to be sent down the runway. If the producer has done a thorough job, he or she has hired people who are invested in the success of the show. It is important to remember that professionals and volunteers alike—essentially every person working the show—feel like their job or responsibility is the most important one in the room. Although this is an admirable trait, trouble can arise from such a view. For example, if an overzealous makeup artist or hair stylist pulls a model out of the lineup to fix the hair, or stops the model on the way, this will cause a break in the flow of the show. Eager dressers may take things into their own hands and add to a look, thus diverting from the model board direction. Issues like these can ruin the pacing of the show, throw off the lineup, and alter the ultimate vision. All team members and others working backstage must be clearly informed of how critical are the timing and direction provided from the stylist and producer (Figure 7.17).

FIGURE 7.16 *Angel Sanchez backstage with garments.*
Courtesy of Angel Sanchez

CALLING THE SHOW

The person in charge of calling the show, sending the models on the runway, and setting both the pace and tone needs to have all models in order, styled according to the model boards, and sent to the line on time to keep the show on schedule.

FIGURE 7.17 *Angel Sanchez waiting to send models out on the runway.*
Courtesy of Angel Sanchez

Breakdown

It may be all champagne and parties post show for the designers and VIP attendees; however, the production team still has a great deal of work to accomplish after the show. The dressers must change their models and make sure all inventory is returned in perfect condition to the model's track. The models are then checked out and are the first to leave. Once the majority of people have left the backroom, the breakdown crew arrives. (More on post-show duties will be discussed in Chapter 8.)

BREAKDOWN CREW

A breakdown crew is a group of individuals hired or acting as volunteers to physically deconstruct the backroom. Breakdown crew can be as little as two people and as many as ten. They are in charge of taking down the dressing tracks, packing up inventory and accessories, and emptying the backspace, leaving only the large items for the décor company, or hotel staff, to handle. The breakdown for shows can take up to several hours. It is important to have some fresh, energized staff to help move the process along. Inventory is either immediately returned to the designer's showroom or stored in a secured location for return within twenty-four hours.

Understanding the general backroom setup, showtime, and breakdown process helps a new producer be prepared for setting up and running his or her own backroom. Working within a confined arena with dozens of people is a challenge in and of itself. Keeping a cool head and referring to all the prepared materials will aid in getting the proper outcome that is created out of the organized chaos. All producers strive for this.

review

Chapter Review

Decisions about where to place the staging, runway, lighting, and all other décor for the fashion show or event are crucial to any producer's success. Creating a front of the house and back of the house that make for an easy working environment while visually supporting the theme is of paramount concern. This chapter discussed the basic layout for both the front of the house and the back of the house. The front of the house is the public location where the audience and attendees will interact. The back of the house is the private area in which the production team, models, dressers, and hair and makeup people work to prepare for the show. The chapter detailed what is included in both the front of the house and back of the house areas. It discussed the different types of runways, seating, and staging, while touching on the roles and placement of the lights, tech table, and entertainment. The vision of the show is determined in part by the effective use of space and placement. The more unique and exciting these aspects are, the more engaged the audience will be, leading to sales and creating a memorable, newsworthy event.

case

Case Problem

The Tastemakers Production Company was preparing for a big charity fashion show at the Luxury Lifestyle Shopping Center. The show was the first of its kind in the city. The producers decided to have a round runway constructed and had several meetings to discuss the width of the actual runway. The client who was a marketing director from the center itself asked if the models could come out at a minimum of two at a time. The reasoning was that this was a retail center and they wanted as many retailers as possible to take part in the event, but only wanted a thirty-minute show. The producer agreed. The runway dimensions were ordered and the muslin to cover the top and the draping for the side was ordered to fit the predetermined measurements.

The morning of the show, the producer saw the runway being constructed and noticed that four feet appeared very narrow considering this was a raised circular runway with seating on the inside and outside of the circle. To have models passing on this runway could be very dangerous not only for themselves but perhaps for the audience as well.

When the producer became aware of this challenge, she approached the décor company who was in the process of building the runway and asked if they could add to the staging. She was informed this would be impossible as the pieces they had only came four foot and they did not have enough with them to accommodate her needs. In addition, there would be no time to order the additional pieces nor did they have enough muslin and draping. After some further discussion and looking at what was in their trucks, one additional two-by-four-foot piece was found. They also were confident that if angled correctly there would be enough muslin and draping to cover the addition.

Questions to Consider

1. How can you utilize the one two-by-four-foot runway piece to your advantage?
2. How should you pace the show so that it still meets the client's demands and provides a safe platform for models?
3. How could this situation have been avoided?
4. Using Figure 7.18 as an example, create a new runway layout including the extra platform. Use grid paper or the websites listed in the Web resources at the end of the chapter.

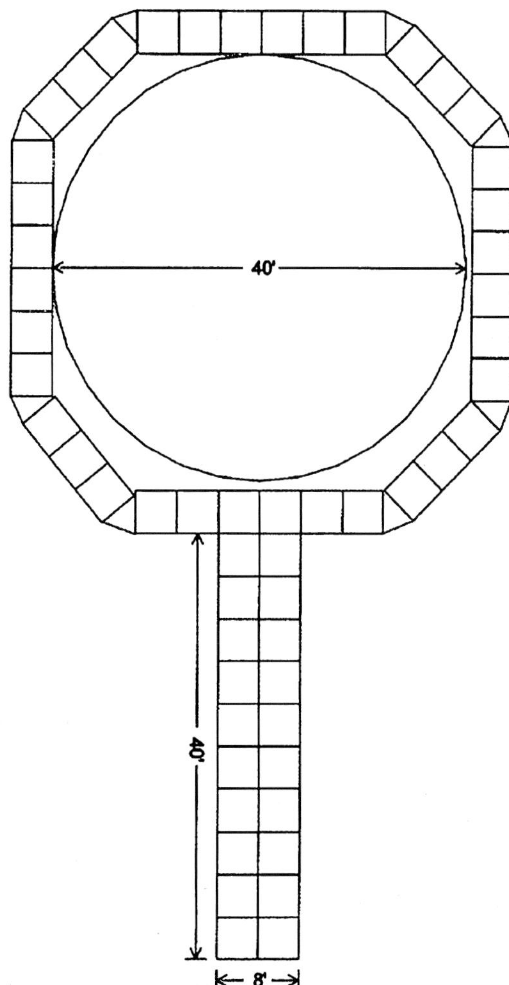

FIGURE 7.18 *Circular runway example.*

Courtesy of Melanie Cortel

Questions for Review and Discussion

1. Name several different types of runways and discuss the pros and cons of each type.
2. What are the components that need to be in a layout and floor plan?
3. What type of seating is most commonly used in runway shows and why?
4. Discuss some unique and creative ideas for seating, locations, and staging.
5. Why are headsets a necessity for producers and coordinators during fashion/runway events?
6. Who should be on the headsets?
7. Discuss the role of the dresser and why it is such a key position backstage. What are some of the items a dresser must have in his or her apron?

Out and About Activities

1. Go online and research the latest lighting trends for fashion shows.
2. Attend a local fashion show or event and take notice of the layout of the room.
3. Write a three-page summary about the event. Consider these questions to be answered:

   Did the layout work?
   What could be improved and why?
   What type of stage and runway was used?
   What type of seating?
   Where is check-in or registration?
   Was there entertainment live music or a DJ?
   Was there commentary on the runway?
4. Schedule an interview with two industry professionals in your area such as:

   Lighting technician
   Décor/event company
   Sound engineer
   Disc jockey
5. Volunteer to be a dresser at an up-and-coming fashion event.
6. Start stocking your dressing apron.
7. Visit the website http://acwworldwide.com and compare and contrast the most recent Hugo Boss runway shows to those from 2011.

In Class Activity

Evaluating the Fit of the Model

Break the class into teams of two with one student playing the seamstress and the other the model. Practice taking proper measurements. Evaluate the fit of the model using the form given at the end of the text.

Ongoing Fashion Show Project

Creating the Show Space, Selecting the Music, and Final Lineup

Add sections in the production folder titled Layout, Floor Plan, Dressers' List, Tech Team, Lighting Plan, Music List, and Supplies for the Backroom

1. Create a basic layout and floor plan for both the back of the house and front of the house for your event. Remember to consider all the relevant elements discussed in the chapter. Consider the staging, lighting, runway, tech table, seating, backroom area, and all additional décor.
2. Create a song list for the DJ or band.
3. Using the template at the end of the text, create a supplies list for the backroom.

Terminology of the Trade

audiovisual 125
back of the house 118
calling the show 133
DJ 125
décor 126
dresser 130
dresser track 129
final fitting 132
fitting 132
floor plan 119
front of the house 118
headset 125
inventory sheet 131
layout 119
lighting 124
model board 131
muslin 120
public address system 126
runway 120
set up 127
setup crew 127
stage 120
staging 120
swag bags 123
tech table 125
theater seating 123
the breakdown 127

Web Resources

www.floorplanner.com
www.smallblueprinter.com
www.totallightingsupport.com

Bibliography

Brody, C. (2010, March 16). Fashion's 10 Most Dramatic Runway Shows. In *Flavorwire*. Retrieved August 4, 2011, from http://flavorwire.com/77895/fashions-10-most-dramatic-runway-shows

Clott, S. (2010, January 15). Erin Wasson to Ditch Tents for ABC Carpet & Home. In *New York Fashion*. Retrieved June 20, 2011, from http://nymag.com/daily/fashion/2010/01/post_15.html

Fashion Week's Musical Guests. (2011, February 9). *Issac Mizrahi Says I Do*. Retrieved March 7, 2011, from http://www.wwd.com/fashion-news/fashion-scoops/name-that-tune-issac-says-i-do-plastic

Foreman, K., Bonet-Black, T., & Baraga, T. (2011, March 21). *On the Scene: Sounding Off.* Retrieved September 15, 2011, from http://www.wwd.com/fashion-news/fashion-features/on-the-scene-sounding-off-3559963

Lacoste Fetes Collaboration with Adler. (2011, June 25). *WWD*. Retrieved June 25, 2011, from http://www.wwd.com/fashion-news/fashion-scoops/lacoste-fetes-collaboration-with-adler-3686380

Mower, S. (2011). Hermes Fall 2011 RTW. In *Vogue*. Retrieved August 4, 2011, from http://www.vogue.com/collections/fall-2011/mhermes/review

Phelps, N. (2010) *Erin Wasson X RVCA.* Retrieved September 18, 2011, from http://www.style.com/fashionshow/reviews/f2010RTW-EWRVCA.

SHOWTIME

LEARNING OBJECTIVES

After completing this chapter, you will be able to:

- Know the importance of the day of the show schedule, timeline, script, and contingency plan
- Discuss the different types of rehearsals
- Gain knowledge about how to have a rehearsal
- Describe opening, closing, and striking the show
- Know about the views of an industry insider
- Understand the terminology of the trade

It's about how you prepare, how you think and your inspiration. Are you the designer who wants to be the person who designed the royal wedding gown, or are you the person who does not believe in the white dress?

—YEOHLEE TENG, fashion designer

You've spent months preparing for the show. You worked with the clients, created the budget, secured the press, hired the models, held fittings, and put together the perfect team. Every detail, contract, and plan is well documented in your production binder. Your goal is to execute the designer's, client's, or retailer's vision beyond their expectations. This is the day all your hard work pays off. The endless hours of styling perfect looks and running the model lineup over and over in your head and on paper all are to guarantee a seamless well-timed event. It will be over sooner than you think. However, until the final parade of models heads down that runway, the team has a long day ahead of it. Forget about sleep! It's showtime!!

This chapter outlines the day of the show. It addresses how all of the elements of the show come together. The focus is on the steps necessary to produce a runway show; however, it should be noted that many of the requirements to produce a fashion show and the differing types of fashion events are the same for any industry that requires a presentation of a product or needs to have an event for any other purpose.

The chapter reviews the day of show timeline, scripts keeping in mind any last-minute needs or changes, and contingency plans. It continues with profiling the importance of check-in, sound check, rehearsals, choreography, *and pacing of the models. In Chapter 7 we discussed in detail the setup of the front of the house and the back of the house. This chapter, however, is on the specifics of running the show and how to troubleshoot last-minute problems that may arise. Problems like a model no show, fitting disasters, and staff challenges all will be scrutinized. Finally, the chapter explores closing the show, the finale, and striking the show. (See Figures 8.1 and. 8.2.)*

FIGURE 8.1 *Jeremy Scott models at Milk Studio.*
Courtesy of Carly Otness/BFAnyc.com

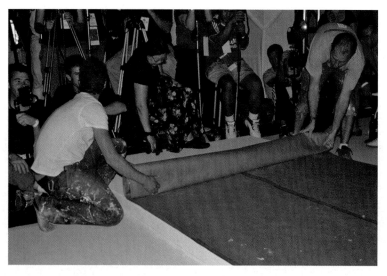

FIGURE 8.2 *Rolling out the runway.*
Courtesy of John Calder

Day of Event Timeline

Timelines are schedules of activities and events. It has been established that a timeline is one of many beneficial tools a producer uses to organize the planning of the show. An ongoing timeline is essential to meeting deadlines. The timeline is necessary to stay on schedule during the long hours of preparation and meetings. The timeline must be shared with all key figures involved in both the front of the house and the back of the house. The rough timeline should be e-mailed to all management and contracted workers such as hair and makeup stylists, technical staff, entertainment people, dressers, and events and décor people at least a week prior to the event. It must be kept updated in real time. Often two timelines are needed: a general events timeline and a specific timeline. A general events timeline and a specific production timeline can vary. For example, when coordinating charity shows, the organization may create a day of event timeline. Such timelines are general in nature and include schedules for the MC, lighting cues, sponsor announcements, and thank-you(s) prior to the runway show itself. It is important that the production team be familiar with this timeline and each member have a copy in the events binder. On the other hand, a **production timeline** is much more detailed. It is a written schedule documenting all production happenings and events beginning with the production team load-in and ending with the breakdown of the show. Both timelines are important because they enable coordinators to stay on schedule. All timeline formats should be simple and easy to understand. The function is to keep everyone informed and organized. It is common to have one person on the production team ensure that the producer/coordinator is sticking to the timeline and those all-important rehearsals, talent, and technical meetings are met. Determining the length of the runway show is done weeks prior to the event and built into the timeline (Figure 8.3).

Day before Show		Contact
Time:	**Event**	
11:00 AM	Total lighting load-in	
11:30 AM	Sound wave load-in	
12:00 PM	Design definitions load-in	
1:00 PM	Communications load-in	
TBD	Cirrus Visual deliver programs	
TBD	Tucson Lifestyle delivers magazines	
3:00 PM	Furniture delivery	
Day of Show		
Time:	**Event**	
10:00 PM	Set up	
	Position racks and model boards	
	Position work lights	
	Position fans	
	Craft services	
	Set up makeup and hair area	
	Set up changing area for alterations	
	Set up sign-in and management area	
10:30 AM	Break	
11:30 AM	Dressers arrive	
	Unload and rack clothes	
	Generate tape labels for every garment bag	
	If hangers are proprietary, ID# of hangers	
	Inventory and sequence outfits	
	Bag jewelry accessories and marry to looks	
	Place model names above appropriate racks	
1:00 PM	10 min. break	
3:00 PM	Professional dresser sets alterations area	
3:30 PM	Female models arrive	
	All models sign in	
	Production sound check	
	Models meet dressers and fitting begin	
	Models will be sent to alterations area as needed	
	Models sent to hair and makeup	

FIGURE 8.3 *Production day timeline example.*

Courtesy of Paula Taylor Productions

Day of Show		
5:00 PM	Male models start arriving	
5:30 PM	Model meeting and quick rehearsal with producer	
7:00 PM	All volunteer dressers are present	
	Dressers familiarize themselves with all outfits and complete inventory	
8:00 PM	Producer address models	
8:15 PM	All models in first looks	
8:45 PM	Top of show!	

FIGURE 8.3 *(Continued)*

Scripts

A script is defined as the written text of a stage play or screenplay. Scripts are beneficial to all shows no matter what the size. If the show has any production elements beyond traditional modeling, a script is helpful. The script can be written by the director and/or producer and is distributed to all the talent and technical staff by the stage manager. For the function of fashion events and runway shows, a script is the basic text outlining lighting, audio, verbal, and visual cues for the technical team and the performers. It is a written outline of the roles for the talent,

London Calling Production Sequence Script Example
Siren sound (DJ queue)
Show opens
Stage /Runway dark (Lighting queue)
House lighting dimmed (Lighting queue)
30 seconds of pre-recorded British street sounds with English newsboys calling out "Extra! Extra!" (DJ queue)
Siren sound (DJ queue)
Scene starts with soft lighting (Lighting queue)
First image (A/V queue)
Carnaby Street image black and white on screen (A/V queue)
Characters and models are frozen until the Dandy character (downstage) will bring characters to life (production note)
Opening music plays for 2 min. and 24 sec. (DJ queue)
Siren sound (DJ queue)
Special lighting effects begin (Lighting queue) as
Union Jack Flag image on screen (A/V queue)
A/V Model wearing British flag gown goes down the runway (production note)
Runway show begins store logos projected while exclamation points and mod art swirl image alternated throughout the slide presentation. (A/V queue)
Union Jack image appears on screen (A/V queue) as
"God Save the Queen" by the Sex Pistols plays (DJ queue) as
Rotating light show highlighting garments (Lighting queue) as
The finale parade of models with British flags head out (production note)
House light up (Lighting)

FIGURE 8.4 *Script for production team.*

Courtesy of Paula Taylor Productions

dancers, actors, MCs, and performances. The script provides another means to stay on schedule and prepares the talent and technical team, prior to rehearsal, in all the nuances of the show. Scripts can be very simple, highlighting important transitions and functions. Scripts act as the voice of the director and producer. They can also be incredibly detailed, leaving nothing to interpretation. Scripts should be sent out prior to the day of the show and reviewed during rehearsals to make sure they work in real life. Often the script or performance needs to be modified. Big-budget shows may have rehearsals prior to the day of the show, but for most fashion events the location is rented for one day only. Therefore, it is not in the budget to arrange for the models, talent, and tech team to be together for a full rehearsal before the day of the event. See Figure 8.4 for an example of a production team script.

The Contingency Plan

The contingency plan is the backup plan or plan B as it's known in most events planning business (Figure 8.5). The contingency plan is a comprehensive course of action to be followed if the chosen plan fails or an existing situation changes. In the fashion world you can bet that situations will change and plans will fail. It is essential that the coordinator create an ongoing plan B, for every detail of the show. The backup plan should be written and made available weeks before the show. It is generally used on the day of the event. For example, if there is a model no show or a model isn't fitting into the clothing selected for him or her, having scheduled a few replacements with similar measurements is a plan B. If the show's location is set outside and the forecast calls for rain, a tent readily available and built into the budget is a plan B. If the DJ's hard drive crashes, having the music backed up on disk is a plan B. In this business the production team must be prepared for anything and everything to go wrong. A contingency plan will address issues when and if they happen.

	Problem	Plan B
Runway	Problems with runway: Muslin yardage insufficient, runway unsafe, runway insufficient in size	Order extra yardage and staging components.
Models	A model unavailable.	Hire extra models with similar measurements
Music	Music failure	The producer saves multiple copies of the music on disc, flash drive, and computer.
Production Team	Staff falls ill during show, staff no show, staff sent home	Cross training, extra staff on call
MC/Entertainment	No show	Have backup MC and Entertainment on call
Lighting	Lighting fails	Lighting tech utilizes emergency backup equipment Location provides in-house support
Sound	Sound failing, not synchronized	In-house backup PA Refer to prerecorded sound on jump drive or disk
Volunteers	No show, failing at duties	Have other volunteers on call Relocate to different job position or send home
Hair & Makeup	No show, Pulling models out of lineup causing a delay in show	Have backup Hair and Makeup on call. Work with a limited crew. Change pacing of show while backstage management corrects problem. Send out fill-in model to keep correct timing of the show.

FIGURE 8.5 *Contingency plan example.*

Once all the plans and timelines are in place, your day can begin. It starts with the production staff check-in, a simple yet important task. After the setup crew is finished and gone, the staff check-in begins. A sign-in sheet is the easiest form of check-in. Each staff member once checked in is given a name badge with his or her job description printed on it and an identifying **lanyard** to wear. A lanyard is a neck cord that attaches to the name badge and is worn around the neck. In most backrooms, if you do not have an identifying nametag, you will not be allowed backstage. Once the management team checks in the dressers, hair and makeup people, and seamstresses following the same process as check-in for the team, everyone can then get to work. Each show and production team has a different approach. Following the timeline is important to stay on track for rehearsals among other things. One key item that appears on most timelines is a **rehearsal**. There are several types of rehearsals: technical rehearsal, run-through rehearsal, and dress rehearsal.

The **tech rehearsal** is a practice session that consists of testing all the technology being used in the performance, that is, lighting, sound, and special effects. Its purpose is to identify and prevent mistakes from happening during the actual fashion show. The technical rehearsal gives the technical team a dry run to see how all the elements such as lighting, sound, and special effects will impact each other. The practice session allows for last-minute changes to be made prior to the dress rehearsal and showtime. The **run-through** is a rehearsal of the show in the order of the script. It includes showing the models the choreography and pacing of the show. Models are not dressed in the garments for the show during run-throughs. The **dress rehearsal** is a term taken from the stage or theater, which is the final rehearsal or practice of a live show, in which everything is conducted as it would be in a real performance. Models or talent are dressed in garments or costumes for this rehearsal. It is often held a day before the actual event, or very early in the morning the day of the event. The majority of fashion shows do not have dress rehearsals, as they are costly. If a full dress rehearsal is scheduled, it should be organized and executed as quickly as possible. The longer the rehearsal takes, the more money it will cost. Time ought to be allotted with the production staff prior to the rehearsal to set up and break down a modified dressing area for the models to change into garments. Professional models and technical professionals are paid to participate in rehearsals, and are best scheduled for only the time they are needed. Following timelines and schedules will help keep the rehearsal moving and within the budget. Many planners schedule time to practice pacing the models down the catwalk during the run-through or dress rehearsal. It is important to run-through the detailed big openings, closing, and any large production fundamentals of the show, such as dancers, movie clips, and other performances or presentations. The coordinator and stage manager need to be certain that all cues are following the script and are workable. It is during rehearsal that a producer notices issues that are not working and he or she will need to make adjustments to the script. For instance, the planner might realize that the lighting is too dramatic, taking away from the garments, or the music is not loud enough to make the impact that he or she was seeking. In addition, the rehearsal gives the models and talent an opportunity to practice the pacing and posing of the show. It is during rehearsal that the models will receive detailed direction on their walk, and inspiration for the show. This is the moment to make certain the show is paced according to the scheduled allotted time.

Show Length

As discussed in a previous chapter, fashion shows vary in length of time. They vary based on which category of show is being produced and the product highlighted. Generally, professional fashion week shows are no longer than fifteen to twenty minutes, highlighting thirty to sixty garments. Larger production shows incorporating more than one retailer and designer can showcase up to 100 garments and may last thirty-five to forty minutes. The length of the show depends upon the number of looks sent down the runway, how many models are out at once, and how many changes there are for each model. As a general rule, a show with fifty-five looks or more is considered a medium to large show and requires a minimum of fifteen to twenty models. Once the producer, model coordinator, or stage manager determines the pacing of the models—for example, are they heading out one at a time or two or more at a time—a rough estimation of the length of the show can be calculated. Like everything in fashion, calculating a show is not an exact science. The person in charge of pacing the models needs to make quick decisions regarding timing according to how quickly the changes are made, poses or marks are scheduled, and the models are walking. Additional elements that affect the length of a show are detailed choreography and music selection.

Choreography

Choreography is the sequence of steps or movements in the show. Properly executed creative choreography can highlight important aspects of the show, help with cues, and keep the attention of the audience. Poorly executed choreography may make the show appear dated and unprofessional. New designers, students, and charities often overdo choreography on the catwalk, creating theatrics that take away from the garments. Movement and dancing on the runway have come in and out of popularity depending on the trends in the industry. In Betsey Johnson's "Le Tour de Betsey" spring 2011 ready-to-wear show, her opening scene began with her on a bicycle and continued with models on skateboards highlighting the ecofriendly, well-choreographed theme. Big-budget production shows have incorporated and scheduled dance performances, talented gymnasts, and other nontraditional movements on stage. These elements, when selected to complement the target market and well rehearsed, will leave the guest with a memorable experience. Most heavily choreographed segments happen at the opening of the runway show, capturing the attention of the audience and signifying the beginning of the show.

Opening the Show

Minutes prior to the top of the show, the models must be dressed in their first looks. Only a skeleton crew from hair and makeup stay to perform quick hair-style changes and makeup touchups. All challenges with models and fitting issues have to be resolved by this point. It does not matter from where the coordinator plans to call, whether from the show, from out front, or backstage. Now it is time to grab the clipboard, check the headsets with the technical team, and begin having the models line up in order. The room goes dark, the music starts, and the lighting cues begin; it's **showtime**!

The opening of a runway show should grab the attention of the audience and keep them engaged. The opening should use powerful music, lighting, choreography, and styling. Designers have their strongest, most recognizable models open a show, setting the stage for an unforgettable event. The pacing and calling of the runway show is now in the hands of the producer/coordinator. According to the needs of the show, the coordinator is calling the show and is cueing all technical personnel. This includes the DJ, audiovisual, and the lighting technician; it is imperative that the dressers, staff, and stylist continue to have models change into their proper look and send them to line up in order. The person calling the show is only as good as the team preparing the model. No models or talent should arrive at the lineup with tags on their clothes, ill-fitted shoes, in the wrong outfit, or with flyaway hair, unless that is the desired look given to hair and makeup. Garment changes occur within minutes. Even with all the detailed preparation, unusual things that were not considered in the planning can happen. A model can fall, hurting herself or himself, thus slowing down the pacing of the show and drawing attention away from the event. The music can stop, skip, or be wrong. If a live band is playing, a guitar string can break. An amp might blow. A steamer not turned off, as a result of a staff member's lapse of memory, can spit extremely hot water on backstage help or ruin an expensive garment. Any number of issues can and will happen. The real solution is simple. The show must go on. The producer must have backup models, extra clothes, a DJ that can quickly keep the beat, and a band that understands some music is better than nothing. A drumbeat, for instance, could provide a dramatic pause and give the guitarist time to change strings. Only with experience and planning can a coordinator get in the habit of asking all the right questions and attempting to foresee all the challenges. A clear-headed, quick-on-the-feet producer will learn, grow, and know better next time. What took months in planning is over in what seems an instant. When the script and model lineup are approaching their final scene, then it is time to cue for the closing sequence.

Closing the Show

The closing of the show is a major celebrated milestone. It should be highlighted with lighting changes, dramatic styling, and adjustments in the tempo of the music, alerting the crowd that the show will soon be over but not soon forgotten. Creating an extraordinary ending is a perfect way to keep your brand in the minds of the consumers, leaving your audience wanting more and looking ahead for next season's collection or next year's show. A charity or student show may include sponsor acknowledgments and closing remarks and announcements.

Finale

Once the last model walks the runway, and the show has ended, it is common for designers to send all models to walk one after another in a parade manner called a finale. Traditionally it is at this time that the designer follows the last model out and takes a much-deserved bow. The house lights go up and the audience heads to one of many after parties (Figure 8.6).

After Parties

Whether it's swimming in the pool on the roof of the Gansevoort Hotel for the Nycked Swimwear's "dip into cool" spring summer 2010 after party or an intimate dinner for twenty at the Zadig and Voltaire after party at the standard hotel, the after party is as important as the show itself. Such parties are smattered with celebrities, editors, and bloggers. Getting into the hottest after party is on every fashionable A-lister's mind during fashion week. For the designers and brands, these parties are excellent public relations tools. They are a natural progression from the catwalk. After parties keep people talking about the show and give the

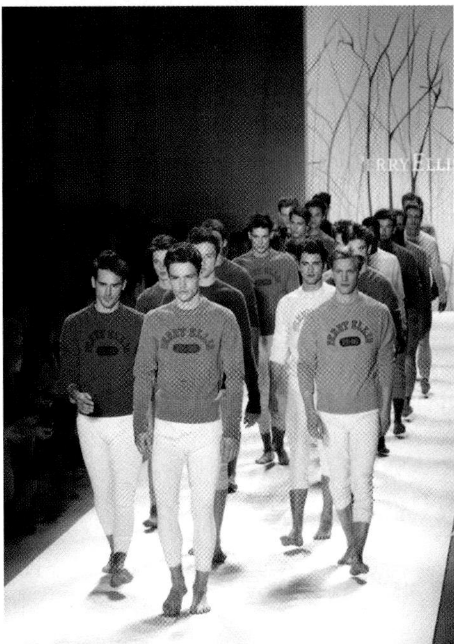

FIGURE 8.6 *Perry Ellis models on the runway.*
Courtesy of Richard Brown Phonography

designer time to connect with clients and press, creating a buzz around the brand. A distinctive after party will get the show talked about, blogged about, and tweeted about for weeks. As for the production team, they won't be playing Def Jam rock star with Charlotte Ronson or sipping champagne at the new Chanel boutique in Soho with Karl Lagerfeld. They have a show to **strike**.

Striking the Show

"Striking a show" is a phrase taken from the theater industry and refers to physically taking down the set, backroom, and stage. Every breakdown or strike is different, depending on the location of the show.

Professional crews are contracted to break down the major structures. However, individual designers, stage managers, and backroom managers are responsible for striking their own collections, racks, and backroom materials. The production team is expected to leave the dressing area in its original state. Most producers hire breakdown crews to strike a show. Coordinators negotiate with all contracted parties such as lighting, sound, and décor people to schedule breakdown and include it in the budget and agreements.

Hotels and convention locations have service crews that are contracted in advance to clean and break down. Even then, however, the show staff is responsible for returning the dressing area to its original state and returning all merchandise to designers, specialty boutiques, and retailers. If contracted to produce the front of the house elements, the production team should work closely with hotel staff and contracted professionals to ensure a seamless breakdown of décor, props, staging, and materials.

Retail shows, trunk shows, and pop ups require less time to break down. However, these shows usually incorporate direct selling post show. They demand that the producer return garments to the rack, clearing the sales area quickly. They require getting garments to the floor for anxious customers to try on.

Merchandise Return

Once the show is over, the merchandise should be removed from the off-site location and returned to retailers and designers as quickly as possible. Clothes must be returned to the retailers in the condition they were borrowed. If any damages occurred, the garment should be dry-cleaned, pressed, and steamed before it is returned, and all hang tags and buttons reattached. Many professional producers hire a service to wrap the clothing and return it to the retailers. It is important for the producer to schedule ahead of time the day and time to return the garments. Garments are to be "signed off" upon return to the retail store, on the merchandise selection record, by a manager or owner of the store. Both parties should inventory all items returned to the sales floor promptly.

Accessories Handling

Accessories are small items carried or worn to complement a garment or outfit. Scarves, hats, handbags, jewelry, and shoes are considered accessories for the runway. Special care should be taken when using borrowed accessories. These delicate items are easily misplaced or broken. The stylist, dressers, and backroom team should make certain that accessories are clearly marked, bagged, and kept on or near the models track. The majority of retailers will not lend shoes for a runway show. If shoes are on loan it is common practice to tape the bottom of the shoes to protect them. This tape must be removed prior to returning the shoes. Seasoned show planners have style closets or storage spaces full of accessories to complement certain looks and provide variety for styling. These items are best kept in plastic bins and clearly labeled for easy identification. The style closet accessories ought to be packed up post show, inventoried, and returned to the storage location. Keeping a running inventory of items on an Excel inventory sheet will allow for members of the styling team to review the inventory without having to physically go to the storage location.

Keeping Connected

As a fashion coordinator, staying in contact and thanking the clients that hire you is important. Never assume you will always get the job. Thank-you notes should be sent to all clients; they should never be a stock form letter. Make each thank-you personal. Simple touches like a photo from the show or framed invitation will show you care and consider them important. Thank-you notes and e-mails should also be sent to the participating retailers, designers, and specialty boutiques that lend merchandise for charity shows. A written message of appreciation is a polite and kind signal that you appreciated all they have done to make the show a success.

Canceling Shows

In the rare instance that a show must be cancelled as a result of severe weather conditions, world events, or monetary issues, the PR people should send out announcements and notices via social media, print, and in some cases by phone as soon as the decision to cancel has been made. Alternative dates should be announced as soon as possible, and tickets refunded. All matters concerning the possible cancellation of a show should have been addressed within the contingency plan.

Industry Insider

Fashion Designer Yeohlee Teng

Fashion Designer Yeohlee Teng discusses her departure from the tents at Bryant Park and her experimental subway show as well as her approach to design from an independent perspective. She speaks about the ongoing process of creating and her collaboration with artists and galleries.

WHAT IS YOUR HISTORY WITH NEW YORK FASHION WEEK?

I was on the 7th on 6th board, the entity that created the shows and New York's Fashion Week for many years; I showed at Bryant Park from the beginning. On September 11, I remember being at my studio, when Jose, our messenger, came to me and said a plane had flown into the World Trade Center. I remember wondering if it was an accident. Half an hour later the second plane crashed into the second tower. At that point we knew that nobody was getting into the city—the assistants, the models, etc. I walked over to Bryant Park to see what was coming. Fern Mallis who ran the shows was outside the tents. The nine o' clock show had come down. I don't think the ten o'clock show started. A decision was made to shut down the shows and the tents, as no one quite knew what was happening. My show at eleven was cancelled and that was the last time I showed at the tents. It was time to do something in a different and more experimental venue and an opportunity presented itself. The following show happened underneath the tents at Bryant Park in the 42nd Street Subway Station.

CAN YOU TELL US HOW THE SUBWAY SHOW MATERIALIZED?

It was the MTA's (the Metropolitan Transit Authority) 100th anniversary and they contacted us because they wanted to do something connected to fashion. I suggested doing something in the Subway Station and they agreed—it was the first and possibly the last show to happen in an active subway station. The insurance was a nightmare. We also could not close down the station. There was no way to bring in power, so we had to forgo runway lighting and sound. It was noisy as the trains were running. Luckily we found a group of guys playing on buckets one night in the 34th street station. They were loud and great. They played for us at the show and got everyone to dance.

AFTER THAT SHOW, DID YOU FEEL LIKE YOU FOUND YOUR MEDIUM FOR PRESENTING YOUR CLOTHING?

To a degree it is a process. If you want to equate shows with dollars and cents, I may not be the best person to talk to. I do it for the experience. For me it is about learning how to look at something and creating a context for looking at the work. That said, the commercial aspects of showing should not be overlooked.

DO YOU SEE FASHION SHOWS AS AN EXTENSION OF THE PROCESS OF CREATING THE CLOTHING?

Pretty much, however, fashion shows are also a way to sell your image and brand. It is an opportunity to showcase your latest creations and a platform to present your products to the world. Huge fortunes get made from the right kind of recognition received from a successful show.

HAS IT ALWAYS BEEN THERE FOR YOU, THIS CONNECTION WITH ART, ARCHITECTURE, AND FASHION?

Yes from the very beginning it has been a seamless connection. April 2011 the Gagosian Gallery did a show called "Malevich and the American Legacy." They found out that the inspiration for my fall 2010 collection was the artist Kazimir Malevich and I was invited to do an installation in the Gagosian Store to launch the event. It was wonderful. My collection was in the store for the duration of the Malevich exhibition and it was a very successful collaboration. We actually sold the pieces and my book *YEOHLEE: WORK*.

WHO IS YEOHLEE'S TARGET MARKET? WHO'S YOUR CUSTOMER?

I think that the market is design and the medium is clothing and fashion. For me design is a universal language and I design clothes without any prejudice.

WHY DID YOU CHOOSE TO OPEN YOUR RETAIL BOUTIQUE?

It was always a dream and my dream became a reality when the opportunity to have a store with my design and production all in the same neighborhood presented itself.

The future of the Garment District lies in re-invention and I saw that having fashion more visible at the street level would help our cause (MadeinMidtown.org). To that end we also had the 1920's façade restored and Architect Joerg Schwartz designed and constructed the store with material ubiquitous in the neighborhood, namely galvanized studs and piping.

HOW DO YOU SEE YOUR FASHION SHOWS EVOLVING?

Fashion shows will continue to evolve with the designs of the clothing and with my inspirations. We held our Fall 2012 show in our boutique and showroom. We installed a Fred Sandback inspired red string *virtual runway* in the space above the models, connecting the boutique to the showroom to and leading viewers through the space. The show, which also celebrated Made in New York, brought a lot of people and press to the store, and to the Garment District.

Excerpt from interview, May 2011.

Chapter Review

In this chapter we have discussed the importance of showday timelines, scripts, and having a plan B. It is critical to the organization of the show that all members stick to the timelines, scripts, and day of show schedules. Definitions and explanations of technical, run-throughs, and dress rehearsals were given. It was addressed that most producers do not have time or money in the budget to hold a full dress rehearsal prior to the show. However, during run-throughs and technical rehearsals, time can be spent giving cues to the models on pacing, movement, and choreography. The chapter reinforced the importance of a strong opening and big finale, and touched on the after party as a PR tool. The chapter closed with how to strike a show, the process of returning merchandise, and finally the importance of staying in communication and thanking clients.

Case Problem

Steven is a new intern for H&K Productions. He has been chosen by previously experienced interns and was informed his job duties would start at the ground level. He was assigned to be a backstage helper, dressing models and working on accessories. On showday he checked in with the backstage manager and was given his ID lanyard. He had a change of clothing with him and told the other interns and volunteers that they were for going out after the show. The seasoned help reminded him that they will all be backstage helping with the breakdown process until very late. He didn't seem fazed by this comment and was much more concerned with getting over to the alterations and fitting area, where the professional dressers were beginning fittings on the models. He asked one of the professional dressers if they would steam his suit and she said yes. She stopped the fitting with the model and began steaming the new intern's suit. It was at this point when the producer's assistant walked back to the fitting area and was shocked to see one of the paid professionals steaming a new intern's garment. When Steven was asked by the production assistant what he was doing, he proudly responded, "Oh I am getting my suit steamed because I switched jobs with another volunteer who was working out front tonight. I just really think I should be out front and not stuck in the backroom. I have worked on other shows before and know tons of the people in the audience. I know I will be of much better use to all of you out front during showtime."

Questions to Consider

1. At this point in the conversation what should the production assistant do?
2. How could this situation have been avoided?
3. What should happen to Steven?
4. Who decides what is the job of interns and volunteers?
5. What is the importance of starting from the ground up in production? Why do you think the producer has his or her interns start in the backroom?

Questions for Review and Discussion

1. Please discuss some critical items that must be on a showday timeline.
2. How are production timelines different from general event timelines?
3. What is a script and how is it beneficial to fashion production? Who on the technical team needs copies of the script and timeline? Why is it so important for the technical team to have scripts and timelines?
4. What key issues should be considered in a contingency plan?
5. Please review and discuss the three different kinds of rehearsals outlined in this chapter.
6. How can choreography hinder a runway show? How can it help?
7. What factors determine the length of a show?
8. What are different ways to send or pace models down the catwalk?
9. Please discuss the importance of a strong opening of a show.
10. What is the function of a finale?
11. Why are after parties considered PR tools?
12. Explain the process of striking a show.
13. Why are thank-you(s) important?

Out and About Activities

1. Go online and research blogs and websites given here for current fashion shows. What are the trends in pacing, movements, and choreography?
2. Go online and research instances of show cancellations. Summarize the various reasons for these cancellations.

www.style.com
www.nymag.com
www.trendspotter.com

Ongoing Fashion Show Project

Running the Show

Using the template examples provided at the end of this text, create a production show timeline, and a contingency plan for your fashion show. Make certain you create folders for your fashion show binder.

1. Prior to the day of your show, create Check-in Sheets for models, staff, and volunteers using the blank templates provided at the end of the text.
2. After a successful show, have the production team write a thank-you to all volunteers, staff, and designers who helped execute the show.

Terminology of the Trade

dress rehearsal 144
contingency plan 143
choreography 145
lanyard 144
production timeline 141
rehearsal 144
run-through 144
showtime 145
strike 147
tech rehearsal 144
timelines 140

Bibliography

Brody, C. (2010, March 16). Fashion's 10 Most Dramatic Runway Shows. In *Flavorwire*. Retrieved August 4, 2011, from http://flavorwire.com/77895/fashions-10-most-dramatic-runway-shows

Catlin, A., & Charlotte, C. (2010 September 8). *Fashion Week's Best Parties.* Retrieved August 12, 2011, from http://nymag.com/daily/fashion/2010/09/fashion_weeks_best_parties.html

AGYNES

IT'S A WRAP!

LEARNING OBJECTIVES

After completing this chapter, you will be able to:

- Understand the importance of evaluations
- Discuss the types of evaluations
- Gain knowledge about reviews
- Understand the terminology of the trade

I came to New York and thought I would be one of a million people but I quickly realized I was one in a Million

—ANDREW WEIR, ACM worldwide

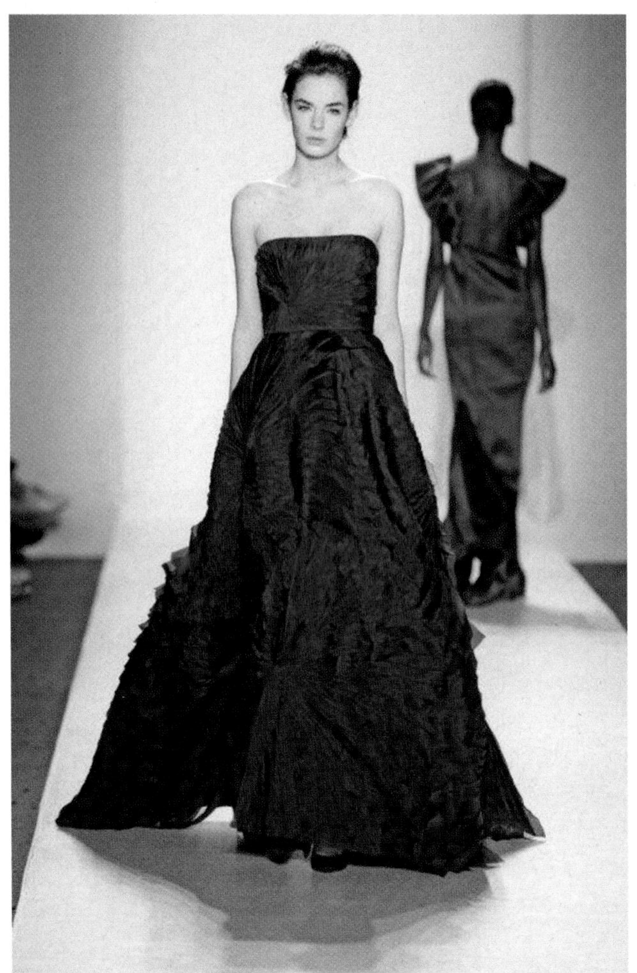

FIGURE 9.1 *Angel Sanchez New York Fashion Week 2008.*
Courtesy of Angel Sanchez/ Dan Lecca

The production team has struck the show, and returned the merchandise. Now is the moment to honestly evaluate and analyze the process and the outcome of the event (Figure 9.1). Create your final divider in the production binder titled **Evaluations**. *Before diving into critical analysis and reviews it is suggested to take off a few days. Take time to enjoy your success. Once you have rested, grab your postshow timeline and begin the process of evaluation. Keep in mind, evaluations are not about placing blame. Success can have many definitions even if the show had hiccups such as missed cues, cumbersome pacing, or the overall production exceeded budget. The bottom line is that only the inner circle knows the details. The producer, the clients, and the designers know the particulars. The audience never saw the script, identified the specifics of the budget, or had any previous knowledge of the in-depth choreography that was planned. The chapter discusses the importance of post–fashion show evaluations and reviews as solution steps in understanding the overall success of an event. It addresses the specific questions asked when creating evaluations and it outlines the diverse types of evaluations that should be conducted. It concentrates on the different groups of people to be evaluated.*

Evaluations

Evaluation involves assessing the strengths and weaknesses of programs, policies, personnel, products, performances, and organizations to improve their effectiveness. In the case of fashion show production these assessments of people and product involved in the production and the show will give the coordinator real insight to the challenges and success of the event. The information obtained will help determine what needs to be addressed, improved upon, or completely changed for the next show. Several evaluations should be performed for different categories to obtain the most accurate results. How detailed the evaluation process should be is determined by the fashion show coordinator. The vehicle for evaluations is an **evaluation form**. Evaluation forms are written or printed documents developed to assess the strengths and weaknesses of an event. Evaluations can produce qualitative and quantitative results. Qualitative surveys or evaluations address among other things the question of how well the event did. They are generally subjective in nature. Quantitative evaluations are number based and among other things address the question of how much the event earned or how many people attended. They are objective in nature. Evaluations can be surveys or questionnaires. A **questionnaire** is a set of printed or written questions with multiple choice answers or with room for a written response. Examples of some possible types of evaluations to be performed are listed below. With each type of evaluation, a custom form should be created.

Audience Evaluations

The audience or attendees are the spectators watching, listening, and observing the fashion show. Audiences may differ according to the type of show being presented. For example, during fashion week ready-to-wear shows in New York, Paris, London, and Milan, the audience may

Thank you for attending our event. We appreciate your support and we would be grateful for your responses to the questions below. Contact information optional.

	Circle One			
	Strongly Agree	**Agree**	**Disagree**	**Strongly Disagree**
1. The key message/purpose of the show was clearly communicated.	4	3	2	1
2. The event met my expectations.	4	3	2	1
3. I would purchase the clothing I saw.	4	3	2	1
4. The event was worth the ticket price.	4	3	2	1
5. I would recommend this event to a friend.	4	3	2	1

The best thing about this event was ______________________________

____

I would have enjoyed this event more if ______________________________

____

Contact Information:

Name ______________________________

Email/ Phone Number: ______________________________

FIGURE 9.2 *Audience evaluation example.*

Courtesy of Paula Taylor

include buyers, press, bloggers, celebrities, and VIP customers. Regional charity show attendees might consist of committee members, family members, local press, and the general public. Student shows generally have an audience of teachers, parents, community members, and students. Evaluating the audience can be as simple as providing an evaluation form or questionnaire asking some of your attendees for their feedback on what was effective and what could be improved upon in the future (Figure 9.2). The printed survey on hand asks specific questions of a selected and qualified group of attendees. Most questionnaires include blank spaces left for answers to the questions from the audience. Questions may require a written answer or a simple yes or no. Some questions that producers might pose to the audience when creating an audience questionnaire or evaluation are listed below. It is important to keep survey questions short and instructions easy to understand; for example, yes or no answers or rating from 1 to 5.

Was the key message/theme/purpose clearly communicated to your audience?
Did the audience members enjoy the MC or guest speaker?
Was the event worth the ticket price?
Did the event meet their expectations?
Would they purchase the clothing they saw on the runway?
Did the show keep their attention?
Would the audience come back next year?

Vendor Evaluations

A vendor is a company that provides products or services to another. For the purpose of fashion shows, vendors are technical people, décor companies, entertainment, disc jockeys, suppliers, and retailers. It is important that the fashion show coordinator or producer evaluate the vendors. It is also important to give the vendors a survey for them to fill out addressing specific questions regarding the vendor's overall point of view concerning the event. Some questions that may appear on a vendor survey are:

Did you have enough time for load-in and breakdown?
Did you have enough support from the production team?
Were your responsibilities clearly defined by the fashion show coordinator?
Did you have enough rehearsal time?
Were garments presented and styled appropriately for your target brand?
Were garments returned and inventoried properly?
Would you work on this event again next year?
Upon what could the production team improve?

Client Evaluations

The client is the person, company, or organization hiring the services of another professional person or company. In short, the clients in fashion show productions are designers, charitable organizations, community organizations, manufacturers, and retailers. The client is that person or entity that hires you and sets your budgets and goals. It is important to ascertain real feedback and evaluations from the client, to secure the job for next year or season. Evaluations for clients should include the following questions:

Did the production team/coordinator or event manager provide the agreed-upon services?
Did they work within the budget provided?
Are there any services that they could have performed better?
Were prior issues resolved before the event?
Was it a positive experience working with them?
Was the event a success?
Would you consider hiring them again?
See Figure 9.3 for a *client evaluation example*.

Staff Evaluations

Staff are all the people employed and working for the producer or fashion show coordinator. All staff members should have a clear understanding of what is expected of them during the show. Producers should evaluate each of their staff members. In addition, each employee should complete peer evaluations for fellow staff members. Peer evaluations as well as an evaluation from the management team and producer are very helpful analytical tools.

Thank you for hiring us for your event. We appreciate your support of our company and we would be grateful for your responses to the questions below.

	Circle One			
	Strongly Agree	**Agree**	**Disagree**	**Strongly Disagree**
1. The agreed-upon services were provided.	4	3	2	1
2. Our event stayed within the budget.	4	3	2	1
3. We were satisfied with the team.	4	3	2	1
4. Our event was a success.	4	3	2	1
5. We will recommend your service.	4	3	2	1

We will use/not use your services again because ______________________________

____

Services that could have been better were ______________________________

____

FIGURE 9.3 *Client evaluation example.*

Courtesy of Paula Taylor

QUESTIONS FOR PRODUCER TO EVALUATE STAFF MEMBERS

Did they meet their goals and objectives?

Did they attend all meetings?

Did they complete their task in a timely manner?

Did they communicate clearly and in a professional manner?

Did they dress and act in a professional manner?

QUESTIONS FOR PEER EVALUATIONS

Did they have a positive attitude?

Did they participate in all staff meetings?

Did they share information and ideas openly?

Upon what might this team member improve?

Volunteer Evaluations

Volunteers are individuals who donate their time for free. They do so to gain experience and to support and work with organizations or companies in which they believe. Among other things they may want to learn more about them or simply support them. Every coordinator should evaluate with their management team how effective and beneficial the volunteers were to the overall event. According to Jan Strimple, she and her team create a Hit or Miss list regarding interns and volunteers. If a volunteer or intern ends up on the Miss list, they are not asked back. The Hit or Miss list can be used for a quick evaluation regarding any aspect of the show (J. Strimple, Personal communication October 24, 2010). In addition, it is important to ask all volunteers to answer survey questions that assess their experiences while helping with the event.

QUESTIONS FOR COORDINATORS TO CONSIDER

Was the volunteer trained and knowledgeable in what was expected?
Did they listen and do their job effectively without being a burden?
Would you ask this volunteer to return next year? Why? Why not?

QUESTIONS TO ASK VOLUNTEERS

Were they properly trained?
Did they feel they had ample support from the production team?

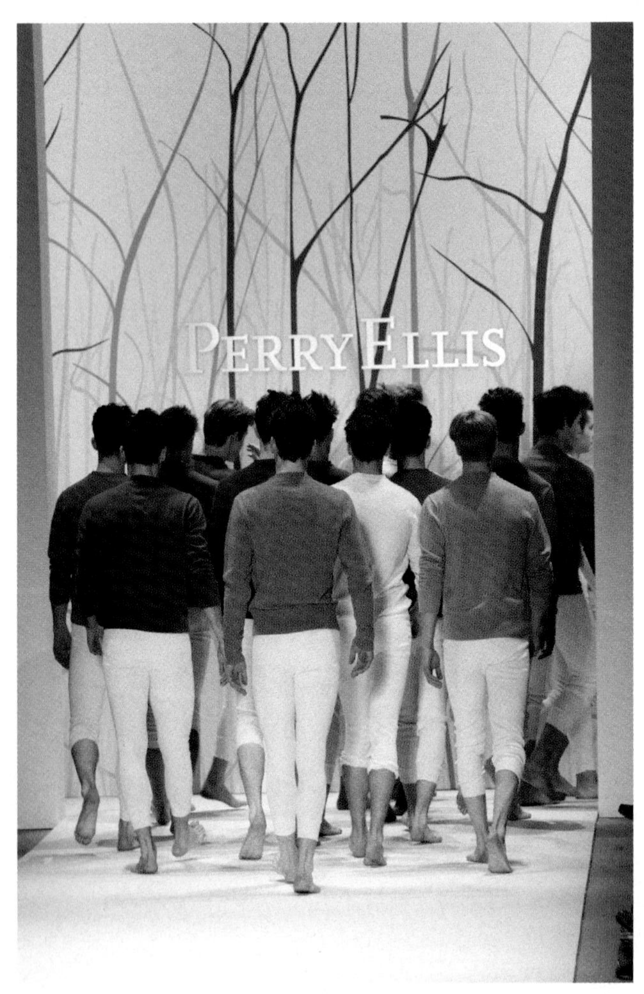

FIGURE 9.4 *Perry Ellis exiting the runway.*
Courtesy of Richard Brown Photography

Model Evaluations

The **models** are the live mannequins who wear the clothing that is highlighted in the show. A great model can take the runway show to the next level. Evaluating models will help the team decide whether or not the model will be asked to walk in another show (Figure 9.4).

QUESTIONS TO CONSIDER ON A MODEL'S EVALUATION

Did they arrive on time?
Were their measurements consistent with the model card?
Were they prepared for fittings?
Did they bring a shoe tote?
Were they professional?
How was their walk?
Would you use this model again?

Budget Evaluation

The event may have gone over budget, meaning the expenses have exceeded the allocated amount listed on the budget. The actual numbers should be reviewed, recorded, and compared to the proposed budget.

QUESTIONS TO CONSIDER

Was the event profitable?
Were there unforeseen expenses?
Was the budget realistic?

Music Evaluation

Music is an important element in runway shows and other fashion productions. Regardless of whether a DJ was hired to mix live or play prerecorded music, or a live band played, the music should be evaluated. Including a question regarding music on the attendee's survey is also suggested. The production team should also conduct its own evaluation.

QUESTIONS TO CONSIDER

Were the sound levels suitable?
Did the DJ or band meet their contracted obligation?
Did the music make sense with the merchandise, theme, or vision of the show?

Location Evaluation

Reviewing the location of the fashion show is a necessary process for the production team. Look over the layout plan and compare it to the reality of the actual physical show. Critical issues such as space for the backroom, proximity to the runway, and sight lines should be addressed. Other issues such as parking, seating, cooling, heating, and the locations for staff should be considered as well.

QUESTIONS TO CONSIDER?

Did the facility meet the needs of the production team?
Were there any major issues with the location?
Were restrooms easily accessible?
Would you conduct the event at this location again?

Merchandise Evaluation

The production team should evaluate merchandise borrowed from retailers and specialty boutiques as well as those items from designers' collections.

Was the merchandise appropriate for the target market?
Was working with the retailers easy?
Was the merchandise delivered and returned without any problems?
Would you use this type of merchandise again?

Additional Evaluations

Any aspect of the show can be evaluated. If the production team or coordinator was responsible for something then it should be evaluated. Matters such as PR, advertising, staging, and guest speakers are just a few additional evaluations to consider.

It is important to summarize and quantify your evaluations. If the majority of your surveys had the participants rate from 1 to 5 or answer yes or no, calculate those results and summarize the overall success of the event. Create a summary document that highlights the strongest and weakest parts of the show. Keep in mind you should segregate the quantitative analysis from the qualitative. Financially you could have a great success. You could have sold a lot of product for the client, increased branding, and/or made money for the charity. This quantitative analysis does not mean the entire production was a success. If the audience learned branding but disliked the brand, there is a problem. If the feelings of all relative participants were negative—that is, they simply did not like the production, yet spent money to support a charity—there is yet a bigger problem. These qualitative results can destroy the effect of a quantitative success. There must be both a quantitative and a qualitative positive outcome in order to have a production really considered successful. This analysis is an excellent and quick tool for understanding and solving problems for the future. It is important to remember that some items are beyond the production team's control and ability to change. If a hotel donates the runway for a charity fashion show, any feedback or suggestions on the evaluations for changing the actual runway may be unrealistic, as the use of the runway was a donation and is not in the producer's power to change. However, if the audience wasn't pleased with the merchandise, models, or music, all of these elements are easily addressed and changed by the coordinator, designer, and production team. Keep the summary in your show folder with the notes and changes to be used as a resource for next year.

Tips for creating an evaluation are as follows:

1. Make the instructions clear and easy to understand.
2. Keep it short and concise.
3. Keep answers either "yes or no" or as a simple rating from 1–5.
4. Leave a space for additional comments.

Reviews

In the world of fashion shows, few things are as important as reviews. A review is an assessment of an event after it happens by a third party. Fashion reviews are seen in trade publications and newspapers like *WWD* and *The New York Times* as well as on websites such as Style.com. They are also seen on numerous influential blogs. The traditional gatekeepers of fashion, the fashion press, who originally wrote reviews have changed. This change has come with the inception of young bloggers and the immediacy of their response in blogs and tweets. Although a majority of trade magazines and fashion press have created blogs and joined the tweeting revolution, many of the new nonindustry bloggers have little fashion industry knowledge. However, their voices are heard.

Successful bloggers have hoards of followers listening to their continuing updated opinions on designers' latest presentations. These new breeds of fashion experts also affect a label's sales and brand awareness. Conventional fashion writers and editors, like fashion veteran Lynn Yaeger, fashion editor of the *Herald Tribune* Susie Menkes, and former host of Fashion File Tim Blanks are just a few of the most notable and vital voices in fashion. These knowledgeable editors, journalists, and bloggers continue to guide and educate the public—as well as buyers and retailers—on current fashion trends. They dispel uninformed beliefs and opinions on whether the shows were successes or failures. Although producers are less directly affected by fashion reviews, if their client receives negative feedback or mixed reception to a collection this may influence the stability of the brands and impact negatively on the coordinator's job security. On the other hand, positive reviews can highlight the production achievements and drive additional sales, educate on the latest trends, and build awareness for the collection. The more positive a review, the further attention the producers, casting agents, and all additional support staff will garner. A seasoned coordinator understands the importance of reviews, but should never compromise the client's needs, or his or her own creativity in an attempt to gain positive reviews. This is the fashion industry. New ideas in clothing displayed on the runway, no matter how outlandish, unique, and unusual, are commonplace in this business. All fashion industry people should learn the skills it takes to write a critique. A strong review goes beyond one's personal opinion. It teaches the reader something and captures his or her attention. Suggestions for writing a review are:

1. Use industry language or terminology of the trade.
2. Open strong! As an example, Tim Blanks in his review of Channel's spring 2012 wrote, "Karl Lagerfeld gets a lot of his inspiration from dreams, but he didn't need any help from them today, because he already had *Last Year at Marienbad*, that hallucinatory slice of avant-garde celluloid from the early sixties, on his mind. Some would say that, despite its storied reputation, it's the most boring movie ever made, but for Lagerfeld—and Chanel—it inspired a breathtakingly surreal setting" (Blanks, 2010).
3. Include the who, what, where, when, and why.
4. Tell the readers something they didn't know.
5. Tie it all together.
6. Use constructive criticism.

The Wrap-up Meeting

Wrap-up meetings with the production team and client should be scheduled for no later than a week after the show. The longer you wait to have the wrap up, the less feedback you will receive. Coordinators should be taking notes during the meeting, highlighting positive feedback and constructive criticism. Again, some feedback is subjective and no matter how hard you try to please everyone involved, it can be guaranteed you won't.

After the evaluations are summarized and the final wrap-up meeting has taken place, the show is now over. Permanently file this production folder, store the flash drive, and start again, with all new forms, templates, and contact list. Keeping files updated and in order will ease the transition from one show to the next.

Chapter Review

Evaluations, assessments, and reviews are important tools to gauge the strengths and weakness of an event. There are numerous evaluations that one can perform. Ultimately the production staff and client will determine how in depth the surveys of the show should be and what aspects must be evaluated. It is important to summarize the results of questioners and surveys. Fashion journalists, bloggers, and editors review designers. After fashion week shows, these reviews can help drive labels sales, educate the public on the latest trends from a specific designer, and build the brand's awareness. It has been mentioned throughout this text that the traditional gatekeepers of fashion news and reviews have evolved with the addition of the fashion blogger, and their tweets. Whether experienced in the industry or not, these very vocal voices are heard and results from their opinions can be seen in sales, trend adoption, and brand awareness. Wrap-up meetings are the last step in production and mark the end of a show. Keeping organized files and starting with a new production folder and templates will help ease the move from one show to the next. On to the next show!!

Questions for Review and Discussion

1. Why are evaluations a key element to gauging the strengths and weaknesses of a show?
2. What type of questions should be asked on an audience's evaluation form?
3. What is the difference between quantitative evaluations and qualitative evaluations?
4. How do reviews educate the buying public?
5. Are reviews still relevant in the modern fashion show environment with so many bloggers and the public access to shows?
6. Why are wrap-up meetings crucial to the evaluation process?

Out and About Activity

1. Write a review. Visit a local retail store and write a one-page review of how the merchandise is presented in the store, the type of merchandise they carry, and the overall feel of the store.
2. Go online and research current fashion show reviews. Highlight the key criticism and the praise.
3. Attend a local fashion show and write a one-page review.

   www.vogue.com
   www.style.com
   www.elle.com
   www.nymag.com
   www.wgsn.com
   www.wwd.com

In Class Activity

The Production Checklist Exercise

Use this list of essential fashion show production elements on the blank checklist provided in the proper order. Begin with those elements that can be completed well in advance of show day. Conclude with everything that must wait until show day, listing show day items in the proper order. Do you notice any elements missing from your lists? If so, add them. Are there elements that should be combined? If so, put them together.

Production Checklist Exercise

Proposal	Contingency plan
Create timeline	Order food and get water, juice, and power bars
Create press release/media kit	Theme and vision
Merchandise selection	Budget
Provide hair and makeup direction	Model fittings
Secure lighting, technician, sound, and audio/visual	Create a backroom checklist (refer to checklist)
Addressing pacing of the show/choreography	Staff check in
Final model lineup	Hire hair and makeup
Create production team and job assignments	Set up backroom
Pitch proposal	Tech rehearsal and dress rehearsal
Utilize merchandise loan record	Story board your vision
Create model boards	Save the date invites /card invites
Tentative model lineup	Secure entertainment, MC, DJ, and additional talent.
Provide hair and makeup direction	Planning calendar
Styling garments and creating look book	Create layout for front of the house and back of the house.
Hire professional dressers, schedule volunteer dressers and seamstress	Create models application form for volunteers and/or contract agency if professional.

(See Figure 9.5 for an example of a production checklist.)

Production Checklist Example	Complete
Create a theme	☐
Build a team	☐
Storyboard theme and vision of show	☐
Create a timeline	☐
Create a planning calendar	☐
Budget	☐
Cast models	☐
Secure merchandise / Designers	☐
Pull merchandise	☐
Create a "Merchandise Selection Record" sheet for all merchandise	☐
	☐

FIGURE 9.5 *Production checklist example.*

Production Checklist Example	Complete
Style looks	☐
Model fittings	☐
Create model board	☐
Model application form (if volunteers)	☐
Sign contract if working with a professional agency	☐
Create press release	☐
Rough model lineup	☐
Secure backstage staff	☐
Dresser	☐
Seamstress	☐
Make contact sheet for all additional staff, models, and production team	☐
Secure hair and make-up	☐
Provide hair and make-up direction	☐
Secure backstage supplies	☐
Secure IT	☐
Create stylebook	☐
Create a detailed contingency plan	☐
Create backstage layout	☐
Pace the runway	☐
Secure craft services	☐
Tech rehearsal—headset test	☐
Call the show	☐
Evaluate show	☐
Return merchandise	☐

FIGURE 9.5 (*continued*)

project

Ongoing Fashion Show Project

Evaluating the Show

1. Use the Hit or Miss Template at the end of the text and make a general list of what worked and did not work for the show.
2. Create two custom evaluations using the evaluation template at the end of the text as a reference.
3. Write a show summary.
4. Send thank-you notes to the appropriate people.

Terminology of the Trade

audience evaluation 154
budget evaluation 158
client evaluation 156
evaluation 154
evaluation form 154
location evaluation 159
merchandise evaluation 159
model evaluation 158
music evaluation 159
peer evaluation 157
questionnaire 154
review 160
staff evaluation 156
vendor evaluation 156
volunteer evaluation 157
wrap-up meeting 161

Web Resources

www.allbusiness.com
www.marketingplaybook.com
www.eval.org
www.style.com
www.nymag.com/fashion/?f=fashion

Bibliography

Field, A. (2011, February 28). Do Fashion Show Reviews Matter? In *Huffpost Style*. Retrieved August 4, 2011, from http://www.huffingtonpost.com/adrien-field/do-fashion-show-reviews-m_b_829277.html

Blanks, T. (2010, October 5). *Chanel.* Retrieved August 4, 2011, from http://www.style.com/fashionshows/review/S2011RTW-CHANEL

How to Identify Your Small Business Target Market (2011, June 30). Retrieved August 4, 2011, from http://www.allbusiness.com/marketing/segmentation-targeting/2588-1.html

ongoing fashion show project chapter breakdown

(The instructor will provide the details for this project.)

CHAPTER 2: THE BEGINNING

1. Instructor introduces the project.
2. Instructor assigns students to production teams.
3. Each student is assigned a job on the production team using the Production Team Job Responsibility Worksheet.

CHAPTER 3: THE SHOWS, THE PRODUCER, AND THE TEAM

1. The class holds a brainstorming session on the purpose and message of the show.
2. Students create a theme (Use Theme/Vision Worksheet).
3. Storyboard the theme.
4. Create a working title/name the show.

CHAPTER 4: PLANNING THE SHOW

Using the templates and worksheets at the end of the textbook:

1. Create a planning calendar.
2. Create a timeline.
3. Create a budget.

CHAPTER 5: GETTING THE WORD OUT

1. Create a press release (use Press Release Worksheet).
2. Create a media kit.
3. Design invitations, save the date, and e-vites.
4. Create a Facebook fan page or blog.

CHAPTER 6: MODELS AND MERCHANDISE

Using the templates and worksheets at the end of the textbook:

1. Hold a model casting.
2. Create a custom contact sheet.
3. Create a custom model release form.
4. Create a custom model application form.
5. Create a model lineup for the show.
6. Pull and inventory merchandise (Use Merchandise Selection Record Sheet).
7. Create style boards.
8. Begin the style note book.

CHAPTER 7: THE FRONT OF THE HOUSE AND THE BACK OF THE HOUSE

1. Create a basic layout and floorplan for both front and back of the house.
2. Create a song list for the DJ or band.
3. Create a backroom supplies list.

CHAPTER 8: SHOWTIME

Using the templates and worksheets at the end of the textbook:

1. Create a production show timeline.
2. Create a contingency plan.
3. Create check-in sheets for: models, staff, and volunteers.
4. Write all thank-you notes post show.

CHAPTER 9: IT'S A WRAP!

Using the templates and worksheets at the end of the textbook:

1. Complete a general hit or miss list for the show.
2. Create and distribute two evaluations for the show.
3. Write a show summary.

glossary

Advertising—The act of attracting public attention to a product or business by paid advertisement in print, broadcast, or electronic media.

Advertising Model—An editorial or runway model that is hired to promote clothing brands, fragrances, and other merchandise through print, online, point of purchase displays, and other media like billboards.

Anchor Text—The link title or clickable text in a hyperlink. This provides an easy ranking for search engines and a way for media to access more information regarding the occasion.

Assistant—A person who works closely with the producer on the needs of the production team.

Audience Evaluation—A simple questionnaire given to the spectators seeking their opinion about the event.

Audiovisual—Provides all sound, visual components and equipment for a show or event.

Back of the House—The workroom or backroom.

Backroom Coordinator—The person in charge of the backroom and responsible for creating the backroom layout, schedules, dressers, and dressing track.

Behavioral Patterns—The complex motivations causing certain reactions of the expected target audience.

Bill Blass—One of the first American designers to brand the trunk show and use it to his advantage.

Blog—A website that contains an online personal journal with reflections, comments, and often hyperlinks provided by the writer.

Body Part Model—A model specializing in modeling specific body parts such as hands or feet.

Bonnie Cashin—An American designer that brought creativity and ingenuity to her clothing during wartime rationing.

Brand Ambassadors—Customers that advertise for a designer or retailer by wearing their clothing and representing it in a positive light.

Breakdown crew—A group of individuals hired or acting as volunteers to deconstruct the backroom.

Bridge Clothing—An apparel price zone that falls in between designer prices and moderate prices.

Budget—An essential planning tool used to define precise expenses and expenditures.

Budget Evaluation—An assessment of the use of funds for the show or event used to determine if the expenses have exceeded the allocated amount.

Calling the Show—Sending the models on the runway and setting both the pace and the tone of the show.

Carnaby Street—Active London street in the 1960s that housed popular stores.

Casting Director—The person in charge of hiring and casting models for fashion shows, presentations, photo shoots, and events.

Celebrity Models—A high-profile person such as an actor or musician chosen by a designer to model with the intention of providing inspiration and solidifying branding with the consumer.

Charity Show—An event with the main purpose of fundraising, education, and branding.

Charles Fredrick Worth—An Englishman who became known as the father of haute couture; he was renowned for the custom clothing he produced for elite clientele.

Child Model—A model that represents the merchandise for babies, toddlers, children, and preteens.

Choreography—The sequence of steps or movements in the show by the models, entertainment, and other performers. When properly executed, it can highlight important aspects of the show, help with cues, and keep the attention of the audience.

Claire McCardell—An American designer that brought creativity and ingenuity to her clothing during wartime rationing. Helped popularize sportwear clothing.

Clare Potter—An important American designer during wartime rationing.

Claude Montana—French designer of the 1980s who staged grand production shows.

Client Evaluation—A written assessment by the employer that ascertains the strengths and weaknesses of the production team.

Commercial Model—A commercial model represents a brand. This model is not held to editorial and runway size requirements.

Composite—Informative card listing of all of the imperative information about a model and his or her agency contact information.

Comprehensive Information—The detailed procedures and data that must be collected and formed in the timeline of the event.

Contact List—A compilation of local and national press contact information.

Contemporary Clothing—Up-to-date, modern apparel.

Contingency Plan—The backup plan.

Décor—The decoration consisting of the layout and furnishings of an interior or exterior space.

Demographics—The aggregation of specific personal information about an individual such as age, race, educational background, and household income of the individual who is the expected or targeted attendee to the fashion show.

Department Stores—Brick and mortar centers selling differing products from a variety of vendors under one roof.

Designer Clothing—Styles or designs accepted as such by fashion leaders and elite consumers.

Disc Jockey (DJ)—The person who selects and plays recorded music or mixes music for the event.

Discretionary Income—The income received that remains after all expenses/necessities have been paid and which thereafter can be spent at will for anything desired.

Dlivir.it—A resource for bloggers, which does away with having to manually post updates to separate social media sites.

Dress Rehearsal—The final rehearsal or practice of a live show, in which everything is performed as it will be in the actual performance.

Dresser—The person who is responsible for getting the models dressed quickly and correctly.

Dresser Track—The rack delineated for each model that holds all the clothing or looks that the model is wearing in the show and has his or her model board and name attached to it.

Editorial Fashion Model—A model primarily used in high-fashion print magazines and in the magazine's online divisions.

Evaluation—A written assessments of the strengths and weaknesses of the people and product involved in the production.

Evaluation Form—A written or printed document developed to assess the strengths and weaknesses of an event.

E-vite—An electronic invitation.

Fashion Dolls—Miniature dolls that were used to show dressmakers' work to high society before live mannequins were introduced.

Fashion Mart—A building or buildings where clothing is produced, manufactured, and sold on a wholesale level.

Fashion Model—A person who wears and presents clothing of a specific brand or designer.
Fashion Presentation—A static presentation where designers and manufacturers use models to wear the clothing and stand on elevated platforms for hours while the press and important buyers observe the clothes.
Fashion Show Director—The person in charge of coordinating the show, delegating responsibilities, and maintaining strong communication with all members of the team.
Fashion Week—Is a fashion industry event, occurring twice a year, lasting approximately one week, held in major fashion capitals throughout the world.
Fashion's Night Out—Special late-night retail events held all over the city and the world; launched by Anna Wintour, *Vogue*, and the Council of Fashion Designers of America to expand the reach of fashion week.
Finale—Final parade in which each model walks down a runway one after the other, signaling the end of the show.
Final Fittings—The day of show fittings.
FIT Models—Live models that try on clothing for designers and manufacturers prior to production.
Fitness Model—A type of model that represents the fitness industry. This type of model is athletic and muscular, works in print promoting fitness-related products, and at trade shows.
Fitting—The act of trying on clothes for the purpose of tailoring the clothing to ensure a proper fit.
Fixed Costs—Needed nonvariable expenses that always must be paid.
Floor Plan—A simple line drawing of a space as if seen from above and used to organize the layout of the front of the house and the back of the house.
Formal Runway Show—An event that presents a traditional and straightforward parade of models walking the runway. Most commonly seen during fashion weeks across the globe and best suited for ready-to-wear collections.
Front of the House—That portion of the location of a fashion event where the audience views the event and experiences all the performance.

Gatekeepers—A name referring to the fashion press, bloggers, and journalists. These are the holders of information regarding fashion news.
Geographics—The area and climate in which the consumer resides.
Gimbels—A department store located in Philadelphia that held as early as 1910 extrovertly themed productions based on Paris fashions.

Haute Couture—The French term literally meaning, "fine sewing." It refers to "high fashion."
Headsets—Hands-free equipment that allows open communication and mobility.

IMG—A marketing agency and management company who produces The Mercedes-Benz Fashion Week and others.
In Kind Donation—Payment of goods or services instead of money.
Informal Show—A more simplified presentation of garments and accessories on a model. This kind of show rarely has any theatrical elements and can be held at retail locations, restaurants, showrooms, hotels, and alternative spaces.
Intern—A person who works in order to obtain course credit from his or her college or high school. This person will also work for the purpose of getting real-world experience.
International Trade Show—A show for the trade and industry professionals located throughout countries around the world.
Inventory Sheet—A list of all of the garments and accessories that are used in the fashion show and details the garments' descriptions.
Invitation—A simple, clear, and informative request to attend an event.

Jean Patou—First French fashion designer to employ American business ideas and concepts by hiring the American mannequin/model for his Parisian shows.
Jeanne Paquin—One of the first women of haute couture who took her models/mannequins out of the couture house to unique locations and created what is known today as the "finale" of a fashion show.

Key Events—Specific milestones that must be met within the timeline for the event.
Kings Road—A fashionable London street for the 1960s hipster youth.

Lanyard—A neck cord that attaches to the name badge and is worn around a person's neck.
Layout—A plan or arrangement of an area, often completed as a schematic on a computer.
Lewis Leonard—Renowned hair stylist who became popular in the 1970s.
Lifestyle Collection—Secondary and divisional collections such as hats, furs, and accessories.
Lighting—The equipment used to provide artificial illumination.
Location Evaluation—An assessment of the strengths and weaknesses of an event location.

Mannequins—Term coined by Charles Fredrick Worth in reference to the first live models to work with designers and model clothing.
Mary Quant—Influential British designer who defined the Youth Movement in the 1960s and permanently changed the runway show by removing commentary, and adding music and props.
Mass Market—A potential source of consumers containing very large numbers of buyers.
Media Kit—An informative self-contained packet holding everything needed to enable the press to write a story about you and/or the event, and as a result learn more about the company or the event.
Mercedes Benz Fashion Week—A fashion week sponsored in many parts of the world by the Mercedes Benz Company.
Merchandise Evaluation—The assessment of the strengths and weaknesses of merchandise borrowed from retailers, specialty boutiques, and designers' collections.
Merchandise Pull—The physical act of selecting garments for the show.
Model—A person who is an idealized version of a designer's clients, who wears and presents the designer's clothing.
Model Application/Information—A form that is filled out for all volunteer models, listing all measurements, notes about the model, and vital contact information.
Model Board—A board that contains a photo of the model, photos of the looks, and styling notes attached for the dresser's reference, which is also referred to as a model style board
Model Card—Cards listing all the imperative information about a model with agency contact information. It also contains a headshot and additional photographs, and is often called a composite or comp card.
Model Contract—A legal agreement that sets forth the detailed responsibilities and expectations of the model.
Model Evaluation—A written assessment of the strengths and weaknesses of a model.
Model Lineup—A list delineating the order in which the models are sent to walk the runway.
Model Release—A legal document that allows producers and designers to use the model's photographs for publication and promotional purposes.
Modeling Agency—A company that represents a variety of models.
Modeling School—A formal training facility for models.
Muslin—A thin, cotton fabric that can be white, dyed, or printed. Muslin is often placed on top of the runway and gives it a crisp look and feel.

"New Look"—Dior's revolutionary design reaction against wartime silhouettes.
National Show—A show/event held in major fashion capitals within a specific country.

Ossie Clark—Influential designer of the 1960s who was the first contemporary designer to use celebrities to promote and model his collection.

Paul Poiret—One of the first fashion designers to travel to other countries to present his collection with live models.
Peer Evaluation—A written assessment of the strengths and weaknesses of a colleague.
Pitch—The act of selling an idea, theme, or vision for the fashion show or event theme.
Planning Calendars—A daily, weekly, or monthly schedule containing important dates and deadlines taken from the timeline and put into a calendar/time format.
Plus-Size Model—A larger, well-proportioned model.
Pop Up Shop—An extension of the trunk show. Pop ups utilize a temporary retail space or can be held in an existing retail store. They may be open for as little as one day or as long as six months. Like trunk shows, pop ups can highlight a specific brand, retailer, or a number of products all at once.
Portfolio—A collection of the model's best, professionally produced photographs.
PR Coordinator—The person who communicates the company's needs to the publicist; a staff member, volunteer, or student in charge of the public relations needs for the event.
PR Firm—The hired organization or group that is in charge of public relations.
Press Release—An article constructed by a company or public relations person on a newsworthy event distributed for the purpose of free advertisement.
Press Show—An event, held exclusively and specifically for the press, with the primary focus of encouraging press coverage of a designer's latest collection.
Press Week—A publicity/fashion event initiated by Eleanor Lambert in the 1940s to promote American designers.
Producer—The person in charge of executing the event, who coordinates and directs every detail of the show.
Production Services—The services offered by a company for a production.
Production Show—A professional fashion show that highlights, brands, advertises, and sells collection of a particular designer, or retailer. These shows are generally for the trade, buyers, press, and VIP customers.
Production Team—The staff that coordinate, work, and present a fashion show or event.
Production Timeline—A written schedule documenting all of the production happenings and events beginning with the setup team load-in and ending with the show breakdown.
Program Editor—The person in charge of the written program.
Promotional Model—A model hired to work events such as trade shows, conventions, sporting events, and concerts. He or she represents items and brands like automobiles, beauty products, alcoholic beverages and sports drinks.
Proposal—A written offering for production services.
Psychographics—The analysis of the potential attendees' lifestyle.
Publicist—The person responsible for highlighting or making public a client, or a client's products such as a runway show.

Questionnaire—A set of printed or written questions used to evaluate an event.

Ready-to-Wear—Apparel made in factories to standard size measurements.
Regional Show—A show/event in a town that is outside of major fashion capitals.
Rehearsal—A practice run-through of an event.
Revenue—The gross amount of money a business receives before deductions for cost of goods and services.
Review—A post assessment by a third party of an event.
Rose Bertin—The French dressmaker to Marie Antoinette; notable for using fashion dolls to present her designs.
RSS Feed—A format for delivering regular changing Web content. A RSS feed lets the reader acquire content from a blog or other websites daily.
Run-through—A rehearsal of the show in the order of the script; it includes showing the models the pacing and choreography of the show.
Runway—The physical extension of the stage where models walk. It can also be a freestanding elevated element.

Salon Style Show—An informal fashion show without the runway. Models walk around tables while customers are enjoying lunch or dinner. Often used for charity luncheons or as sales tools in retailer's establishments.
Separates—Fashion focused on pieces such as blouses, skirts, pants, and suits.
Set up—The physical act of arranging, placing, and readying all physical elements required for an event, such as setting up chairs for the audience in a predetermined order.
Set up crew—A core group of individuals who begin the setting up process, before the models, hair and makeup people, seamstress, or other auxiliary staff arrive.
Showroom Models—An informal presentation in sales wherein a model wears sample garments for the buyer's review and consideration for purchase.
Showroom—Category of informal show exclusively used for wholesale trade or industry professional. This is where buyers visit a showroom during market week and periodically throughout the season to order merchandise.
Showtime—The start of the fashion show; when the lights go down, the music starts, and the lighting cues begin.
Silhouette—The shape or form of a garment.
Social Media—A free and measurable PR tool for modern public relations utilizing the Internet, phones, and their varied applications.
Sponsorship—Supporting the fashion show or event by providing money or other resources that are of value to the sponsored event. This is often in return for advertising space at the event or on printed materials.
Sportswear—A term created by American designers in the 1930s and the 1940s highlighting ready-to-wear affordable separates that mirrored a more casual and active lifestyle.
Staff Evaluation—A written assessment of the strengths and weaknesses of the individuals working on an event.
Stage—Raised platform on which the show will take place or on which theatrical performances are presented.
Staging—The act of building a stage, runway, and a background. It can also include setting the lighting cage.
Stage Manager—The person in charge of managing actors, talent, and stage crew technicians during the production.
Stage Manager—The person responsible for conducting and controlling all the activity and talent on the actual stage or runway.
Storyboard—A visual summary and outline of the concept of the fashion show. Developed in the early stage of production, it is used to help organize inspiration and solidify the theme.
Strike—The process of breaking down the show.
Student Show—A fashion event coordinated by students under the supervision of faculty of a specific educational institution such as a college, university, or high school.
Stylebook—A book that includes detailed information on garments and how the garment will be displayed on the model.
Supermodel—A name given to represent a group of models that quickly rose to fame in the late 1980s and early 1990s.
Swag Bags—Promotional gifts and materials placed on each seat prior to the attendee's arrival.
Swimsuit Model—An editorial, runway, commercial, or catalog model who models swimwear.

Takada Kenzo—Designer of the 1970s who broke haute couture tradition and presented a major ready-to-wear show on stage rather than a traditional runway.
Target Audience—A specific group of consumers or potential customers to whom a company aims to sell its product.
Tear Sheets—A tool models use to promote themselves. Published photographs from past assignments torn out of magazines.
Tech Rehearsal—A practice session that consists of testing all of the technology used in the performance including lighting, sound, and special effects in order to prevent mistakes from occurring during the actual fashion show.
Tech Table—The one central area where sound, lighting, and audiovisual control and run their aspect of the show.
Teen Models—Girl and boy models between the ages of twelve and fifteen representing a variety of demographic segments of the population. The market they represent is called the junior market.
Theater Seating—The place where the audience sits. Often chairs are placed side by side next to the runway and stage.

Theme—Overall concept, vision, and mood for a show.

Thierry Mugler—French designer who became popular in the 1980s and who staged grand shows, selling tickets to the public. He started the trend for fashion shows to become inclusive public events and vehicles for entertainment.

Timeline—A tool used to help organize dates and deadlines for all the important facets of the show.

Trade Show—An industry-only exhibition for manufacturers and designers to showcase their new collections. Trade shows can only be attended by company representatives, retail buyers, and members of the press.

Trunk Show—A one-time presentation of clothing used in a variety of settings. One of the most effective direct sales tools for retailers and designers. Its purpose is to highlight specific pieces of a collection, or unique items not normally featured in the retail establishment.

Variable Costs—Certain charges that are not constant and are subject to fluctuation.

Vendor Evaluation—A written assessment of the strengths and weaknesses of all service or product providers.

Vera Maxwell—An American sportswear designer who brought creativity and ingenuity to her clothing during wartime rationing.

Vertically Integrated—A business that is in control of production from raw material to retailing.

Volunteer—A person who offers his or her services for free without any recompense. Often the intent is to acquire experience or to contribute to a good cause.

Volunteer Evaluation—An written assessment of the strengths and weaknesses of nonpaid staff.

Volunteer Models—A model that is not signed to a professional agency and may offer his or her services for free. Also known as amateur models.

Wanamaker—A department store located in New York City. In the early 1900s it held big-budget fashion shows based on Parisian fashion.

Wrap up meeting—A post-show gathering of staff for the purpose of evaluating the strengths and weaknesses of the production.

Youth Quake—A name given to the young people or new youth market that was part of Mary Quant's clientele in the sixties.

perforated worksheets

Production Team Job Responsibility Signup Sheet

Name of Show ____

Location ____

Type of Show ____

Title	Name	Phone	Email
Show Coordinator			
Merchandise Coordinator			
Styling Coordinator			
Model Coordinator			
PR/Promotion Coordinator			
Stage Manager Coordinator			
Photo Coordinator			
Dressers			
Volunteers			
Type of Production in the show			
Retail Store	Name		
	Type of Merchandise		
Designer Show	Number of Designers		
	Number of Garments		

Notes

Theme/Vision Worksheet

General Theme/Vision: ____________________

____

____

____

Intent: ____________________

____

____

____

Audience: ____________________

____

____

____

Potential Mood/Atmosphere: ____________________

____

____

____

Potential Buzz Factor: ____________________

____

____

____

Timeline Blank Template

Events	Notes
Start:	
End:	
Start:	
End:	
Start:	
End:	
Start:	
End:	
Start:	
End:	
Start:	
End:	
Start:	
End:	
Start:	
End:	
Start:	
End:	
Start:	
End:	
Start:	
End:	

(continued)

Timeline Blank Template

Events	Notes
Start: End:	
Start: End:	
Start: End:	
Start: End:	

Fashion Show Budget Template

	Budgeted	Actual
INCOME:		
Donations		
Ticket sales		
Sponsorships		
Other		
Income Total		
EXPENSES:		
Front of House		
Location rental		
Insurance		
Food & beverage (catering)		
Entertainment		
Audiovisual		
Lighting		
Sound		
Security		
Videographer		
Photography		
Décor		
Staging and runway		

(continued)

Fashion Show Budget Template

	Budgeted	Actual
Guest speaker(s)		
Master of ceremony		
Phone & fax		
Printing		
Front of House Expenses Total		
Back of House		
Staffing		
Producer		
Production assistant(s)		
Stage manager		
Backroom manager		
Stylist(s)		
Dresser(s)		
Seamstress		
Intern(s)		
Other		
Hair & makeup		
Models		
Costumes and custom designs		
Shipping		
Miscellaneous		
Back of House Expenses Total		
General/Other		
Promotional materials		
Advertisement		
IT support		
General Other Expenses Total		
Total Expenses		
Profit (LOSS) before Taxes		
Taxes		
Net Profit or (LOSS)		

Planning Calendar Template

Sunday	Monday	Tuesday	Wednesday	Thursday	Friday	Saturday

Press Release Worksheet

Use the press release provided or one of your own.

Who is the contact person?

What is the headline?

What is the positioning statement?

How did you end the press release?

What are the 5 Ws of the event and are they listed in the first two paragraphs?

Who? ______________________________

What? ______________________________

Where? ______________________________

When? ______________________________

Why? ______________________________

What is the lead? Is it buried?

Are there any surprises?

Hyperlinks, anchor texts, or multimedia?

What would you change, add, or delete to make this press release as effective as possible?

Model Application Template

Name of Show Goes Here

Name: ______________________________

Phone: ______________________________

Address: ______________________________

E-mail: ______________________________

Date of Birth: ______________________________

Measurements:	Women:	Men:
Height: ______	Bust: ______	Chest: ______
Weight: ______	Dress: ______	Shoe size: ______
Waist: ______	Shoe size: ______	Inseam: ______
Pant size: ______	Inseam: ______	Sleeve length: ______
Hair color: ______	Hips: ______	
Eye color: ______		

Model's Experience: ______________________________

____

____

____

Coordinator's Notes: ______________________________

____

____

____

You will need to attend a dress rehearsal on ______________

Model applicant's initial here: ______________

Signed release form: ______________

Model Release Template

I, ______________________________________, hereby give ____, its successors, and assigns the absolute and irrevocable right and permission with respect to the photographs taken of me or in which I may be included with others during the rehearsals and production of (*name of event*) on (*date[s] of event*):

(1) To copyright the photographs,

(2) To use, reuse, publish, and republish the photographs individually or in conjunction with other photographs,

(3) To use my name in connection therewith.

I understand that any and all photographs taken become the property of ____ .

I hereby release and discharge ____ , its successors, and assigns from any and all claims and demands arising out of or in connection with the use of photographs, including but not limited to any and all claims for libel or invasion of privacy.

Name (of individual being photographed): ____

Signature: ________________________________ Date: __________________________________

Address: ____

City: ____________________________________ State: _____________ Zip:_______________________

Telephone: ___________________________________ Date of Birth: _______________________________________

E-mail: ____

If the person named above is a minor, the parent or guardian shall sign below:

Name: ____

Signature: ____ Date: __________________________________

Address: ____

City: ____________________________________ State: ____________ Zip: _________________________

Telephone: _________________________________ Date of Birth: ____

E-mail: ____

Merchandise Selection Record Sheet Template

Store: ____________________

Date: ____________________

Show: ____________________

Issued to: ____________________

Model Name	Size	Color	Description

Received in Stock by: ____________________ **Date:** ____________________

From: ____________________

Supplies for Backroom Template

	Complete
	☐
	☐
	☐
	☐
	☐
	☐
	☐
	☐
	☐
	☐
	☐
	☐
	☐
	☐
	☐
	☐
	☐
	☐
	☐
	☐
	☐
	☐
	☐
	☐

Evaluating the Fit of the Model Worksheet

Question	Yes	No
1. Does the neckline lie smoothly around the base of the neck?	Yes	No
2. Is the waist of the garment at the waist of the model?	Yes	No
3. Do the shoulder seams bisect the shoulder—that is, lie straight, directly on top of the shoulder?	Yes	No
4. Do the armhole seams line up with the tip of the shoulder?	Yes	No
5. Does the garment pull across the bust?	Yes	No
6. Do the darts point to an end slightly before the fullest part of the bust?	Yes	No
7. Does the shoulder dart fall in the center of the shoulder?	Yes	No
8. Is the front waist dart at the princess line seam on the model?	Yes	No
9. Is the center back seam centered and perpendicular to the floor?	Yes	No
10. Does the back shoulder dart line up with the front shoulder dart?	Yes	No
11. Does the back strain across the shoulder blade?	Yes	No
12. Is the back waist dart straight?	Yes	No
13. Is there enough ease at the side seam under the arm?	Yes	No

Notes:

Contingency Plan Template

	PROBLEM	PLAN B
Runway		
Models		
Music		
Décor		
Staff		
Lighting		
Sound		
IT		
Hair & Makeup		

Day of Production Timeline Worksheet

Day before Show		Contact
Time:	Event	
Day of Show		
Time:	Event	

Backstage Sign-in Sheet

POSITION	PRINT NAME	SIGNATURE	TIME

Model Check-in Form Template

NAME	SIGNATURE
WOMEN	
MEN	

Evaluation Template

	Circle One			
	Strongly Agree	Agree	Disagree	Strongly Disagree
1.	4	3	2	1
2.	4	3	2	1
3.	4	3	2	1
4.	4	3	2	1
5.	4	3	2	1

HIT or MISS List Template

HIT	MISS

Index

Q

R

S